New York Road Runners
Complete Book of
Running and Fitness

"*This book has it all!* It gives the combined wisdom of the NYRRC's many experts to the serious runner, the beginner exerciser, and for those seeking to keep the entire family fit."
—Grete Waitz, nine-time New York City Marathon champion

PRAISE FOR THE PREVIOUS EDITIONS:

"For the serious, recreational, or neophyte runner...a comprehensive effort...a great service to runners."—*USA Today*

"The new testament."—*American Health Magazine*

"One of the most comprehensive guides to the sport ever published."
—*New York Newsday*

"It's the last word on running...the best book for the money."
—*Free Press,* Detroit, Michigan

"I know it works because I've recommended it to others who have ended up running the 5K distance easily after ten weeks."—*Telegraph,* Macon, Georgia

"Provides information on how to build a personally-tailored running program, and details exactly how to reach personal goals."—*Journal,* Providence, Rhode Island

New York Road Runners
Complete Book of
Running and Fitness
Fourth Edition

By
Gloria Averbuch

Random House Reference
New York   Toronto   London   Sydney   Auckland

Grateful acknowledgment is made to the following for permission to reprint previously published material:
> *Susan Foster*: Fifty black and white illustrations. Reprinted by permission of Susan Foster.
> *Bob Glover*: Excerpts from training brochures. Reprinted by permission of Bob Glover.
> *Human Kinetics Publishers*: Excerpts from *Nancy Clark's Sports and Nutrition Guidebook* by Nancy Clark, Champaign, IL: Human Kinetics, 1990. Copyright © 2003 by Nancy Clark. Reprinted by permission.
> *New York Road Runners*: Excerpts from *New York Running News* and *New York Runner*. Reprinted by permission of New York Road Runners.
> *The Quaker Oats Company*: "Gatorade Heatwave Fluids: The Inside Story" and excerpts from "Beat the Heat Infocard." Reprinted by permission of the Quaker Oats Company.
> *Road Runners Club of America*: Excerpts from *Children's Running: A Guide for Parents and Kids*. Copyright © 1989 by Road Runners Club of America. Reprinted by permission.
> *Running* magazine: Excerpts from "Cliff Temple's Guide to Running," Parts 1–3. Reprinted by permission of *Running* magazine.
> www.whartonperformance.com: "Stretching and Strengthening." Reprinted by permission of Jim and Phil Wharton.
> www.hartman-international.com: "Peaking Past Forty." Reprinted by permission of Gerard Hartmann.

Library of Congress Cataloging-in-Publication Data
The New York road runners complete book of running and fitness. — 4th ed.
   p.   cm.
   Rev. ed. of: The New York Road Runners Club complete book of running. 3rd ed, 1999.
   Includes index
   ISBN 0-375-72024-3
   1. Running.   2. Physical fitness.   I. New York Road Runners Club complete book of running.
GV1061.N43 1997
613.7'172—dc21   91-23114
                                       CIP

In memory of my father, Bernard Averbuch, my strength and inspiration (1919–91). And to Fred Lebow, who so artfully blended running and life.—G.A.

Throughout the book, frequent references are made to *New York Runner* (formerly *New York Running News*), published quarterly, the official magazine of New York Road Runners.

- New York Road Runners (NYRR) was formerly known as the New York Road Runners Club (NYRRC) and is occasionally referred to by its former name.

- All information in this book—including statistics and records—is the most current available as of November 2003.

- All photos are printed with the permission of New York Road Runners.

CONTENTS

Part 3—The Distances

Part 4—The Psychology of Running

Part 5—Nutrition

Part 6—Fitness and Safety

Part 7—Health and Medicine

Part 8—Aging and Exercise

Part 9—Children's Running and Fitness

Part 10—Women's Running

Part 11—Walking

Part 12—The Running Lifestyle

Part 13—Running Equipment

PREFACE TO THE FOURTH EDITION

Welcome to the fourth edition of *New York Road Runners Complete Guide to Running and Fitness*. Continuing in the spirit of the book's earlier success, the goal of those who have authored, organized, and contributed to this volume is to share the latest in the areas of running, fitness, and health.

Innovations at NYRR reflect growth and trends in the running and fitness movement. While maintaining its status as one of the largest and most prestigious organizations of its kind worldwide, since the last edition of this book was published, NYRR has continued to serve runners and active people in all categories—professional athletes, beginners, youth, the elderly, the physically challenged, and underserved populations. As the running movement has evolved, so has the organization, which seeks to instill a lifelong health and exercise program among the general population.

People are continually discovering the joy, ease, and benefits of running. The numbers prove our community remains vast and strong. According to the latest statistics from the USATF Road Running Information Center and American Sports Data, Inc., nearly 10.5 million Americans ran on 100 days or more in 2002. And once discovered, the commitment appears to be lifelong: More than 11 million runners have been in the sport for ten or more years.

This book provides even more for those who want to take their running one step further—the 7.74 million people who completed a road race in 2002.

The fourth edition of the book also reflects the increasing trend toward running for fitness. Running is continuing to gain in popularity, especially among women, but there is more of an emphasis on fitness than on performance. That's according to New York Road Runners' Technologies Administrator Tom Kelley, who says that while NYRR membership continues to grow and more people attend its races, the number of runners participating in the sport at a competitive level is going down, while the number of runners participating for fitness and social interest is going up.

Understanding these trends is just one of the reasons NYRR is uniquely qualified to bring you this book. NYRR is the leading organization worldwide for running and fitness. Not only is the organization located in the area of the country with the greatest number of runners, but its scope is international. The New York City Marathon alone draws runners from nearly 100 nations.

From earlier volumes of this book, thousands of readers have benefited from the knowledge and expertise of NYRR and its associates. It is with great enthusiasm that we continue to provide the latest cutting-edge information available in this new volume.

—Gloria Averbuch

ABOUT THE CONTRIBUTORS

New York Road Runners Complete Book of Running and Fitness is based on original interviews, articles, and adapted writings of some of the running world's best and brightest. The advice and insights conveyed in these pages are the words not of one author, but of a panel of contributors connected to NYRR by having run in its events or otherwise worked with the organization. Below is an alphabetically arranged list of these contributors. Grateful acknowledgment is made to all of them, and to the publications that have granted permission to reprint articles and excerpts from previously published magazines and books.

Mark Allen is the six-time winner of the Ironman Triathlon in Hawaii. He was also the winner of the NYRRC's first triathlon and has been among the top finishers in the NYRR 10-mile Twosome. In 1997, *Outside* magazine called Allen "the World's Fittest Man."

Lauren Wallack Antonucci is a registered dietitian and sports nutritionist in private practice in New York who serves as nutrition consultant for New York Road Runners, as well as other running and triathlon teams and events. She has run in marathons and competes in triathlons, from international to the ironman distance.

Gordon Bakoulis has represented the United States in World Cup and World Championship competition and has run 2:33:01 for the marathon. She is an eight-time recipient of the NYRR Runner of the Year award. She is currently editorial director of *New York Runner,* the official publication of NYRR.

Beryl Bender Birch has been NYRR's wellness director since 1981. She has been a specialist in the field of yoga for athletes and yoga therapy since 1980 and is the author of *Power Yoga* and *Beyond Power Yoga.*

Amby Burfoot, who won the 1968 Boston Marathon, is the executive editor of *Runner's World* magazine. In his 40 years of running on the roads, he has covered more than 100,000 miles.

Nancy Clark, M.S., R.D., sports nutritionist and runner, is the author of *Nancy Clark's Sports Nutrition Guidebook,* third edition (2003), and

Nancy Clark's Food Guide for Marathoners (2002). She is the director of Nutrition Services, SportsMedicine Associates in Brookline, MA, one of the largest athletic injury clinics in New England.

Eamonn Coghlan was the world indoor record holder in the mile (3:49:7), the 1983 World Champion in the 5000 meters, and a three-time Olympian for Ireland. A 10-year resident of New York, Coghlan ran many NYRR races. He currently works with Our Lady's Hospital for Sick Children in his native Dublin.

Ted Corbitt, one of the founders of New York Road Runners and its first president, at one time held the American record in the 50-mile, 100-mile, and 24-hour runs. In addition, he was an Olympian in the marathon at the 1952 Games in Helsinki. Corbitt is a retired physical therapist who set a six-day race age-group record at age 82.

Margaret Dessau, M.D., is a certified internist and has been a member of the faculty of Columbia University Medical School in New York. She was also a contributor to *New York Running News* and an accomplished runner. At her peak, she won a 10K race in Tokyo in 36 minutes.

Tom Fleming, a 2:12:05 marathoner, is a two-time winner of the New York City Marathon and has held five American road bests at various distances. He is currently a teacher and high school coach. He has coached at all levels, from world class to recreational runners, and has served as a U.S. coach in international competition.

Susan Foster, a graphic designer and illustrator, is also a sub-three-hour marathoner and NYRR Runner of the Year nominee in her age category.

Peter Gambaccini is a writer for *Runner's World* and the *Village Voice* and a contributing editor of *New York Runner.* Gambaccini is also the author of *The New York City Marathon: Twenty-five Years.*

Thom Gilligan, a 2:30 marathoner, heads Marathon Tours, a travel agency specializing in trips to races around the world. He has been associated with NYRR for over two decades.

Bob Glover is the program director of Running Classes and City Sports for Kids at NYRR. He is also the author of *The Runner's Handbook, The Competitive Runner's Handbook,* and *The Runner's Training Diary.*

Gerard Hartmann is a physical therapist to 400-plus Olympic athletes and world record holders in distances ranging from 100 meters to the marathon, including some of the contributors to this book. He is largely credited by Paula Radcliffe as a driving force in her successful world marathon record runs. In his own athletic life, Hartmann is a seven-time national Irish triathlon champion.

Don Imus is the host of *Imus in the Morning,* syndicated on over 100 radio stations across the country. He has also done live broadcasts of the New York City Marathon.

Howard "Jake" Jacobson is a coach to Olympians and former men's national racewalk coach. A champion age-group racewalker, he introduced Healthwalking to the nation in 1982 and has taught over a million people to Healthwalk and Racewalk. For many years he conducted sold-out classes for NYRR. His protege **Lon Wilson** now oversees and conducts NYRR walking classes.

Deena Kastor set the American women's marathon record by running 2:21:16 at the 2003 London Flora Marathon. She made her marathon debut in 2001 at the New York City Marathon and ran 2:26:58, the fastest debut time for a U.S. woman. Kastor also dominates the world stage on both the roads and cross-country. In 2002, she ran a world 5K road best, set an American 10,000-meter track record, and won a silver medal in the 8K at the World Cross-Country Championships.

Meb Keflezighi, one of 11 children, moved with his family from Eritrea to San Diego in 1987. He is the U.S. record holder for 10,000 meters (27:13.98) and was the top American finisher in the 2002 New York City Marathon. Also in 2002, Keflezighi won five individual U.S. titles: 15K, 5K, and 7 miles on the road; 10,000m on the track; and the 12K cross-country. In 2003, Keflezighi won the U.S.A. Men's 8K Championship in Central Park.

Nina Kuscsik is the winner of the first official women's Boston Marathon (1972), a two-time winner of the New York City Marathon, a former 50-mile world record holder, and on the USATF Women's Long Distance Running Committee. She is also on the board of directors of NYRR.

Lewis Maharam, M.D., is the medical director of NYRR and the New York City Marathon, as well as a number of other prestigious road races and the New York City Triathlon. He is the chairman of the Board of Governors of the International Marathon Medical Directors Association (IMMDA) and president of the New York chapter of the American College of Sports Medicine. Dr. Maharam has a private sports medicine practice in New York City.

David E. Martin is professor of physiology in the Department of Cardiopulmonary Care Sciences at Georgia State University in Atlanta. He has had a lifelong research interest in the physiology of athletic performance, particularly with runners and jumpers. Martin, who also heads several committees of USATF, has been an adviser or coach to some of the nation's top distance runners for the past 30 years.

Stu Mittleman achieved an extraordinary string of ultramarathon successes in the 1980s. During that decade, he set American 100-mile, 1000-mile, and six-day records, of which the latter two still stand. He is the three-time national 100-mile champion and set a world record in the 1000-mile run in 1986. Mittleman is a personal trainer, author, and motivational speaker.

Gary Muhrcke is the winner of the first New York City Marathon (1970) and the winner of the first Empire State Building Run-Up (1978). He is the founder and owner of the Super Runners Shop chain of stores, located throughout the New York metropolitan area.

PattiSue Plumer is a two-time Olympian and multi-time American national champion in the 3000 and 5000 meters. She previously held the American record for 5000 meters. She is the winner of the 1990 Fifth Avenue Mile in 4:16.68, an event record that still stands.

Bill Rodgers is one of history's most accomplished road runners. He is the four-time winner of both the New York City and Boston Marathons. An Olympian and winner of other numerous prestigious road races and awards, he is still a top age group competitor.

Marla Runyan, who is legally blind, captivated the world's attention in 2002 when she ran 2:27:10 at the New York City Marathon. Runyan finished 2002 ranked number one in the U.S. in the Marathon and 3000m and 5000m on the track. She also holds the American indoor record in the 5000m, which she set at the Armory Track and Field Center in Manhattan.

Alberto Salazar changed the face of marathoning worldwide in the 1980s by winning three New York City Marathons: The first, in 1980, was then the fastest ever for a first-time marathoner, and the second was a then world best of 2:08:13. He simultaneously held the American record in the 5000 and 10,000 meters. He currently works for Nike sports marketing coaching elite young distance runners.

Norbert Sander, M.D., is the president of The Armory Foundation, which oversees the largest indoor track and field program in the nation. He is also the winner of the 1974 New York City Marathon and an NYRR board member. Sander still maintains his medical practice, located in City Island, New York.

Mona Shangold, M.D., who has spoken at NYRR clinics, has long been at the forefront of research and information regarding women and exercise. She is currently director of the Center for Women's Health and Sports Gynecology in Philadelphia. In addition, Shangold is the author of a number of books in her area of expertise.

George Sheehan, M.D., the renowned running philosopher, died in 1993. He was a regular columnist for *Runner's World* magazine and the author of numerous books. He was also a top runner in his age group for many years.

Frank Shorter is the 1972 Olympic gold medalist in the marathon and the 1976 Olympic marathon silver medalist. His gold medal performance has been credited as a major catalyst for the American running boom.

Francie Larrieu Smith can boast a running career with the greatest longevity and versatility of any American runner ever, man or woman. She made five Olympic teams and two World Championship teams for distances from 800 meters to the marathon. She held 36 U.S. records and 12 world bests, which she set from age 16 to 38.

Mickey Lawrence, also an avid runner, heads Image Impact, Inc., a special events marketing company, and works with NYRR.

Allan Steinfeld, New York Road Runners president and CEO since 1993, has been on the staff since 1978. Over a 20-year-period, he worked together with Fred Lebow to develop renowned events, such as the New York City Marathon. He is one of the world's leading authorities on the technical aspects of road racing and has developed many of the methods that are now standard for road races around the world. A former competitor, and lifelong runner, he is also an officer of several national running associations and serves as a technical adviser for television broadcasts of the Olympic Games.

Doug Stern is an aquatics consultant and competitive athlete. His swim instruction is extensive and includes all ages from high schoolers to senior citizens, and people from various sports backgrounds. He is a contributing writer for several publications, and his deep water running classes are part of the NYRR program.

Felicia Stoler, M.S., R.D., is the nutrition captain for the New York City Marathon. She is the sports nutritionist at the New York City

Marathon Health and Fitness Expo, which is visited by 75,000 people annually, including all marathon participants. She is also a clinician and the expert speaker for the RUN NYC program.

Kathrine Switzer is perhaps best known for being one of the first women to run the Boston Marathon. Switzer, the winner of the 1974 New York City Marathon, is also head of the highly successful Avon women's running circuit. She has also worked on running events for television.

Cliff Temple, a journalist and coach, died in 1994. He had been the Track & Field correspondent of the *Sunday Times* (London) since 1969. He covered six summer Olympic Games and coached—among others—a number of British Olympians.

Grete Waitz is the nine-time winner of the New York City Marathon and the six-time winner of the New York Mini 10K. In those NYRR events alone, she set a total of five world bests. Waitz is also an Olympic silver medalist and 1983 World Champion (both in the marathon), and the five-time winner of the World Cross-Country Championships. She is chairwoman of the NYRR Foundation.

Dan Weiner, M.D., is a New York City plastic surgeon and avid runner.

Jim and Phil Wharton have been worldwide leaders in musculoskeletal therapy since 1988. They have personally worked with all level of athletes, from recreational to over 150 Olympic medallists. Since 1993, the Whartons have taught active-isolated stretching classes for NYRR. They are the authors of books on stretching and strengthening, published by Random House, including *The Whartons' Stretch Book*. Their latest is *The Whartons' Back Book* (Rodale Press).

Thanks also go to Paul Friedman, Gabriel Sherman (editorial assistant), Lewis Maharam, M.D., Ian Jackman, Gordon Bakoulis, and Angela Miller for their various contributions.

ABOUT NEW YORK ROAD RUNNERS (NYRR)

New York Road Runners (NYRR) is a not-for-profit corporation that believes in and promotes the sport of running for health, recreation, and competition. Founded in 1958 with a membership of 47, NYRR has since grown into the world's largest running organization with more than 40,000 members from every U.S. state and dozens of countries around the world; it serves 250,000 runners and walkers annually.

NYRR is dedicated to keeping runners and walkers on the roads moving strongly, healthfully, and happily; introducing the sports of running and walking to new and young runners; and encouraging and advancing the performances of talented and competitive runners.

NYRR fulfills its mission through a host of events, programs, and communications. NYRR is also a leading source of information and education on the sport. The organization is run by a staff of pacesetters and innovators in the sport.

RACES AND FUN RUNS

NYRR offers a complete calendar of events with races nearly every weekend—and sometimes two. Among the most prominent are the New York City Marathon®, which treats over 34,000 finishers to a tour of New York City; New York Mini 10K, the longest-running and most prestigious all-women's race in the world; the Fifth Avenue Mile, where both elite and everyday runners enjoy a fleeting glimpse of New York City's Museum Mile; the Empire State Building Run-Up; and the New Year's Eve Midnight Run, which starts as the clock strikes 12 and the new year begins.

NYRR annually publishes a race calendar, which includes all NYRR races. (Check on the Web at www.nyrrc.org.)

CLASSES AND CLINICS

NYRR hosts Running, Power Yoga, Deep Water Running, Active-Isolated Stretching, IM=X Pilates, and Healthwalk/Racewalk classes to educate runners and walkers and to keep them moving properly and smoothly. In addition, NYRR offers several clinics per year ranging from running injury-free to marathon preparation.

Running Classes, which began in the 1970s, cater to runners of all levels—from beginners to advanced competitors.

Power Yoga, the total strength and flexibility workout for mind and body, combines a flowing sequence of postures with dynamic breathing techniques. Power Yoga classes are recommended for prevention and rehabilitation of injury. (For more information, see Chapter 12.)

Deep Water Running, which is a modified non-impact form of running, is perfect for runners recovering from or trying to prevent injury. (For more information, see Chapter 11.)

IM=X Pilates (puh-LAH-teez) is a means of improving posture, lengthening muscles, and developing core abdominal and back strength.

Active-Isolated Stretching is a full-body flexibility program created to complement running and other activities.

Easier to begin and not as jarring as running, **Healthwalking** provides total fitness and is virtually injury-free. (For more information, see Chapter 39.)

PUBLICATIONS

In 1958, noted marathoner Ted Corbitt put out the first edition of a running publication on a mimeographed sheet. It became the first issue of *New York Runner*, the nation's oldest running magazine. Today, the quarterly magazine, received by members of NYRR, contains informative and entertaining feature stories, race coverage, event schedules, and medical and training columns.

NYRR also publishes a thrice-annual newsletter, "In the Loop," which is sent to all NYRR members and features news of members and member programs and services. A bimonthly race mailing is available to members on request.

MERCHANDISE

The Running Gallery, featuring a wide selection of official NYRR and New York City Marathon merchandise, is located in the lobby of the New York Road Runners at 9 East 89th Street. The store offers everything from T-shirts, both cotton and technical fabrics, to hats and ties. NYRR members enjoy a 10 percent discount on all non-sale merchandise. Items may also be purchased online at www.nyrrc.org/merchandise or by calling toll free at 1-800-405-2288.

COMMUNITY SERVICES

The Safety Program

NYRR Safety Program is dedicated to the security of Central Park and all those who use it. Through the *Safety Patrol* program, as well as its daily *Informal Group Runs*, NYRR works with staff and volunteers in cooperation with police and park personnel to offer safety options. The community service kiosk is located at Engineer's Gate in Central Park (5th Avenue and 90th Street). NYRR Community Services Manager Steve Boland says the program is a "running neighborhood watch for Central Park."

New York Road Runners Foundation

The New York Road Runners Foundation is a series of community-based running programs within underserved populations throughout New York City, with the goal of disseminating its expertise to interested parties across the country and around the world. The Foundation serves youth of all fitness and athletic abilities. As of 2003, over 1,000 youth participate weekly in the Foundation's flagship after school program, *Running Partners*, which has been established in more than 50 schools and community centers throughout the city.

City Sports for Kids

City Sports for Kids, part of the New York Road Runners Foundation, is a youth track and field program based at the Armory Track and Field Center in Manhattan. Founded in 1990, the program offers skills training for children of all ability levels in running, sprints, hurdles, long jump, high jump, shot put, and javelin. Each session includes low-key meets with age-group categories and colorful ribbons for all.

Senior Fitness

Free and open to men and women age 60 and over, this program features guided walks of up to three miles through Central Park. Groups meet throughout the week and are taken on diverse routes by walk leaders. The program began in 1997, in response to both an aging demographic and NYRR's desire to expand its fitness role to include all facets of the population. This "walk and talk" program also includes the social benefits of exercise. "Graduates," that is, those who desire a more ambitious exercise program, are referred to NYRR's Healthwalking classes. NYRR recommends that participants check with their physician prior to starting an exercise program.

ACHILLES TRACK CLUB

One of the most remarkable success stories of NYRR is the Achilles Track Club. Perhaps no aspect of the running movement better demonstrates the range of the sport's potential.

The Achilles Track Club began in 1983 as a NYRR program to introduce disabled people to the sport of running. It is now a worldwide organization that encourages people with all types of disabilities to participate in running with the general public. The organization provides training, encouragement, and technical expertise to disabled runners.

Achilles includes people with all types of disabilities, such as visual impairment, stroke, cerebral palsy, paraplegia, arthritis, amputation, multiple sclerosis, cystic fibrosis, cancer, traumatic head injury, and organ transplant. Runners participate with crutches, in wheelchairs, on prostheses, and without aids.

Since its founding, Achilles has expanded into several chapters in the United States and over 100 chapters in 63 countries. There is also a youth program called Achilles Kids. In New York, 2,600 disadvantaged children with disabilities train at 78 public schools. Achilles 65, a relatively new program for disabled seniors at senior citizen centers, is currently operating.

Membership in Achilles is free and includes races, coaching, workouts, team T-shirts, and the newsletter, *The Achilles Heel.* Contact Achilles at ACHILLES@aol.com, www. AchillesTrackClub.org, 212-354-0300, 42 West 38th Street, Fourth Floor, New York, NY 10018.

One of the most dramatic Achilles stories is that of Trisha Meili, better known as the "Central Park Jogger." In her best-selling autobiography, *I Am the Central Park Jogger,* which details her brutal attack while running in Central Park, Meili writes of beginning to run again, only shortly after beginning to walk again after having to use a wheelchair. Her first tentative runs were with a chapter of the Achilles Track Club. In 1994, she became a volunteer guide for Achilles, much like the volunteer who had helped her start to run again. She joined Achilles members at their Saturday morning workouts in Central Park.

In 1994, Meili escorted Achilles Track Club founder Dick Traum as his guide in the New York City Marathon. In 1995, Meili joined the Board of Directors of Achilles, and through that organization became involved in co-authoring a scientific article outlining research that demonstrated the positive results of exercise on brain-injured people.

In 1995, Meili ran the New York City Marathon with an Achilles guide. As she wrote in her book, "Six and a half years after I had nearly lost my life in this park, had lost 75 to 80 percent of my blood, had nearly lost an eye, had lain in a coma from which some doctors believed I would never emerge—indeed, after doctors had predicted I would never regain my physical or mental capabilities—I crossed the New York City Marathon finish line in four hours, thirty minutes, and one second . . ."

At mile 16 of that race, Meili was joined by another Achilles guide, Jim Schutz, the man who would eventually become her husband.

Meili continues to run. On June 29, 2003, she participated in the Hope and Possibility 5-Mile in Central Park, a race produced by the Achilles Track Club. The race passed by the site of her attack.

NYRR MEMBERSHIP

For more information about NYRR, please send a self-addressed stamped envelope with your query to NYRR, 9 East 89th Street, New York, NY 10128, check on the Web at www.nyrrc.org, or call 212-423-2292.

REMEMBERING FRED LEBOW

Like so much at NYRR, this book began with Fred Lebow. Fred was also the mastermind behind events like the New York City Marathon and was one of the figureheads of the running movement.

During the many hours and months it took to write the original edition of this book, and the years spent promoting it, Fred's energy and commitment never waned. In fact, he was a tireless promoter—speaking at clinics and attending numerous book signings. After all, he believed in what he was promoting. Despite his four-year battle with brain cancer, or maybe because of it, Fred had so much he wanted to share. What better place than in a book? When he delved into the project, he devoted the same talent and energy he gave to all of his creative work. And the result was equally successful.

On October 9, 1994, Fred lost his battle with cancer. But, in a larger sense, he had won the war—against time. That's because he left the world his legacy. From a handful of diehard runners circling Central Park, he created and developed the New York City Marathon, one of the country's largest and among the world's most prestigious events of its kind. Fred was at the forefront of the running boom, blending all-comers with world class athletes to create a variety of events that still endure—including runs up New York City's Empire State Building and down posh Fifth Avenue. His support for women's running resulted in the Women's Mini Marathon, the original all-women's race in this country. His events have served as prototypes for other such endeavors around the world. As president and later chairman of the New York Road Runners Club, Fred built the organization into an international resource for running and fitness events and information.

Fred's true genius was the way he blended sport and life. He was an impresario in the grandest tradition. He took a simple sport and, with a stroke of daring and imagination, made it a global passion. Those who have ever run, walked, or watched a road race, or enjoyed the sport on any level, benefit from what he created.

Fred was an unlikely race director who, while wearing running shoes, brought his message of health and fitness everywhere and to everyone—

from meetings with several presidents in the White House to an audience with the Pope at the Vatican.

It was with the same remarkable spirit that Fred dealt with his illness. No amount of running or fitness could have cured his ultimately-fatal brain cancer. But Fred achieved so many victories in the race against this disease. Determined to regain his fitness after extensive cancer treatments, his will was remarkable. From the few halting steps, to the loops of the hospital corridors he circled, Fred built his stamina. He vowed to realize a seemingly impossible dream: to run his own marathon.

In 1992—in celebration of his 60th birthday—Fred Lebow did just that. With the help of his friend and coach, nine-time Marathon winner Grete Waitz, he completed the 26.2-mile New York City Marathon in 5:32:34. His race was a gift he gave himself; moreover, it was the ultimate statement he made to the rest of the world. Fred's message to us all was simple yet profound: to live life to its fullest.

There are many markers to honor Fred Lebow. Among them are a life-size bronze statue in Central Park and the display of the shoes he wore to run his last marathon at the USATF Hall of Fame, to which he was inducted. The street going by New York Road Runners headquarters was renamed in his honor. This book, which endures and has been reborn in its latest revision, is yet another of those markers.

In Fred's honor, and because his advice and anecdotes will always be a part of the history of the sport of running, some of his contributions have been left as they were first written in earlier editions of the book.

Each of the contributors to this book—and everyone involved—participated in Fred's honor and on behalf of NYRR to create the most complete volume on running and fitness. Fred would be grateful to those contributors who continue to update their material, and also to the new contributors who provide their insights and expertise. We continue to dedicate our efforts to our dear friend, whose spirit remains everywhere.

—*Gloria Averbuch*

FOREWORD

On behalf of New York Road Runners, the authors, the more than 40 contributors to this book, and the scores of others who helped create it and make it such a success, I would like to express my deep gratitude, as well as pride and satisfaction. We at New York Road Runners are gratified that our work has been so well received. As we celebrate the fourth edition of this book, we acknowledge the accomplishments of our organization, and also of its revered former leader, the late Fred Lebow.

As president of NYRR, and as an avid, lifelong runner, I know the value of expert running and training advice. I am gratified to say that this book provides this advice, and so much more. From running to walking, from cross training to travel, from health and injury prevention to words of wisdom for all runners of all levels and ages—this book truly lives up to its claim of being "complete."

But you need not just take my word for it. I have written this introduction for the latest revision—the fourth edition of this book. The fact this volume is being reissued yet again is testimony to the many thousands who have read, and benefited, from the book—using it continually as a resource guide. We at NYRR know that the running and fitness community need and want solid and useful advice. Based on the positive response to the book, we trust that they have found it. It is this response, together with the ringing endorsement of many of the world's best runners and experts, that has made this book so popular and such a success.

As times have changed, and running has expanded to include other activities, NYRR has accommodated these changes. In all our events and programs, we are striving to meet the changing needs of our community. From cross training to family fitness, the Road Runners prides itself in being on the cutting edge of the latest additions and developments in our sport. Because I believe in our organization's ability to reflect these developments, I am confident that this book will continue to serve our community successfully.

The latest development as this book goes to press is the first-time title sponsorship of the ING New York City Marathon. The agreement between New York Road Runners and ING, a major global bank and financial organization, is the largest sponsorship deal in the history of the race. In line

with New York Road Runners' emphasis on community service, which is detailed in the book, the sponsorship agreement includes ING Run for Something Better, the aim of which is to advance running and fitness programs
in both the local and global running communities.

As you learn all there is to know about NYRR and the sport of running,
it is my sincere belief that you will gain the knowledge to run far, fast, and
healthfully into the future.

—Allan Steinfeld, president and CEO, New York Road Runners;
race director, ING New York City Marathon

INTRODUCTION

When I lined up to run my first marathon in New York in 1978, I was amazed when I looked around at the huge number of people on the starting line. Until that time, I had only run races on a track with no more than a handful of other competitors. It was that day in New York that I realized there was a movement, and a level of running, totally different from mine.

"Why would all these people run 26.2 miles?" I remember thinking. Who was the 45-year-old who would finish in four hours, or the age group competitors trying to win in their category? I had never related to a certain type of running—for personal goals and satisfaction, for fitness, even to develop one's own level of athleticism.

Today I understand all those people, because I am one of them. I'm a much slower runner than I was in my competitive days, but equally devoted to my recreational running. When I do participate in a race, I start and finish in the middle of the pack. I have come to enjoy running on another level than world class, and find that I, too, train for personal satisfaction.

The running boom changed a lot of people's lives—not the least of which was my own. Running that first marathon so many years ago opened a new door for me. Instead of retiring from the sport as I had previously planned, I was reborn as a road runner and enjoyed another decade of success. During that time, I was joined by millions of others who found themselves similarly reborn through road running and the fitness movement.

There has been yet another development in the running movement. In the 1980s, the average runner trained to take part in races and to improve and run faster times. Today, running is part of a total fitness program and lifestyle—which may, or may not, include competition.

Today, the running movement continues with very solid participation numbers. However, based on my experience in clinics and among thousands of runners, many people have different motivations for running than in the boom years of the 1980s. There are several reasons. One, I believe, is that the average person is not as fit as he or she was 25 years ago. So instead of competition or to improve running times, people run now more for health and fitness. In addition, there is a large expansion of charity races and cause-related organizations (such as Fred's Team), and this brings in an entire new population of people who might not otherwise participate. It creates an extra motivation and commitment for participants.

New York Road Runners, whose expertise is the foundation for this book, understands these latest developments in the running movement. Their programs reflect these changes. What NYRR has to offer—from its races for all ages to its classes and educational clinics—is phenomenal. NYRR is also a health-oriented and a social organization. Although I have belonged to a wonderful running club in my native Norway since I was 12 years old, it doesn't have nearly the reach and scope of NYRR.

I can personally testify to that reach, and to the expertise of New York Road Runners. I often say New York is my second home. After winning the Marathon several times, people started to know me. I would go running in Central Park and be greeted by strangers who called out, "Welcome back!" The friendship that I developed with New York Road Runners' former president, Fred Lebow, has extended itself to the organization. Although Fred has passed away, I am still actively involved in NYRR events, such as the Norway Run and Grete's Great Gallop, the JPMorgan Chase Corporate Challenge, and the NYRR Foundation. I consider New York Road Runners unique in all the world.

Like Fred and NYRR, *New York Road Runners Complete Book of Running and Fitness* is on the pulse of the running movement. It covers everything. All the book's expert contributors—those "born and raised" in the early running boom and those who are part of the next generation—make it reliable and trustworthy. It is with pride that I am one of the contributors to this book. As an author myself, I know how thorough this volume is. I appreciate how much work that takes.

From my competitive days and years of doing clinics and coaching average runners, I know the value of good training, and the quality results that come from that training. In the years of giving advice to others, I have also learned the importance of helpful, cutting-edge running and fitness information. Between these covers, you have just that.

—Grete Waitz

PART 1
TRAINING

1
FOR BEGINNERS

Every runner, at one time or another, is a beginner. As a beginner, you can reap all the benefits that the seasoned runner enjoys, plus you may appreciate elements of the sport long forgotten by the veteran. As a beginner, you also bring a special freshness and excitement to the sport that you should indulge and appreciate.

WHERE TO BEGIN...?

What can you expect as a beginner? For starters, you will gain a new awareness of your body. Running will improve your stamina. It will help you control or reduce your weight (most beginners lose one half to one pound per week). And running provides a new relationship with nature; if you've never really felt the sun, wind, or rain on your face, you will now!

So how should you begin? Grete Waitz, nine-time New York City Marathon champion, has outlined a ten-week program specifically for beginners.

Waitz says her "running" program is actually a "jogging" program because you must jog before you can run. Both running and jogging are enjoyable and beneficial, but one precedes the other, and then they are done in balance. In fact, every running program, no matter what level, includes some jogging. Before beginning this program, be sure you have a physical and consult your physician about your basic health and fitness. Also, consider a few of Waitz's facts and tips:

Run at a conversational pace. While jogging you should be able to talk comfortably without being winded. Make a commitment to train with a friend. When motivation is low and excuses are easy to find, that commitment to meet your training partner will see you through.

There is a saying in Norwegian, **"Hurry slowly."** Getting fit is done by gradually and progressively increasing training. Beginners often feel Waitz's program is too slow; however, although the heart and lungs respond quickly to exercise, muscles and joints take much longer. That is why those who run too far and too fast too soon often end up injured, burned out, or both. On the other hand, if the program is too strenuous, take your time, even longer than ten weeks, if necessary. Stay with a given session as long as you feel you must, and move ahead when you feel you are ready.

This program is designed to bring you from your armchair to running 3 1/4 miles (five kilometers plus) continuously. It is based on running three days per week. You should space those days out to allow for sufficient recovery between efforts. If you are not using a track to gauge the distances, you can approximate them. With experience, you will begin to get a sense of how long it takes you to run each segment and to complete the workout. Then you will be able to use time as a basic indicator of distance. (The point, however, is not to run for time.)

Studies have shown that the ideal amount of exercise for optimum fitness is 20 to 30 minutes three times a week, done at a moderate level of intensity. This program will get you fit. You should realize that those who run more than this amount are doing so for reasons beyond fitness. (If this eventually becomes the case for you, you can explore more advanced programs in this book.)

Use the first four weeks to get a general education. Pay close attention to your body; learn to read its signals of fatigue and stress, or when you can push beyond them. It's like studying another language. It may seem foreign at first, but eventually you will learn to understand the meaning of various physical sensations. (If you discover a particular week is especially difficult, feel free to repeat it. There is no need to enforce the ten-week schedule if you would feel better modifying it.)

After ten weeks, you may either stay at the level you have reached or you may want to increase your running with a goal, for example, running a race. To maintain basic fitness, however, simply continue doing the schedule for week nine.

Ten-Week Beginner's Program

Week 1
- Alternately jog/walk (eight of each) 100-yard segments, for a total of 1 mile.
- Same workout for all three days.

Week 2
- Alternately jog/walk (five of each) 200-yard segments, for a total of 1 1/4 miles.
- Same workout for all three days.

Week 3

- Alternately jog/walk, varying the segments between 200 and 400 yards, for a total of 1 1/2 miles.
- Same workout for all three days.

Week 4

- Alternately jog/walk, but walk only half the distance of each jog. Vary the segments between 1/4 and 1/2 mile, for a total of 1 3/4 miles.
- Same workout for all three days.

Week 5

- Day 1: 1/2-mile jog, 1/4-mile walk, 1/2-mile jog, 1/4-mile walk, 1/2-mile jog, for 2 miles total.
- Day 2: 3/4-mile jog, 1/2-mile walk, 3/4-mile jog, for 2 miles total.
- Day 3: 2-mile jog, no walk.

Week 6

- Day 1: 1/2-mile jog, 1/4-mile walk, 3/4-mile jog, 1/4-mile walk, 1/2-mile jog, for 2 1/4 miles total.
- Day 2: 1-mile jog, 1/4-mile walk, 1-mile jog, for 2 1/4 miles total.
- Day 3: 2 1/4-mile jog, no walk.

Week 7

(Only jogging, no walking from this point on; however, you can vary the pace of the jog.)

- 2 1/2-mile jog.
- Same workout all three days.

Week 8

- 2 3/4-mile jog.
- Same workout all three days.

Week 9

- 3-mile jog.
- Same workout all three days.

Week 10

- 3 ¼ miles total (5 kilometers plus).
- Congratulations! You're no longer a beginner.

GRETE WAITZ'S RUNNING FOR FUN AND FITNESS

I've noticed that for some people the physiological motion of running is very easy. I've watched a very big man, 220 pounds, run very economically with a very good gait. Usually these people are naturally athletic. They find running simple. There's no batting a ball. There's no fielding. All you need is yourself and a decent pair of shoes. I think that's why running is so appealing to most people. Obviously, it must be easy if so many people attain an acceptable level of fitness and stay with the sport so long.

Is there any personality trait that makes someone a good runner? That's probably one of the hardest questions to answer. There are some people who have excelled who don't have the greatest talent, but they're bright enough and realistic about their goals. They know what they have to do to achieve those goals. And this is true for all levels.

Are the really good runners smarter? Not necessarily. I've known some who weren't. But then you've got to factor in an incredible God-given innate ability. There's something else that makes the great ones different. I think that, number one, they had a good mother and father; the genetics are right. Of course, they also have great desire. I can spend hours talking about the nature of desire, will, and guts.

What makes running an integral part of someone's life? That may be an unanswerable question. Some people have no idea why they wake up every morning and have to get in their run. But they'll tell you what the end result is: They feel better and they don't get the headaches they used to at their jobs. The average person is running for both fitness and stress relief.

After an initial time period, running does become easier. You can always remember that first week, those first few runs. What people enjoy, whether you're talking about an elite runner or a jogger, is that you do improve fairly quickly.

How long this takes varies from person to person. I've seen some rather overweight people, for example, who weren't athletic at all, who started running and within three months made big changes. I don't just mean in how they looked, but their entire attitude. They felt more confidence in themselves and more confident about exercising.

The point is to take it gradually, particularly for those people who want to lose weight. Many times I advise them to begin with a walking program, because running may be too difficult. But I'll promote the activity either way. I know, sooner or later, they're going to want to start jogging or running.

Regardless of your reasons for wanting to begin a program of running, use some common sense:

1. **Start at the doctor's office.** A thorough checkup is recommended before undertaking an exercise program. It is useful to explain to your doctor the details of any exercise program you intend to do. A stress test is recommended if you are over age 40.

2. **Keep a diary, a running/exercise log.** You can track your progress by recording the times and distances you run, even how you feel, who you run with, and the weather. Be accurate about what you write, as this record can greatly instruct you in the future.

3. **In terms of clothing, always put comfort before fashion.** Wear loose clothing. Your feet will expand during a training run, so make sure you purchase shoes that are large enough. You should run in well-cushioned training shoes.

4. **Never push it.** Use the talk test to determine if your pace is appropriate: You should be able to converse comfortably while running. Run with the same style you use to walk, a relaxed effort with your own natural form and rhythm. Do not hesitate to alternate running and walking.

5. **Know your body.** Get in the habit of checking your pulse—in the morning before getting out of bed, during daily tasks, and during running. This will give you a gauge of both your general health and your fitness level. (To determine your pulse rate, see Heart Rate Monitor Training, Chapter 4.)

6. **Four feet are better than two.** Train with a friend. It makes the running easier and the commitment and motivation stronger.

7. **Develop your own training routine.** Any time of day and any place is fine, as long as you are consistent in exercising. If you pre-

fer to vary your fitness routine, do other exercises or sports on nonrunning days.

8. **Practice good exercise habits,** such as organized and thorough warmups and cool-downs, to avoid aches and pains. Easy-paced running is an effective warmup. The cool-down is most essential, and should include a stretching routine for muscle flexibility.

9. **To avoid injuries,** heed the following: Don't run in worn-down shoes; avoid uneven surfaces; don't be impatient and run too far or too fast too soon. If you feel a suspicious pain, or if you feel ill, take time off from running until the condition improves.

10. **Set no limitations.** While using common sense and being cautious is the best guarantee for long-term enjoyment and acquiring the benefits of running, don't underestimate your potential ability. There are times it feels great to go for it!

For the total newcomer to running, Cliff Temple, journalist and coach, offers these six golden rules:

1. Run more slowly than you think you should.
2. Don't run as far as you think you should.
3. Run more often than you think you should.
4. Exchange experiences with other runners whenever practical (shared training runs are ideal).
5. Try to find a local running club that offers coaching that is specific to newcomers.
6. Read running magazines and books from cover to cover, and always keep issues handy in case an injury or training query turns out to be *your* problem or question next week.

NYRR SAYS SLOW AND STEADY

Beginners should learn to love the sport. Like other endeavors, if running is not undertaken properly, it can be difficult and discouraging. It sometimes takes a while to learn to enjoy it. That doesn't necessarily happen overnight.

GRETE WAITZ'S 2-MILE WALKING AND JOGGING PROGRAM

Week	Day 1	Day 2	Day 3	Day 4 (optional)
1	10 min walk 5 × 1 min jog with 2 min walk between 10 min walk	40 min fast walking or other aerobic activity like biking, swimming, soccer, etc.	10 min walk 7 × 1 min jog 2 min walk between 5 min walk	same as day 2
2	10 min walk 5 × 2 min jog 2 min walk between 5–10 min walk	40 min fast walking or other aerobic activity like biking, swimming, soccer, etc.	same as day 1	same as day 2
3	5–10 min walk 6 × 2 min jog 1–2 min walk between 5–10 min walk	40 min fast walking or other aerobic activity like biking, swimming, soccer, etc.	5 min walk 8 × 2 min jog 1 min walk between 5 min walk	5 min walk 4 × 3 min 1–2 min walk 5 min walk
4	5 min walk 5 × 3 min jog 1 min walk between 5 min walk	5 min walk 3 × 5 min jog 1–2 min walk between 5 min walk	5 min walk 4 × 4 min jog 1 min walk between 5 min walk	40 min fast walking or other aero- bic activities
5	5 min walk 8–10 min jog 1–2 min walk 5 min jog 5 min walk	5 min walk 10 min jog 1–2 min walk 8 min jog 5 min walk	5 min walk 10 min jog 1 min walk 10 min jog 5 min walk	40 min fast walking or other aero- bic activities

(continued)

GRETE WAITZ'S 2-MILE WALKING AND JOGGING PROGRAM (CONT.)

Week	Day 1	Day 2	Day 3	Day 4 (optional)
6	5 min walk 10 min jog 1 min walk 10 min jog 5 min walk	5 min walk 15 min jog 1–2 min walk 5 min jog 5 min walk	5 min walk 20 min jog 5 min walk	40 min fast walking or other aerobic activities

You can follow this program if you have not exercised for some time and would like to get in shape again. The program starts conservatively, and it is something the whole family can do together. The relatively slow start is designed to improve your aerobic condition without the risk of injury. After all, your muscles, joints, and ligaments need a little time to get used to being active again.

If you are 50 or older and fairly new to exercise, you may prefer a slower progression than the program suggests. Make your own adjustments; use the program as your guideline.

Make sure you have a recovery day or two between the workouts and don't forget to stretch after each walk/run.

In order to start properly, the beginners in NYRR running classes combine running and walking. Most novices make the mistake of deciding right away to run one mile. That's the number, the distance, that they have in their head. But most don't realize how far one mile really is. This kind of approach—taking on too much too soon—usually results in feeling pain, or becoming injured or discouraged.

The goal of the class is to get beginners eventually running 20 minutes without stopping, and to be introduced to the sport in a positive and enjoyable way.

GORDON BAKOULIS'S CONVENIENCE APPROACH

To me, the beauty of running is that you can do it anywhere. Other exercises seem so cumbersome in comparison: you have to go to a gym, or change into a bathing suit, or buy expensive equipment. Although each person has to find his or her own exercise formula, the simplicity of running gives it a great advantage.

Here are some tips for beginners:

1. Find a training partner.
2. If necessary, join a health club and run on an indoor track or treadmill.
3. Seek out local road races.
4. Join in group runs, or set up groups of your own.
5. Take a fitness vacation or attend a running camp.
6. If you're injured, try to adopt a "Zen-like" attitude. Keep in shape with crosstraining.

FRANCIE LARRIEU SMITH'S ADVICE FROM EXPERIENCE

Be patient; don't expect too much too soon. I highly discourage young people from competing in road races. I think it's great to expose them to fun running, but it kills me to see a child running the marathon.

A lot of beginners don't realize that some pain is natural. Even the most seasoned runners experience pain. When I come back after a lay-off due to injury and I'm forced to start at the bottom, I, too, experience some aches and pains. It's important to know that it passes. Just make sure to go by the book, building slowly by adding only ten percent a week.

I think you can know the signs of injury trouble with experience. Exercise helps you to get to know your body. I know when something is serious or not. I believe I've come to know my body so well that I can judge if and when it's time to see a doctor. This is the case not only with running injuries, it's true even with illnesses, like the flu.

I hope that people gain some sound training knowledge with this book. I meet people every day who still basically don't seem to know what to do. They read about someone's training in a running magazine and they copy it. One thing people need to realize is that there is no one program that works for everyone.

Another thing I tell runners is that no matter how inexperienced a runner you may be, there is nothing wrong with being intense. You don't know what you might discover. True, there are those who just don't have the genetics to be great. But then there are the "late bloomers." In running, as in any athletic event, there may be latent talents you never expected would blossom.

Do It Together

Exercise programs are followed better when working out with a spouse. In one study, nearly 50 percent of men who exercised alone quit their program after one year, while two-thirds of those exercising with their wives stuck with it.

RUN ROVER

Runners who are not content to let sleeping dogs lie are increasingly taking pets along for their runs and workouts. Why not? Dogs are great company, offer visible security, and make no running demands, conversational or otherwise. But is this fitness trend fair to your animal companion?

Yes, according to the Humane Society of the United States. Regular aerobic exercise, such as running and walking, is the best way to promote cardiovascular fitness and keep your dog's weight in check (sound familiar?).

For runners with like-minded canines, the Humane Society offers the following guidelines for a safe and satisfying running partnership:

- Be sure to check with your veterinarian before starting your pet on an exercise program. The vet will confirm if your pet is fit enough for regular exercise.

- Not all dogs are runners. Short-legged breeds are less suited to the sport, and pug-nosed pooches have trouble breathing. Make sure that running is the right kind of exercise for your pet.

- Consider investing in some of the gear that can help your running dog—a hands-free leash, reflective wear, a portable drinking bowl, running booties.

- Even if you do not warm up (and of course, you should), your dog might want to. Put the animal through a few sprints to loosen up its muscles and get its heart pumping.

- Build up slowly and watch for signs of fatigue. If your dog lies down during a workout, end the session.

- Keep water on hand before, during, and after a workout to avoid doggie dehydration.

- Avoid temperature extremes. Because dogs do not sweat, they can easily become overheated.

- If your canine is corpulent—i.e., you can't feel its ribs—cut out the dog's snacks and follow your vet's advice about putting your pet on a reduced-calorie diet. Be aware that most "people food" is too high in fat and calories for a dog.

- While running, watch the surface—your dog is barefoot! If your dog is not accustomed to running on pavement, build up gradually.

- Keep your dog on a leash and by your side when running. Your dog should wear an identification tag and, of course, should be licensed by your local Department of Health.

- Do not overdo it. Animals don't always know when to quit, so don't let your dog run until it drops.

STRIDING THROUGH THE DECADES: THE 20s AND 30s.

Masters runner and writer Gail Waesche Kislevitz wrote a series of articles for *New York Runner* called "Striding Through the Decades," which covered the twenties to the seventies. Here's what she discovered for your twenties and thirties:

- To make running a constant you can count on during these decades of change, set up a schedule and stick with it.

- Motivate yourself with a meaningful goal, such as running a race.

- Be willing to accept changes in the role of running, especially if you're coming from a competitive sports background. Career, relationships, and other lifestyle demands may simply be more important at this stage of life.

- If you are young and want to run forever, take care of yourself. Treat injuries at the onset, incorporate a stretching routine, and make sure to warm up before a race or workout.

- Establish healthy habits—such as stretching—and maintain them.

- Lift weights to strengthen the major muscles of the legs and upper body, and to maintain a stable core.

- Apply sunscreen every time you run outdoors. The cumulative effects of sun damage can lead to skin cancer down the road. (For the forties and fifties, see page 372.)

FRED LEBOW'S FIRST EXPERIENCES

My most vivid memories of beginning to run are of how little anyone seemed to know about the sport and how little was available in the way of information and equipment. Not only did I have trouble getting any decent shoes, but when I went to a newsstand to try to find a running magazine, it was hopeless. "Running," I told the vendor, who looked quite puzzled. "You know, track and field." His eyes lit up in seeming recognition. Then he handed me *Road & Track,* a magazine about cars.

I started running one mile along the Central Park reservoir. In one of my first runs, I saw an old-time runner and we started talking. He was a regular racer who ran events at Van Cortlandt Park. He encouraged me to race too. "But I'm 38 years old," I told him. "Well, I'm old enough to be your father, and I'm doing it!" he replied.

When I started running, I had the idea I had to be very good to participate. I remember how embarrassed I was the first time I called to inquire about a race and had to tell the official I was 38 years old. One of my first races was a five-miler near Yankee Stadium. People who raced were fairly serious in those days. There were only 60 people, and I came in 59th, beating a 70-year-old. But I was pleased I was able to finish without walking.

These days, it's perfectly acceptable to do a five-hour marathon. People run 4:59 and they're ecstatic. When I ran my first marathon (4:09), I was depressed that I didn't break four hours. A majority of runners in New York don't break four hours. I think it's great that now time no longer determines or affects participation.

When I began running, I sought advice from a multitude of people—athletes and coaches. Running was so foreign to me and to those around me. It seemed hard to get advice. The questions were very basic then, like: Why do this sport in the first place?

In 1970 I was talking with Gary Muhrcke and Norb Sander (two early winners of the New York City Marathon). Gary took me outside to show me how to run, how to lift my legs. Like many people at the time, I used to believe running wasn't natural, that you had to learn how to do it. I was surprised when Gary finally said, "It's nothing special. Just do it. It's a natural movement."

The great thing about this sport is that it's never too late to begin, and there's so much support to do so. Jack Rudin is one of our Marathon sponsors and has been involved with running and racing for years. His father was a marathoner. It's only recently that he's started walking (inspired, no doubt, by his wife, Susan, an avid racewalker). I see how he gloats over his achievements, how happy he is. It's great.

2

INTRODUCTION TO TRAINING TERMS

A variety of training philosophies, advice, and programs are followed by beginners, as well as advanced runners. Many programs are similar in principle, and many experts' views support each other. Yet different athletes stress different aspects of the sport—its benefits, techniques, and goals. Remember, no training program can account for the individual circumstances of each runner. As with any training program, the ones in this book can be adapted to suit specific needs.

The basic training techniques are defined below.

FARTLEK

Fartlek, which means "speed play" in Swedish, was popularized as a form of training by Gosta Holmer, a longtime Swedish Olympic coach. In essence, it consists of incorporating bursts of speed into the middle of a long run. You may do these bursts, for example, for the distance of certain markers—several trees or light posts—or for a particular time (30 seconds or one minute). "Fartlek brings us back to the games of our childhood," according to Cliff Temple. "A child plays while sitting, walks some steps, runs to its mother, walks or runs back to the playground, makes a longer excursion to get a toy....The swift but short runs dominate and develop the inner organs."

What appeals to so many runners about fartlek training is that it takes the pressure off of doing more structured, timed intervals on the track. In addition, it's a good alternative to a track workout in bad weather. Whereas you might cancel a track workout on a rainy, windy day when the desired times would be impossible to achieve, there is no reason to skip a fartlek workout; in fact, in this case, it's also good practice for racing under tough conditions.

While fartlek is an effective method of quality training, at the same time it also seems a natural extension of the recreational aspect of running, as the name "speed play" indicates.

INTERVAL TRAINING

While most elite runners begin their careers on the track, the majority of average runners have been introduced to the sport via the roads and road racing. A good number of these runners find the track foreign and intimidating. The track can be a rewarding new challenge and an important tool in training. What's more, for a true test of ability, nothing surpasses running the 400-meter oval.

According to Cliff Temple, whose ideas about interval training are given here, many runners have an aversion to running on the track; however, by using that simple 400-meter oval, you can improve your distance-running performances more effectively than with yet another road run. In addition, many still have the impression tracks are for the elite. That is simply not so.

How does track running help a runner? On a track, you most likely will run a series of relatively short repetitions over distances from 400 to 1000 meters. Due to the brevity of each effort compared to your normal 45 minutes of steady running on the road, each run can be at a considerably faster pace than you are used to.

On a steady road run, your pulse rate might remain around 120–140 beats per minute most of the way. But at the end of a single hard 600- or 1000-meter run, you could push your pulse up to 180 or more. As your body adapts to the higher demands, it becomes still more physiologically efficient. And don't forget, these shorter intervals can be done on the road if a track is unavailable, and that same purpose will still be served.

CLIFF TEMPLE'S GOLDEN RULES OF THE TRACK

1. Always run in a counterclockwise direction.
2. Never warm up on the inside two lanes. Use an outer lane or the grass infield.
3. If you have to cross the grass infield, make sure no one is throwing a javelin, discus, or hammer.
4. If, during a hard training run, someone is walking, standing, or running more slowly on the inside lane ahead of you, shout "Track!" which is the standard warning signal.

At first, it is best to be conservative. You'll know you've succeeded if you finish the session feeling you could have done a little more. If necessary, adjust the sample workouts outlined in this chapter and throughout this book to achieve that feeling. As you gain conditioning, you can increase, and eventually move ahead to the next level of program.

Interval Training Tips

1. Don't use the same interval session every time; allow yourself three or four variations of a session to check progress. (The programs and philosophies in this book allow for such variations.)

2. You don't necessarily need to use a track, but do employ permanent and easily identifiable landmarks.

3. Be strict with yourself in timing your recovery period.

4. If possible, get someone to time your runs and the recoveries.

5. Make sure you warm up properly before the beginning of each session.

6. Interval training has countless variations, which can be adjusted as you become fitter; you can increase the number of runs, amend the distance of run, or reduce the amount of interval recovery.

7. Don't expect every single session to show an improvement in times. The fitter you get, the more difficult that becomes.

8. Make allowances for diverse weather conditions; e.g., run with the wind rather than against it where possible, but note the conditions in your training diary.

One caveat: If you're new to the track, take the opportunity to get used to running on turns. This can be quite stressful, particularly on the inside leg, which incurs a torque not experienced when running in a straight line. This is even more the case on indoor tracks, which are usually smaller and have more and tighter turns than outdoor tracks. The risks of injury on an indoor track are higher as a result. You might want to take a few weeks to adapt by running an increasing number of easy laps on the track before beginning hard efforts.

Balance is another way to avoid potential injury. You can lessen stress by alternating directions. Cliff Temple's golden rules point out that track etiquette and safety require running in the counterclockwise direction; however, if the track isn't crowded, or you're willing to run your workout in outside lanes, it's possible to change directions. Olympic 1500-meter bronze medalist and New York City Marathon champion Rod Dixon related that he would run 20 quarters on the track during his building phase, alternating five in the clockwise direction, five in the counterclockwise direction.

This caveat applies even if you're not taking up speedwork. Many people run recreationally on the track or are tempted to find an indoor facility in inclement weather. Often personnel at these tracks will switch the running direction periodically throughout the day. If staff at your facility does not, request it, explaining why.

HILL TRAINING

Like the program outlined in Chapter 3, Cliff Temple advocates the use of hill training. He recommends a one- to two-mile warm-up jog, and stretching exercises for gluteal (buttocks) muscles, quadriceps, hamstrings, calves, and Achilles tendons. Afterward, a one- to two-mile jog is recommended for a cool-down. But he cautions against hill work if you have existing calf or Achilles injuries.

According to Temple, the muscle groups used to tackle the resistance provided by a hill are virtually the same as those used for sprinting, although their range of movement is different. By running a series of uphill efforts, it is possible to simultaneously improve strength and, indirectly, speed. Hill running should give the well-conditioned runner a good return for the time and effort invested in it.

Variations on Hill Running

To avoid running steep downhills and to allow for sufficient recovery from an uphill leg, Temple advocates running hills in a "D" shape. Athletes run hard 80 to 100 meters up the straight line of the D, then gently jog around the curved part in a gradual descent to the start of the next circuit. If the course is grass and free of hazards like stones and glass, Temple encourages athletes to run in bare feet to allow the fullest range of natural leg movement. If this type of "D" course is impractical, one variation to running up a hill and straight back down can be running up and down two short, parallel roads that are connected at top and bottom in a square-shaped course.

When racing, some runners tend to slow down when they go up a hill. Yet according to Running Tips on Anglefire.com, that is one of the worst and most common mistakes that a runner makes. A hill is supposed to be one of the best places to speed up. If you keep your pace going up a hill, chances are you won't get passed. In fact, you will pass other runners. Being passed on a hill "burns" a runner's mind more than almost any other racing strategy.

While sprinting short hills is designed to develop dynamic, blazing speed, there are other methods and purposes for running hills. Training should reflect the nature of its use. Thus, you need not always run hill workouts that require you to charge up at full speed. Temple points out that for the distance runner, the hill must be looked on as something to be negotiated effectively and economically with as little disruption to the running rhythm as possible. In this case, don't view a hill as something that has to be climbed as quickly and vigorously as possible.

A good hill session for the distance runner includes a number of hills or a short loop with hills that can be run a number of times. As you approach each hill, concentrate on keeping the upper body relaxed and letting the legs do as much of the work as possible. As you reach the top of each hill, concentrate on running over the top until the gradient eases. Then pick up natural rhythm again. Temple points out that it is almost like trying to pretend the hill isn't there.

Running hills has many benefits. In addition to building stamina and strength, it also contributes to injury prevention (the stronger quadriceps muscles gained from running hills can minimize knee injuries). However, what goes up must come down. Many runners put all their effort into getting up a hill, only to ease off upon reaching its apex, as if the run or race ended there. Downhills can be used to your advantage as well.

The most important elements in running downhill are form and control. You should lean forward slightly and relax the neck and shoulders. Your stride length should increase slightly, but not so much that you are placing too much additional stress on your legs and lower back. If you want to work on downhill running, it is best to do so on grass or some other natural surface.

THE BUDDY SYSTEM

What appeals to so many people about running is that you can do it alone, at any pace you like, and let your mind wander or problem-solve. There's no need to make and keep appointments, to chat when you don't feel like it, or to run slower or faster than you want to in order to accommodate someone else's pace. So it's easy to see why runners get hooked on the solitude.

On the other hand, there's nothing like the "support system" of a training buddy or group. This is true for a myriad of reasons, from safety and companionship to getting the encouragement to go the distance or get through a tough workout.

Then there's the balance that comes from socializing with a group. Francie Larrieu Smith says, "I'm pretty intense during interval sessions, but I like the socializing with a group when we step off the track."

The support of a running partner or group is always useful, especially for speedwork; however, it isn't always easy to find a partner who trains at the same pace or is on the same rhythm on a given day. In addition, even among equally matched runners, some excel over shorter distance intervals, some over longer stretches.

So try this buddy system. Use each other for incentive by giving one runner a head start or varying the distance for each runner. For example, when planning to do 400-meter intervals, one runner could take a 200-meter head start. Or, setting off together, one runner could finish with 200 meters, while the other continues on for 400 meters (or, in the case of fartlek, three light poles and six light poles). Both runners benefit from being pushed and from encouraging each other.

Gordon Bakoulis on Training Partners

When I first started running, what kept me going was a commitment to meet someone. I was a high school girl trying to stay in shape in the off-season from team sports. I met my running partner every day for months at exactly 6:30 A.M. We didn't miss a day, except for illness. If one of us overslept, the other would throw pebbles at the bedroom window to wake up the tardy partner. After a few months of this, I was hooked on the running routine for good.

I think running partners or groups are so important. The most crucial reason is safety. In addition to the safety factor, we run together for com-

panionship, and to remind each other how important a part of our lives this
activity is.

Tom Fleming on Running with a Group

Group running encourages consistency. Throughout my entire career I've
run with partners and groups. Currently, our group trains together several
times a week. It's a weekend ritual.

Most people like to run with others. Just the act of meeting makes the
workout more enjoyable. When it comes to the hard work, I think people do
it better when they're together. They drive off each other's energy. Then
they share a light moment. Even if the individual workouts are different, it's
worth it just to start and finish together. Obviously, the advantages are more
psychological than physical, but nonetheless, it gets the job done.

Bob Glover on Running with a Group

Sometimes the social aspect of running is an important aspect of the workout. From coaching NYRR running classes and coaching a team, I've seen
how much it helps to be in a class or to be on a team. Particularly in the winter months, it's easy to quit or taper off. But when runners come out to the
Tuesday night class, even if they're not full of energy, they usually do better than they thought they would. Even if a person swears he or she is totally unmotivated to run on a particular occasion, I say just come out and do
stretching exercises with the class.

3

TRAINING PROGRAM FOR 5K
TO THE MARATHON

Although running—and sports training in general—has made enormous advances since the early days of the running boom, the basic principles of training have not changed. "From the mile to the marathon, sound training principles are the same," says Tom Fleming.

The focus of Fleming's training program is a strong mileage base. Fleming feels that although some may be able to run long-distance events on relatively low mileage, it is not advisable. According to Fleming, "What seems to be getting a lot of attention is how good you can be by doing the least amount of work. What I say is, let's look at how much better you can be by doing the proper amount of work."

To experience steady improvement in your running, and to enjoy a long, healthy running career, Fleming believes you have to put in a relatively substantial amount of mileage at some point in your training cycle. This is especially true with running a race, like a marathon or even a 10K. "If you are short on time or motivation, it is wiser to adjust your goals rather than to try to do more or longer racing with less training," he says.

In the late 1960s there were two important trends in distance running that gained wide popularity. One is called LSD (long, slow distance), the American equivalent of a system embraced most notably by New Zealand coach Arthur Lydiard. A joke began to circulate that if you ran long enough and slow enough, you'd become long and slow. That's why the second trend was important, to balance the first. It is called interval training.

Although Fleming points out that he doesn't completely agree with everything in the Arthur Lydiard system, he feels the basis of that philosophy is absolutely sound. As a beginner, as well as at the beginning of a training cycle, you need to develop endurance and strength. There's only one way to do that, and Lydiard gave the same prescription to everyone, from half-milers to marathoners—two or more months of base-building, consisting of long, slow distance running.

If you're a runner who, for example, does one marathon a year, Fleming believes you will get the best results from a solid, progressive training program characterized by relatively high mileage training. Because you've built a strong base rather than taking risks by cutting corners with lower mileage, he contends you can then be successful and have a healthy career. The question Fleming gets asked most often by the beginners is, "How do I get faster?" He says he always tells them, "Get stronger and you'll get faster." To do that, you've got to build a good mileage base.

If you're a serious runner, you may be asking, "What about speedwork?" Of course you need the fast running, acknowledges Fleming, "but you can't build a house without a foundation."

Fleming is even a believer in what is called "overdistance training." He defines it as spending a week or two at some point running relative maximal mileage, i.e., the most you can comfortably tolerate. This is not mandatory in his training program, but it is an option for the serious runner.

For example, for a 30-mile-a-week runner, this might mean slowly building (no more than ten percent per week) to a couple of 50-mile weeks. This is not meant to be a permanent rise, just a brief period of heavier training. In building your base mileage, you build strength and conditioning. In testing your upper limits with overdistance training, you can gain both conditioning and confidence.

"World-class athletes are always trying to go right to the limit. That's what it takes to make it to the top," Fleming reflects. At some point in their training, distance runners may try overdistance training. Runners like Bill Rodgers experimented with running as much as 50 percent more than their usual mileage for one to two weeks. "Eventually they go right to a ceiling, and bump into it, but they learn not to go over it," comments Fleming. One of the benefits of heavy training is that you quickly learn to read your own body.

In addition to the training benefits, many runners try overdistance training for the mental edge to gain the confidence that comes from their ability to reach their limit. And this applies to everyone, not just the elite.

THE PROGRAM

Tom Fleming's program is based on some of the most successful methods of distance running. In designing the system, Fleming incorporates elements popularized by running pioneers Arthur Lydiard, New Zealand coach and proponent of high mileage training, and the late Bill Bowerman, famed Oregon distance-running coach and inventor of Nike's waffle-soled shoes, with other well-established training elements to create a multi-phase program. The phases are not meant to be done simultaneously. Although some can be done together, others absolutely should not (e.g., hill work and fartlek). Some need not be done at all, for example, a beginner could experience significant improvement simply by doing Phases One and Two. Imperative, however, is balance. Balancing mileage, intensity, and rest is essential to making this—and any training program—successful.

Bowerman's Hard/Easy Method

Hard/easy is generally recommended as the premise of all training programs. (Indeed, it is sound advice for all exercise and sports.) It simply means that for every hard effort, a sufficient rest period is required to recover and assimilate the benefits of training. This easy period varies in length, depending on the individual as well as the intensity of the effort. A runner might follow a hard effort one day with an easy run or a day off the next, or easy running for two or more days following.

Phase One: Lydiard's Endurance Mileage

This distance phase, which builds endurance, ultimately helps a runner to become more efficient—therefore faster—by developing aerobic capacity. As a result of a recent emphasis on shorter, faster mileage, Fleming feels this essential base training has been compromised. "Although this phase is generally accepted as being essential, very few do it thoroughly," he says.

Studies have shown that athletes often need to slow down their distance runs (a claim also substantiated in Chapter 4, Heart Rate Monitor Training). Therefore, Fleming emphasizes that the base phase should not consist of anaerobic (literally, without oxygen, as in a sprint) running; Phase One should be run at conversation pace, generally for six to eight weeks.

Phase Two: Tempo Runs

A tempo run is done at a strong pace, approximately 20 seconds per mile slower than 10K race pace. This pace is held for about 15 to 25 minutes in the middle of a longer distance run (with the segments before and after used as warmup and cool-down periods). This type of running is done in the first third of the season, as a way of adapting to faster interval running.

Phase Three: Hill Repeats

Hill repeats should be done on a sufficient grade but not on a steep hill, a maximum of one-quarter mile in length from base to top. One- to one-and-a-half minutes per repeat is an adequate amount of stress. These efforts should be strong, but not done at full speed. After running uphill, a slow jog down minimizes jarring to the quadriceps and knee joints. In this phase, Fleming's athletes average eight hill repeats, one time per week, for six weeks. The hill phase begins at the end of the base distance phase. Fleming has found that initially runners are able to do four repeats. They can generally add two more repeats per session.

Phase Four: Fartlek

Fartlek is basically interval training, but with less structure. While many runners are familiar with the term *fartlek,* some do it incorrectly. Fleming's top athletes run a total distance of nine miles, five at most of fartlek effort; however, computing with either time or distance is possible. As an example of time, the workout Fleming's athletes do consists of a total running time of one hour, with three minutes hard, two minutes easy for 30 minutes in the middle of the run. This is done one time a week for four to six weeks. This type of run is done in cycles throughout the year, except during the endurance phase, when it is not done at all.

Phase Five: Interval Training

Interval training usually starts at the beginning of the competitive season. Prescriptions here for distance runners are to do 800- to 3000- meter repeats, once each week for six to eight weeks, depending on the length of the competitive season. The recovery phase for Fleming's athletes is based on time, but it is also common to use distance for recovery, e.g., jogging a 400-meter recovery lap around the track. Although intervals are customarily done on a track, there is no need to be restricted to one. Fleming's team also does intervals on measured distances in a park.

An advanced runner might do four times 800 meters at race pace, for example. It is recommended, however, that a beginner might want to do the intervals slower than race pace. If a runner tolerates a workout well, Fleming shortens the rest period rather than speeding up the interval. "Psychologically, it seems to be easier on the athlete," he says.

In the beginning of the season, runners concentrate on longer intervals; during the actual racing phase, the intervals become shorter and faster. This aids "sharpness" by developing the speed and efficiency of leg turnover.

TRAINING TIPS

1. Training should be progressive and consistent.

2. All training programs should be individualized. Each runner can learn to identify a perfect blend of ingredients to develop his or her specific strengths. This is done through coaching and personal experience.

3. Each type of training has its own specific effect.

4. Each program should be tailored to the event for which the runner is training.

5. Carefully planned, realistic, short- and long-range goals are the best approach to guarantee successful results.

6. With an experienced eye, a coach or training partner who knows the athlete's individual running style and mechanics can help that person determine when to cut back, or when to push on. If running form begins to fall apart, it is often a sign the workout is falling apart as well.

7. Build on strengths; don't waste time trying to improve weaknesses. If a runner has great endurance but limited speed, Fleming believes it is more productive to develop the ability to maintain a high level of aerobic running than to spend time and effort trying to develop a kick or sprint ability.

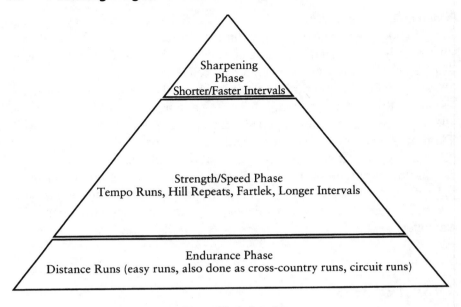

**Tom Fleming's
Training Pyramid**

Tom Fleming's Training Pyramid

Percentage of Yearly Training

Endurance Phase: 35%

Strengths/Speed Phase: 55%

Sharpening Phase/Racing: 10%

Easy run—conversation pace.

Tempo run—hard, but in control.

Hills—should be approximately 200–400 meters long, not extremely steep.

Intervals—are given in minutes, so you may use a watch and do them on a training loop, or go to a track and convert them into specific distances.

Pickups—150 to 200 meters in length (or pick objects for distance, such as five light posts). The pace is quick, but not an all-out sprint. They are inserted during a distance run at will, and should not be so taxing as to require stopping for recovery. Shorter pickups of 50–100 meters should be done before hard workouts and races.

A FIRST TIME MARATHONER'S STORY

One spring, 31-year-old Angel Jimenez met Tom Fleming. Jimenez was clearly an athlete of some kind, and turned out to be an Olympic-style Tae Kwon Do champion who ran about 25 miles a week for fitness. He told Fleming he wanted to run a race and added, "I'm entering the New York City Marathon." The New York City Marathon was in November, less than six months away.

ANGEL JIMENEZ'S TRAINING CHART

Week of	Days Running per Week	Total Miles (with races)
7/1	7	58 (5-mile race)
7/8	6	50
7/15	7	62
7/22	7	60
7/29	6	56
8/5	7	61 (5K race)
8/12	6	57
8/19	7	68
8/26	7	68
9/2	7	67 (5-mile race)
9/9	7	65
9/16	7 *	70
9/23	7	70 (10K race)
9/30	6 **	67
10/7	7 ***	78
10/14	7	54 (10K race)
10/21	7	55
10/28	7	31 + 26.2 mile NYC Marathon in 2:41:50

*First 20-miler; **Second 20-miler; ***Third 20-miler

Fleming felt it was too soon for him to run the marathon. He tried to discourage him, but to no avail. Jimenez announced he wanted to start to do speedwork to prepare for racing. Fleming managed to quash that idea. He cautioned Jimenez against doing any interval running for at least four months and put him on the high-mileage buildup outlined in the table on page 29. Fleming stressed that for a novice like Jimenez, the object of the marathon is to complete it, not race it.

After building his base of training, Jimenez was invited by Fleming to run with his team once a week during their medium efforts. His ability to keep up with top-class athletes became his "speedwork" (a tempo run) and served to bolster his confidence. By September, Jimenez had participated in 5K and 10K races to feel the difference between racing and training.

Little did Fleming anticipate the emergence of Jimenez's talent. He responded very well to training. He lost 18 pounds from his already muscular body. He was well prepared for the marathon and ran a smart race, going out slowly. He experienced the joy of passing people throughout the second half of the race, which he finished in 2:41:50.

To prevent the almost universal mistake of taking up training too quickly after the excitement of running a successful marathon, Fleming emphasized several weeks of easy running before Jimenez rebuilt his mileage base for the next goal.

TRAINING CHARTS

Advanced Beginner

The 26-week advanced beginner level training program is designed for the 50- to 55-minute 10K runner. At this level you've probably already run several races. This program will help you to gear your training toward improving your race times.

Fleming uses a 26-week time frame because, as he emphasizes, there are no shortcuts. If you want to experience steady improvement, you have to have both the patience and determination to stick to a plan. It is often the case that people are tempted to change suddenly because of what some friend is doing or because of a program they read about in a running publication.

Patience is particularly important as you may need to hold yourself back. Stick to the schedule, even if at times you feel so good you'd like to skip a phase or part of the program.

The first 12 weeks of all the programs are strictly devoted to building the base. On the advanced beginner level, base building continues right through to the 17th week. It is Fleming's view that runners at this level can improve tremendously simply by being consistent. No fancy workouts are needed in this stage.

During the 17th week, short pickups during the normal distance run are included once a week to help give you a sense of the faster pace you will encounter in a race. The pickups can be done for several light posts, with plenty of jogging and resumption of normal training pace in between each.

Racing every three to four weeks is probably plenty at this level. Mixing up the distances—for example, 10K, 5K, five miles, four miles, etc.—will help give you a variety of opportunities to test your new endurance.

Intermediate

The intermediate-level runner is someone in the 44- to 50-minute range for 10K. The intermediate level training program is basically the same as the beginner's program, but the mileage is slightly higher. During the initial 12-week base building, training mileage slowly increases from 25 miles per week to 35 miles per week. Daily training amounts can be varied according to your personal habits and preferences. Fleming tends to make the Sunday run the long one for the week.

26-Week Advanced Beginner Level 10K Training Program*

Wk	Monday	Tuesday	Wednesday	Thursday
1	2 miles easy	2 miles easy	3 miles easy	2 miles easy
2	2 miles easy	2 miles easy	3 miles easy	2 miles easy
3	2 miles easy	2 miles easy	4 miles easy	2 miles easy
4	2 miles easy	2 miles easy	4 miles easy	2 miles easy
5	2 miles easy	3 miles easy	4 miles easy	3 miles easy
6	2 miles easy	3 miles easy	4 miles easy	3 miles easy
7	2 miles easy	3 miles easy	4 miles easy	3 miles easy
8	2 miles easy	3 miles easy	4 miles easy	3 miles easy
9	3 miles easy	3 miles easy	4 miles easy	4 miles easy
10	3 miles easy	3 miles easy	4 miles easy	4 miles easy
11	4 miles easy	4 miles easy	4 miles easy	4 miles easy
12	4 miles easy	4 miles easy	4 miles easy	4 miles easy
13	4 miles easy	4 miles easy	4 miles easy	4 miles easy
14	4 miles easy	4 miles easy	4 miles easy	4 miles easy
15	4 miles easy	4 miles easy	4 miles easy	4 miles easy
16	4 miles easy	4 miles easy	4 miles easy	4 miles easy
17	4 miles easy	4 miles easy	4 miles w/4 pickups	4 miles easy
18	4 miles easy	4 miles easy	4 miles w/4 pickups	4 miles easy
19	4 miles easy	4 miles easy	4 miles w/5 pickups	4 miles easy
20	4 miles easy	4 miles easy	4 miles w/5 pickups	4 miles easy
21	4 miles easy	4 miles easy	4 miles w/6 pickups	4 miles easy
22	4 miles easy	4 miles easy	4 miles w/6 pickups	4 miles easy
23	4 miles easy	4 miles easy	4 miles w/6 pickups	4 miles easy
24	4 miles easy	4 miles easy	4 miles w/6 pickups	4 miles easy
25	4 mile easy	4 miles easy	4 miles w/6 pickups	4 miles easy
26	4 miles easy	4 miles easy	4 miles w/6 pickups	4 miles easy

In the 13th week, moderate interval training begins. These intervals can be done on the track or on the roads or trails, wherever you normally do your workouts. The intervals should be done at approximately your current 10K race pace. It is not so important to determine exactly how fast you are going, as long as you've increased your pace substantially, but without straining in the effort. Recovery between intervals should consist

26-Week Advanced Beginner Level 10K Training Program* (cont.)

Wk	Friday	Saturday	Sunday	Total for Week
1	Rest day	2 miles easy	4 miles easy	**15 miles**
2	Rest day	2 miles easy	4 miles easy	**15 miles**
3	Rest day	2 miles easy	5 miles easy	**17 miles**
4	Rest day	2 miles easy	5 miles easy	**17 miles**
5	Rest day	2 miles easy	5 miles easy	**19 miles**
6	Rest day	2 miles easy	5 miles easy	**19 miles**
7	Rest day	3 miles easy	6 miles easy	**21 miles**
8	3 miles easy	Rest day	**Race**	**21 miles**
9	Rest day	3 miles easy	6 miles easy	**23 miles**
10	Rest day	3 miles easy	6 miles easy	**23 miles**
11	Rest day	3 miles easy	6 miles easy	**25 miles**
12	3 miles easy	Rest day	**Race**	**25 miles**
13	Rest day	3 miles easy	6 miles easy	**25 miles**
14	Rest day	3 miles easy	6 miles easy	**25 miles**
15	Rest day	3 miles easy	6 miles easy	**25 miles**
16	2 miles easy	Rest day	**Race**	**25 miles**
17	Rest day	3 miles easy	6 miles easy	**25 miles**
18	Rest day	3 miles easy	6 miles easy	**25 miles**
19	Rest day	3 miles easy	6 miles easy	**25 miles**
20	2 miles easy	Rest day	**Race**	**25 miles**
21	Rest day	3 miles easy	6 miles easy	**25 miles**
22	Rest day	3 miles easy	6 miles easy	**25 miles**
23	Rest day	3 miles easy	6 miles easy	**25 miles**
24	2 miles easy	Rest day	**Race**	**25 miles**
25	Rest day	3 miles easy	6 miles easy	**25 miles**
26	2 miles easy	Rest day	**PEAK RACE**	**25 miles**

* For the 50–55-minute 10K runner.

of very easy jogging for at least the same amount of time as the hard effort. Perhaps a little more recovery will be needed in the beginning, until you become accustomed to such efforts. (Note: You should expect to feel a little sore or sluggish in the legs in the early going. Don't worry, this is the body's natural adaptation to the increased training effort.)

26-Week Intermediate Level 10k Training Program*

Wk	Monday	Tuesday	Wednesday	Thursday
Distance/Base Building Phase				
1	3 miles easy	4 miles easy	3 miles easy	4 miles easy
2	3 miles easy	4 miles easy	3 miles easy	4 miles easy
3	3 miles easy	4 miles easy	4 miles easy	4 miles easy
4	3 miles easy	4 miles easy	4 miles easy	4 miles easy
5	3 miles easy	5 miles easy	4 miles easy	4 miles easy
6	3 miles easy	5 miles easy	4 miles easy	5 miles easy
7	3 miles easy	5 miles easy	4 miles easy	5 miles easy
8	3 miles easy	5 miles easy	4 miles easy	5 miles easy
9	3 miles easy	4 miles easy	5 miles easy	4 miles easy
10	3 miles easy	5 miles easy	4 miles easy	5 miles easy
11	4 miles easy	5 miles easy	4 miles easy	5 miles easy
12	4 miles easy	5 miles easy	4 miles easy	5 miles easy
Intervals/Speed Introduction Phase				
13	3 miles easy	4 miles easy	5 miles, 6×1 min.[a]	4 miles easy
14	4 miles easy	4 miles easy	6 miles, 6×1 min.[a]	4 miles easy
15	4 miles easy	4 miles steady	6 miles, $4 \times 1{:}30$ mins.[a]	4 miles easy
16	4 miles easy	4 miles easy	6 miles, $4 \times 1{:}30$ mins.[a]	4 miles easy
17	4 miles easy	4 miles easy	6 miles, 3×2 mins.[a]	4 miles easy
18	4 miles easy	4 miles easy	6 miles, 3×2 mins.[a]	4 miles easy
19	4 miles easy	4 miles easy	6 miles, 2×3 mins.[a]	4 miles easy
20	4 miles easy	4 miles easy	6 miles, 2×3 mins.[a]	4 miles easy
21	4 miles easy	4 miles easy	6 miles, 3×2 mins.[a]	4 miles easy
22	4 miles easy	4 miles easy	6 miles, $4 \times 1{:}30$ mins.[a]	4 miles easy
23	4 miles easy	4 miles easy	6 miles, 6×1 min.[a]	4 miles easy
24	4 miles easy	4 miles easy	6 miles, 2×3 mins.[a]	4 miles easy
25	4 miles easy	4 miles easy	6 miles, 3×2 mins.[a]	4 miles easy
26	4 miles easy	4 miles easy	5 miles, 4×1 mins.[a]	4 miles easy

*For the 44–50-minute 10K runner.
[a]@ 10K race pace.

(continued)

26-WEEK INTERMEDIATE LEVEL 10K TRAINING PROGRAM* (CONT.)

Wk	Friday	Saturday	Sunday	Total for Week
Distance/Base Building Phase				
1	3 miles easy	3 miles easy	5 miles easy	**25 miles**
2	3 miles easy	3 miles easy	6 miles easy	**26 miles**
3	3 miles easy	3 miles easy	6 miles easy	**27 miles**
4	4 miles easy	3 miles easy	6 miles easy	**28 miles**
5	4 miles easy	3 miles easy	6 miles easy	**29 miles**
6	4 miles easy	3 miles easy	6 miles easy	**30 miles**
7	4 miles easy	3 miles easy	7 miles easy	**31 miles**
8	4 miles easy	2 miles easy	**Race**	**30 miles**
9	5 miles easy	4 miles easy	7 miles easy	**32 miles**
10	5 miles easy	3 miles easy	8 miles easy	**33 miles**
11	5 miles easy	3 miles easy	8 miles easy	**34 miles**
12	4 miles easy	2 miles easy	**Race**	**32 miles**
Intervals/Speed Introduction Phase				
13	5 miles easy	4 miles easy	8 miles easy	**33 miles**
14	5 miles easy	4 miles easy	8 miles easy	**35 miles**
15	4 miles easy	3 miles easy	**Race**	**33 miles**
16	5 miles easy	4 miles easy	8 miles easy	**35 miles**
17	5 miles easy	4 miles easy	8 miles easy	**35 miles**
18	4 miles easy	3 miles easy	**Race**	**33 miles**
19	5 miles easy	4 miles easy	8 miles easy	**35 miles**
20	4 miles easy	3 miles easy	**Race**	**33 miles**
21	5 miles easy	4 miles easy	8 miles easy	**35 miles**
22	4 miles easy	3 miles easy	**Race**	**33 miles**
23	5 miles easy	4 miles easy	8 miles easy	**35 miles**
24	4 miles easy	3 miles easy	**Race**	**33 miles**
25	5 miles easy	4 miles easy	8 miles easy	**35 miles**
26	3 miles easy	2 miles easy	**PEAK RACE**	**30 miles**

*For the 44–50-minute 10K runner.
[a]@ 10K race pace.

26-WEEK ADVANCED LEVEL 10K TRAINING PROGRAM*

Wk	Monday	Tuesday	Wednesday	Thursday
Distance/Base Building Phase				
1	4 miles easy	6 miles easy	4 miles easy	6 miles easy
2	4 miles easy	7 miles easy	4 miles easy	7 miles easy
3	5 miles easy	7 miles easy	5 miles easy	7 miles easy
4	5 miles easy	8 miles easy	5 miles easy	8 miles easy
5	6 miles easy	8 miles easy	6 miles easy	8 miles easy
6	6 miles easy	8 miles easy	6 miles easy	8 miles easy
7	6 miles easy	8 miles easy	6 miles easy	8 miles[a]
8	6 miles easy	8 miles easy	6 miles easy	8 miles[a]
Hill Work Phase				
9	7 miles easy	6 miles easy	7 miles, 4 × uphill	7 miles easy
10	7 miles easy	6 miles easy	7 miles, 5 × uphill	7 miles easy
11	7 miles easy	6 miles easy	7 miles, 6 × uphill	7 miles easy
12	7 miles easy	6 miles easy	7 miles, 6 × uphill	7 miles easy
Long Interval/Strength Phase				
13	7 miles easy	6 miles steady	7 miles, 3 × 4 mins.[b]	7 miles easy
14	7 miles easy	6 miles steady	7 miles, 4 × 3 mins.[b]	7 miles easy
15	7 miles easy	6 miles steady	7 miles, 6 × 2 mins.[b]	7 miles easy
16	7 miles easy	6 miles steady	7 miles, 8 × 1:30 mins.[b]	7 miles easy
17	7 miles easy	6 miles easy	7 miles, 3 × 4 mins.[b]	7 miles easy
18	7 miles easy	6 miles easy	7 miles, 4 × 3 mins.[b]	7 miles easy
19	7 miles easy	6 miles easy	7 miles, 6 × 2 mins.[b]	7 miles easy
20	7 miles easy	6 miles easy	7 miles, 8 × 1:30 mins.[b]	6 miles easy
Faster Interval/Peaking Phase				
21	5 miles easy	5 miles easy	7 miles, 4 × 2 mins.[c]	5 miles easy
22	5 miles easy	5 miles easy	7 miles, 6 × 1:30 mins.[c]	5 miles easy
23	5 miles easy	5 miles easy	7 miles, 8 × 1 min.[c]	5 miles easy
24	5 miles easy	5 miles easy	7 miles, 4 × 2 mins.[c]	5 miles easy
25	5 miles easy	5 miles easy	7 miles, 6 × 1:30 mins.[c]	5 miles easy
26	5 miles easy	5 miles easy	7 miles, 8 × 1 min.[c]	5 miles easy

*For the 38–44-minute 10K runner.   *(continued)*
[a]With two-mile tempo run.
[b]@10K race pace.
[c]@5K race pace.
[d]With pickups enroute.

26-WEEK ADVANCED LEVEL 10K TRAINING PROGRAM* (CONT.)

Wk	Friday	Saturday	Sunday	Total for Week
Distance/Base Building Phase				
1	4 miles easy	4 miles easy	8 miles easy	**36 miles**
2	4 miles easy	4 miles easy	9 miles easy	**39 miles**
3	5 miles easy	4 miles easy	9 miles easy	**42 miles**
4	5 miles easy	4 miles easy	10 miles easy	**45 miles**
5	6 miles easy	4 miles easy	10 miles easy	**48 miles**
6	6 miles easy	6 miles easy	10 miles easy	**50 miles**
7	6 miles easy	6 miles easy	10 miles easy	**50 miles**
8	6 miles easy	6 miles easy	10 miles easy	**50 miles**
Hill Work Phase				
9	7 miles easy	6 miles easy	**Race**	**50 miles**
10	7 miles easy	6 miles easy	10 miles easy	**50 miles**
11	7 miles easy	6 miles easy	10 miles easy	**50 miles**
12	7 miles easy	6 miles easy	**Race**	**50 miles**
Long Interval/Strength Phase				
13	7 miles easy	6 miles easy	10 miles easy	**50 miles**
14	7 miles easy	6 miles easy	10 miles easy	**50 miles**
15	6 miles easy	4 miles easy	**Race**	**47 miles**
16	7 miles easy	6 miles easy	10 miles easy	**50 miles**
17	7 miles, 4 short[d]	6 miles easy	10 miles easy	**50 miles**
18	6 miles easy	4 miles easy	**Race**	**47 miles**
19	7 miles, 5 short[d]	6 miles easy	10 miles easy	**50 miles**
20	6 miles easy	3 miles easy	**Race**	**45 miles**
Faster Interval/Peaking Phase				
21	7 miles, 6 short[d]	5 miles easy	10 miles easy	44 miles
22	4 miles easy	3 miles easy	Race	39 miles
23	7 miles, 7 short[d]	5 miles easy	10 miles easy	44 miles
24	4 miles easy	3 miles easy	Race	39 miles
25	7 miles, 8 short[d]	5 miles easy	10 miles easy	44 miles
26	4 miles easy	3 miles easy	**PEAK RACE**	**39 miles**

*For the 38–44-minute 10K runner.
[a]With two-mile tempo run.
[b]@10K race pace.
[c]@5K race pace.
[d]With pickups enroute.

26-Week Competitive Level 10K Training Program*

Wk	Monday	Tuesday	Wednesday	Thursday
Distance/Base Building Phase				
1	6 miles easy	6 miles easy	6 miles easy	6 miles easy
2	6 miles easy	7 miles easy	6 miles easy	7 miles easy
3	6 miles easy	7 miles easy	7 miles easy	7 miles easy
4	6 miles easy	7 miles easy	7 miles easy	7 miles[a]
5	7 miles easy	7 miles easy	7 miles easy	8 miles[a]
6	7 miles easy	8 miles easy	7 miles easy	8 miles
7	7 miles easy	8 miles easy	7 miles easy	8 miles[a]
8	7 miles easy	8 miles easy	8 miles easy	8 miles[a]
Hill Work Phase				
9	7 miles easy	8 miles easy	8 miles, 6 × uphill	8 miles easy
10	7 miles easy	8 miles easy	8 miles, 8 × uphill	8 miles easy
11	7 miles easy	8 miles easy	8 miles, 10 × uphill	8 miles easy
12	7 miles easy	8 miles easy	8 miles, 10 × uphill	8 miles easy
Long Interval/Strength Phase				
13	7 miles easy	8 miles easy	9 miles, 3 × 5 mins.[b]	6 miles easy
14	7 miles easy	8 miles easy	9 miles, 5 × 3 mins.[b]	6 miles easy
15	7 miles easy	8 miles easy	9 miles, 6 × 2:30 mins.[b]	6 miles easy
16	7 miles easy	8 miles easy	9 miles, 10 × 1:30 mins.[b]	6 miles easy
17	7 miles easy	8 miles easy	9 miles, 3 × 5 mins.[b]	6 miles easy
18	7 miles easy	8 miles easy	9 miles, 5 × 3 mins.[b]	6 miles easy
19	7 miles easy	8 miles easy	9 miles, 6 × 2:30 mins.[b]	6 miles easy
20	7 miles easy	8 miles easy	9 miles, 10 × 1:30 mins.[b]	6 miles easy
Faster Interval/Peaking Phase				
21	7 miles easy	8 miles easy	9 miles, 6 × 2 mins.[c]	6 miles easy
22	7 miles easy	8 miles easy	9 miles, 8 × 1:30 mins.[c]	6 miles easy
23	7 miles easy	6 miles easy	9 miles, 12 × 1 min.[c]	6 miles easy
24	7 miles easy	8 miles easy	9 miles, 6 × 2 mins.[c]	6 miles easy
25	7 miles easy	8 miles easy	8 miles, 8 × 1:30 mins.[c]	6 miles easy
26	6 miles easy	6 miles easy	8 miles, 12 × 1 min.	6 miles easy

*For the 34–38-minute 10K runner.
[a]With tempo run.
[b]@10K race pace.
[c]@5K race pace.
[d]With pickups enroute.

(continued)

26-Week Competitive Level 10K Training Program* (cont.)

Wk	Friday	Saturday	Sunday	Total for Week
Distance/Base Building Phase				
1	6 miles easy	5 miles easy	10 miles easy	**45 miles**
2	6 miles easy	6 miles easy	10 miles easy	**48 miles**
3	7 miles easy	6 miles easy	10 miles easy	**50 miles**
4	7 miles easy	6 miles easy	12 miles easy	**52 miles**
5	7 miles easy	7 miles easy	12 miles easy	**54 miles**
6	7 miles easy	7 miles easy	12 miles easy	**56 miles**
7	7 miles easy	7 miles easy	14 miles easy	**58 miles**
8	8 miles easy	7 miles easy	14 miles easy	**60 miles**
Hill Work Phase				
9	8 miles easy	5 miles easy	**Race**	**54 miles**
10	8 miles easy	7 miles easy	14 miles easy	**60 miles**
11	8 miles easy	7 miles easy	14 miles easy	**60 miles**
12	8 miles easy	5 miles easy	**Race**	**54 miles**
Long Interval/Strength Phase				
13	9 miles easy	7 miles easy	14 miles easy	**60 miles**
14	9 miles easy	7 miles easy	14 miles easy	**60 miles**
15	7 miles easy	5 miles easy	**Race**	**52 miles**
16	9 miles easy	7 miles easy	14 miles easy	**60 miles**
17	9 miles, 6 to 8 short[d]	7 miles easy	14 miles easy	**60 miles**
18	7 miles easy	5 miles easy	**Race**	**52 miles**
19	9 miles, 6 to 8 short[d]	7 miles easy	14 miles easy	**60 miles**
20	7 miles easy	5 miles easy	**Race**	**52 miles**
Faster Interval/Peaking Phase				
21	9 miles, 6 to 8 short[d]	7 miles easy	14 miles easy	**60 miles**
22	7 miles easy	5 miles easy	**Race**	**52 miles**
23	9 miles, 6 to 8 short[d]	7 miles easy	12 miles easy	**58 miles**
24	6 miles easy	4 miles easy	**Race**	**50 miles**
25	7 miles, 6 to 8 short[d]	7 miles easy	12 miles easy	**55 miles**
26	5 miles easy	4 miles easy	**PEAK RACE**	**45 miles**

*For the 34–38-minute 10K runner.
[a]With tempo run.
[b]@10K race pace.
[c]@5K race pace.
[d]With pickups enroute.

26-Week Intermediate Level Marathon Training Program*

Wk	Monday	Tuesday	Wednesday	Thursday

Distance/Base Building Phase

Wk	Monday	Tuesday	Wednesday	Thursday
1	3 miles easy	4 miles easy	3 miles easy	4 miles easy
2	3 miles easy	4 miles easy	3 miles easy	4 miles easy
3	3 miles easy	4 miles easy	4 miles easy	4 miles easy
4	3 miles easy	4 miles easy	4 miles easy	4 miles easy
5	3 miles easy	5 miles easy	4 miles easy	4 miles easy
6	3 miles easy	5 miles easy	4 miles easy	5 miles easy
7	3 miles easy	5 miles easy	4 miles easy	5 miles easy
8	3 miles easy	5 miles easy	4 miles easy	5 miles easy
9	3 miles easy	4 miles easy	5 miles easy	4 miles easy
10	3 miles easy	5 miles easy	4 miles easy	5 miles easy
11	4 miles easy	5 miles easy	4 miles easy	5 miles easy
12	4 miles easy	5 miles easy	4 miles easy	5 miles easy

Intervals/Speed Introduction Phase

Wk	Monday	Tuesday	Wednesday	Thursday
13	3 miles easy	4 miles easy	5 miles, 6 × 1 min.[a]	4 miles easy
14	3 miles easy	4 miles easy	6 miles, 6 × 1 min.[a]	4 miles easy
15	3 miles easy	4 miles steady	6 miles, 4 × 1:30 mins.[a]	4 miles easy
16	3 miles easy	4 miles easy	6 miles, 4 × 1:30 mins.[a]	4 miles easy
17	3 miles easy	4 miles easy	6 miles, 3 × 2 mins.[a]	4 miles easy
18	4 miles easy	4 miles easy	6 miles, 3 × 2 mins.[a]	4 miles easy
19	3 miles easy	3 miles easy	4 miles easy	6 miles, 2 × 3 mins.[a]
20	3 miles easy	4 miles easy	6 miles, 2 × 3 mins.	3 miles easy[a]
21	3 miles easy	3 miles easy	6 miles, 3 × 2 mins.[a]	4 miles easy
22	3 miles easy	4 miles easy	6 miles, 4 × 1:30 mins.[a]	4 miles easy
23	3 miles easy	3 miles easy	3 miles easy[a]	5 miles, 6 × 1 min.

Tapering Phase

Wk	Monday	Tuesday	Wednesday	Thursday
24	3 miles easy	3 miles easy	5 miles, 2 × 3 mins.[a]	4 miles easy
25	2 miles easy	3 miles easy	5 miles, 3 × 2 mins.[a]	3 miles easy
26	3 miles easy	3 miles easy	5 miles, 4 × 1 mins.[a]	3 miles easy

*For the 3:30–4:00 marathon runner.
[a] @ 10K race pace.

(continued)

26-Week Intermediate Level Marathon Training Program (cont.)

Wk	Friday	Saturday	Sunday	Total for Week
Distance/Base Building Phase				
1	3 miles easy	3 miles easy	5 miles easy	**25 miles**
2	3 miles easy	3 miles easy	6 miles easy	**26 miles**
3	3 miles easy	3 miles easy	6 miles easy	**27 miles**
4	4 miles easy	3 miles easy	6 miles easy	**28 miles**
5	4 miles easy	3 miles easy	6 miles easy	**29 miles**
6	4 miles easy	3 miles easy	6 miles easy	**30 miles**
7	4 miles easy	3 miles easy	7 miles easy	**31 miles**
8	4 miles easy	2 miles easy	**Race**	**30 miles**
9	5 miles easy	4 miles easy	7 miles easy	**32 miles**
10	5 miles easy	3 miles easy	8 miles easy	**33 miles**
11	5 miles easy	3 miles easy	8 miles easy	**34 miles**
12	4 miles easy	2 miles easy	**Race**	**32 miles**
Intervals/Speed Introduction Phase				
13	5 miles easy	3 miles easy	10 miles easy	**34 miles**
14	5 miles easy	3 miles easy	10 miles easy	**35 miles**
15	4 miles easy	3 miles easy	**Race**	**32 miles**
16	5 miles easy	3 miles easy	12 miles easy	**37 miles**
17	5 miles easy	3 miles easy	14 miles easy	**39 miles**
18	3 miles easy	2 miles easy	**15K or 10-mile race**	**36 miles**
19	4 miles easy	3 miles easy	16 miles easy	**39 miles**
20	4 miles easy	3 miles easy	18 miles easy	**41 miles**
21	4 miles easy	2 miles easy	20 miles easy	**42 miles**
22	3 miles easy	2 miles easy	**20K or half mar. race**	**37 miles**
23	4 miles easy	3 miles easy	17 miles easy	**38 miles**
Tapering Phase				
24	4 miles easy	3 miles easy	15 miles easy	**37 miles**
25	4 miles easy	2 miles easy	13 miles easy	**32 miles**
26	2 miles easy	Rest day	**THE MARATHON**	**42.2 miles**

*For the 3:30–4:00 marathon runner.
[a]@ 10K race pace.

26-WEEK ADVANCED LEVEL MARATHON TRAINING PROGRAM*

Wk	Monday	Tuesday	Wednesday	Thursday
Distance/Base Building Phase				
1	4 miles easy	6 miles easy	4 miles easy	6 miles easy
2	4 miles easy	7 miles easy	4 miles easy	7 miles easy
3	5 miles easy	7 miles easy	5 miles easy	7 miles easy
4	5 miles easy	8 miles easy	5 miles easy	7 miles easy
5	6 miles easy	8 miles easy	6 miles easy	8 miles easy
6	6 miles easy	8 miles easy	6 miles easy	8 miles easy
7	6 miles easy	8 miles easy	6 miles easy	8 miles[a]
8	6 miles easy	8 miles easy	6 miles easy	8 miles[b]
Hill Work Phase				
9	7 miles easy	6 miles easy	7 miles, 4 × uphill	7 miles easy
10	7 miles easy	6 miles easy	7 miles, 5 × uphill	7 miles easy
11	7 miles easy	6 miles easy	7 miles, 6 × uphill	7 miles easy
12	7 miles easy	6 miles easy	7 miles, 6 × uphill	7 miles easy
Long Interval/Strength Phase				
13	7 miles easy	6 miles easy	7 miles, 3 × 4 mins.[c]	7 miles easy
14	7 miles easy	6 miles easy	7 miles, 4 × 3 mins.[c]	7 miles easy
15	5 miles easy	6 miles easy	8 miles, 6 × 2 mins.[c]	7 miles easy
16	5 miles easy	6 miles easy	8 miles, 8 × 1:30 mins.[c]	7 miles easy
17	5 miles easy	6 miles easy	8 miles, 2 × 6 mins.[c]	7 miles easy
18	5 miles easy	6 miles easy	8 miles, 3 × 4 mins.[c]	7 miles easy
19	4 miles easy	6 miles easy	7 miles easy	8 miles, 4 × 3 mins.[c]
20	4 miles easy	6 miles easy	8 miles, 6 × 2 mins.[c]	6 miles easy
21	4 miles easy	6 miles easy	8 miles, 2 × 6 mins.[c]	5 miles easy
22	5 miles easy	6 miles easy	8 miles, 3 × 4 mins.[c]	7 miles easy
23	4 miles easy	6 miles easy	7 miles easy	8 miles, 6 × 2 mins.[c]
24	3 miles easy	6 miles easy	8 miles, 2 × 4 mins.[c]	5 miles easy
Tapering Phase				
25	3 miles easy	6 miles easy	8 miles, 3 × 3 mins.[c]	5 miles easy
26	3 miles easy	6 miles, 6 × 1 min.	5 miles easy[c]	4 miles easy

*For the 3:00–3:30 marathon runner.
[a]With two-mile tempo.
[b]With three-mile tempo.
[c]@10K race pace.
[d]With pickups enroute.

(continued)

26-Week Advanced Level Marathon Training Program* (cont.)

Wk	Friday	Saturday	Sunday	Total for Week
Distance/Base Building Phase				
1	4 miles easy	4 miles easy	8 miles easy	**36 miles**
2	4 miles easy	4 miles easy	9 miles easy	**39 miles**
3	5 miles easy	4 miles easy	9 miles easy	**42 miles**
4	5 miles easy	4 miles easy	10 miles easy	**45 miles**
5	6 miles easy	4 miles easy	10 miles easy	**48 miles**
6	6 miles easy	6 miles easy	10 miles easy	**50 miles**
7	6 miles easy	6 miles easy	10 miles easy	**50 miles**
8	6 miles easy	6 miles easy	10 miles easy	**50 miles**
Hill Work Phase				
9	7 miles easy	4 miles easy	**Race**	**50 miles**
10	7 miles easy	6 miles easy	10 miles easy	**50 miles**
11	7 miles easy	6 miles easy	10 miles easy	**50 miles**
12	7 miles easy	4 miles easy	**Race**	**48 miles**
Long Interval/Strength Phase				
13	7 miles easy	6 miles easy	10 miles easy	**50 miles**
14	7 miles easy	6 miles easy	10 miles easy	**50 miles**
15	8 miles easy	4 miles easy	13 miles easy	**51 miles**
16	8 miles easy	4 miles easy	15 man easy	**53 miles**
17	8 miles, 4 short[d]	4 miles easy	14 miles easy	**52 miles**
18	8 miles easy	4 miles easy	**15K or 10-mile race**	**53 miles**
19	7 miles easy	4 miles easy	16 miles easy	**52 miles**
20	8 miles, 5 short[d]	4 miles easy	18 miles easy	**54 miles**
21	7 miles, 6 short[d]	4 miles easy	20 miles easy	**54 miles**
22	5 miles easy	3 miles easy	**20K or half mar. race**	**51 miles**
23	7 miles easy	4 miles easy	17 miles easy	**53 miles**
24	6 miles, 6 short[d]	4 miles easy	15 miles easy	**47 miles**
Tapering Phase				
25	6 miles, 6 short[d]	4 miles easy	13 miles easy	**45 miles**
26	4 miles easy	3 miles easy	**THE MARATHON**	**51.2 miles**

*For the 3:00–3:30 marathon runner.
[a]With two-mile tempo.
[b]With three-mile tempo.
[c]@10K race pace.
[d]With pickups enroute.

26-WEEK COMPETITIVE LEVEL MARATHON TRAINING PROGRAM*

Wk	Monday	Tuesday	Wednesday	Thursday
Distance/Base Building Phase				
1	6 miles easy	6 miles easy	6 miles easy	6 miles easy
2	6 miles easy	7 miles easy	6 miles easy	7 miles easy
3	6 miles easy	7 miles easy	7 miles easy	7 miles easy
4	6 miles easy	7 miles easy	7 miles easy	7 miles[a]
5	7 miles easy	7 miles easy	7 miles easy	7 miles[a]
6	7 miles easy	8 miles easy	7 miles easy	8 miles [a]
7	7 miles easy	8 miles easy	7 miles easy	8 miles[a]
8	7 miles easy	8 miles easy	8 miles easy	8 miles[a]
Hill Work Phase				
9	7 miles easy	8 miles easy	8 miles, 6 × uphill	8 miles easy
10	7 miles easy	8 miles easy	8 miles, 8 × uphill	8 miles easy
11	7 miles easy	8 miles easy	8 miles, 10 × uphill	8 miles easy
12	7 miles easy	8 miles easy	8 miles, 10 × uphill	8 miles easy
Long Interval/Strength Phase				
13	6 miles easy	8 miles easy	9 miles, 3 × 5 mins.[b]	6 miles easy
14	6 miles easy	8 miles easy	9 miles, 5 × 3 mins.[b]	6 miles easy
15	6 miles easy	8 miles easy	9 miles, 6 × 2:30 mins.[b]	6 miles easy
16	6 miles easy	8 miles easy	9 miles, 10 × 1:30 mins.[b]	6 miles easy
17	6 miles easy	8 miles easy	9 miles, 3 × 5 mins.[b]	6 miles easy
18	7 miles easy	8 miles easy	9 miles, 5 × 3 mins.[b]	6 miles easy
19	6 miles easy	6 miles easy	8 miles easy	9 miles, 6 × 2:30 mins.[b]
20	6 miles easy	8 miles easy	9 miles, 10 × 1:30 mins.[b]	6 miles easy
21	6 miles easy	8 miles easy	9 miles, 3 × 6 mins.[b]	6 miles easy
22	6 miles easy	8 miles easy	9 miles, 4 × 4:30 mins.[b]	6 miles easy
23	6 miles easy	6 miles easy	8 miles easy[b]	9 miles, 6 × 3 mins.
24	6 miles easy	8 miles easy	8 miles easy[b]	8 miles, 6 × 2:30 mins.
Tapering Phase				
25	6 miles easy	8 miles easy	7 miles easy	8 miles, 6 × 2 mins.[b]
26	6 miles easy	8 miles easy	6 miles, 6 × 1 min.[b]	6 miles easy

*For the 2:40–3:00 marathon runner.   *(continued)*
[a]With tempo run.
[b]@10K race pace.
[c]With pickups enroute.

26-WEEK COMPETITIVE LEVEL MARATHON TRAINING PROGRAM* (CONT.)

Wk	Friday	Saturday	Sunday	Total for Week
Distance/Base Building Phase				
1	6 miles easy	5 miles easy	10 miles easy	**45 miles**
2	6 miles easy	6 miles easy	10 miles easy	**48 miles**
3	7 miles easy	6 miles easy	10 miles easy	**50 miles**
4	7 miles easy	6 miles easy	12 miles easy	**52 miles**
5	7 miles easy	7 miles easy	12 miles easy	**54 miles**
6	7 miles easy	7 miles easy	12 miles easy	**56 miles**
7	7 miles easy	7 miles easy	14 miles easy	**58 miles**
8	8 miles easy	7 miles easy	14 miles easy	**60 miles**
Hill Work Phase				
9	8 miles easy	5 miles easy	**Race**	**54 miles**
10	8 miles easy	7 miles easy	14 miles easy	**60 miles**
11	8 miles easy	7 miles easy	14 miles easy	**60 miles**
12	8 miles easy	5 miles easy	**Race**	**54 miles**
Long Interval/Strength Phase				
13	9 miles easy	6 miles easy	16 miles easy	**60 miles**
14	9 miles easy	6 miles easy	16 miles easy	**60 miles**
15	7 miles easy	5 miles easy	**Race**	**53 miles**
16	9 miles easy	6 miles easy	18 miles easy	**62 miles**
17	9 miles, 6 to 8 short[c]	6 miles easy	18 miles easy	**62 miles**
18	7 miles easy	5 miles easy	**15K or 10-mile race**	**56 miles**
19	8 miles easy[c]	6 miles easy	20 miles easy	**63 miles**
20	9 miles, 6 to 8 short[c]	6 miles easy	20 miles easy	**64 miles**
21	9 miles, 6 to 8 short[c]	6 miles easy	20 miles easy	**64 miles**
22	7 miles easy	5 miles easy	**20K or half mar. race**	**57 miles**
23	8 miles easy	6 miles easy	18 miles easy	**61 miles**
24	8 miles easy	6 miles easy	16 miles easy	**60 miles**
Tapering Phase				
25	8 miles easy	6 miles easy	14 miles easy	**57 miles**
26	4 miles easy	4 miles easy	**THE MARATHON**	**60.2 miles**

*For the 2:40–3:00 marathon runner.
[a]With tempo run.
[b]@10K race pace.
[c]With pickups enroute.

Advanced

The advanced-level runner is capable of running 10K in 38 to 44 minutes. It is at this level that Fleming believes you can benefit from the addition of some tempo running during the seventh and eighth weeks. Four weeks of hill work is introduced as a prelude to the faster work done during the Long Interval/Strength Phase. Note also that the mileage of the advanced level is slightly higher than that of the intermediate.

The strength intervals are done once a week at 10K race pace either on the road or track, whichever is the preference. To determine what distances to run on the track, simply estimate how much distance you cover, for example, during a three-minute interval. If you are a 42-minute 10K runner and thus averaging about seven minutes per mile, half-mile repeats would be done at about 3:30. Therefore, a workout of 4 × 3 minutes could be 4 × 800 meters (half-mile) in 3:30 with three to three-and-a-half minutes of rest between each. When done on the road, the rest should be the same amount of time or distance as the interval.

Also added to the schedule are short pickups done during your normal Friday run, but only during weeks when there is no race.

The final Faster Interval/Peaking Phase is added during the last six weeks. During this phase, the mileage is cut slightly, which should help you feel a little more spring in your legs, and the intervals are done closer to 5K race pace.

Competitive

The competitive runner is one who is classified as a 34- to 38-minute 10K runner. The difference between this level program and the advanced program is, as for the others, more mileage. In the beginning, you do 45 miles per week and build to a maximum of 60 miles per week. During the initial eight-week Distance/Base Building Phase, you do tempo runs once per week from week four through week eight. The hill work and intervals are similar to the advanced level, except that the amount increases on the competitive level.

MARATHON TRAINING

It is Tom Fleming's belief that, first and foremost, everyone doing these programs is a distance runner, so whether you are training for the 10K or the marathon, the initial 12 weeks are always the same. After about 12 weeks, you have built enough of a base to add some speedwork with the goal of running a 10K, or to increase the long run to become accustomed to the demands of a marathon. Therefore, you'll note that on each level the 10K and marathon programs are almost identical, except that for the marathon, an allowance is made for the Sunday run to become increasingly longer. In addition, longer races are suggested to accustom the body to the marathon race experience.

4

HEART RATE
MONITOR TRAINING

When heart rate monitors first came on the market, Grete Waitz, one of history's most successful distance runners, told herself, "I don't need that little helper." But time and experience changed her mind. After trying one of the devices, she was surprised to discover that despite her experience, she was making consistent training errors (mostly training too hard and without sufficient rest).

For the past decade Waitz has been a strong advocate of using a heart rate monitor (HRM) for athletes and exercisers on all levels, and in any fitness activity. Since retiring from competition, she has seen the benefits herself, such as in her indoor bike workouts or on the ski machine.

Waitz prescribes the device to any athlete she coaches. Her most successful model of heart rate monitor training was world class runner Liz McColgan. McColgan used a heart rate monitor when Waitz began coaching her in 1995. In April 1997, McColgan ran a personal best in the London Marathon, 2:26:52, one of the fastest times in the world that year.

On the beginner level, the guidelines for the proper amount of running and exercise are fairly clear. What's more difficult, but equally important, is to establish a safe, effective pace. As runners progress and become more serious, the questions become even more refined and specific. How do I train most efficiently? How much speedwork should I do? How hard should it be done? How much long-distance running will best maximize my potential? How can I get the most out of training without getting injured?

Overtraining is a common and understandable mistake. And it's a classic one. Who hasn't acted on that feeling that if a little is good, more must be better? With the excitement and enthusiasm that come from fitness and athletic achievement, it isn't always easy to tell when we're overdoing it. In fact, sometimes it seems almost impossible to avoid that trap.

Even experienced runners know the rules of preventing overtraining and overracing, which is all well and good on paper. But many runners are complex people—very often compulsive overachievers. Therefore, it will come as little surprise that Waitz estimates that almost all the serious athletes she has encountered often run too hard, particularly with their speedwork. "Their perception of training effort is not accurate. In fact, runners are notoriously inaccurate," she says. It is no wonder, then, that probably 95 percent of all injury results from overtraining.

For the beginning runner, the goal is also to prevent overtraining so that he or she will not become "turned off" to the sport by injury or illness. For the more experienced runner, the issue is how to achieve a high level of fitness without crossing that fine line into the injury zone.

For recreational, or even serious runners, who have the tendency to stay in the "comfort zone" but want to improve, the HRM is effective in forcing them to work harder. Waitz coached one woman who wanted to better her marathon time. Using the HRM as a guide, she was assigned some harder, but not especially rigorous, workouts. After achieving her marathon goal, she admitted to Waitz the HRM kept her "honest."

There has long been established a sound basis of scientific information on the proper amount and intensity of training. It was very difficult to apply it accurately, however, until training became more scientific. That's because it was based on perceived effort. With the use of a heart rate monitor, there is no guessing. Guidelines are all in the numbers, precise and specific.

Exactly what is a heart rate monitor and how does it work? There are various types of heart rate monitors, but the most popular device fits like a belt right below the chest and is accompanied by a watch that picks up the heartbeat signals from the belt. Based on heart rate formulas, once your set of numbers is determined for various workouts, you merely program the device. It then emits a beep if your heart rate either rises above or falls below the desired zone.

Follow the directions for operating and maintaining the device and do not store the monitor in a plastic bag after training. The moisture from perspiration will adversely affect the device.

Science has determined a great deal of what we need to know about exercise and heart rate. We know that there are optimal training zones based on heart rate. Once maximum heart rate (MHR) has been determined, other heart rate information for training can be gleaned.

You can determine your MHR by using the simple formula in this chapter, which gives a rough figure, or for greater accuracy, you can take a stress test on a treadmill. For those who are a bit more ambitious, or who do not want to spend money on a stress test, here is a possible self-test. Find a long hill and run up it as hard as you can. When you truly feel you are giving it your absolute maximum effort and cannot run a step harder, check your heart rate. That should be a fairly accurate reading of your MHR. Waitz stresses that it is important for serious runners to determine their maximum heart rate more accurately, not just use the formula on the following page.

At the other end of the heart rate scale is the resting heart rate (RHR). RHR, like MHR, is an indicator of health and fitness. Trained athletes tend to have low resting pulses, some in the 40s or even 30s in beats per minute. You should become familiar with your RHR to know what your norm is when you are fit and healthy. Resting pulse rate should be measured before getting out of bed in the morning as often as possible—ideally every day. If you wake up and it's high—as high as 75 beats per minute in the case of a fit person—you'll know that you're either sick, on the verge of being sick, or have overtrained. When you are fatigued, ill, or injured and are forced to cut back training, tracking your MHR and RHR can help you stage a proper comeback.

Like any single method, using heart rate to gauge training is most effective with experience. But how do you best gain that experience? It is inefficient to stop mid-run to measure your pulse and compute your heart rate. That's when the ease and effectiveness of a heart rate monitor is most apparent.

PURCHASING A HEART RATE MONITOR

When deciding which heart rate monitor (HRM) to purchase for the Running Gallery at NYRR, Beth Creighton, NYRR's merchandise director, conducted a sampling test with NYRR staff. She had them run with a variety of HRMs until she came up with a consensus of four or five different models, which the Running Gallery now sells. Creighton says the testers found the information the HRM provided valuable, particularly the novice runners, who liked having much of the guesswork taken out of their running.

Creighton points out you can get anything from the very simple HRM, which checks heart rate and includes the basic features of a running watch, to the most sophisticated, which logs a variety of information for a number of training runs, which can then be downloaded to a computer. Of the price range—$100 to $500 as of 2003—says Creighton, "You're paying for the technology." What you choose depends on your level of comfort with that technology, she adds. "Some people live and die by the information, while some can't even use a VCR, so they would never use a heart rate monitor to download information into a computer."

TRAINING ZONE

Training zone refers to the range in which aerobic benefit is achieved. The high end of the training zone is MHR. The low end of the training zone is 60 percent of the MHR.

Grete Waitz, as well as other coaches, prescribes workouts based on percentages within the training zone. Any time you exercise within the low limit to the MHR, you are acquiring cardiovascular benefit. Below that 60 percent, though you're burning calories, you are not attaining aerobic benefit.

The heart rate monitor keeps a runner from training too hard, as well as from "sandbagging," or taking it too easy. In most cases, with a heart rate monitor, runners initially feel that they are doing just that—running too easily. They are often surprised that the device directs the body to run slower than they are used to, yet they are still within the training zone. Use of the heart rate monitor assures proper pace and training benefits, as well as sufficient (and safe) recovery from strenuous efforts.

The heart rate monitor confirms that quality is more important than quantity. "I've seen runners do a lot of miles a week, but a lot of those are 'junk miles,' " says Waitz. "The monitor proves it's better to do fewer quality miles."

HEART RATE FORMULA

There are various formulas for measuring heart rate. A number of them add or subtract for a whole list of variables—from current health to different levels of fitness. While some of these formulas may be more accurate than the one used here, most are more difficult to compute. Besides, the only way to determine exact maximum heart rate is to take a stress test. Otherwise, this formula has proved fairly accurate—and it is definitely simple.

- Men—220 minus your age (Add ten points if you are already fit; i.e., running or involved in another exercise program.)

- Women—226 minus your age (Add ten points if you are fit.)

- Beginners, do not add ten.

Because these formulas were determined using the average population, if someone is physically fit, he or she adds ten points. (i.e., 230, 236). This ten-point addition has proved to be fairly accurate.

Thus, a 40-year-old fit woman charts the following as a scale of her training zone, which is used to determine all workouts:

MHR is 196 beats per minute.

90%—176

80%—157

70%—137

60%—118

For a 40-year-old fit man, the numbers are:

MHR is 190 beats per minute.

90%—171

80%—152

70%—133

60%—114

TRAINING WITH A HEART RATE MONITOR

Below you will find various recommendations for heart rate monitor training.

Beginner

First, consult a physician before taking up running or any exercise program. If you are over age 30, and/or overweight, or if you have been sedentary for ten years or more, get a checkup. Do not use a heart rate monitor as a substitute for a fitness test.

It takes a beginner at least six months to get completely acclimated to running. During this time, speed is not important. The point is gradually to increase mileage at a safe pace.

If you're just getting into the sport, *never run above 70 percent of your MHR*. Sixty to 70 percent is recommended. Maintain that level for at least three months. After that, you may continue to maintain basic training at that heart rate level, or add one to two workouts per week during which you intensify your effort to raise your heart rate five to ten beats.

You should stay at this level for at least six months before moving on to the intermediate phase. Otherwise, you can stay where you are and continue to maintain basic fitness.

Intermediate

Use of the heart rate monitor is not necessary for a warmup or a cool-down. A warmup and cool-down can be 1 to 1 1/2 miles of easy jogging before and after the workout. But use the monitor for speedwork.

1. Most intervals should be done at 90 percent of maximum heart rate, but not higher. (Depending on the type of workout, intervals usually total 1 1/2 to 2 1/2 miles of hard running.)

2. For mile intervals and fartlek—which are longer intervals—run at 80 to 85 percent of maximum heart rate.

The heart rate monitor is especially effective to gauge the length of recovery between efforts. Often the key isn't how hard you work out, but how long you recover. For example, if you run 880 yards, with a two-minute recovery, how do you really know if that is too much or too little rest? Recovery is achieved as soon as you drop to or below 120 beats per minute. Then you're ready to go again.

Also, use the heart rate monitor for a long sustained effort, whether it is six or 18 miles. Your pace should be comfortable, conversational, 65 to 70 percent of MHR for advanced beginners, up to 80 percent for more experienced runners; for your regular run (not recovery from hard runs) 65 to 75 percent of MHR, and recovery run (done the day after a hard workout or race) 60 to 70 percent of MHR. (If the pace feels like you're walking, add a ten-beat increase.)

RESULTS

Is the heart rate monitor successful? According to the improvement Grete Waitz has seen of runners on all levels, it is. In addition, with heart rate monitor training there is often a significant decrease in the number of aches and pains.

Waitz believes in the device because of personal experience and because she has seen other athletes get good results with it. Waitz concludes, "Perceived exertion is too subjective a measure. Heart rate monitors are logical. They make sense."

While the heart rate monitor certainly would seem to be the most logical training tool, be aware that it is just a training device. You don't have to get locked into it. You don't have to use it every time you run.

For all but those who make a living at it, the first and foremost aspect

IF YOU'RE MEASURING YOUR PULSE BY HAND

While you're exercising, check your pulse at the wrist, not the neck. Studies have shown that applying pressure to the carotid artery in the neck can slow your heartbeat by three to twelve beats per minute, which can cause you to miscalculate the intensity of your workout. Also, use your fingers, not your thumb.

***

Don't bother to check your pulse every time you exercise. For one thing, particularly if you are doing it by hand, it can be very inefficient. Some people fail to find their pulse for 20 to 30 seconds after they've slowed down. In the meantime, the heart rate quickly comes down, making any kind of calculation inaccurate. For the same reason, count for six seconds only and multiply by ten. Many teachers and trainers use the rate of perceived exertion (RPE) instead. This rating system—based on a scale of 0 to 10—indicates how hard you *feel* you're exercising. One expert believes that RPE puts the focus back on the exerciser, encouraging her or him to tune into the body rather than rely on a theoretical figure.

That's not to say that target heart rate should be abolished altogether. Pulse rate is helpful in initially determining your own RPE for a certain activity. Pulse counting is also recommended for pregnant women or those with chronic health conditions such as diabetes (because small increases in pulse can have adverse effects), or when exercise conditions change: Heat, humidity, and altitude can all affect heart rate.

of running is that it should be fun and enjoyable. Sometimes you just want a pleasant, slow run and a nice chat with a friend. For those times, you don't really need a heart rate monitor.

And of course, like all training methods, nothing is absolute. No one factor always directly correlates to results. There are too many other variables, like weather, mood, and general health. And, as with any endeavor, there's the psychology of success, and just plain luck.

Also, keep in mind that the heart rate monitor is a training tool, not a training plan. How well you use the tool depends on how skilled the advice is you're getting, or how well you stick to a program. But in general, anything that is more training-specific betters one's chances of success.

5

YOUR TRAINING DIARY

Keeping a diary can be a valuable training aid. A diary provides you with both knowledge and perspective. It helps you to analyze your training and discover what works best for you. By analyzing your diary, successful cycles can be repeated and cycles that lead to breakdown, injury, or poor performance can be eliminated.

For every level of runner, the diary is an important tool. For the beginner, getting into the habit of keeping a diary reinforces the fitness lifestyle. For the intermediate runner, it is a motivation to improve further and to set new goals. And for the advanced, it is essential in tracking and evaluating intense, complicated training. "Because you invest so much in your sport, the diary is also important in its function as a coach, psychiatrist, and conscience. It gives you the opportunity to contemplate your training and to be counseled by it," according to Grete Waitz.

It is also important not to become a slave to the diary. A diary should be a motivator, not something that goads you to do more and more just to be able to write it down. It should be a record of sensible achievement, effective training regimes, and relevant feelings and reflections.

Training can be recorded on anything—from a book designed as a running diary to a loose-leaf notebook or desk diary. Some runners use computers to record their training and racing. Whatever format you choose to record your running, it should include the following information:

1. Date and day of the week.
2. Distance or time run; the course or place running occurred.
3. Overall evaluation of the run: weather, type of effort (e.g., hard, moderate, easy), feelings, comments (e.g., felt sluggish on uphills), training partner or group.
4. Pulse—resting (taken in the morning while still in bed), training pulse, when and where relevant or of interest to you.
5. Weight, measured before run.
6. List of planned upcoming races.

7. Long- and short-term goals. Chart goals with a suggested time frame of up to one year. Significant goals should be written in the front of the book as a reminder. Never lose track of where you want to go, and how you want to improve.

While most serious and elite runners know the value of a diary, it can be an extremely useful tool for everyone. Mary Ellen Howe took up running with great enthusiasm, particularly after losing 25 pounds in less than one year. A new job and an arthritic condition in her knee, however, caused her to run with more care.

To monitor her training, she kept a diary, of which she said the following: "Staleness in my running is almost always due to overtraining, lack of sleep, or crossing multiple time zones during business travel. Recognizing the problem should be easy, but often is not unless I check the comments in my running log. When I see too many notations saying 'felt slow, tired, or legs were dead,' I know that it is time to cut my mileage 25 to 50 percent, catch up on sleep, and get a massage."

I keep a training diary. I buy a standard running log that you can find at most running stores. But I find a weekly log doesn't present a complete picture of the training cycle. Looking at a week isn't enough information. I like looking at six weeks at a time. My husband is my coach, and he'll make a grid for eight weeks at a time with all the key workouts highlighted in yellow. What happens when runners only look at one week is that people get caught up in mileage. You think more is better, and if you miss a day, you try to make up and add more miles. If you step back, you'll get a better picture of your training program.

It's not just about hard runs and easy runs. You have to include cycles of hard and easy weeks. Recovery doesn't always take place in two days. Especially as runners get older, they don't recover as quickly.

—*Marla Runyan*

Tom Fleming says, "I'm a stickler. I've got 24 years' worth of my own very detailed training diaries. My main reason for keeping a diary is to record all workouts and races. This enables me to look back over the work done, and evaluate if and how it has brought me toward my goals."

It is important to evaluate your running in this regard. Good results don't just happen by accident. They are the product of a consistent, progressive training program, one which can best be built and improved by analyzing past results.

Tom Fleming, as a coach, reads his athletes' diaries, but asks that they keep them mostly for their own benefit. "I ask them to write down—in their own handwriting—their goals. It's always great to see something like Anne Marie Lauck's diary. Together we decided on a goal, which she wrote down: to make the World Championships team and to run 32:20 for 10,000 meters (nearly a minute faster than her previous best time). She improved her time to 32:26, made the World Championships team, and she won the World University Games. We specifically set a time goal because I believe she needed something that she could grasp. Time is something all runners can understand. We all live by the clock."

One of the main uses of a training diary is to gain perspective. It is very difficult for any athlete, no matter what level, to assess the overall effectiveness of training while it is being done—despite years of experience. That's because so many factors—goals, aging, relative progress—are constantly changing.

Anne Marie Lauck looks back over one year to get a good benchmark of her training progress. After about a year training seasons and cycles begin to repeat, so there is an aspect of completion. Thus, she can use the diary as a source of comparison to new cycles. She sees what she did right, and when she was at her peak. And she sees what preceded trouble, like a down period in performance or the onset of an injury.

"Athletes forget," says Fleming. "They improve, and later when they are stuck on a plateau, they forget that improvement. With a diary, if they get stuck in a rut, proof of their better days is in black and white. In addition, it is important for an athlete to verbalize his or her aspirations."

But one of the most important factors for keeping a diary is a positive attitude. "If I'm feeling down in September, not doing well, I'll look back at May—a great month," says Lauck. "Then I fully understand that you can't always be that up. I still had that great period of time on which to look back." With this perspective, she can be more patient and wait for a peak cycle to come again, as it inevitably does.

"Can you talk yourself into a performance? Absolutely," says Fleming. "I've done it myself. 'Boston Marathon' reads the heading in large letters in my 1983 diary, which I wrote down months before the race as a source of inspiration. I weighed 170 pounds, 15 pounds overweight, as I stood on the starting line of that race. I had only done one or two good long runs. My diary entries reflect the fact that I absolutely talked myself through that race, and I managed to run in the low 2:14s. That has to be a record for the fastest fat man in the world!"

Anne Marie Lauck also uses her diary to enhance her confidence. For example, she looks back at what she did during last year's cross-country season immediately preceding the upcoming cross-country season. "I look at the good workouts, and I see what results came from them. I feel better prepared for the upcoming season. Just seeing how I progressed knocks down a lot of psychological barriers."

Although using the diary's past performances is a good learning tool, it is not a precise guide for the future. "I don't necessarily duplicate what I did the year before," says Lauck. What Lauck and Fleming do seek to do is duplicate the *pattern* of success, not necessarily the workouts and races themselves.

Confidence, inspiration, and patience are also the privilege of other runners who keep a diary. Says Lauck, "A lot of average runners really get into keeping a diary. Maybe they don't need to study it every day, but it can keep them feeling up. If you're sitting inside in January and there's a blizzard, and maybe you're sick, you can get out the diary and look back at what you did in the spring. It can make you realize that a time like that will come again."

You don't always have to use a training diary as an educational tool. "Sometimes you like to look it over just for the heck of it," she says. Lauck feels that it has an even deeper value than as a training guide. "Even if you don't write down all the details of your day—and I try not to do that in my training diaries for specific reasons—you can still look back at what you wrote and recall other things that were going on in your life." For Lauck, looking at the places, and the people she was with, evokes an entire range of memories. "I can visualize how it might be when I'm 45, retired from competition. I'll look back at my diary when I was in my prime and be able to say, 'This is what I once did.' "

ANNE MARIE LAUCK'S DIARY

To illustrate Tom Fleming's point and show how athletes and their coaches use athletes' handwritten perceptions and expressions in their diaries, Anne Marie Lauck has provided samples reproduced here in facsimile.

WEEK #27 (see figure on page 61)—This week is unique, says Lauck. Although it was a mid-season period, in which the emphasis was on

YEAR TOTAL

2243

TOTAL MILEAGE
FOR WEEK #27

93

JULY

Am - Ran 7¾ mile loop {49:00}; felt OK; hot tub
Pm - DEL VAL TRACK; warm up about 3 miles + strides;
1000m→69, 2:19, **2:53** jog 400; 8x400m w/200 jogs between
warm down after 400's   {69, 69, 69, 68, 69, 68, 68, 67}

17

MONDAY 1

Am - Ran about 8 miles very slow w/ Jim; humid; tight + sore
Pm - Ran Hampton loop (4.9 miles) {30:50} very rainy
lifted weights downstairs; sauna

13

TUESDAY 2

Pm - Ran 4 miles very easy {26:45}
Ran 4x strides + jog to make 5 miles total
hot tub

5

WEDNESDAY 3

Am - Ran 2 miles slow in early morning (at home)
9:30 → LONG ISLAND 5K → 1st: 15:40 [4:55, 10:00, 15:05]
course record; felt pretty comfortable, eased last
mile + picked up last 200m.
Pm - Ran 5 miles easy

15

THURSDAY 4

Am - Ran 10 miles at Gorge {6:30 pace}; feel good
from race
Pm - Ran Hampton loop easy; sauna

15

FRIDAY 5

Am - 9.7 mile loop at Tom's {53:30}; very humid!
Pm - 5 miles on Del Val trails; 4x400 w/200 walk/jog
on track [66.5, 66.8, 65.5, 66.1] warm down

18

SATURDAY 6

Am - Ran 10 miles easy at Gorge (about 6:45 pace)
sauna   very humid 😔!

10

SUNDAY 7

Week #27*

*Please note that Anne Marie Lauck is an elite runner and her schedule reflects this
status. Do not attempt to duplicate her mileage, but learn from her notations
regarding weather, partners, and her own physical condition.

YEAR TOTAL
27 23

TOTAL MILEAGE
FOR WEEK # 34
68

AUGUST

Am - Ran about 5 miles
Pm - TRACK; warm up 2 miles + strides
800m - 2:18; 3×400m - 65,66,66
4×200m - 29.8, 30, 31, ? warmdown

11

MONDAY 19

Am - Ran about 5 miles on indoor track ⊕ (typhoon in town!)
Pm - Ran 5 miles w/ Tom
Stiff & sore

10

TUESDAY 20

LEAVE FOR TOKYO FROM CHIBA TRAINING BASE
Am - Ran about 5 miles very slow w/ Tom (an absolutely
horrible run)
Pm - Ran about 5 miles in Yoyogi Park w/ strides
on grass.

10

WEDNESDAY 21

Am - 6½ miles easy   VERY HOT + HUMID TODAY!
Pm - TRACK AT OHI - warm up 1½ miles + strides
1600m - 4:52
800m - 2:19
2×400m - 64.3, 64.5

12+

THURSDAY 22

Ran about 8 miles with Tom — very slow

8

FRIDAY 23

Am - 5 miles easy w/ Jim
Pm - YOYOGI track : warmup 2+ miles + strides
4×400 — 65,66,65,65
4×200 — 30's
warm down.   Good workout - felt good

12

SATURDAY 24

Ran about 5 miles easy with Jim

5

SUNDAY 25

Week #34

strength work, she ran a race. "It was a fantastic week," says the athlete of the high-volume running and the successful race. But yes, it does go against sound training principles. This is not generally a period during which she would race. "It shows I broke the rules," says Lauck. "We're all crazy. I bet if you analyzed the programs of other top runners, you would see they break the rules, too. But it gives them confidence. Here I had a high-mileage, high-quality week, and I ran a race. I felt good; I ran fast. The race didn't seem to affect me adversely. The fact I did it gives me a sense of invincibility."

WEEK #34 (see figure on page 62)—This is a week that represents the tapering period. "I was at full speed capacity," says Lauck. This is also a special week in her career as it precedes the 1991 World Championships in Tokyo. The workouts here provide her with special memories as well as confidence because they were done after traveling to a nice place, yet she succeeded in doing them in oppressive weather conditions. The week ends on August 25. Two days later, in the heats for the 10,000 meters, she ran her personal best time, 32:26. In 1993, Lauck ran 31:23 at the Peachtree Road Race, as of 2003 still the second fastest American woman of all time for the distance.

See figure page 64 for Lauck's diary entry for actual schedule/events in April and May:

April: Boston Milk Run 10K—1st place, 32:48

Mt. Sac 10K—passed

Penn Relays 10K—3rd in 32:43

May: Nike Women's 8K—5th place, 25:48

On the next three events she listed, she passed. Instead, Lauck ran a 3000-meter time trial, alone on the track, in 9:03:05—a personal best. Fleming commented that "It was early in the season, so instead of undergoing the pressure of a race, and risking getting beat, I preferred to emphasize confidence. She proved to herself she could run fast." In fact, her time was better than the winning time at the Boston 3000-meter race, which she chose not to run.

In June, Lauck passed on the Boston and New York races. Instead, she ran a 1500-meter time trial, alone on the track, on May 28. Her time of 4:18 was a personal best. Says Fleming, "When she did that by herself, without being pushed by anyone else, she gained the confidence to realize she could perform well in a race."

Lauck's diary entry for June 13 (See figure page 65):

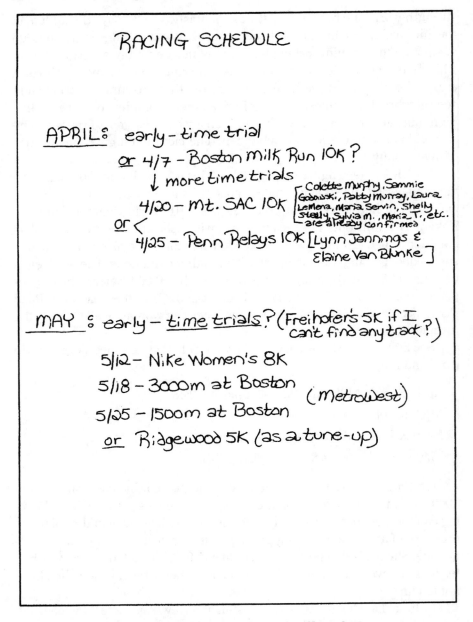

RACING SCHEDULE

APRIL: early - time trial
or 4/7 - Boston Milk Run 10K ?
↓ more time trials
4/20 - Mt. SAC 10K [Colette Murphy, Sammie
Godowski, Patty Murray, Laura
Lemena, Maria Servin, Shelly
or < Steely, Sylvia M., Maria T., etc.
are already confirmed
4/25 - Penn Relays 10K [Lynn Jennings &
Elaine Van Blunke]

MAY : early - time trials ? (Freihofer's 5K if I
can't find any track ?)

5/12 - Nike Women's 8K
5/18 - 3000m at Boston   (Metrowest)
5/25 - 1500m at Boston
or Ridgewood 5K (as a tune-up)

Actual Schedule/Events in April and May

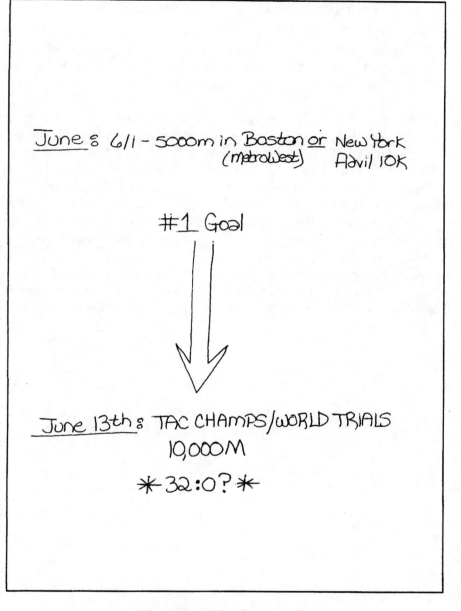

June : 6/1 – 5000m in Boston or New York
            (metroWest)   Advil 10k

#1 Goal

June 13th : TAC CHAMPS/WORLD TRIALS
            10,000M
         ✻ 32:0? ✻

Diary entry for June 13th.

TAC/US CHAMPS/WORLD TRIALS 10,000m.

AM—ran 4 miles very light; hot tub

PM—race at 7:55 P.M. cooler & breezy. 3m warm-up + strides. 32:50, 3rd place, Going to Tokyo! (with Lynn Jennings + Francie Larrieu Smith). Last 400m in 67 secs. I *can* sprint!

Racing Schedule—This represents a unique feature. Tom Fleming believes in having Lauck write down her tentative racing schedule, and her year-end goal (again, in her own handwriting). Writing down the goal solidifies it in her mind. Fleming says, "*I* don't write it, nor does she just say it. *She* puts it down in black and white. Then, I can hold it up to her in the end as proof." In February, Anne Marie Lauck's 10,000-meter best time was 33:05. Her goal sheet for a target race one-half year later reads, "32:0?" In that race, she ran 32:26. Not only is this a substantial improvement, but her prediction is extremely accurate.

Anne Marie Lauck went on to make the 1996 U.S. Olympic Marathon team. She placed tenth in the Games; she was the first American woman. Since these diary entries, she also bettered her 10,000-meter time to 31:37:26.

6
COACHING

A coach brings out the best in an athlete—physically and mentally. There's an art to the craft of coaching. As former Stanford University coach Brooks Johnson once said, "Coaching is no different from what a choreographer does with a dance or what a playwright does with a play." A coach also serves as a supporter, a mentor, a friend, and a psychologist. According to Francie Larrieu Smith, "Having a coach helped my longevity and the direction of my training and career. I get more from myself if someone like a coach is watching me during my workouts. I don't always do this—only for interval sessions. The hard-paced and other runs I do by myself. For every runner, whether jogger or world-class athlete, there are ups and downs. Those who are self-coached can become stagnant or bored. At least occasionally, it might be good for those people to seek out some coaching advice."

Do you need a coach? One of the beauties of the sport of running is that you can do without a coach—and be a success. Take, for example, Olympic gold medalist Joan Samuelson. "I train alone a lot of the time," she says, "and I am currently self-coached. I have never thrived in an atmosphere of a lot of runners. I have always chosen to live away from that. I have very few friends who run. My philosophy on running is, I don't dwell on it, I do it."

While coaching is not mandatory, would you benefit from having a coach, or from coaching advice? Based on the experience of most of the athletes in this book, and on observing the thousands of runners who have been guided by coaches in NYRR classes, the answer to that question is a resounding yes. Longtime age-group champion Toshiko D'Elia puts it like this, "Everyone needs a good coach. That person is like an outside observer, an evaluator, another set of eyes. I would not have been running this long without a coach."

While having a coach may seem impractical for most runners on all but the advanced or elite level, that does not preclude seeking and acquiring coaching advice. There are many types of coaching situations. In addition to one-on-one private coaching, there are running classes, clubs, Y's, running camps, and other organizations through which informal coaching is available. More experienced runners can offer some valuable advice and insights, which can be considered a form of coaching.

In addition to the educational aspect of coaching, there are other benefits you can derive—from motivation to the camaraderie of sharing your experience. A coach can provide not only advice, but also perspective and support.

"As a coach, I try to keep people from taking their running too seriously," says Gordon Bakoulis, who has coached runners at all levels. "New Yorkers in particular can be such an intense bunch. Typically they are very successful in their work, used to putting out a hard effort and getting positive results. You tell people like this that improvement in running is a gradual process, but sometimes they don't get it. They throw themselves into it too intensely, getting injured or disillusioned. Those with some athletic background get the most caught up. Women are usually more sensible than men. I find this in their approach to sports in general. I have no concrete evidence, but they seem more willing to listen to reason."

Grete Waitz cautions that a coach/athlete relationship should not be built on blind faith, but on communication—an exchange of ideas and information. She suggests that you work together with a coach to construct a training program, even if you are a beginner. You know yourself better than anyone—from your body to your time commitment and training goals. Fill your coach in and be sure to understand the training exercises and goals your coach suggests for you.

And remember, not all coaches will be right for you, nor will you be right for them. "I have a few requirements about who I will coach," says Tom Fleming. "I think a person has to stay with a program at least one year. That's the only way to know if it works."

"When I think of coaches who are most inspiring, I think of Fred Thompson, the outstanding mentor of the Atoms Track Club, based in Brooklyn," recalled Fred Lebow. For years, the Atoms have nurtured young local talent. "Fred has made Olympians and shaped young lives."

CASUAL COACHING FOR THE ALL COMER

Whether it's a professional coach, an amateur, an experienced runner, or just a friend—getting some coaching help can be useful.

Coach Tom Fleming believes that a lot of casual runners (and walkers) would like coaching help or advice but are often afraid to ask. But, he claims, "From the casual jogger to the runner who graduates to doing a marathon, to the twice-a-year marathoner, everyone can benefit by getting coaching help." He points out that the many decisions a runner is forced to make are a lot easier when shared with a coach. "Coaching is more than just being able to give a workout," he says, referring to the support, encouragement, and understanding that a good coach can provide.

Fleming uses the example of the casual jogger who decides to train for a marathon. That's because each spring, he meets people who have decided to run the New York City Marathon in the fall. In discussions with some of these people, he assesses their ability, and then he zeros in on their goals. In terms of the viability of those goals he says, "Some are totally off, and some right on." No matter which is the case, he believes coaching advice is helpful. "Everyone needs an objective set of eyes." For some this advice can be casual—like those who drop by a running store. Others, often the less experienced, need more structured advice, he says.

Once you decide to seek it, though, how do you go about finding a coach? "The best resource is people the coach has already helped." When you think you've got someone, try to provide the person with as many details as possible. Do you have a running diary to show, for instance? Finally, Fleming believes the ideal situation is to let someone watch you run. "I don't understand how people get coached by phone or by fax. The best way is to have someone see you run. Analyzing a running effort in writing is one thing, but having someone see you is another. An experienced coach can have a pretty good eye."

Michael Koehane, a 1989 age-group NYRR Runner of the Year, is a personal coach who has conducted a class in Central Park for runners of all levels since 1996. He advises, "You should expect your coach to ask a lot of questions about your entire schedule, life schedule included—everything from shoes to nutrition, stretching, injuries, and so on. This is because every runner is different, and his or her running schedule needs to be structured accordingly."

INTERNET COACHING

Whether it's because you like to go it on your own, or your area is without a conveniently located running club, or you want to supplement the coaching advice you are already getting, you might want to consider online coaching. Online coaching may do more than improve your times. You can also work on other goals like maximizing training to complete a race, or losing weight through your exercise.

Online coaching, or "Virtual Coaching," is gaining in popularity, even over running clubs and personal trainers. E-mail, sometimes supplemented by phone calls, can be a convenient way to develop a one-on-one relationship with an experienced coach. Because it costs less than a personal trainer, even an average runner can hire a virtual coach, with no geographic limits.

While some feel Internet coaching may be impersonal, creating a constant dialogue made possible by e-mail can allow you to spend more time with a coach than you would in person. Choosing a coach, or an online coaching company, may be more challenging, however, as you cannot meet with the person. So, consider the bottom line first: cost. Keep in mind that you get what you pay for; if the service is very inexpensive, chances are you will not get much of the coach's time. To avoid overpaying, however, make sure that the amount of interaction you want seems in line with the price.

You should try to find out as much as you can before making a commitment. Ask if the coach has relevant experience and certification and establish how much time you are paying for.

(Adapted from: www.coolrunning.com)

7

POST-WORKOUT
STRETCHING PROGRAM

This routine takes 10 to 20 minutes total and should be done after every run. Unless otherwise indicated, hold the stretch for 30 to 45 seconds and repeat three or four times. "Progression" refers to the transition from one exercise to another. This routine is taken from the Craftsbury Running Camp.

WALL PUSHUP

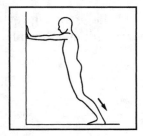 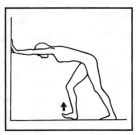 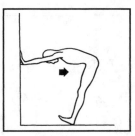

Stand three feet from wall, feet apart and flat on ground, hands on wall, arms straight for support. Lean hips forward, and bend knees slightly. This exercise stretches the calf.

 Progression: Bring one foot forward, with knee bent. Lift front foot's toes up. Lower your upper body to waist height. Stretches muscle under calf.

 Progression: Feet together, rock back on heels, hands on wall, forming a jackknife with the body. Stretches hips, shoulders, and lower back.

BACK SCRATCH

Place palm of hand on bottom of opposite bent elbow; gently push the arm up until it touches the ear, and your hand reaches down, or "scratches," your back. Guide your hand down your back as far as comfortably possible by gently pushing on the elbow. Change hands and repeat. Stretches triceps and shoulders.

HAMSTRING STRETCH

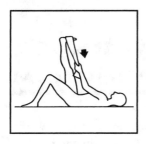

Lie down with one leg straight up in the air and the other leg bent with your foot on ground. Lay towel over arch; gently pull the towel as you push against it with your foot (to the point where muscles contract). Hold 30 seconds; relax. Pulling on the towel encourages hamstring to increase range of motion and strength.

Progression: Turn foot outward so the toes point away from body to stretch outer hamstring fibers. Stretches and strengthens hamstrings and calves.

TRACE THE ALPHABET

With the foot in the air, circle it in large tracings of A-B-C-D...Z. Develops ankle strength and flexibility.

FOOT CRUNCH

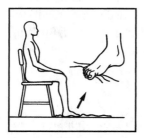 

Lay the towel on ground. Grab the towel with the toes until the arch tires. Strengthens foot muscles, good for those who suffer from plantar fasciitis.

Progression: Hook toes under a chair. Keep knees bent (sit-up position). Hold position until shin tires. Good for those who suffer from shin splints.

QUADRICEPS STRETCH

Kneel (do not sit) on knees; lean back with body erect, arms to the side. Hold 15 seconds. Come back to original kneeling position. Repeat three times.

HEEL TO BUTTOCK

Stand on one foot. Lift the other foot (bend knee) with the opposite hand. Attempt to raise the heel of the lifted foot to buttocks. Keep the trunk upright. Hold 30 to 40 seconds. Repeat three or four times. Change legs and repeat. Also stretches the quadriceps.

HIP/LOWER BACK STRETCH

Get into a sitting position. Cross left leg over right bent leg. Hug the left knee to the chest. Twist the trunk of your body and look over your left shoulder. Change legs and repeat, looking over your right shoulder.

ILIOTIBIAL BAND STRETCH

Lie on your side with both legs bent in running position. Bring the bottom bent leg up toward your chest. Then bring the top bent leg up back toward buttocks in back. Hold for 30 seconds.

Progression: Lie on your back, knees bent. Hug your shins to your chest. Stretches hamstrings and lower back.

Progression: With your feet on the ground, raise your hips up in the air until your torso forms a flat plane. Hold 30 seconds, lower. Repeat ten times. Stretches quadriceps and lower back.

GROIN STRETCH

Seated, draw your feet together until the soles are nearly touching. (They can touch completely if you are flexible enough.) Place your elbows on the inside of your knees. Lean forward gently, simultaneously pressing your knees toward the ground.

8

RUNNING FORM

Running is natural, right? For the most part that's true. If there is something to teach in running, however, it is good form. The biggest problems in most runners is their upper body form. Most coaches do not alter lower body form. To change lower body form is too unnatural and too highly technical for the average runner. In addition, it is almost impossible, even on an elite level, to change foot plant without extensive retraining. You practically have to teach someone to walk in an entirely different way. Therefore it is probably best to let your feet alone and concentrate on your upper body.

Can improving upper body form make a difference? Here's one analogy: How many times do you swing your arms back and forth in one run? Thousands of times. If every arm swing were more efficient, and thus could result even in a hundredth of a second improvement, if you add up all those hundredths, you could improve your overall 10K time by seconds, even minutes.

Coach Tom Fleming, for one, recommends that his athletes work on upper body strength by using lightweight dumbbells. Fleming also claims that just the act of running itself will aid in developing form.

Can upper body form ultimately make a difference in performance? According to Fleming, "If you were to ask Emil Zatopek, who had horrible form, he would probably say no. And he won five Olympic gold medals. The point is, I'll take a great engine with a beat-up-looking body any day." Despite exceptions like Zatopek, however, Fleming agrees that the average runner can benefit by improving upper body form.

The upper body ultimately affects what runners do from the waist down. Improper upper body movement during running results in improper leg lift. Since it is unreasonable to expect a person to correct all mechanical errors at once, it's useful to focus on improving one aspect of form at a time.

The biggest form problem is improper use of the shoulders and arms. The shoulders are too high and the arms are too low or too high. This creates inefficient use of the upper body. Proper upper body movement consists of two elements:

1. **Proper arm swing.** Bend the elbow at a right angle, but do not lock it in this position. Always keep body parts relaxed and fluid. When swinging the arm, the hand should brush the area just below the side of the running pants' waistband.

2. **Shoulders.** Tight shoulders cause tension in the neck and upper back. To make sure shoulders are relaxed, take a deep breath and exhale hard. The shoulders will automatically drop. While running, they should remain in an upside-down "U" shape, not in a "T" shape. In addition, the shoulders should not move during running.

To relax your upper body, think of something soothing. For example, some people visualize running in a serene forest or near tranquil water. This takes the focus away from the running effort.

Many runners on all levels have weak upper bodies. Many experts believe that weight work can improve upper body efficiency, and, thus, your running. One former NYRR coach invented what he calls the "THI" system of weight training. The letters refer to the shape the body makes when doing the exercises. It's the working person's weight training system for upper body strength. It's short yet effective, because most runners have many other obligations and can't spend a great deal of time and money going to fancy gyms.

As was pointed out earlier, a runner swings his or her arms thousands of times in the course of a run. You need strength to do that. With the exercises that follow, in six weeks you'll notice a significant difference. Many runners have had tremendous results with this program.

To do these exercises, you will need two simple dumbbells, from three to six pounds. Test the proper weight by going into a sporting goods store's free-weight department. Hold the dumbbells at your sides. If they are too heavy, they will pull you down; if they are too light, you'll be able to raise them with no effort. You want something that feels like a weight, but is not oppressively heavy.

Try doing the following exercises no more than three times a week, for 15 to 20 minutes, preferably on the days of your easy runs. It's also recommended that you do *not* do them in conjunction with your run; do them any other time of day, a minimum of one hour before or one hour after a run, in front of a mirror if possible.

EXERCISES

1. Sit on the floor with your back straight and your legs straight out in front of you. Put the weights in your hands and swing them in the running motion. Count to 15, maximum (right hand up and back, left hand up and back is one). Take a deep breath, and repeat. (Fifteen repetitions is an advanced workout. In the beginning, you may want to do less. Start with three or five—whatever is comfortable—and build up slowly.)

    Using the running motion while sitting guarantees that the mechanics of the arm swing are correct. If your arms fall too low, the weights will hit the floor; if you bring your hands up too high, you won't be able to move.

2. Standing up, do the same exercise, watching that the weights do not fall below hip level. (You may choose to do both #1 and #2, or only one of them.)

    Now you're ready for the "THI" series. Go through each movement once, completing the T-H-I for one set, up to a maximum of 15 repetitions.

3. "T": With the weights at your sides, bring both hands up sideways simultaneously, reaching shoulder height, so your body looks like a "T" shape. Then bring them down. Pay attention in this and all exercises not to let the weights fall back down with gravity. You should slowly bring them down, maintaining control.

4. "H": Bring your arms out straight in front of you (Frankenstein style) and open them to your sides, then close again, as if you were playing the accordion.

5. "I": Hold the weights resting on the front of the thighs, so you see the backs of your hands. Raise them in front of you to shoulder height (Frankenstein style). Bring them back down.

POSTURE PERFECT

Maintaining good posture, both in the act of running and the rest of the time, is crucial for the serious and recreational runner alike. Without good posture, your running form will suffer and you will never reach your full potential. Injuries, whether to your knees, back, or neck, are much more likely. Still, many runners pay little attention to posture. They slouch over their desks at work; they slump while waiting for the train, and when it comes time to run, their shoulders are hunched and their arms swing wildly.

When at work, you should try getting up from your seat every hour, and stretch out your back and neck. Since a strength imbalance contributes to bad posture, runners should find a way to exercise the entire body—especially the back, which is frequently neglected. Weak stomach muscles can be firmed up with bent-knee stomach crunches (see page 87), which strengthen abdominals without placing heavy strain on the back. Strong abdominals are important because they divert stress from the back, which has more ligaments and muscles than anywhere else in the body.

Staying relaxed and concentrating on your form will not only prevent injuries and fatigue, but also improve your performance.

Keep these basics in mind to ensure proper (and efficient) running form:

1. Keep your trunk erect, with arms, shoulders, and neck relaxed with head up. You should not be looking at your feet.

2. Arms should swing directly forward and backward, never across the body.

3. Keep elbows at a 90-degree angle at your sides, and hold your hands loosely. Your hands should swipe the bottom of your shorts as they swing.

4. Always wear appropriate running shoes, making sure they are in good condition and fit your feet correctly.

(Adapted from "Stop Slouching!" by Rob Jennings, *New York Runner,* Nov./Dec. 2000.)

9

ACTIVE-ISOLATED STRETCHING AND STRENGTHENING EXERCISES

At today's fast pace of life it is often difficult to find time for fitness and health. The father-and-son team of Jim and Phil Wharton are internationally known personal trainers and therapists who have devised exercises that anyone can fit into their schedule. The Whartons have worked with countless sports figures from pro football players to Olympic gold medal winners, and they run clinics all over the United States—in New York City, Florida, and California—and across the world.

The Whartons' exercises can protect the busy runner and help prevent a good cross section of most injuries that occur in runners. Says Phil Wharton, "If we have only five to ten minutes a day, these simple exercises enhance our daily lives, keeping us fresh and injury-free, so we can enjoy our personal lives. If you spend your day sitting down, and then you go out running, it's like going from zero to 60 miles per hour," Phil says. "The muscles do not have the proper blood flow and flexibility. By properly preparing muscles before and after activity, you can increase blood flow and alleviate the possibility of injury."

The following exercises are examples from the fuller program that can be found in the Whartons' books, at Wharton clinics, or in NYRR classes.

PRINCIPLES OF ACTIVE-ISOLATED STRETCHING

Picture the last time you saw a runner stretching before he or she trotted over to the track. It's a familiar scene. He stands to the rear of his car and throws his leg up onto the trunk, his knee straight and locked. Or she stands in front of a fence and reaches her leg up and holds it on the top. Then she reaches out toward her toes. She bounces. Then she holds. Bounce. Hold. Hurt. Hold longer.

The man uses the weight of his torso, and, grabbing onto his calf and pulling himself lower and lower, his hands get closer to his toes with every bounce. This looks like a successful stretch. His hamstring, the massive muscle in the back of his thigh, is getting warmed up and ready for the explosive workout just about to happen. Right?

Wrong.

Simply put, a muscle, when it is being statically stretched with it being bounced and pulled, has a natural tendency to protect itself from this (albeit well intentioned) violence by quickly contracting back to the range that feels normal to it. It is important to realize that only a relaxed muscle will allow itself to be stretched. And the hamstring was not the relaxing muscle in this old, standard leg-up-on-the-trunk-stretch. It was the muscle on the other side of the thigh—the quadricep. All that our runner succeeded in doing was alarming the hamstring so that it tightened to protect itself. Each of them relaxed the quadricep for a good stretch that never happened. The guy would also get a nasty heel print on the trunk of his car.

There's more bad news. Our runner's leg-up-on-the-trunk-stretch involved literally hundreds of muscles from his ankle to his back, from his arms to his neck. The human body has a remarkable ability to compensate and adapt when something is not quite right. In this situation, not one muscle was isolated and worked. In fact, many other muscles besides the hamstring were contracting into their protective postures. (This stretching method is particularly bad for runners with back problems. Your back is protected by lying down to stretch.)

And the final clincher. After our runner's workout, stretching would have allowed his muscles to increase their blood flow and oxygenation, and let them flush out waste products such as lactic acid. Static stretching with bouncing and pulling tightens up every system the muscle uses to heal itself. In short, nothing good happens. Our runner is not going to recover quickly. Not only that, but he is setting himself up for an injury.

There is a better way: a revolutionary, yet remarkably simple flexibility system called active-isolated stretching. (Technically, this is not stretching; it is lengthening.)

Here's how it works:

1. It works one muscle at a time.

2. It actively contracts the muscle that is opposite the targeted muscle, which will relax in preparation of its stretch. (All muscles work in pairs.)

3. You stretch gently and quickly.

4. You release before the muscle realizes it has been stretched and goes into its protective contraction.

5. Then you do it again.

6. Then you go out and win.

(We told you it was simple.)

A flexible body that is stretched effectively is more efficient. It is more easily trained to maximize strength and endurance, it enjoys greater range of motion, it stays balanced more easily, it is less prone to injury, it recovers from workouts more quickly, and it feels better. Also, there'll be no more heel marks on the trunks of cars.

Why do it?

"We are always told to brush our teeth to prevent cavities. But there's no owner's manual for our muscles," says Phil Wharton. We are constantly using our body, and gravity alone causes us to get tight, so muscle care should be our motto. Wharton says we should think of dogs and cats. Innately, they know to stretch before moving. It's just a two-second stretch, and it follows the principle of active-isolated stretching.

As Wharton explains, we have what is called the myotatic stretch reflect—a protective mechanism that basically stops our body from overstretching. (Cats and dogs have this reflex too.) In the past, we overrode this reflex with static stretching—holding a stretch for extended periods of time. In the 1940s and 50s, ballistic (or bouncing) became the popular method of stretching. This caused muscle pulls and tears and led to the 1970s method of stretching, which was a yoga derivative. In the 1980s, static stretching became the prescribed method. Now, there's an even better way.

Problems with stretching, like muscle pulls, led people to think, "Maybe we shouldn't stretch." But research confirmed that we should, with the condition that we not stretch cold muscles. We were told to warm up, then stretch, then run, then stretch again. "But who has the time?" says Wharton.

"The Kenyans and the Ethiopians—the best runners in the world, don't intellectualize about stretching," he says. "They know how to stretch and warm up."

TO STRETCH OR NOT TO STRETCH

Wharton says that there's good reason for elite runners, and all runners, to stretch. Think of the compression every time you take a running step—the forces exerted equal two to three times your body weight. If your muscles are in a shortened state (contracted, not lengthened), they are more predisposed to strains, tears, and micro-damage. A warmed muscle, with blood flow deep in the capillaries, is one that's ready to work. Lengthened muscles allow longer, freer strides and less effort to go through your stride. So, you run with nonrestricted movement.

Too Busy?

If you have only five minutes a day, says Phil Wharton, it's worth it to invest them in stretching. Start with the hamstring stretch. "You're sitting all day. Give yourself the benefit of stretching. You'll feel so much better."

THREE GREAT STRETCHES
AND THREE GREAT LIFTS

Here are some of the exercises in the Active-Isolated stretching program:

Gastrocnemius Stretch

What you stretch: Calf muscles (Gastrocnemius)
What you contract: The muscles in the fronts of the lower legs (the ankle; foot dorsal flexors, especially the tibialis anterior)
Equipment you need: Length of rope
How many repetitions: 10 each side
How long to hold each stretch: 2 seconds
Sit with both legs straight out in front of you. To take pressure off your back, you may want to relax your non-exercising leg by bending your knee and putting the sole of that foot flat on the surface on which you are sitting. Loop your rope around the foot of your exercising leg (still straight) and grasp each end of the rope in your hands. From your heel, flex your foot back toward your ankle, aiming your toes toward your knee. Use your rope for a gentle assist at the end of this movement. Remember to keep your knee locked and upper body still. For an advanced stretch, you may bend forward at your hips and lean your upper body closer to your locked knee.

Straight Leg Hamstring Stretch

What you stretch: The large muscles in the backs of the thighs (the hamstrings)
What you contract: Muscles from the fronts of the hips down the fronts of the thighs (hip flexors, including the quadriceps)

Equipment you need: Length of rope
How many repetitions: 10 each side
How long to hold each stretch: 2 seconds
Lie on your back. Begin with your non-exercising knee bent with that foot flat on the surface on which you are lying. Take your rope and hold the ends together so that it forms a loop. Place the foot of the leg you're exercising into the loop. Lock your knee so that your leg is extended straight out. From your hip and using your quadriceps, lift your leg as far as you can. Aim your foot toward the ceiling. Grasp the ends of the rope (to maintain the loop) with both hands and "climb" up the rope, hand over hand as your leg lifts. Keep slight tension on the rope. Use the rope for gentle assistance at the end of the stretch, but do not pull the leg into position and irritate the back of your knee.

Quadriceps Stretch

What you stretch: The muscles in the fronts of the thighs (rectus femoris)
What you contract: The muscles in the buttocks (gluteus maximus) and
   the backs of the thighs (hamstrings)
Equipment you need: Length of rope
How many repetitions: 10 each side
How long to hold each stretch: 2 seconds
Lie on your side with your knees curled up against your chest in a fetal position. Relax your neck, resting your head on the surface or on a pillow. Slide your bottom arm under the thigh of your bottom leg and lock your elbow around the back of your knee. Contract your abdominal muscles to keep from rolling. Reach down with your upper hand and grasp the shin (or ankle or forefoot) of your upper leg. If you are unable to bend your knee sufficiently in order for you to reach with your hand, use your rope as an extender. Wrap it around your ankle and grasp the ends. Keep your knee bent and your leg parallel to the surface on which you are lying. Contract your hamstrings and gluteus maximus and move the upper leg back as far as you can. You may use your hand to give a gentle assist at the end of the stretch.

GREAT LIFTS

Rhomboids

What you strengthen: The inner group of muscles that steadies and controls the upper back, and the connection of the shoulder (rhomboids major and minor, supraspinatus, infraspinatus, levator scapulae, and pectoralis minor)

The action: Bent elbow, horizontal shoulder abduction

Equipment you need: Two handheld weights (dumbbells)

The Workout: Lie down on your stomach on a bed or a table, and hang over the edge until you are suspended out as far as your armpits. You are going to work both arms simultaneously. Dangle your arms down over the edge. Relax your neck so that your head drops down. Take one weight in each hand. (Remember, they must be equal.) Your palms should face up and your thumbs should point forward. Lock your elbows at 90-degree angles and touch the weights together in line with your nose. This is the starting position. Bring your locked elbows up toward the ceiling as far as you can go, separating the weights. Hold for a moment. Return slowly to starting position.

Managing your sets: Ten reps constitute one set. Plan to rest 30 seconds between each set. How long does it take when Jim and Phil work out?

First set: 40 seconds / Rest: 30 seconds
Second set: 40 seconds / Rest: 30 seconds
Third set: 40 seconds
Total time: 3 minutes

Taking it to the gym: You can stand and use a cable and pulley system. Remember to bend forward 90 degrees at the waist, contract your abdominals to stabilize your body, relax your neck and drop your head, lock your elbows into 90-degree angles, and keep your back straight. You'll work one arm at a time. Place the hand of your non-exercising arm on the thigh of your exercising side to help balance you.

We think the seated machines can help you do the job, but they can put pressure on your back. Even though you're upright, keep your neck relaxed and your head down to isolate the rhomboids and keep other muscles (like your trapezius) from engaging to help do the work. Lying down is better than standing. And standing is better than sitting.

Lower Leg Triple Play

What you strengthen: Lower leg (tibialis anterior and posterior, peroneus tertius, extensor hallucis longus, extensor digitorum longus, and peroneus brevis, tertius, and longus)

The action: Ankle dorsi flexion and foot supination and pronation

Equipment you need: A tube sock with a weight in the toe

The workout: This workout is designed in two parts for two reasons. First, these muscles always function as a team, working in concert to stabilize your foot and support your weight to keep you upright and balanced. And second, because once you're in position in the workout, it's efficient to continue from one exercise to the next.

Before you begin, you're going to need to construct a piece of personal workout equipment. Take a long tube sock and stuff a 1-pound weight down into the toe. If you don't have a weight, you may use anything that weighs a pound and is small enough to fit.

Tie the sock onto your exercising foot by dangling the weight under the ball of your foot and threading the sock between your big toe and the toe next to it. (The "second metatarsal" for those who enjoy technical accuracy or "the little piggy who stayed home" for all the rest of us.) It doesn't matter how far down the weight hangs, but make certain that you have plenty of sock left to loop around your foot. Continue to wrap by looping the end of the sock around the outside of your foot, under your arch and back up over the top of your foot. Then fasten it securely by tying under the top wrap. It's really simple. (see www.whartonperformance.com)

Note: You can work out both sides at the same time if you use two equally weighted socks.

Part 1

Sit on any surface that allows your thighs to be parallel to the floor, your knees to bend at 90-degree angles, and your feet and sock-weights to dangle well above the floor. Sit up straight and contract your abdominals to keep your torso stable. You might want to place a rolled towel underneath your knees. This padding will take pressure off the kneecaps (patellae). Also, any time you sit with your knees slightly higher than your tailbone (coccyx), you reduce stress on your back. Slightly separate your knees and feet. Point your toes down straight to the floor. This is the starting position. Now, slowly raise the front of your foot until you can go no further. Your heel will be down and your toes will be up. You'll feel contractions in the outside of your lower leg and the top of your foot. Hold for a moment and then slowly return to the starting position: toe pointed down.

Part 2

Maintain the same basic position, but this time you want to point your toe straight down and come up by sweeping your foot to the inside and pointing your big toe to the ceiling. It's a diagonal movement. You'll feel contractions in your arch and in the inside of your lower leg. Sweep back down until your big toe is pointing straight to the floor. Hold for a moment. Then continue the sweep up and to the outside as far as you can go. Again, this is a diagonal movement. You'll feel contractions in the outsides of your ankle and lower leg. Slowly return to the starting position: toe pointed down.

Managing your sets: Ten of Parts 1 and 2 combined constitute one set. There is no need to rest between sets unless you feel fatigued.

How long does it take when Jim and Phil work out?

First set: 1 minute
Second set: 1 minute
Third set: 1 minute
Total time: 3 minutes

Taking it to the gym: To our knowledge, there is no equipment that isolates the muscles so effectively as this simple exercise.

Gluteals

What you strengthen: Buttocks (gluteals, primarily the gluteus maximus)

The action: Hip extension with bent knee

Equipment you need: Ankle weights

The workout: Bend over a bed or workout table with your pelvis on the edge and the ball of the foot of your non-exercising leg on the floor. Keep your non-exercising leg relaxed. Bend your exercising leg to a 90-degree angle and let it do all the work. (Resist the temptation to brace the foot of your non-exercising leg against the floor so you can push against it.) Move the exercising leg up toward the ceiling to the point where the buttock muscles engage but not beyond parallel with your back and pelvis.

Managing your sets: Lift ten reps with one leg. Lift the next ten reps with the opposite leg. Working both sides constitutes one set. There is no need to rest between sets if you alternate legs unless you feel fatigued. How long does it take when Jim and Phil work out?

First set: 50 seconds right / 50 seconds left
Second set: 50 seconds right / 50 seconds left
Third set: 50 seconds right / 50 seconds left
Total time: 5 minutes

Taking it to the gym: Machines at the gym work well here, where a locked position helps isolate and track muscles properly . . . as long as you use machines that allow you to work out one leg at a time and put no strain on your back.

To see photos of these exercises, go to www.whartonperformance.com, from which these exercises are excerpted. They are samples of a more complete program, which can be found in *The Whartons' Stretch Book* and *The Whartons' Strength Book,* both published by Random House.

CRUNCH!

This simple exercise can work wonders for your running (and likely your walking, too). Though vanity provides many people with the motivation to build a strong midsection, runners have a far more compelling incentive. Strong abs keep you running strongly—upright and with efficient running mechanics. In contrast, a weak trunk can lead to sloppy running form, which can sap endurance and predispose a runner to a host of injuries throughout the lower half of the body.

There are many ways to work the abdominals. The simplest, and perhaps most effective if done correctly and consistently, is the crunch. Here are the four elements of a safe, effective crunch:

Body Position

Lie on your back with knees bent to about 90 degrees. There should be a space between your lower back and the floor. Contract the abdominal muscles to draw your back toward the floor. This puts the body in the pelvic tilt (or posterior tilt) position, which engages the transverse abdominus muscle and keeps undue pressure off the lower back.

Arm Position

You can see people hold their arms in many different ways—behind the head, folded on the chest, raised toward the ceiling, and other positions. They are all acceptable, depending on your desired resistance load—that is, how hard you want to work. The easiest arm placement is alongside the thighs. Across the chest is slightly more challenging, hands behind the neck offers that much more difficulty in terms of resistance (but makes up for it by offering neck support), and finally, extended up over your head is the most difficult. No matter what your position, the arms should move as part of the torso unit, and not initiate any of the effort. Working the arms defeats the purpose of working the abdominals.

Neck Movement

To avoid straining the neck, you must raise the head and neck, rolling up one vertebra at a time so the muscle action is smooth instead of jerky. Rise up until there's roughly the space of a tennis ball between your chin and chest. Maintain that position throughout a set of crunches or return your head to the floor between crunches if you need a brief rest.

The Effort

Performing the crunch is simply a matter of squeezing your ribs to your hips and exhaling. (Holding your breath increases blood pressure and decreases oxygen to the brain.) Once this is done, the crunch is done. Anything more is a sit-up, which works the hip flexors rather than the abs.

Choose quality over quantity. Do each crunch in a slow, controlled manner (two seconds up, hold two seconds, two seconds down). Beginners can start with a set of 15 crunches, and gradually work up to three sets of 15 to 20. Three times a week is sufficient.

You should include crossovers in your crunches—i.e., crunches on a diagonal. Start by putting your right ankle on your bent left knee (which will stabilize your hip), do your pelvic tilt, put your left hand behind your head and stretch your right arm out against the floor or ground, then twist and lift your left rib to your right hip, as much as you can (there's no need to try to touch your elbow to your knee). Crossovers target the obliques and develop rotational strength, which will keep your kinetic energy going forward when you run.

(Adapted from "Crunch! What This Simple Exercise Can Do for Your Running," *New York Runner,* May/June 2001.)

STRETCHING TO PREVENT MUSCLE TEARS

To avoid chronic muscle tears the athlete should be fastidious about stretching, especially the main locomotive muscles which cross two joints, i.e., the hamstrings, gastronemius, quadriceps and adductors. Muscle strength imbalances between opposing muscle groups should be corrected. The strength balance between hamstring and quadriceps is very important and serious athletes should have their strength ratios tested on a Cybex or similar strength testing machine. At all times, but especially when doing speed work, it is imperative to be adequately warmed up. Prevention is better than cure, but for the runner who has the symptoms of a developing chronic muscle tear a little treatment early on saves time out and a great deal of agony later on.

—Gerard Hartmann

ELITE STRETCHING

Gerard Hartmann claims that now at competitions worldwide, the system described as active isolated stretching is preferred by most athletes. He cites the career of 400-meter legend Michael Johnson.

"Behind the glamour of the amazing Michael Johnson is a warm-up routine that has 40 minutes of isolated stretching as the main ingredient. Eighty percent of Michael's pre-race warm-up is done stretching on a treatment table—with very minimal running before going onto the start blocks."

10

CROSS TRAINING

Why cross train? Why engage in other sports? Why expend time and energy swimming and biking when running seems sufficient to promote well-being? According to writer Peter Gambaccini, who elaborates on cross training options in this chapter, complementing or even partially replacing running with some other form of workout can make sense for every level of footracer. The injured runner, forced to forsake the weekly road mileage, can choose from a wide array of cross training activities to work muscle groups and tax cardiovascular capacity. Many cross training options require low or even no impact; they offer a welcome respite from the pounding of the pavement.

> People think running is just about getting out there, but it's all of the other factors—sleep, proper nutrition, and cross training—that allow you to get the most out of the sport.
>
> I take ice baths every day, for example. I find they significantly boost my recovery. I'll also try and get a massage three times a week, and I'll get in the weight room six days a week. Three of those are spent doing core strength workouts. The other days I'll do plyometrics and weight exercises.
>
> —*Deena Kastor*

Cross training can also prevent injuries caused by a muscular imbalance or other physical irregularities. A knee injury, for example, can be an alignment problem traceable to the relative power and weakness of adjacent muscle groups. Pure long-distance runners tend to have mighty hamstrings and feeble quadriceps. Muscle groups that work together need to be compatibly strong. It is risky to overdevelop one set and neglect the other. There are cross training solutions to this potentially disastrous problem.

Wisdom and purpose should guide your cross training. There is probably a cross training option for whatever particular weakness plagues your

MORE CROSS TRAINING TIPS

I usually go to the weight room two to three times per week. I'll do 30 minutes of weights with 15–20 repetitions at each exercise. I also do a lot of exercises with my own body weight for resistance. For core and stability training, I use the therapy ball. I also go to the pool and lap swim for 20 minutes. It helps loosen up my back and increases my freedom of motion in my muscles.

I am pretty flexible; I was into gymnastics when I was younger, so I do stretches I know work for me to help my hip, which has been a trouble area. I can grab my foot and bring my ankle to my forehead. I stretch four to five times per week for an hour.

—*Marla Runyan*

running. The more specific that cross training is to your needs, the more benefits you'll reap.

In addition to preventing future injuries and alleviating the stress of current ones, cross training can also make you a superior runner. Swimming enhances flexibility and even lengthens the running stride. Reasonable weight workouts give the upper body strength and tone that will keep running form intact. Bicycling fortifies the quadriceps needed to attack the tough hills. And cross-country skiing, if done properly, produces an even greater oxygen intake capacity than does running.

There's also the matter of diversion. Running is supposed to be fun. A second or third sport can alleviate monotony and inject a little joy into training.

Runners on all levels report greater success and fewer injuries by reducing their mileage and cross training to make up the difference. Each runner will need to experiment, but it may be reasonable to cut running by 20 percent and substitute another sport for what's being omitted. And by alternating two aerobic activities, it virtually guarantees that all of the muscle groups are brought into play.

When embarking on a new regimen to supplement running, remember that cross training should not be an added excuse to exhaust oneself. Trying to handle a regular run and some cycling in one workout, for example, is just a hybrid form of overtraining.

Finally, start doing some serious stretching before your cross training. Your musculature will be working in entirely new ways; don't ask tight, cold, untested muscles to do new tricks.

I think a current fallacy is the use of cross training to achieve success in running. You can't replace the need for higher-mileage running with another sport; however, I don't consider light weight work, such as with dumbbells, to be cross training. That is part of a runner's overall training.

Cross training is great when you're injured, during an off-season, or for general fitness, but I don't believe in it as an integral part of a running program. I definitely believe that an athlete is a good runner because he or she runs.

I'm not a big believer in extensive cross training to prevent injury, even if athletes claim to have injury problems that can be solved by it. For example, if an athlete comes to me with chronic muscle soreness, I examine the previous phase of training and probably discover that training wasn't done properly.

If you want to be a better runner, you've got to run more—it's as simple as that. To prove this point, I cite as an example those who are best succeeding in distance running—the Africans. The day I walk into the home of any runner in any African city, town, or village and find a stair climbing machine, rowing machine, or wet vest near a swimming pool, I'll be proved wrong. Until that day, I stick by my belief in the need to concentrate on putting in the running miles.

—*Tom Fleming*

CYCLING

Bicycling has become one of the most popular and beneficial cross training options for runners. Like many runners, Dan Glickenhaus says, "I had always looked on cycling as a form of transportation, not really a way to train. I had no idea what RPMs (pedaling revolutions per minute) were." Glickenhaus has learned and then some. He's a former president of Team Red Line, New York's talented triathlon squad, and he won what was then the Central Park Triathlon in 1989, 1990, and 1991.

Glickenhaus tasted victory as a frequent winner in New York City road races. He took up bicycling as a break from the impact of running while his injuries healed.

In the same way that many running injuries can be traced to incorrect form, cyclists will suffer if they aren't properly fitted to their bikes. Too many beginners ride with bike seats that are too low or too high, or with handlebars at an improper angle, which can cause back pain. Get an expert to fit your bike to your needs.

Is cycling strenuous enough for athletes accustomed to running's rigors? Glickenhaus often wears a heart rate monitor, and has found that some of his highest heart rates are at the end of hill climbs on the bike. But Glickenhaus, who once ran 80 miles per week, warns that an equivalent cycling regimen takes a lot of miles. For example, Hawaii's Ironman Triathlon includes 112 miles of cycling and 26.2 miles of running; that four-to-one ratio

I cross train with bike riding. My recommendation is pretty simple. I take about 40 percent of my current aerobic training, and this includes a weekly two-hour run, and convert it into biking. For example, the two-hour run is sometimes replaced by a three-hour bike ride; however, this conversion does not include the anaerobic running—my twice-weekly interval training. The reason I have made this adjustment to biking is to relieve the stress of the pounding. Biking helps one avoid injuries because it allows more recovery time between running workouts and puts less overall stress on the body.

It's the cumulative stress that causes injuries. I believe that it's not so much that you're more prone to injury as you get older, it's that the amount that you've done builds up. Everybody has a certain saturation point. Then you get hurt.

Ask [top masters runner] John Campbell. He started running when he was 38. He was accumulating stress at the same rate and in the same way as if he had been 24 when he started. He had the same four or five years of excelling without major injury problems, and then he got hurt—just like someone in his 20s would in the same situation.

The other aspect of biking for me is that I participate in the multi-sport events. It's another way to have a training goal, and an area in which I can still improve. The frustration for me, and perhaps for many others, is that at some point, we cannot improve our running times. The guy who ran 2:36 for the marathon at age 32 is likely running about three hours when he's over age 40. Maybe if he starts to ride the bike now, and he enters biathlons, he can feel he's improving. He gets better on the bicycle, and that's a way to improve his training and competition goals.

—*Frank Shorter*

between the two disciplines is fairly common. Therefore, you can assume that the effort of a 10K run is equal to that of a 25-mile bike ride. So cycling is definitely the sport for people who wish to train a lot and don't care about investing the time.

Cycling complements running quite well. The effort of long-distance athletes in both sports is similar to a degree; they are both essentially dependent on lower body strength. Cycling, however, is a more thorough muscular workout than running. The quadriceps drive most of the cycling stroke, but the calf muscles are working as the pedal is pulled back up. In the tuck position assumed by serious cyclists, the lower back is conditioned as well. In hill climbs, the arm and shoulder muscles do a great deal of the pulling. For variety, use a light bike ride as a warmup before a run.

Although the sports go well together, a cycling workout shouldn't be too intense if you plan to run hard the following day. Conversely, a serious track session might be followed the next day by an easy spinning bike ride with no intervals or challenging assaults on hills.

"Runners who start cycling should have some concept of what a workout is," states Glickenhaus. Bike computers and watches can help calculate pedal revolutions. It's wise to start with an easy warmup loop before following with a tough one. On the flats, a cyclist may, as runners do, sprint hard for the space between two telephone poles, ease off, and then speed up again.

Hills can be a real challenge. "When you're climbing a hill, you still want to maintain 60 to 80 RPMs in lower gear," warns Glickenhaus. The urge to stand up on the pedals should be avoided. It's more efficient, and more athletically beneficial, to remain seated. It's no secret that biking, in which legs encounter resistance as they rotate and with the knee driving higher than it does in running, will help a runner's leg rotation.

It is even possible to do a type of interval training on bicycles. In a low gear, increase the RPMs of your pedaling. If normal is 60, try 80 for one minute. A cyclist can alternate 60 RPMs and 80 RPMs for one, five, or six sets, and then finish off with a slow ride home. Both in running and cycling, speed is a product of increased turnover. This kind of bike workout will do wonders for the quadriceps, helping to balance the overdeveloped hamstring from running.

The injury-free runner will still want to do his or her serious long runs and speed workouts. But to lessen the impact and add variety, the 30- or 45-minute "easy" recovery run can give way to, for example, a two-hour bike ride.

For the more serious athlete, cycling requires extra concentration. An opponent's surge in a road race may seem like a decisive move, but Dan Glickenhaus suggests, "In cycling you have to watch even more closely. If someone makes a break, he can be gone in a matter of seconds." It's also important in bike racing to be extra attentive for safety reasons. Taking an elbow in a crowded pack of runners is one thing. In a throng of cyclists, the same thing at high speed can cause a massive collision and serious injury.

CROSS-COUNTRY SKIING

Cross-country skiing is a cross training option that many runners quite sensibly turn to in winter—and even in summer, with skis mounted on roller-skate wheels. Cross-country skiing is an excellent fitness substitute for road running. It's a long-distance sport that enhances cardiovascular fitness and utilizes many of the same muscle groups as distance running. Not surprisingly, good long-distance runners very often tend to make outstanding cross-country skiers.

Cross-country skiing has been traced back thousands of years to Siberia and Scandinavia. Later, it was a big asset to the Vikings in their eleventh- and twelfth-century conquests. And it can be the biggest boon of all to the cross trainer. Tests have shown that cross-country skiers have oxygen intake capabilities surpassing those of long-distance runners.

The rudiments of cross-country skiing are not difficult to master. In the beginning, it is quite like walking on skis. Going straight ahead, be advised not to lift the ski tips; keep them in contact with the snow at all times. This is facilitated by keeping your weight slightly forward.

More advanced, quicker skiing approximates the motion of running. The thrusting leg has a stronger push or kick, and the steps and the glides are longer. The weight can be well forward, and although the backs of the skis come out of the snow, the angle between the lower leg and the front of the ski should never exceed 90 degrees.

On uphill climbs with poles, the arms and shoulders get plenty of work. For going up steep, seemingly insurmountable slopes, switch to a "herringbone" technique, in which a V-shaped wedge is formed with the backs of the skis together and the fronts wide apart. For this, the poles are positioned behind the skis.

Two world-renowned Norwegian distance runners, Ingrid Kristiansen

As time goes on, I am more into alternative training. Biking—and mountain biking—and skiing have been my main activities in addition to running. Cross-country skiing is a way of life for many Norwegians, and I have done it recreationally for years. I have also done the Nordic ski machine as an alternative workout when I was injured from running.

During injury, you can stay very fit with alternative sports, but be aware that resuming running still requires some adjustment. When you start running after a layoff, even if you are fit, your "tires are flat." You have to take time to get your legs used to running again. When I started running again after a period of alternative training, I wasn't breathing hard, but my legs were aching. To use the analogy of a car, it was like the engine was tip-top, but the tires were without air.

Since I retired from serious competition, I have really enjoyed doing other sports. I've had some "marathon" cross training sessions. For example, in December of 1991, I took a holiday vacation with my husband, Jack. In three weeks in Austria and Germany, we covered a lot of miles: 250 skiing, 100 running, and 100+ walking.

—Grete Waitz

and Grete Waitz, have many years of cross-country ski experience; Kristiansen even won skiing titles before becoming a top runner. Waitz recalls that all the years that she lived in Oslo, she went skiing as part of training in winter months. She estimates that of every 12 distance workouts she would do, three or four were on skis. "That was one of the reasons I stayed injury free. Runners who have the opportunity should try cross-country skiing," she concludes.

On skis, Waitz discovered, "You get tired in a different way. You spend more time out there." She calculated that to get the equivalent exercise value, she would have to spend two minutes on skis for every one minute she'd run. "A ten-mile run would be like two hours skiing," she figured. Cross-country skiing, in which legs tend to be closer together and the body is less erect than in running, sometimes left Waitz with soreness in her inner thighs and lower back, strengthening those areas in the process. Skiers who use their poles to propel themselves can strengthen the upper body and firm up their abdomen. To regain her running form, Waitz would not ski during the week of an important race.

Much of the United States gets enough snow for you to try this sport in winter months. A mere two or three inches on the ground in a local park or woods is enough to merit giving cross-country skiing a try.

DOWNHILL SKIING

Downhill skiing isn't usually considered a valuable form of cross training, but if you've seen Bode Miller whooshing down a slope faster than a car can legally travel on most highways, you begin to perceive that this is physical work. Two of cross training's greatest benefits, a break from pounding and a chance to enhance flexibility, are features of downhill skiing. And few sports are as exhilarating as skiing. In training, skiers do an exercise in which, from a frog-like posture, they leap up and down repeatedly. The goal is to develop "explosive" quadriceps.

WEIGHT TRAINING

Runners are not advised to "pump up" their bodies with heavy iron weights, but weight training with moderate weights and numerous repetitions is often recommended. Some people are now recommending heavier weights and fewer repetitions for runners. A coach or an observant running partner may be able to point out a flaw in your form that is traceable to weakness in a particular muscle group. Training with weights can alleviate such a weakness.

Many runners who do no other exercise have underdeveloped upper bodies; these athletes often overlook the fact that what happens from the waist up also matters in running. Arms are steering mechanisms; they provide balance and prevent toppling over or veering to one side. In addition, vigorous arm motion is part of a powerful finishing kick. So strengthening the upper body by weight training can contribute to better running performance. Toning and strengthening muscles with weights can assist in preventing injuries. Weight training has its cardiovascular benefits, too.

While lifting weights, concentrate on regular breathing, really filling your lungs with oxygen. Breathe deeply during the easy part of lifting/lowering, and expel the air during the effort. A comprehensive weight workout can become even more strenuous and aerobically beneficial if you move very quickly, or literally dash, from one weight station to another, not pausing to rest and completely catch your breath. Triathlete Bill Noel goes through his series of 17 separate Nautilus exercises in under 30 minutes.

Bench presses, or overhead presses with free weights, will not only give the arms and shoulders strength but will also add tone and coordination. Rather than striving to lift your absolute maximum, as a runner you're better off working with about two-thirds of what you can lift. If 150 pounds is your best press, you should try sets of 100-pound lifts, perhaps four to six lifts per set. Make it feel like an effort, but don't strain yourself and risk injury.

There are specific weight exercises that condition each muscle group. With "squats," the bar of weight is placed on the shoulders behind the neck, and the weight is taken down by bending the knees and then raising up again. The quadriceps provide most of the upward thrust. Experimentation will determine what's comfortable, but it's unwise to bend until the thighs dip below a 90-degree angle; to do so may put undue strain on the knees and negate the positive effect on the quadriceps. Runners can also try "lungers," again for the quadriceps. In this exercise, with the weight on the shoulders, the athlete steps forward nearly as far as possible with the left leg, then steps back, and does the same maneuver with the right.

LIFT FOR LIFE

Runners benefit from weightlifting and so does everyone else. Guidelines from the office of the Surgeon General of the United States recommend that all Americans incorporate two sessions of weekly resistance training into their exercise programs. Resistance training has been shown to be a major preventive measure against osteoporosis and the loss of muscle strength as a result of aging.

As the director of Corporate Health and Fitness at Rodale (publisher of *Runner's World* magazine) for over two decades, Budd Coates knows something about strength training. Coates, whose marathon best is 2:13, continues to excel as a masters runner, recording a 2:22 at the 2001 Boston Marathon, and winning the JPMorgan Chase Corporate Challenge in Central Park.

Coates says he has been supplementing his running with a strength training program "forever" (25 years): two to three times per week, for about 20 minutes per session. He always ends his session with Active-Isolated Stretching (see Chapter 9).

According to Coates, there are two main reasons strength training is valuable. First, it complements a running program by creating balance in muscle strength (such as working the areas of the legs not strengthened by running). Second, particularly over time, most adults create for themselves a forward posture, with a rounded back. Strength exercises—those done for the upper back and shoulders—can offset this. This keeps the chest cavity open, and as big as possible, which maintains lung volume.

Strength training is even more important as we age. "You need to make sure you pay more attention to balanced strength, as the effects of any muscle weaknesses are multiplied as we age."

Does strength training help running? Says Coates, "What improves running is running, but the ability to run can be improved through strength training. It keeps you generally more fit, and allows you to keep running."

Coates offers the following insights and suggestions:

- The best way to get started in a strength program is to get help from an expert. Even if you've been at it for a while, it helps to be occasionally evaluated by someone with a professional eye. You may not realize you have acquired poor posture or bad habits.

- Just as with running, you won't feel the same each time you strength-train. Some days will seem like a breeze; on other days, the weights may feel heavier than usual. Consider that you need not lift the same amount of weight each time. And don't judge progress by individual sessions, but rather, by looking at an entire month.

- You should see progress within three to four weeks of undertaking a strength program. It takes about that long for the body to adapt and get rid of what Coates calls, "new program soreness."

- There is an abundance of strength and weightlifting programs, and you could end up doing one that takes hours. But if running is your goal, don't lift to lift—lift to supplement your running.

Lift Right

Research has shown that you can make substantial strength gains with only two weightlifting sessions a week. For runners, these sessions should be done on days you don't do a long run, a race, or a hard workout. Each session should include one to two sets of exercises for every major muscle group—leg and trunk muscles. It doesn't really matter for beginners whether you use free weights or machines; just make sure you're using them properly: This means performing each repetition in a controlled, slow manner (two seconds for the positive or lifting part of the exercise; four seconds for the negative or lowering part of the exercise). Choose a weight you can handle for eight to 12 repetitions. Always remember to stretch—preferably both before and after—a weight training session.

(Adapted from "Weight Training," *New York Runner,* July/Aug. 1998.)

LIFTING FOR CALORIE BURN

Although super-slow weightlifting has its proponents and its benefits, if you're hoping for maximum calorie burn when lifting weights, forget the slow strength training regime (lifting for 10 seconds, lowering for 5). In one study, researchers a the University of Alabama at Birmingham found that conventional lifts (e.g., lifting up in 2 seconds, 8 to 12 reps) used 45 percent more energy than did super slow lifting, which had an energy demand equivalent to a walk.

Pull-downs are one of the most dependable exercises for developing all of the major upper back muscles and the biceps. From a sitting position, the weight is pulled from over the head down behind the neck to the shoulders, then raised up again. Leg curls are the best weight routine for the hamstrings. Lying on the stomach on a bench, the athlete places his or her feet behind the weight apparatus and "curls" it by pulling the weight up toward the hamstrings.

It's not unusual to see runners or walkers carry weights in their arms as they stride down the road. This makes some sense, but only if proper form is maintained, and heavy weights are not recommended. Alternating left and right arm curls with light dumbbells in synchronization with your natural running motion is fine. But those athletes who run while weights dangle at their sides, with elbows virtually locked and little arm movement at all will be rewarded for their efforts with nothing but strained elbow and shoulder joints.

STAIR TRAINING

At New York's Downing Stadium, the site of the 1991 TAC/USATF Championships, onlookers watched admiringly as a pair of hardy athletes ran up and down the concrete stairs in every one of the stadium's 50-odd sections.

One needn't be quite so ambitious, but stair training is highly recommended. It can tax your aerobic capacity every bit as much as hills do, and, like hills, stair training puts special emphasis on the quadriceps. It also requires a slightly higher than usual knee lift to reach the next stair, thus serving to extend the hamstrings. Stair training can help erase the tendency to run with a shuffle, too close to the ground.

There's a key difference between hills and stairs, however. When running up stairs, only the toes and the forefoot need to strike the ground. The heel is out over the edge of each step, with only air underneath it. Stairs may be a training antidote to regular running, which can aggravate heel, Achilles tendon, and plantar fascia woes.

Stair climbing is now a major activity in health clubs. Maybe it was partly inspired by the Empire State Building Run-Up, a race we started in 1978. Who could have guessed that what seemed then like such a "kooky" idea (and still does to many, I suppose) would become a mainstream form of exercise.

In the late 1970s, someone from one of our public relations companies came to us about holding a race up 86 flights of stairs in the Empire State Building. I immediately loved the idea. In the beginning, we limited it to only ultramarathon runners. I thought those were the people who could best ascend the 1,575 steps. I was actually wrong. A miler could probably do better. Eventually, we opened it up to about 100 qualified athletes from various sports, but mostly runners. The Run-Up has spawned similar events in places like Melbourne, Australia, and Chicago. In fact, every year the winner of the Melbourne event is awarded a trip to our event. The Run-Up has even created talk about having a Grand Prix of stair climbing races in buildings.

This event is probably one of the hardest things I've ever done. There's no air in the stairwell, so it's tough to breathe. Afterwards, you cough like a smoker. It sounds a little gruesome, but it's really a great event. The Empire State Building is one of the most charismatic buildings in the world. It wasn't built for runners, but the fact is, the event has become a permanent feature, just like King Kong, who has also taken part (as a runner in costume). And people come from all over the country, and the world, to run this race.
—*Fred Lebow*

[In 2003, four-time event winner Paul Crake of Australia became the first person ever to ascend the steps in under ten minutes, in an event record 9:33. The women's event record in the Empire State Building Run-Up—12:19—was set in 1996 by Belinda Soszyn.]

Stair training requires that the entire body's weight be lifted to ascend each stair. It's tiring. A session on stairs is not a long-distance haul; these should be short, intense workouts, done after a sufficient warmup.

Recently, the equivalent of stair training has been made possible by variously named products that are essentially platforms set at different heights to approximate a single step on a flight of stairs. These devices are portable and require very little space. On these platforms, you can step up and step down repeatedly, deriving the benefits of a moderately paced run with only a fraction of the usual impact to the lower body.

The height at which you set these platforms determines the difficulty of the workout, particularly the amount of work the quadriceps, hamstrings, and gluteals have to do. Runners with certain injuries to the knee joint find that the afflicted area can be strengthened with this regimen. Doing the stepping in conjunction with light hand weights can create a more complete workout, doing wonders for the deltoids, triceps, and biceps as well.

Realize, of course, that just walking up stairs will have a positive effect on running form. You will still reap the benefits of a moderate aerobic workout, strengthen the quadriceps with each step, and stretch the hamstring and gluteal muscles in a manner that will loosen and lengthen your running stride.

SWIMMING

American distance running champion Meb Keflezighi knows the benefits of hitting the water. "I started cross training last year, and I incorporate plyometrics and bounding into my weekly running schedule. If I'm injured, I'll swim and use the bicycle, but I'll mainly concentrate on swimming."

The attraction of swimming as cross training is obvious on several counts. Swimming is a zero impact sport, a total respite from pounding the road. The most severely stressed running muscles get a bigger break in swimming than in cycling or cross-country skiing. The aerobic and anaerobic effects of running can be virtually duplicated in swimming, if training distances are properly selected. And swimming utilizes many muscles neglected by runners—the shoulder and arm muscles, to be sure, but also other key groups, such as hip flexors and hip abductors, which are needed to propel a swimmer through the greater resistance of water. Well-trained swimmers also have a more complete range of motion in their joints than runners. Their shoulders and ankles are looser.

For the healthy, injury-free runner, swimming may be ideal as the second sport of a single day's exercise. Legs that are too weary to contemplate pedaling a bicycle can still handle a half-hour in the pool or a swim at the beach.

There are also psychological reasons to swim. While swimming, an athlete is quite literally in another element. The water is calm and quiet. A form of sensory deprivation transpires. In this regard, swimming can be a more relaxing and contemplative endeavor than running.

"The pool is fantastic. We've had tremendous results," states John McDonnell, who directs his champion University of Arkansas cross-country and track athletes off the road and track, and into the water. "We simulate an interval workout in the pool, the same effort as on a run." The basis for a swimmer's interval workouts is similar to running's training techniques. McDonnell says, however, "If the kid is a good swimmer, we make him swim, but not if he's swallowing water and he's just trying to survive. If that's the case, we give him an aqua vest." The athlete then runs in water, buoyed by his apparel.

Doug Stern, whose program for deep water running appears in Chapter 11, conducts special classes in New York for runners whom he tries to turn into superior swimmers—and, therefore, superior runners. "Runners come in with handicaps," Stern has found. "They have very inflexible ankles; they can't point their toes out as if they were ballet dancers." It's crucial to increase ankle flexibility, he says, "to get on top of the water." Moreover, according to Stern, "Runners have no upper body strength. They have no upper body localized endurance. Breathing patterns go down the tubes." Unless they adapt to water, even well-conditioned runners tire quickly, and swimming is of little use.

Why is the bendability of ankles important to runners? After a foot has landed on the ground, better ankle flexion increases stride length and frequency by making the push off that foot more forceful and powerful than it would be if the ankle were tight.

To aid ankle flexibility, which diminishes after childhood, Stern himself walks around barefoot almost all of the time at home. When seated, he places his toes as far behind himself as possible, pushing the tops of the toes down on the floor and forcing his heel and calf closer together. As a result, Stern, who is in his late 40s, has greater ankle flexion than most people.

If a runner moonlighting as a swimmer doesn't have a kick in the water, Stern suggests using fins. After the fins come off, kicking should be easier, and so should swimming. A strong kick elevates and stabilizes the swimmer's body. A freestyle sprinter will ride almost atop the water; consequently, the arms turn over faster. One difficult drill, in which, while kicking, the head is up and looking straight ahead and the hands are held together with arms extended, helps the novice swimmer master the desired high position in the water.

There are techniques for directing the physical conditioning of swimming toward a particular muscle group. A "pull buoy" stuck between the legs, rendering them less mobile, isolates the arms and requires them to provide 100 percent of the thrust through the water. Conversely, a kickboard, a floating device held in front by fully extended arms, requires that the legs do all the work.

As in other cross training options, swimming workouts can be geared for local muscular endurance. The huge sweep of the butterfly stroke, in which the arms move in a circular motion away from the shoulders, may be the most aggressive way of training the chest and shoulder muscles. Kicking while laying on one's back, on the other hand, is the most efficient way for a swimmer to condition the hamstrings. And enough freestyling with the correct form—as near to hydroplaning as is feasible—will strengthen the lower back. The runner-cum-swimmer may emerge from freestyle with improved posture and less of a swayback, which means more erect running form.

Since the water through which swimmers glide is far heavier than even the thickest air through which runners stride, swimming can be more taxing to the cardiovascular system The equivalent of a running session in swimming is easy to calculate. It takes four times as long swimming to cover the same distance running. For repeat 400s on the track, substitute repeat 100s in the pool. Instead of a six-mile run, do a mile and a half swim.

CIRCUIT TRAINING

When he was at his peak, winning three New York City Marathons and a Boston Marathon, Alberto Salazar merely supplemented his running with situps and pushups. Situps and pushups are often part of an ingenious supplement to a runner's training that goes by a variety of names, but is commonly known as a "par course" (also called circuit training). The par course shares some of the particulars of the obstacle courses that military boot camp recruits are required to traverse. In essence, the course is a series of exercise stations set along a runner's outdoor trail. Within a half-mile or mile loop, these exercise stations can be staggered at 50- or 100-yard intervals; the precise layout is largely contingent on the available space. The running and the exercises can be fully integrated into a single routine, akin to a cross-country race with miscellaneous obstacles, or perhaps an extremely daunting steeplechase.

The particulars of a par course can include situps on a negative incline platform (on which the head is lower than the feet), chinup bars (at different heights, to accommodate runners of various sizes), a pushup station, a balance beam, and a horizontal ladder, which an athlete crosses hand-over-hand. There is often a platform (or, for rural tastes, an evenly planed tree trunk) on which to step up and down as many times as possible within 30 seconds. Include this par course as part of a run to work the abdominals, shoulders, and arms, and lift knees higher than on a normal run. This is serious cross training. In fact, if you have a running-related injury, it's worth doing the par course all by itself.

The name par course comes from Europe, where Steve Prefontaine, Oregon native and 1972 U.S. Olympian at 5000 meters, first encountered it. A par course was later incorporated into one of the fabled sawdust running paths of Eugene, Oregon, that is now known as Pre's Trail in memory of Steve Prefontaine. Variations of the par course abound; some large corporations, such as IBM, even have them in their headquarters' parking lots.

PILATES

Pilates (puh-LAH-teez) is a means of improving posture, enhancing the elasticity of muscles, and developing core abdominal and back strength. As a runner who has also completed biathlons, Pilates practitioner Melenie Small, who directs NYRR's IM=X Pilates classes, understands firsthand the connection between Pilates and running. She adds that this connection also holds true for walking, or any other sport or exercise program.

Small explains that Pilates is basically an exercise program that focuses on strength, flexibility, and concentration—the latter deriving from an emphasis on breathing technique. Many runners utilize shallow breathing, Small explains, whereas the deeper, fuller breathing pattern that Pilates teaches originates from the chest and rib cage, and engages the deeper abdominal muscles, whether inhaling or exhaling. Consequently, the deeper breathing pattern results in a lower heart rate and a stabilized torso, both keys to more efficient running.

Posture is another area of focus in Pilates. Small explains that, translated to running, the entire concept of working on the abdominal muscles means that, "You are moving your arms and legs, but you're doing it with a strong center. The arm and leg actions affect the spine via the musculature that surrounds the spine. Therefore, if the core abdominal musculature is unstable, the spine will be affected by the forces the limbs create while running. Through Pilates, the musculature surrounding the spine will be stronger, and disallow forces created by limb action to compress or buckle the spine. Therefore, you run with a more stabilized torso, absorbing forces created by lower and upper body activity."

People tend to focus on abdominal strength simply by "working to achieve a six-pack," says Small, but the Pilates system that also strengthens the hips and deeper abdominal (i.e., tranversus abdominis—acts as a girdle surrounding the torso) and back muscles means the entire gamut is covered. "The result is that the spine will be aligned properly, diminishing muscle tension surrounding the spine and reducing poor posture while running" (i.e., leaning forward, forward head, rounded shoulders).

While there are instructional videos on the market, Small believes it is much more worthwhile to test Pilates by finding a beginner mat class. "You'll get the basic principles of breathing and working with the abdominals and torso/shoulder stabilization," she says. Most centers utilize certified Pilates instructors, but if in doubt, you can ask to see proof of that certification.

As for seeing results, Small quotes the founder of this system, Joseph Pilates, who has said: It takes 10 sessions to feel a difference, 20 sessions to see a difference, and 30 sessions for a total body change.

Why Try Pilates?

Pilates is one of the hottest fitness trends. According to the SMGA International, which tracks participation numbers, in 2002 there were a projected 4.7 million Americans aged six and over who engaged in Pilates one or more times, an increase of 169 percent over 2000—by far the highest growth rate monitored for any fitness activity.

Among the key benefits of Pilates are:

- Increased core strength (strength of the abdominal, hip flexor, and lower back muscles)
- Enhanced flexibility throughout the body
- Increased range of motion
- Improved breathing and aerobic endurance
- Better balance and coordination
- Improved ability to concentrate

(Adapted from "Pilates for Runners," *New York Runner*, Sept./Oct. 2002.)

ROWING

Rowing doesn't require a sylvan river or neighborhood pond. Good health clubs have rowing machines that very closely approximate a real rowboat. These devices can be purchased for in-home use as well. Rowing can be done as languidly or as feverishly as suits the cross trainer, but proper form is crucial to avert injury and reap rowing's benefits. A rower should keep the back straight, and make sure to push with the legs to make progress rather than pull with the back. Rowing indoors is a perfect alternative in foul weather, and it's a low impact method of strengthening quadriceps and calf muscles. Sprint intervals can even produce an anaerobic workout. In general, a cross trainer should row two miles for the exercise effects of a one-mile run.

VOLLEYBALL AND BASKETBALL

If rebounding in basketball helps a runner, it follows that volleyball would also be a boon. The constant vertical leaping from a poised and crouched position is clearly helpful to the quadriceps and the calf muscles. Games like basketball and volleyball—pitched team battles—can also help hone a runner's competitive edge.

TENNIS

"You don't play tennis to get in shape; you get in shape to play tennis." That adage is stressed by Peter Sikowitz, a former editor at *World Tennis* and *Men's Fitness*. Sikowitz is an athlete who began jogging to become a better tennis player. He became a "born-again runner at 30," and tennis was reduced to a secondary concern.

To sharpen himself for tennis, Sikowitz would do a four- or five-mile jog, and some side-to-side drills. "I found it really did help my tennis," says Sikowitz. "I'm sort of an endurance athlete anyway. I could stay out on the court all day."

Tennis training and a runner's training can indeed overlap. "A runner who wants to play tennis would be well advised to do some 200-meter intervals," says Sikowitz, since in tennis you go from a stationary position to a full sprint.

A runner not used to playing tennis will feel a bit of stress in the buttocks muscles, which get the conditioning, and Sikowitz figures tennis is half an upper body workout, particularly when a player is stretching to fire a fierce overhand serve.

For a runner, says Sikowitz, the benefits of tennis are mostly psychological and social. "Those are very important benefits. You're still outdoors; you're able to hang out with people of different ability." The latter is not true, of course, during a training run.

A runner's schedule can probably accommodate two tennis sessions weekly, an hour apiece for singles or two hours each for doubles. On the court, the runner is able to concentrate on another activity. "It's a mental vacation from running," explains Sikowitz.

SQUASH

Squash may be a more reasonable alternative to tennis, especially for urbanites. In a crowded metropolis, squash requires less space than tennis. It tends to be less expensive, and even a half-hour can be a useful workout. Having a less talented playing partner is less of a problem than in tennis; keeping the squash ball in play with easy volleying is simpler.

Like tennis, squash is a racket game, with smaller implements—a hard rubber ball and a playing surface in which all four walls, including the one behind you, are part of the game. It may require quicker reflexes and a better sense of geometry than tennis. But both games reward sharp, precise, intelligent shotmaking, and an athlete who excels at one game is often an ace at the other.

In squash, players are on their toes, ready to move in any direction in an instant. There is a lot of short sprinting involved, and the quadriceps are taxed.

Typically, a 60-minute squash game is equal in energy expenditure to a five- to eight-mile run.

Depending on your purpose, and that of your partner, squash and tennis can be played either ferociously or quite lackadaisically. It should be easy to fit in a game of whatever intensity is appropriate for your training.

IN-LINE SKATING

At the dawn of the '90s, it often appeared that runners and reckless daredevils on in-line skates were competing for the same premium recreational space on American roadways. Runners didn't appreciate these new athletes, who careen down hills in near kamikaze fashion, apparently expecting the runners to get out of their way.

By the early '90s, more and more avid runners had sheepishly revealed a little secret. They also fancied Rollerblades. The proper appellation for this new sport, which features boots with a single row of hard wheels from front to back, is "in-line skating." Skating shouldn't hurt runners and can actually be a useful exercise respite.

In-line skating has already become a serious competitive sport. For example, the International In-Line Skate Association sponsors a 50K Championship in Central Park in New York. Its most prestigious event is the Athens to Atlanta 85-Mile Marathon in Georgia in October.

Steve Novak, the president of the New York Road Skaters Association, states that in-line skating is an excellent cross training activity for running, as well as a literal change of pace. "And as opposed to running, in-line skating permits more of a sense of freedom," says Novak.

The muscles that drive in-line skaters are similar to the ones brought to bear in cycling. "You use a little more of the quadriceps. You are generally bent over, supporting your upper body weight with your back," Novak explains. The necessary arm swing, from the elbow forward, resembles what one strives for as a runner.

On in-line skates, the hips are behind the arms. An in-line skater's knees are bent for a lower center of gravity to improve balance and make it easier to recover from stumbles. People in a more upright posture will be flailing their arms wildly to keep from crashing.

Because of the single line of wheels, the motion of in-line skating is closer to ice skating than to traditional roller skating, which uses four wheels. In fact, the story goes that in-line skating was developed by hockey skaters in the mid-1970s.

As for stopping, the preferred method is to turn the hard rubber heel brake towards the pavement. Another option is "T-stopping," in which one foot turns sideways at a 90-degree angle to the forward position.

Sprint races of 200, 400, or 800 meters for in-line skaters are not unknown, but a more common and popular distance is 10,000 meters. Good 10K times are under 17 minutes, corresponding to a good runner's expectations for 5K. In-line skaters will not charge from the start as quickly as runners, but it is easier for them to maintain racing speed once it has been reached. The quality of the pavement will have an effect; ripples and bumps will slow down a competitive in-line skater. Pack drafting, with tactics and strategy similar to cycling, will also cause a variance in racing times.

A no-impact sport, in-line skating generates few if any knee injuries, shin splints, or Achilles tendon ailments. A talented in-line skater will compete at distances from 5K to 150K. To handle that range, a day's training could include intervals, long distance at medium exertion, and sprints.

"Technique is so critical," stresses Steve Novak. "You can be in aerobic shape, but if you don't have technique, you can be defeated easily. Therefore, it is sometimes advisable to skate slowly or moderately and concentrate more fully on form."

Novak observes, "When you skate, it's not like running. You push straight out to the side. Keep the knees bent all of the time. The more bent the knee, the more you can push out to the side with your legs." Keep your body weight on the back of your heels. The ideal knee bend forms a 90-degree angle between the upper and lower legs, with the upper body bent slightly forward for wind resistance. A beginner should merely start by standing on the skates to practice balancing. Begin skating on a flat, smooth area, free of foot traffic and other obstructions.

Novak concedes that running "is a more concentrated exercise. You would have to skate for a longer period of time to equal running effort. In skating you have the opportunity to cease exertion, because you're rolling. In running, you're either running or you're not." Still, in-line skating can be a tonic for the runner's spirit. One of the primary attractions of the sport, concludes Novak, is that skating harkens back to our youth.

ROLLER SKATING

Long before in-line skating became a recreational phenomenon of the '90s, Irene Jackson's Central Park Track Club teammates would see her weave in and out of their midst on more traditional four-wheel roller skates. Jackson, a medalist at the Colgate Games and in the women's masters race at the Fifth Avenue Mile, suffers periodically from knee problems. Skating is not a high impact sport, but the impetus of forward force exercises the quadriceps. Jackson also discovered that with roller skating, she uses her upper body a lot.

With all forms of skates and skis, the foot is essentially stabilized; there's no forefoot or heel striking, and far less stress on the arch. Skating and skiing may be an alternative training method for runners whose Achilles tendons or plantar fascia are ailing.

ICE SKATING

Ice skating is a pleasant complement to running, particularly if you can find a rink that isn't overcrowded. Again, the thrust comes from the quadriceps, and the arm swing required for balance can loosen upper body muscles. This is a sport where form counts, so concentration is key. And concentration—so essential as the mind wavers in the fourth and fifth miles of a 10K—is a quality worth practicing.

SNOWSHOEING

The list of winter alternatives goes on. Janis Klecker, the Minnesotan who won the 1992 U.S. Olympic Marathon trials, customarily included two four-mile sessions on snowshoes in her weekly training regimen. The meshed snowshoes often sink three or four inches into frozen snow. With that kind of resistance, a step out of the snow must be a high and wide step. Any such exaggeration of a normal step taxes the muscles in a new way. The quadriceps feel the weight as they pull out of the snow, and the hamstring and buttocks muscles are exercised by the necessary high knee lift. Snowshoeing, which could be considered a type of winter hiking, is also another respite for runners with foot and lower leg ailments. The wide, flat surface of the snowshoes disperses the impact of each footstrike.

BOXING

Any exercise that doesn't hurt a runner is likely to help. The great jazz trumpeter Miles Davis trained as a boxer for decades. He wasn't going to risk his embouchure by getting pummeled in the ring, but he did punch the light and heavy bags, utilizing his fast on-the-toes footwork as he did so. Listen to any of his albums and you can hear that he was cardiovascularly fit. Punching the bags develops the shoulder and arm muscles so often neglected by runners, as well. In fact, a number of New York runners also work out with boxing.

Undoubtedly, you can conjure up even more physical endeavors that can serve as complements and alternatives to running. The only requirement is to always keep in mind that cross training should be aimed at preserving and protecting your body, and conditioning it in ways that the running motion is not able to do.

Hitting the bags with a regular cadence requires coordination, the same coordination a runner prays for when his or her form is going to pieces late in a race. Because coordination is such a prized commodity, another bit of a boxer's training, jumping rope, can also help runners. The wrists and forearms, which should drive a racer forward in pistonlike fashion, get plenty of work as they turn the rope, and the jumping itself does wonders for the calf muscles. This is another form of training in which an athlete can alternate slower, leisurely segments with the equivalent of speed sessions. A 30-second interval, in which you swing the rope as quickly and jump as lively as you can, certainly has the anaerobic benefits of a 200-meter run.

To burn calories, get fit, add variety to your running—why not jump rope? Here are a few tips on the activity from *Running and FitNews*. To be sure the rope is the right length, stand on the middle of it and raise the ends up the sides of your body. The handles should reach your armpits. When jumping, don't grip the handles too tightly. Also, use your wrists, not your arms, to turn the rope. Your shoulders will get sore if you use your arms too much. Jump lightly and only as high as you need to clear the rope. Maintain good posture and keep your knees slightly bent. Try to jump for one to five minutes, working your way up to a total of 20 minutes for a good aerobic workout. Vary your workouts. Learn to jump using one and two feet, alternating feet, skipping, jumping double time, and crossing over the rope.

DEEP WATER RUNNING

Doug Stern began teaching deep water running in 1970 when one of his high school students was forced off the track due to injury. That student was Steve Williams, who went on to become a world-class sprinter. Since the inception of this program with NYRR through the end of 2003, more than 3,000 people have attended Stern's classes.

Following the New York City Marathon in 1990, Stern began conducting deep water running classes for runners in the New York area, initially to aid marathoners' recovery. The benefits of deep water running and a do-it-yourself workout are described in this chapter by Stern.

"As a swimming teacher and coach, I've been surrounded by water all my life. I have always been a believer in the general power of water. Water is our most natural environment. It is where we are initially reared, in the womb, and it remains the most supportive and relaxing medium in which to be," Stern explains. "Water takes the stress off the body. When I am in the water, I feel I'm being cradled, held there. Therefore, it makes sense to use water to bring us back to health (in the case of injury) and to develop strength and stamina, while simultaneously benefiting from this sense of being nurtured."

Deep water running is exactly what the name says. It is not aqua jogging, nor is it aqua aerobics. It is a system meant to most accurately simulate and enhance the act of running. It provides all the benefits of the land activity, yet with the safety and ease of an exercise performed in liquid.

Water has certain characteristics that make it ideal for non–weight-bearing resistance training. The most obvious is its buoyant effect. Because you float at, or near, the surface of the water, you can run suspended in the water without pounding or jarring your feet or joints. Water is also viscous, or thicker than air. As you move your arms and legs through the water, you encounter tremendous resistance. This resistance can be used to strengthen both muscles and joints. The faster you move your arms and legs, the greater the resistance, and, therefore, the harder the workout and the greater the strength gain.

The attributes of deep water running are many. Not only does it allow you to run without the stress of pounding, but it also enhances flexibility and helps speed the blood flow to the heart. That's because on land, gravity concentrates the blood in the lower body. Because of more efficient blood flow to the heart, all water activity promotes faster recuperation from bouts of intense exercise.

Another advantage of water is its cooling effect. On land, the body temperature rises more quickly; thus, you are forced to intersperse hard running with jogging or walking, largely to allow for cooling of the body. In water, because body heat is more quickly dissipated, one needs a fraction of the time to recover. It's also a lot safer in regulating body temperature during critical times, such as in the hot summer months or during pregnancy (pregnant women can also avoid stress on muscles and joints by doing light deep water running).

The properties of water afford an excellent opportunity to work on running form. On land, how can you stop in mid-stride to check your form? Impossible. But in water you run as if in slow motion, facilitating a better examination and development of running form. Better form means more efficient running. This translates to longer and faster running.

The benefits of deep water running are many. It increases range of motion and builds strength and cardiovascular conditioning. It enhances muscular endurance and flexibility—all of this without the risk of injury.

Stern says three types of runners are well served by water running:

1. **The injured,** who can use water to recuperate from biomechanical or overuse injuries. Runners with every type of injury have been represented in deep water running classes, including sufferers of Achilles tendinitis, stress fractures, metatarsal problems, and shin splints. They have often been referred by physicians, chiropractors, and physical therapists—or they hear about the classes through NYRR publicity or by word of mouth.

   In the water, those who would normally be forced to stop running entirely can allow injuries to be repaired by a break from running on land and simultaneously continue uninterrupted cardiovascular fitness activity. One of the additional benefits of deep water running is that muscles, joints, and their supporting structures are strengthened, thus protecting the body from future injury.

2. **The beginner,** who because of obesity or a sedentary lifestyle, is not yet able to run on land. Water running allows this category of runner to develop ability in a more supportive medium. In moving their legs at their own pace, these people don't tire as easily as they may be inclined to do on land. Some people come to running by testing themselves first in the water.

3. **The fit athlete,** who wants to intensify speedwork and fitness, yet avoid injury. The benefits of water running for fit athletes were noticed immediately after a series of classes was first begun—the day following the 1990 New York City Marathon. This system of active rest resulted in much quicker recovery for marathoners.

Instead of spending seven days running on land, a runner may want to replace one day with deep water running; for example, to recover from a harder effort. Not only does this lessen the stress of continuously running day after day, but a change in the training environment also adds variety.

EQUIPMENT

Although it is possible to do deep water running without a flotation device, Stern believes it is best to use one. This is especially true in the beginning when learning proper technique. A flotation device keeps you above the water with little effort, which enhances the supportive nature of the water. There are many flotation devices on the market, from vests to belts.

THE WORKOUT

Stand in shallow water, about four feet deep. Begin by swinging the arms in a pendulum fashion, as you would for running. Emphasize pushing the elbows back and keeping the pendulum close enough to your body to graze the thigh with the thumb on the back swing.

Create intensity. That's what I tell my classes. The faster you do this, the more you get out of it. I quote Shakespeare's Polonius, "To thine own self be true." Be true to yourself; work to your capability. Demand that of yourself. It's easy to "dog" the workout, but you won't get the results. People fear hard work. We're afraid it might hurt. But explore the uncomfortable zone. You're not going to injure yourself. I have a woman in my class who is 88 years old. She does the workouts. It's all within the limits of what you can do.

—Doug Stern

When you are comfortable with the arm swing, begin moving your feet in high stepping fashion, coordinating the stepping with the arm lift (opposite arm and leg, just like in land running). Do this for one to five minutes, working your way down to a shorter time in future sessions after you have perfected the exercise.

Begin moving forward while doing this motion, slowly progressing to deep water until your feet can no longer touch the bottom.

Concentrate on running tall, but with no tension. To do this, keep the chest up and forward and the hips under the shoulders (that is, do not let the buttocks stick out). The facial muscles should remain relaxed—chin dropped and mouth open. Breathe naturally.

As you perform the workout, you may naturally move about, but even if you remain in one place, it is not important. Warm up by gently running for five minutes.

Strength Development

Arm Crossovers

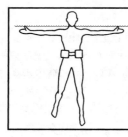 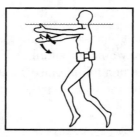

While running, extend arms to your side, keeping elbows straight and palms facing forward. Pull arms until they cross over in front. Then turn your palms outward and push your arms back as far as possible. On each crossover, alternate which arm finishes on top. Repeat for two minutes. This exercise strengthens chest and back muscles and develops shoulder flexibility. (Remember, in this and all water exercises, the faster you move, the greater the resistance, thus the more strength required and developed.)

Crunches (Sit-ups)

With hands paddling (sculling) at your sides to keep afloat, lie on your back and bring your body in a "V" position (that is, buttocks toward pool bottom).

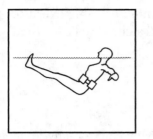 

Flex toes upward as if pulling water toward your chest. Pull your knees as far to the chest as possible, then return to original position. Be conscious of the feet pulling the water in and pushing it away on each movement. Do these crunches for two minutes at a comfortable pace. This exercise strengthens the abdominals.

Abductor (Outer Thigh)/Adductor (Inner Thigh)

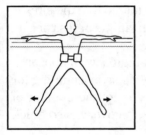 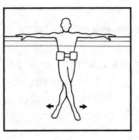

Run to the pool wall. With your back facing the wall, extend your arms straight to the sides and hold on to the side or gutter of the pool. Extend the legs to your sides in a split position. Knees should be straight. Pull both legs together like scissors and cross them, alternating left and right legs in front. Push legs out to return to original position. Do this exercise for two minutes. This exercise strengthens inner and outer thighs, which help stabilize and give balance to the leg, and improves biomechanics.

Leg Crossovers

Maintain the same position as above, with your hands holding the sides of the pool. Point your legs straight under you, toward pool bottom. Pull the right leg across your body, bringing it as far as possible toward the left hand. Rotate the hips to facilitate this movement. Returning to starting position, reverse legs, with the left leg swinging toward the right arm. Do one swing per leg at a time, alternating right and left legs. Do this exercise for two minutes. This exercise strengthens quadriceps and the inner thighs, and stretches hip flexors and shoulders.

Running

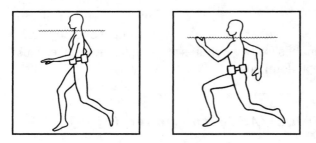

Now you're ready to do a deep water running workout. Begin with three minutes of gentle running, concentrating on form and building speed. Remember to continue to drive the arms, so that the elbows are swinging back. The arm swing often shortens with fatigue or loss of concentration.

Fashion interval or fartlek running of 20 to 25 minutes, with appropriate rest. Check the pulse at your neck during rest, but do so by counting for only ten seconds and multiplying that number by six to get the number of beats for one minute. This is more accurate, as water recovery is so quick that the pulse rapidly slows.

Cadence is leg turnover. According to Doug Stern, it is an important aspect of deep water running. Cadence is also stride frequency—that is, the speed at which your legs are moving, coupled with stride length. Cadence improves by increasing range of motion, which is developed with deep water running.

Check cadence by counting one leg turnover for 15 seconds. Every minute you run, count cadence for 15 seconds to make sure you are continuing to run at the same pace, or faster. As a basis of comparison, and to check progress, it is good to check cadence while running on land as well.

It is good to be aware of the cadence of your legs during fast water running. Checking cadence helps keep you focused, since it can be easy to space out in the water. In addition, good cadence will develop quicker running on land.

After hard running time has elapsed, spend five minutes cooling down with slow running.

Post-Workout Stretch

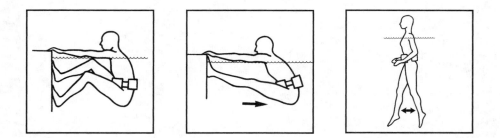

Do this gentle and comfortable stretch by facing the pool wall, and with your arms extended straight out in front of you, hold on to the side or gutter. Start with your feet under the water on the wall, knees bent. Keeping the knees bent, slowly walk your feet up the wall, stopping every few feet to straighten the legs and stretch. Finish when you have walked your legs all the way up to your hands. The entire cycle should take two minutes.

This stretch serves the same purpose as touching your palms to the ground on land. It stretches the hamstrings, calves, and Achilles tendons.

Finish the entire workout by gently shaking your legs out under water.

12

POWER YOGA: THE PRACTICE

Beryl Bender Birch began teaching yoga to one class of three runners in 1981. Today, over 100,000 runners have taken her course, which enables them to incorporate yoga techniques into their fitness and running programs.

"Everyone knows running is great for the cardiovascular system; however, it's also a fact that the sport dramatically tightens certain muscle groups while doing nothing for others." Says Bender Birch, "The Power Yoga Practice® solves this problem by bringing a balance of strength and flexibility to a running program. When you follow the Power Yoga program, there's little need for any other type of training besides running. You don't need to lift weights, do calisthenics, or take stretch classes."

Bender Birch's yoga practice is intended to develop health, strength, flexibility, balance, and mental concentration. It is also designed to ensure that muscles are worked efficiently and safely. As a companion training program to running, the exercises help prevent injury and are therapy for rehabilitation from injury. According to Bender Birch and other experts, this efficiency and safety is something greatly lacking in runners' random stretching exercises.

In addition, this yoga program develops the upper body, which running alone does not do. The routine below is an abbreviated form of the complete program, which includes the yoga versions of pushups and situps, two exercises commonly performed by runners. Adding these two exercises to the modified practice that follows will help develop additional strength and biomechanical balance.

The three laws of Power Yoga are:

1. **Be hot to stretch and stay hot while stretching.** Hot means from the inside out—sweating. Trying to stretch a cold body is like a glassblower trying to shape cold glass—it shatters. This is the risk taken when a runner typically slaps a leg onto a fence and struggles to bring his or her head to the knee in a futile effort to warm up for a run.

    The pre-run routine outlined below is a versatile aerobic warm-up, good for running or any other sport. The entire series of warm-

123

up movements is choreographed. They are coordinated with deep, controlled breathing through the nose, referred to here as yogic breathing.

2. **You must be properly aligned according to biomechanical integrity.** To prevent injury while stretching a muscle, correct alignment is mandatory. Stretching injures you only if you do it improperly, while cold, or without static contraction in the muscle opposing the muscle being stretched. Although the alignment must be precise, the practice described here allows for an individual degree of flexibility.

3. **You must stretch intensely and in concurrence with strengthening in order to stretch safely and effectively.** This yoga practice offers an alternative to passive stretching, in which a person hangs down, hoping for gravity to do all the work. Contrary to Power Yoga, this passive stretching does nothing for the development of strength, flexibility, and concentration.

In order to gain the full benefit, an athlete must stretch with vigor. But to do so without injury, one must be aligned and must be sweating throughout the practice session.

The Power Yoga routine below is adapted from Beryl Bender Birch's book *Power Yoga*. Although it is generally done indoors and preferably with bare feet, it can be done outdoors with running shoes on as well.

PRE-RUN ROUTINE: SUN SALUTATION

Don't worry about getting the breathing sequence exactly right until you have become familiar with the postures. Once you are comfortable with the practice, then work on your breathing and do the sun salutation as a dynamic, continuous routine—that is, do it in one flowing movement. Unlike other forms of yoga, there are no rest periods between poses. Start by repeating the pre-run routine three times. As you progress, move up to six repetitions. In several months, when your arm strength in particular has improved, you may do the routine as many as ten times. All postures that call for a tightened, or contracted, thigh muscle prevent overstretching the hamstring, a common mistake that may lead to injury.

Sun Salutation: Readying Position

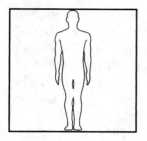 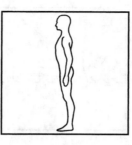

Stand with feet together and arms at your sides. Do ujjay: pranayama (yogic breathing through the nose) to quiet the mind and get yourself centered. This is called the readying position.

Position 1

Inhale. Bring arms up over your head, palms together. Tilt head back and look toward your thumbs. Tighten the thighs and buttocks. Do not arch your back.

Position 2   ## Position 3

Exhale. Bend your knees slightly, bringing your palms to the floor alongside your feet. Tuck your head into your knees.

Inhale. While maintaining position, raise your head, look up, and lift your chest.

Position 4

Exhale. Walk or jump your legs back, making your body straight like a plank. Drop down into a pushup position. (Beginners: Do a modified pushup, with the knees touching the ground.)

Position 5

Inhale. Place the tops of your feet flat on the floor. Lift your torso off the ground with your arms, raise your head, and look up at the ceiling. Make sure to lift your thighs off the ground. (Note: Keep knees on the ground if you have lower back problems or weak arms.)

Position 6

Exhale. Turn toes under so soles of feet are facing the floor. Lift yourself up into an upside-down "V" position, supported by your arms with hands on the floor. Push buttocks toward the ceiling. Hold this position for five breaths. Push down on your heels. (Don't worry if your heels don't touch the floor at first. They will in time.) Flatten the palms. (This is a perfect pose for runners. It stretches the hamstrings, calves, heels, feet, Achilles tendons, shoulders, and lower back.)

Position 7

Inhale. Bend knees, step or jump feet forward until they are between hands, look up in front of you, lift chest (same as position 3).

Position 8

Exhale. Tuck head into slightly bent knees with palms on the floor next to feet (same as position 2).

Position 9

Inhale. Bring arms straight overhead, palms together. Squeeze buttocks, tighten thighs. Look up (same as position 1). Exhale and return to readying position.

POST-RUN ROUTINE

Between each of the yoga positions below, you may insert a full sequence of the pre-run sun salutation. Since you naturally cool down after a run, doing the sun salutation between postures will keep you hot throughout your post-run yoga practice. The contracting of muscle groups is for strengthening.

Triangle Posture

With legs three feet apart, turn right foot out 90 degrees and left foot in 30 degrees. Inhale, extend arms straight to the side. Hold your right thigh contracted. Exhale. Without bending your knees, bend at the hips to your right, placing the right hand on your right ankle (or shin). Hold your right thigh contracted. Look up at your left hand. Take five to ten yogic breaths. (Remember, mouth closed!) Come up, reverse feet position, then exhale, and do the exercise to the opposite side. Don't forget to hold the left thigh contracted as well. This exercise stretches the hamstrings, hips, iliotibial band (side of hip), and side of calf. Good for low back pain, tight hips, and hamstrings.

Inverted Triangle Posture

Turn right foot out 90 degrees and left foot in 45 degrees. Inhale, extend arms to your side. Exhale, turn torso to the right and bring both arms down to shin, ankle, or floor. Do not bend knees. Make sure right thigh is contracted. Reverse and do to other side. This exercise is good for lower back, tight hips and hamstrings, and iliotibial band tightness.

Extended Side Angle Posture

Stand with feet four to five feet apart. Turn the right foot out 90 degrees and the left foot in 30 degrees. Inhale. Extend arms to the side. Exhale, bend right knee directly over the right ankle, bringing the right palm to the floor next to the inside arch of the foot. Extend left arm straight up toward the ceiling (arms and shoulders should form a straight line). If you are not comfortable with your hand coming to the floor, use a phone book or similar object to raise the level of the hand. Hold for five breaths. Reverse and do to other side. This exercise stretches hips, groin, lower back, ankles, and shoulders and strengthens thighs, arms, and back. Good for low back pain.

Warrior Posture

Stand with feet five feet apart. Turn the right foot out 90 degrees, the left foot in 30 degrees. Twist upper body, turning hips to the right. Hold back leg straight. Bend the right knee directly over the right ankle (don't lunge the knee past the ankle). Raise the arms straight over the head, with the palms together. Hold this position for five breaths. Reverse and do to other side. This exercise stretches ankles, calves, hips, and shoulders and strengthens thighs, ankles, arms, and shoulders.

Single Leg Forward Bend Posture

 Sit on floor, extend left leg straight in front, with toes of left foot flexed upward, pointing toward ceiling. Bring the right foot to the inside of the left thigh. Bend down the left leg until your hands reach the knee, shin, or foot. Tighten the left thigh. Grasp the leg and pull gently with arms while concentrating on tightening the left thigh. Take five breaths. Reverse and do other leg. (Note: Do not allow back to round. Keep chest lifted and head up! Extend back and spine. Work toward eventually bringing the chin to the shin.) This exercise stretches hamstrings, lower back, and groin and strengthens shins, quadriceps, and biceps.

13

OVERTRAINING, OVERRACING

"Life," says exercise physiologist David E. Martin, "can be seen as an energy pie—no matter how you cut it, there are only so many slices." In this chapter, Martin explains the crucial principles of rest and regeneration, and how runners must account for the energy spent not only on running, but also in their daily routines. "Stress plus training equals straining," he concludes.

Running is primarily a volume-oriented sport. That is, the more you run, the fitter you get—within limits, of course. And there's the rub: How much is enough, and how much is too much? There's probably not a serious runner who hasn't at some time come down with a case of the blahs. What caused it? Too much mileage? Poor coaching? Too much stress?

Back in the 1930s, the famous Harvard physiologist Walter B. Cannon coined the term "homeostasis" to define "those dynamic self-regulating processes that keep the body's internal environment constant." As this definition is viewed in the context of training, it's easy to see how we get more fit if the training stress is just right. The breakdown caused by the hard work stimulates adaptive processes in the body to help it tolerate more of the same. Scientists call this homeostatic adjustment; runners call it getting fit. It is a system that creates more blood volume, greater numbers of enzymes for fuel metabolism, increased stored fuel in the working muscles, stronger tendons and ligaments, and more.

How can you suddenly end up with tendinitis, a bad cold, or a big-time case of the training blues? Is it really a case of too much stress? Is it the inability to differentiate between good stress and bad stress? Or is it something you're leaving out of the training plan?

Training is a two-step process. There is breakdown and recovery. Runners often are so caught up in the reps and sets and weekly mileage totals—the discipline and hard work or breakdown—that the recovery is forgotten. *Not* training is a part of training, because during the nontraining period regeneration occurs. Without the easy days to permit regeneration, without the high carbohydrate diet to replenish fuels, without relaxing and therapeutic massages to help the sore muscles recover, profound tissue adaptation never occurs to permit better performance.

131

It is also essential to factor into your training program stresses from other activities. Consider your whole life as an energy pie, which contains the sum total of life stresses. You can slice that pie any way you desire, but the pie isn't going to get any larger. If the slice for the workaday job gets larger as the job becomes more stressful, try to reduce the size of other stressful slices to compensate. Excess stress can bring about a breakdown of bodily function as much as physical training. The pie is only so big, and unfortunately, high-achieving, active athletes often eliminate recovery slices to take on more stresses. Soon there are no slices to provide for the stress of sleepless nights, taxing business trips, or a few missed meals. Then fatigue, staleness, some bad race times, or an inability to keep up the training pace *forces* you to relax. So stress plus training equals straining.

According to David Martin, when you are experiencing a performance slump, and wondering what's happening, there are plenty of things that can be done to turn the situation around. It's just a matter of knowing some simple physiology.

"For openers, there's dehydration," Martin explains. "Your working muscles are about 75 percent water. If you have not been rehydrating enough during and after training, the pool of water within your muscles is not as large as it should be. Thus, during interval sessions, for example, in a dehydrated state, lactic acid levels will rise higher than normally seen at the pace being maintained. Be sure you drink adequately to keep the effects of accumulating lactic acid at bay: The solution to pollution is dilution. If you have waited until you're thirsty before drinking, you have waited too long.

"And then there's hemoglobin. Are you anemic? Fully $98\,1/2$ percent of the blood's oxygen is transported by hemoglobin. If your hemoglobin has gotten too low, such that you cannot transport as much oxygen as previously, you can't manage the same pace without working harder. Have you given blood recently? Or is your menstrual flow excessive? Or have you decided to go off red meat for a while? Or have you stopped your iron supplementation? (Iron is part of the hemoglobin molecule).

"Finally, there's carbs. If you have 'upped the ante' in your mileage, and are into a marathon training block, you may need more calories than you are taking in, and your liver and muscles are simply low on energy. The best nutritional advice is never to be hungry (the companion to 'never be thirsty' mentioned above), and to eat half a dozen smallish meals daily so as to ensure a continual energy infusion.

"Next time you have a case of the training blahs, do a 'body check' to see if your fluids, foods, and hemoglobin are being managed in good order. Or better yet, don't ever let them get short shrift in terms of attention. Keep that engine of yours finely tuned. It's often said that our body is a temple; don't live in a shack!"

Below, in outline form, are more typical symptoms of overtraining. These symptoms don't necessarily surface all at once, but combinations of two or more are common.

SYMPTOMS OF TRAINING-RELATED OVERTRAINING

1. Lack of desire to train; thoughts of skipping sessions that aren't even particularly difficult.
2. Inability to complete training sessions that had been well within your grasp a week or two earlier.
3. Unusual muscle soreness following training, with recovery taking much longer than usual.
4. Performance plateau, or even lowered performance decrement, despite increased training loads.

SYMPTOMS OF LIFE-RELATED OVERTRAINING

1. Increased tension, anger, complaining, and negativity.
2. Decreased enjoyment of life.
3. Poor quality of sleep.

SYMPTOMS OF HEALTH-RELATED OVERTRAINING

1. Increased incidence of illness.
2. Decrease in body weight and appetite.
3. Constipation or diarrhea.
4. Swelling of lymph nodes.
5. Increased morning pulse.

Overtraining often is as much a result of attitude as it is a result of training. In the typical psychological stimulus/response paradigm, if schedule

TAKING TIME OFF

Whether for physical or mental reasons, sometimes it is good to contemplate taking a break from running. This is particularly true for serious, long-term runners, who might consider some of the benefits of a break.

Signs You May Need a Break

- Diminished performances, even though you feel like you're trying as hard as or harder than ever.

- At the start of a training run, your legs lack "spring" or they're continually sore.

- Your morning pulse rate is elevated by, for example, five beats per minute.

- You frequently seem to be fighting off a cold or virus.

- You're particularly cranky or otherwise out of sorts.

If you do take a break, consider the following:

- Plan your "down time." A good time to take a break is just after you've finished a big event, like a marathon. If you've not done as well as you hoped, you probably aren't particularly excited about starting running again. If you've run a personal best time, it might also be good to take time off, because when you're all pumped up, it might be tempting to resume strenuous training again, often before you are fully recovered.

- Physiologists talk about Delayed Onset Muscle Soreness (DOMS). This soreness usually peaks between 24 and 48 hours after a strenuous activity, as a result of lactic acid buildup. But DOMS is most likely caused by actual damage to muscle cells. The extent of such damage is difficult to measure, but post-race is a great time to consider taking time off to let micro-tears heal. Muscle damage caused by a hard marathon, for example, can sometimes take four weeks to regenerate.

- Plan a fitness alternative. In order to prevent or lessen "detraining," a lack of activity that causes fitness levels to drop, try to do your running equivalent with cycling, swimming, cross-country skiing, or other physical activities. This will allow you not only to rest the muscles from running, but also to strengthen some other muscle groups not fully utilized in running and still maintain a high level of cardiovascular fitness. An alternative exercise vacation is also a nice mental break from running.

- There are many factors involved in how long your come-back from a break will take. But a very conservative esti-mate is that you'll need two days of running for every day of "down time" to return to your former level of running fit-ness.

- Know when to say when: Too much rest can set you back. One study involving competitive European swimmers found that a group that strayed from the pool for eight weeks (no training at all) after the season ended was un-able to equal their personal records from the previous year once they returned to training and competition. A second group did a mere 30 percent of their in-season volume in some workouts and was able to get back to, and in some cases surpass, their best times from the year before.
  (Adapted from "Taking a Break," Mark Will-Weber, *New York Runner,* July/Aug. 1999.)

overload is the stimulus, overtraining is the response. So often runners look to their training diaries for the answer to their staleness and become frustrated when they see no telltale signs that training is the culprit. They see no sudden increase in weekly mileage and no increase in the number of hard sessions. It is not the running but the approach that has broken the training link of breakdown and recovery.

Awareness of the need for regeneration, coupled with understanding the inherent risks of overachieving, should prompt you to program down-time into your training. Taking a day off from training each week is an ex-ample. Periodizing your running activities is another. This means, perhaps, creating a cycle of a buildup (training), competition (racing), and regener-ation (downtime) over a period of several months.

Other training options may help. If you plod a few early-morning miles and then hope to blast some intervals later in the day, try instead training once a day, but making it meaningful. A fairly quick late-afternoon session of several miles pays off in time economy as well as in improving aerobic stam-ina. In terms of nutrition, ample liquid and carbohydrate replenishment im-mediately following training sessions will help keep energy levels adequate.

Racing entails risk. The most common mistake in addition to overtraining is racing too much too soon. Once novices get a little taste of competition, which is very positive, they may start racing every week. If they don't outright break down, people in this category wonder why they can't run faster. It's because they never recover from one race to another, never build any peaks. It becomes just one big plateau.

Ever notice how some people are always injured, and some people never are? What's that all about? The uninjured are either lucky, they've got a genetic gift, or they know how to strike the right balance. Sure, some inherited good biomechanics help, but largely, the uninjured remain that way because they are running smart.

Conversely, it's unlikely that the chronically injured have bad genes or are simply unlucky; it's more likely they're paying the price for constantly overdoing it.

—*Tom Fleming*

This still leaves the approach problem. Try mixing training activities with family life. How about doing stretching exercises with the children? Organize a warmup or cool-down routine as a family activity. Clearly, the best way to ensure that the energy pie is best sliced is continually to assess where to cut it.

PART 2
RACING

14
WHY RACE?

Why run a race? You race to test yourself, for the ritual, the camaraderie, and for the adventure and discovery. If you didn't compete as a child, the race offers another chance. Once you've raced, the challenge and accomplishment are motivation to continue. Few experiences allow such a range of personal satisfaction, and even fewer are as symbolic. When you race, your effort is singularly your own. In your sparest clothing, and with the power of your own body, you confront the challenge of the race. In a race, no one else and nothing else can do for you what you must do for yourself.

Racing appeals to millions of people. In fact, according to the latest statistics from the USATF Road Running Information Center, 7.74 million people completed a road race in 2002, up from 4 million only five years previously. While the distance that remains most popular is the 5K, followed by the 10K, distances also showing growth even in one year (from 2001 to 2002) were one mile (up 11 percent), 25K (up 10 percent), 15K (up 7 percent), half-marathon (up 5.4 percent) and marathon (up 5.3 percent).

Fred Lebow understood that the beauty of the road race is the oppor-

The reason we changed our name from the New York Road Runners Club to New York Road Runners is because 'club' does not reflect who we are. Runners tended to view us as a competitive club. This gave the perception that to run in our races, you had to be a serious competitor. You don't need to be. Fundamentally, road racing is a chance to gauge yourself, and to be around similar people who run at a similar pace. You're pushing against yourself more than you're racing against anyone else. Everyone does things to better themselves, whatever that may be—whether it's physical or mental. That's what our organization stands for. You go out and run your normal miles, and then enter a race, and find yourself running faster, stronger. The race psyches you up. It's all about expressing your own values, and finding your own self-worth.

—*Allan Steinfeld*

tunity it presents for all-comers and world-class athletes to have the same experience. In this regard, running is unique. In few other endeavors in life can athletes of all abilities undertake the same task and gain the same sense of achievement. "Imagine being able to run for that long," Bill Rodgers once remarked in admiration of four-hour marathoners.

How Often Should You Race?

Races abound—there is probably one somewhere every weekend—so how many should you do? Take the advice of the master, Grete Waitz, who in a racing career of more than two decades not only set world records at distances from 3000 meters to the marathon, but was rarely injured.

First, determine the purpose of a race. "Is it to perform or to get a good workout?" asks Waitz. She has nothing against running a race as a speed workout, if you're disciplined enough not to get caught up. But if the aim is performance, you should limit your racing. "Look at the calendar, check which racing distances are available, map out your training, and set a racing schedule for the next two months."

Of races shorter than the marathon, Waitz suggests no more than two per month. Even in her peak, she never exceeded that amount. In the winter, she raced less, and made sure to give herself six to eight weeks of good training before racing.

The marathon is another consideration. Waitz advises running no more than two a year, which is what serious runners limit themselves to; at the most three, which she did only twice in her career. "You need to recover, both mentally and physically, before you start training for the next one."

Her most important piece of advice is, "Plan in advance and stick to your plan. If you don't, it's like playing the lottery. Good runners have a plan. That's why they are better than those who race on impulse."

If you have never raced, don't hesitate to try. People of every level run races for a variety of reasons. And you may surprise yourself. As Grete Waitz has said, "There is something about the ritual of the race—putting on the number, lining up, being timed—that brings out the best in us."

If the idea of a race looms a bit large, consider an event that puts the emphasis on fun and participation. Fun runs, held almost everywhere, are a good introduction to racing. Races for charitable causes or with unique themes are also popular.

VOLUNTEERS

From group runs, to safety patrols, to races—volunteers are the backbone of NYRR events. The New York City Marathon alone relies on over 12,000 of them. In fact, most running events and running clubs depend on volunteers. So, the next time you run a race, remember to thank the staff—from those along the course who give you water, to those in the finish chutes. Chances are they have donated their time as volunteers. And for a special experience, or if you're sidelined from injury and can't run, why not try volunteering. You can also learn an awful lot about races, and the people who run them.

NYRR conducts a variety of special fun runs and races throughout the year. As the clock strikes midnight on December 31st (and 12:00 A.M. on January 1st), the New Year's Eve Midnight Run begins. The event is complete with fireworks, noisemakers, and a pre-race costume parade. The annual April Fool's Day Backwards Mile treats runners to an alternative perspective with a one-mile race that is run in reverse. There are also races run for a cause; for example, NYRR's Race for the Cure, part of a national series for women that promotes breast cancer awareness and education.

Elite marathoner Gordon Bakoulis points out that while some runners choose never to race, most are inspired to test themselves in some type of competition, be it a short distance fun run or a major marathon in a distant city. And the variety of reasons for racing are reflected in the variety of racing opportunities offered across this country and internationally. Bakoulis says if you're on the fence about running a race, consider what racing offers—on and off the course.

- **Fun.** For many runners, racing is primarily a social event. It's a chance to meet people and participate in the running scene.
- **Education.** Many races are preceded or followed by clinics at which

Anybody who is out there more than 30 minutes at a time three times a week is running for some reason other than physical health. Most runners fall somewhere on the continuum of that minimum amount all the way up to working out 13 times a week, running 140 miles.

I'd say for anyone on that continuum who is running beyond three times a week for half an hour there is a probably a psychological need to set a goal for their training. It helps to have a certain number of times it can be reinforced and improvement can be seen. Racing is a good way to do that.

—Frank Shorter

elite runners, doctors, physiologists, or other experts speak on a variety of topics related to running. These events are usually free and open to all. Expos are offered at larger races, displaying everything from running shoes to the latest carbo-loading beverages.

- **Motivation.** Knowing that you have a race to prepare for can help get you out the door. If you have already met the goal of becoming fit through regular running, congratulations. You may find committing to a race motivates your continued training. After one race, see if you aren't inspired to improve your time in another race, or alter your training for a different type of running contest.

- **Challenge.** Racing provides the satisfaction of taking on a hard task and finishing it, of meeting a challenge at your own level as well as against the clock and other individuals.

Given the nature of running, certain things will never be altered. That's one of the beauties of our sport. There is no judge; it doesn't matter how you look. If you have reconstructive surgery on your nose, for example, you're not going to get the gold medal instead of the silver, like it may be in some other sports. It's still simply training-based, and the only judge is the clock.

—Bill Rodgers

ARE YOU READY TO RACE?

Ready to try a race? Before you do, read this section to help ensure that your first race isn't your last.

Pick a Race You Can Handle

A good rule of thumb is that the race distance should be no greater than one-third of your weekly mileage. That means you can try a 5K (3.1 miles) if you run at least nine miles a week, a 10K if you're logging at least 18. Remember, your goal at this stage is to *complete* the distance, not to *compete*. Avoid longer races your first time; you can try them later. If you enter a race that's over your head, you will probably survive, but may struggle to finish, feel sore, and possibly get injured. Do *not* race if you have never run before or have been sedentary for a month or longer, especially if you smoke, have diabetes, are overweight, or have a family history of heart disease. (As you'll read in the marathon section, it is not a good idea for anyone to try a marathon as a first race.)

Give Yourself Time to Prepare

Even if you are in shape, don't jump into a race on a whim. Instead, pick one at least a few days away to give yourself time to prepare mentally and logistically. Think about the details: a good pair of shoes and the right clothes for the weather, where and when to register, etc. Then on race day you'll be able to relax and have fun. If you're out of shape, pick a race at least a few weeks or months away so you have time to prepare properly. (See the training programs in other chapters.)

Forget Time Goals

Run your first race for the experience, with a goal of making it to the finish line, not of setting speed records. You will have many chances to run fast later, so take this time to learn the following things about yourself: Were you nervous? Did you get thirsty or hungry? Did you talk to other runners, or keep to yourself? When did you feel tired—at the beginning, somewhere in the middle, or at the end? Did you have trouble concentrating at any point? Did you run progressively faster, slower, or stay at about the same speed throughout? Did you ever want to stop? Did you have fun?

Notice things around you. What was the start like? Could you get water along the way? Could you follow the course? What was your time at various points? (Most races have mile markers, often with digital clocks or someone calling out the time. Or you can set your watch at the start to record your time.) Runners of all levels learn something from every race they run.

Take It Easy Afterward

Intentionally or not, you will probably run your race faster than your normal training pace, thanks to the excitement around you. So take it easy for a few days, even after a short race. Run easily or do something else, such as biking or swimming, to let your muscles recover. Even elite runners rarely run hard for four or five days after a race, and for at least a month after a marathon.

15
STRATEGIES FOR
BETTER RACING

You've run one or more races, and you're hooked. Now your goal is to improve race performances through training and motivation. Following are tips for better racing performance:

PLAN YOUR SCHEDULE

Some runners race every weekend, others only a few times a year. Most elite runners divide the year into two or three seasons and aim to race their best at the end of each season. Then they rest, and build up again. For example, at most, serious runners run one marathon in the spring and one in the fall. They choose these races first, then plan others leading up to them to gauge fitness and to prepare mentally and physically for the event.

Top runners usually have the advantages of coaching advice and the pick of races all over the world. But any runner can plan a season. Many running clubs have long-range schedules of local races. You can check NYRR's annual race calendar as well as magazines, such as *Runner's World* and *Running Times,* and on the Web, to find races farther afield.

Many runners divide their year into two seasons, culminating in a couple of fast 10K races in the spring and a marathon in the fall. Pick your big race or races first. They should be at least three months away so you can prepare properly. Then pick at least one or two races between now and then; run these races to evaluate your fitness and to gain strength and experience for the big ones.

Former champion miler Eamonn Coghlan believes planning races is the key to racing success. "Following a carefully thought-out plan of buildup, sharpening, racing, recovery, and rest allows runners to perform at their best," he says. Exercise scientists call this seasonal approach to running (or any endurance sport) *periodization.* Periodization means using a planned program of base training, buildup, sharpening, racing, rest, and recovery to produce fast times without burnout or injury. Even if you don't care about racing fast, planning races lets you organize your life, especially if you travel to races.

145

PLAN RACE STRATEGIES

Top runners often say they win races without having a strategy. Don't believe them! It's rare that a runner has no idea how he or she might reach the finish line first. As Doug Stern puts it, "The strong will take it from the weak, and the smart will take it from the strong. Learn your craft and plan your races."

Some runners go out fast from the start, hoping to build up an insurmountable lead. Others prefer to hang back, then come on strong in the end. Some runners are famous for this "sit and kick" racing strategy.

Your race strategy depends on many things—your strengths as a runner, your personality, the course, the competition, even the weather. For example, it is not a good strategy to try to run your fastest marathon

AGE-GRADED RESULTS

Tom Kelley, Technologies Administrator at NYRR, explains the age-graded results system. "Age-graded scoring is a way to compare your time to a standard for each sex and every age. Each runner's time is adjusted to that of an open division athlete using a factor for age and sex. Thus, older runners' times are adjusted downward and open division runners' times remain the same. Next to a runner's age-graded time on the results page is his or her rank among others of their gender based on their age-graded time. In the final column of our results we show Performance Level Percent. These percentages can be interpreted as follows:"

100% = Approximate World-Record Level
Over 90% = World Class
Over 80% = National Class
Over 70% = Regional Class
Over 60% = Local Class

"Age-graded results are provided as a performance comparison. Awards at NYRR races have continued to be given in our traditional age categories, but age-graded scoring provides runners with a way to compare themselves with others, regardless of age," says Kelley.

in 75-degree heat with high humidity. A better strategy is to go out conservatively and hope to pick off the faster starters in the end. Good cross-country racing strategy involves moving to the front early to avoid getting trapped behind slower runners on narrow trails.

Race strategies don't always work, so make fallback plans. To a large extent, you have to let the race unfold. Anything can happen, particularly in events like the marathon.

TAPER AND PEAK

These skills are part of both race planning and strategy. Tapering, or to taper, means to cut back on running in the time before a race; peaking, or to peak, means planning your training and racing to produce your best possible performance in one or a few races. For a marathon, you should taper for at least two weeks, cutting your mileage at least 20 to 30 percent two weeks before the race, and 50 percent (the marathon mileage not included) one week before. Tapers for shorter races, from a mile to a half marathon, are shorter.

The main thing is to orient your training, preparation, and goal-setting in a way that peaks. The other important aspect is focus. If you're going to do something with a goal that is significant, you have to be training for a significant period of time.

Average runners often use racing as one of the goals in their training. Maybe it is to help them continue through their training, maybe it motivates them to get out there on a consistent basis.

The focus for the average runner should be on consistency; that's all you need to shoot for. It's not necessary to try to achieve an ultimate goal. Consistency is more important than any particular training you do. Between the person who follows a very rigid program for two weeks a month, and the person who just goes out and runs for 45 minutes five days a week for most of that month, the person with the longer, more generally consistent approach is getting better training.

—*Frank Shorter*

There are many different strategies for tapering, but it's a good idea for all runners to do it in some form. Eamonn Coghlan says that no matter what the distance, you should either not run the day before a race, or just jog easily for a couple of miles to feel fresh and loose.

You may hear about runners who also "run through" races, that is, who do not taper. The race thus becomes more of a training run. While an extensive taper isn't needed for races early in your season, remember that racing is both an emotional and a physical experience. No matter what speed you run, a race will get the adrenaline flowing. Why not savor that experience? Some top runners claim they don't favor running through races because they like the confidence a good race gives them, and know running through it means they won't race well. When you taper, you can't log as many miles for that week, and that can make people nervous, especially when they're training for a marathon. But you can gain so much more from a good race. Don't become a "mileage junkie." You should run light and easy the day or two before a race, and you should take it easy afterward.

PREPARING FOR HOT WEATHER

Take ten days to two weeks to get used to hot weather, building workout intensity and duration gradually. Choose intensity in cooler morning hours over easier work during the heat of the afternoon. Monitor core body temperature, which should stay below 102.2° F, immediately after a workout. Higher than that, your performance is deteriorating. Unfortunately, an oral thermometer isn't precise enough, and doesn't take the right reading. Core means core. You will need a rectal thermometer. Avoid lengthy warmup periods on especially hot and humid days. Do not use supplements with ephedra during training or on race day; taking ephedra increases your risk of heat illness.

—*Dr. Lewis Maharam*

FOCUS AND CONCENTRATE

What do you think about during races? Even though your body is doing the work, your mind can help you run faster. Joan Samuelson, Olympic Marathon gold medalist, has talked about the "cocoon" of concentration she enters before a race. Gordon Bakoulis writes, "I've been so focused before races, I can't recognize friends who wish me luck before the start." You don't have to concentrate quite so hard, but focusing helps performance.

Before the race, stretch and warm up with friends, but be sure to take a few minutes to be alone. Talk to yourself about the race, reminding yourself that you have worked hard for this, the big day. Think about the course and review your race strategy. If you are nervous, that's fine. The adrenaline will help you run faster.

During the race, concentrate on your breathing, your pace, the weather, and your place compared to other runners. As you gain racing experience, you will develop an ability to know when you can run a little harder and when you should hold back. There is no magic to doing this, but it cannot happen without focus and concentration. That's why you shouldn't use the race to plan your dinner menu, wonder whether you locked the door, or muse on your neighbors' running attire. Coach yourself through each section of a race, advising yourself to "relax and flow" on the downhills, "keep it steady" on the flats, and "shorten your stride, lift those knees" as you go uphill.

From facing the experience of ultradistance triathlons, I have learned that athletics is about being able to stay relaxed and be patient. Racing is pain, and that's why you do it, to challenge yourself and the limits of your physical and mental barriers. You don't experience that in an armchair watching television.

In any race there are the moments you feel great, and the moments you feel you're not going to make it. You've got to be willing to breathe hard, sweat, and still stay relaxed. You hear it over and over again—a television announcer saying, "Watch that guy, he looks so relaxed." It's a rare athlete who wins who doesn't look relaxed.

I think the point is not to be afraid of the challenge. Fear is probably the thing that limits performance more than anything— the fear of not doing well, of what people will say. You've got to acknowledge those fears, then release them.

When I was a swimmer, I did all the wrong things. I would see the competition pull away, and the fear would grip me. I learned you can't hide from yourself or your ability. You have to accept what you have and be patient with yourself.

—*Mark Allen*

The longer the race, the harder it is to keep concentration throughout and, for most runners, a random thought or two will not ruin your race. Let the thought occur, then gently shift your attention back to the moment. You may want to try using imagery to concentrate. Visualize a string between you and the runner in front of you. See yourself winding the string into a ball as you pull closer. You can repeat a word or phrase in time with your breathing or footsteps: "Stay loose" or "I can do it" are some you might try.

THE CHIP

The ChampionChip race timing system utilizes a small plastic "chip" that contains a transponder that is attached to the runner's shoe. Each chip has a unique seven-digit code that is read by an antenna located under mats placed at the start and finish of each race (and also at split points for some races).

At NYRR races, the ChampionChip system records both the official time, from the starting horn, and the net time, measured from the time each runner crosses the starting line. The official time is used to establish the order of finish and to present awards in accordance with USATF rules. The rule states, "Official timing begins with the start signal." This ensures that the runner who crosses the finish line first is the winner. NYRR provides the net time only as additional information for each runner. For the New York City Marathon, splits are provided at 10K, half-marathon, and 20 miles. All three splits, the official time, and the net time appear on each runner's finisher certificate.

As you practice focusing, you will learn to use your body's feedback to adjust your pace and plan how you will run the rest of the race. When you are well focused, you can pull up your level of performance. When you are having a bad race, focus on things that will inspire you—for instance, the crowds that cheer as you run by. Think back to a hard workout you did and remember how you pushed through the fatigue. Envision the finish line and think how proud you will be to cross it. Focus and concentration keep your mind sharp and your body working to finish the race as strongly as you can.

PACE YOURSELF

How fast should you run races? That is something you will learn by racing; however, the process will be quicker, and racing more enjoyable, if you practice running at race pace or faster in workouts. This is what speedwork is for.

Speedwork can also bring down your race times dramatically, as many runners have discovered after doing interval workouts with NYRR running classes. By timing yourself in workouts, you learn how fast to pace yourself in races. Finally, doing speedwork with others gives you a sample of the adrenaline rush of a race, although it is not a good idea to get in the habit of racing in speed workouts. You want to save your best performances for race day.

A word of caution: don't lock yourself in to performing at a predetermined pace. Sometimes circumstances, like weather or job stress, make it necessary to adjust or slow down. At other times, everything comes together. You feel great, and you run faster than expected.

Remember, in the 5K and 10K, you can always pick it up. In a short race like the mile or a track race, it's over so quickly; you have to hit your pace right out of the gates. But there's always room in longer road races to pick up your pace. If you go out too fast, you'll have a bad day and feel frustrated. It's always more rewarding to finish strong and run negative splits (the second half quicker than the first half). Go out a little bit slower than your desired pace, and when you feel settled into the race, then you can start increasing the speed. That goes for runners at both the elite level and general level.

—*Meb Keflezighi*

REST AND RECOVER

A race taxes your body and mind more than your daily training, including speed workouts. You must rest afterward, no matter how you feel. "This is hard for some runners," says Eamonn Coghlan. "If they have a good race or season, they are pumped up, and want to train hard again right

away. If they did poorly, they want to train hard to redeem themselves."
Coghlan always forced himself to take a month off after each season,
doing little or no running. "For the first week, I felt great. Then I'd get an
itch to run, but I'd hold back. At the end of four weeks, I'd have such an
appetite for running, I could scarcely contain myself. I really believe that
forced rest lengthened my career." Remember the general rule for recovery: one day's rest for every mile of a race (including the marathon)
before you choose to run hard or race again. Cross training can replace
running on those rest days.

TAKE AN ICE BATH FOR RACE RECOVERY

Consider taking an ice bath to speed recovery from races and
hard workouts. Here's how to do it, and why, according to *Runners' World* magazine. Fill a bathtub with six inches of water, and
dump in a tray or two of ice cubes. Make sure the water covers
your heels, Achilles tendons, calves, hamstrings, and buttocks
(some people favor covering the entire legs, quadriceps included)—the places most likely to feel tight after a long or hard
run. Stay in for five to ten minutes. It's intense—painful—in the beginning, but it's effective. Advocates say you'll feel a noticeable difference in your muscles the following day. (It worked for Paula
Radcliffe, helping her to set a world marathon record.) Says physical therapist and ice bather Clint Verran, "The cold initially causes
your blood vessels to constrict. After about five or ten minutes, the
blood vessels in the muscles start to relax, allowing your legs to
gradually return to normal. This results in a 'pumping action' that
rids your muscles of by-products, and makes your legs feel
springy the next day."
(Adapted from *Runner's World,* Sept. 2003.)

A CHECKLIST OF RACING DO'S AND DON'TS

1. Even if you're not racing seriously, it pays to choose a well-
    organized race with a good reputation. Time and accurate distance
    may not be important to you, but adequate water stations are in-
    valuable.

2. Read the race entry blank carefully and note the date, time, and location of the event. (You'd be surprised what nervousness makes you forget!) If you don't know directions, bring a map and the entry blank with you (often the blank includes directions).

3. If possible, scout the course and the location beforehand. It helps to know where that steep hill is, and the location of a friendly neighborhood gas station or restaurant—so you can use the rest room and avoid the long lines at the race site facilities if necessary.

4. The night before the event, pack your bag and check several times to make sure you have everything (even legendary sprinter Carl Lewis once forgot his running shorts). Make sure you have your race number (pin it to your shirt ahead of time), that your shoes and clothing are broken in, and that you have all other necessary or emergency items—a bottle of water, adhesive bandages, petroleum jelly, toilet paper, safety pins, sunscreen, change of dry clothes, etc.

5. If you're planning to meet a friend to run with, select a spot ahead of time—preferably one that is away from the crowded starting area.

6. Stick to your tried-and-true methods of what to eat and drink—or what not to eat and drink—the night before and the morning of the event (avoid alcohol, don't eat too close to the race, don't drink coffee or other caffeinated beverages if you are not used to them).

7. Don't arrive so early that you expend excess energy nervously waiting and braving the elements, such as cold or heat. (Would you believe that every year at least one lone runner arrives at about 3 A.M. at the New York City Marathon starting area? The race starts at about 10 A.M.!) Once at the race site, try to find shelter from either winterlike conditions or direct summer sun. Do not sunbathe before a race.

8. Don't arrive so late that you can't find parking, or that the lines for the toilets are too long. Arriving late exacerbates nervousness and cuts into precious warmup time.

9. Arrange to stash your warmup clothing in a car, baggage check, or with a friend. Especially if it's very cold, keep your outer gear on until the last possible minute.

10. Continue to drink water, even small sips, until race time.

11. After the race, don't forget your crucial cool-down routine. While it's nice to bask in your achievements and share in the camaraderie at the finish, novice runners often make the mistake of standing around after the race and chatting. Elite runners almost never do this—much to the dismay of the media, who often seek out a missing athlete who is off running a cool-down.

WHEN IS IT ALL RIGHT TO DROP OUT OF A RACE?

One of the things running teaches us is to push ourselves, even when body and mind would rather call it a day. But sometimes dropping out of a race makes sense, and in very rare cases, it can be a matter of life and death.

Drop out if you feel acute pain. This will most likely be in the hips, legs, or feet, and can signal an injury to muscle, connective tissue (tendons and ligaments), or bone. Sometimes it's hard to tell injury-related pain from the muscle fatigue that's normal when you work hard. Simple fatigue usually causes a burning sensation that lessens if you slow down. Pain caused by a muscle pull or tear, a sprain, or a fracture will likely get worse with every step.

Stop if you feel dizzy, disoriented, or if you stop sweating. Although these symptoms of heat exhaustion usually strike in hot, humid weather, they can occur anytime. By the time you feel them, you are at risk for heat stroke, a life-threatening condition caused by very high body temperature. Stop running, summon help, and get water in and on yourself as quickly as possible.

Attempt to finish, but you may have to forget it if you get a side stitch. It may hurt like crazy, but chances are it'll go away. Many people just run through the pain, taking deep, relaxed breaths. You can also try slowing down slightly and pressing your fingertips into the area. If that doesn't work, walk a bit, breathing deeply, then ease back into running.

The same is true of stomach problems. This is a tough call. Grete Waitz's 1985 New York City Marathon effort, during which she had diarrhea, proves that it's possible to finish in world-class form with severe abdominal distress. (You do, however, need to assess what is reasonable. For Waitz to stop for a rest room would have meant losing the race.)

"There's a difference between having tendonitis and diarrhea," points out Waitz. "If there is physical pain connected to an injury, you should stop." In terms of an illness, she says, "First of all, you shouldn't even start a race if you have a fever, but if you are ill, and you realize mid-way through it isn't going to work out, you should stop."

But Waitz does not recommend dropping out because you realize your time is not good. "It would be too tempting to get into that habit, to drop out regularly," she claims. Besides, you can always salvage something from a race. If you stay in it, chances are you'll learn something, and approach the next race feeling mentally stronger.

"If it's a marathon, for example, and the weather is bad, or the conditions are awful—it's better not to even start than to DNF (do not finish). Pick another event," says Waitz. She recalls that at one New York City Marathon in the late 1990s, the weather was so windy and cold that it even snowed. "A lot of people didn't even run. They got back onto the buses at the start and went to the finish. I would have done the same thing if I had been running for time, or intended to be out on the course for a while." Be especially careful about deciding to start a marathon if there's a question you'll finish, because as Waitz points out, by the time you decide to DNF, you have probably run so far that you can't do another one soon.

PART 3
THE DISTANCES

16
THE MILE

The lights are dimmed every year for the highlight event at the venerated Millrose Games. In a solemn voice, the announcer intones, "Ladies and gentlemen, the Wanamaker Mile." A rumble, then a roar rises from the crowd at New York's Madison Square Garden.

Fred Lebow was inspired by the Wanamaker spirit. Imagine taking this race out of the arena and to the outdoors? Why not make this spectacle—which ignites the cheering of up to 18,000 fans—available to thousands more (even millions with television) by bringing the mile race to the roads?

"Would you run a mile on the road?" Fred Lebow asked Eamonn Coghlan after he won one of his seven titles in the Wanamaker Mile. "As long as we can run it on Fifth Avenue, so it finishes in front of the Irish Tourist Board," he answered. That's where Coghlan worked at the time and he felt the promotion would be great.

Lebow ran into Coghlan at the Bislett Games in Oslo later that year. "What about that Fifth Avenue Mile?" Coghlan asked. "You're serious, aren't you?" Lebow replied.

In 1981 New York Road Runners staged the first road mile, appropriately enough on one of the world's most elegant thoroughfares, Fifth Avenue. This event, broadcast on network television, has featured some of the world's fastest times run for the distance (although those times are unofficial, since they aren't run on a uniform track). And this racing format has been adopted worldwide.

Over the years, the Fifth Avenue Mile has expanded to allow racers of various abilities and in different divisions—not just the elite—to compete. High school, masters, and top local divisions are now included in the event. In keeping with the "everyone included" spirit of NYRR, in 1991, Lebow and NYRR created an "all-comers" division in the race. Heat after heat of various groups of runners take off, giving everyone who participates an opportunity to experience what Eamonn Coghlan calls "that sheer exhilaration" of running the mile.

THE MAGIC MILE

Many road runners think of a mile as one section of a longer race. The idea of running a single mile for time, let alone on a track, is absolutely foreign. This test of both speed and endurance, however, need not be reserved for only the elite milers. In addition to being a distance worthy of racing by anyone, training for and running a mile can translate to running well at other distances.

Running writer and coach Cliff Temple points out that you may know your best time for 10K, or the marathon, yet you likely have no idea of your ability over the magic mile. In his hometown of Hythe in Kent, England, there is no track, but there is an accurately measured, straight seafront mile, complete with permanent markers. This means that local runners can time themselves over the distance when they feel like it—either in the middle of a training run or in a special time trial. Some runners try it once; others spend all year using it as a training gauge, trying to improve their times.

Across the United States, various running teams and clubs have marked out mile runs on paths, roads, and in parks. Contact those groups to find out where "the milers" head on the roads. If you don't have a spot nearby, seek the aid of your local running club or other group to help mark a mile in your area for everyone's use.

You might also want to check out an all-comers track meet—the introduction to running the mile (and various other distances) for many a runner. Either way, the mile can be a good indication of your current conditioning and your progress.

THE MAGIC—AND MIND-SET—OF THE MILER

"In certain ways, the feeling of running a mile in 3:49 is exactly the same as when I ran my first marathon in 2:25 in New York in 1991. And that sheer exhilaration that you experience is the same for a world-class runner as it is for a jogger," says Eamonn Coghlan of the mile.

The more complex the situation, the more disciplined you must be to go through it, the more you absorb the feedback and responses while going through it, the deeper the feeling of success. Coghlan believes that in the inner mind, this experience is equivalent in all realms of life—be it in sports or education. "When I run a world record in the mile, and I get that feeling of sheer speed and invincibility, it is exactly the same feeling, psychologically speaking, that somebody else gets from running a personal best time," Coghlan explains.

I do love to run indoors. I love the tightness of the track. I love the fact you're going around 11 times for a mile on a short straightaway and a tight turn with a bank. The crowd is right on top of you. I can get a tremendous feeling of exhilarating speed indoors that I don't get outdoors, because you can get the centrifugal force effect from the bank turn. That turn catapults you down the straightaway, and before you know it, you're back into that bank turn again. I enjoy that feeling. The sound of your footstrike on each stride hitting the board, and the speed you get back from that, gives you a great uplift. Some runners sink in it. Some runners feel as if they lose their sense of balance on the turns. I don't. All the elements of indoor running I get a high out of, and as a result of that, I excel.

—Eamonn Coghlan

Coghlan goes on to say "Running a fast mile feels almost like you're flying like a bird, in complete control of everything that's going on, physically and mentally. You feel absolutely fantastic, like a runaway express train that could effortlessly go on and on forever. There's just no pain. You feel as if you could run forever without anybody behind or in front of you. When I do it, it's as if I've gone through a wall. That's the optimal psychological experience."

"I think everyone should try running a mile. People can relate to the mile. That magical four-minute mile barrier has set a universal standard. To run under that time is a phenomenal achievement. For the average runner, to see how close that person can come to the 'almighty' gives them an indication of where they really stand."

CLIFF TEMPLE'S TRAINING FOR THE MILE

To train for the mile, you need to develop your speed endurance. As a distance, the mile is too far to sprint, but if you are looking for significant improvement, it is not far enough to cover at a comfortable aerobic pace. This means you need to rehearse running at a pace that makes you fairly breathless but that is still some way short of sprinting.

Finding that ideal pace may require several attempts. If you push too hard you will go into oxygen debt. This means using oxygen faster than the lungs can send fresh supplies to the working muscles. In this case, you will simply have to slow down until a balance is restored. On the other hand, if you don't push hard enough, you may find when you are close to the finish that you still have a lot left, and will end up making a mad sprint for the line, knowing that you could have run faster earlier. This is not efficient pacing either.

So to start with, you can look for time improvements simply by correcting your pacing. When you can run at a speed you can just about sustain for most of the distance without going into oxygen debt, you will be close to your current potential. Once you feel you have reached that point, the way forward is through improved training, although don't feel you have to get your pacing absolutely perfect before you start specific training.

The mile is also a key component in training. If you go out and run quarter-mile repeats, even though you get benefit, you don't get the same feedback as you get from running mile repeats. I can run quarter-mile after quarter-mile all day long, yet I can try to use that training to run a 5000-meter race, and bomb. But if I change my training repeats to three fourths or one mile, I'll be spent after two of them, because I have to extend my body and mind over four full laps of the track. For a quarter-mile, you don't have to concentrate that long, and the physical pain is over fairly quickly. Mile repeats, on the other hand, provide you with the physical and mental ability to withstand the longer distances in a race.

—Eamonn Coghlan

A typical training session would involve running one or two miles steadily to warm up, and then running hard for 60 seconds. At the end of that, you should walk for 60 seconds, then jog for two minutes, by which time your breathing should return to near normal. Then you run hard again for 60 seconds, walk 60 seconds, and jog two minutes. A first attempt at this session should include a total of four hard runs. As you get used to it, increase the number of repetitions to six or eight, or even divide them into two blocks of four, with a 10-minute jog between the two sets.

Eamonn Coghlan has composed a training program based on a six-week period of four 10-day training cycles. "So many people get caught up in seven-day cycles," he says, "but that can be a trap. Most of us are just too

TRAINING FOR A FIVE-MINUTE MILE

Warm up before all hard efforts and finish with a cool down.

FIRST 10-DAY CYCLE

Day 1: $4 \times \frac{3}{4}$ mile on rolling hills, like a golf course (fast time is not important here, but try to do all the segments in the same time)

Day 2: five miles

Day 3: eight miles easy; 6×100-meter strides

Day 4: 6×400 meters at goal race pace (if your goal is five minutes, do each one at 75 seconds); jog/walk 400 meters' recovery between efforts

Day 5: five miles

Day 6: five miles

Day 7: 10×200 meters in 35 seconds; jog/walk 200 meters' recovery between each

Day 8: rest

Day 9: ten miles

Day 10: five miles, 6×100-meter strides

SECOND 10-DAY CYCLE (REPEAT FIRST CYCLE)

THIRD 10-DAY CYCLE

Day 1: $2 \times \frac{3}{4}$ mile on the track, 80 seconds per lap if possible; complete rest between

Day 2: five miles

Day 3: five miles easy, 6×100-meter strides

Day 4: 6×400 meters in 73 seconds, 400-meter jog/rest between

Day 5: rest

Day 6: six miles

Day 7: 8×200 meters in 35 seconds; 200-meter jog/rest between

(continued)

TRAINING FOR A FIVE-MINUTE MILE (CONTINUED)

Day 8:   five miles
Day 9:   five miles
Day 10: five miles

FOURTH 10-DAY CYCLE

Day 1:   1 × 2000 meters (five laps of the track); 85 seconds per lap
Day 2:   five miles
Day 3:   five miles
Day 4:   4 × 400 meters (73 seconds each); 400 meters' rest; 4 × 200 meters (33 seconds each); 400 meters' rest
Day 5:   rest
Day 6:   five miles
Day 7:   2 × 800 meters (two minutes, 33 seconds each); complete rest between efforts
Day 8:   five miles
Day 9:   three miles; 10 × 100-meter strides
Day 10: five miles

Rest two days with light jogging, then race.

TRAINING FOR A SIX-MINUTE MILE

FIRST 10-DAY CYCLE

Day 1:   warmup jog 15 to 20 minutes, 4 × 3/4 mile on rolling hills, like a golf course (fast time is not important here, but try to do all the segments in the same time)
Day 2:   five miles easy
Day 3:   eight miles easy; 6 × 100-meter strides

(continued)

Training for a Six-Minute Mile (continued)

Day 4: 6 × 400 meters at goal race pace (if your goal is six minutes, do each one at 90 seconds); jog/walk 400 meters for recovery between efforts

Day 5: five miles

Day 6: five miles

Day 7: 10 × 200 meters in 42 seconds; jog/walk 200 meters' recovery between each

Day 8: rest

Day 9: ten miles

Day 10: five miles; 6 × 100-meter strides

SECOND 10-DAY CYCLE (REPEAT FIRST CYCLE)

THIRD 10-DAY CYCLE

Day 1: 2 × 3/4 mile on the track, 96 seconds per lap if possible; complete rest between

Day 2: five miles

Day 3: five miles easy; 6 × 100-meter strides

Day 4: 6 × 400 meters in 87 seconds; 400-meter jog/rest between

Day 5: rest

Day 6: six miles

Day 7: 8 × 200 meters in 42 seconds; 200-meter jog/rest between

Day 8: five miles

Day 9: five miles

Day 10: five miles

FOURTH 10-DAY CYCLE

Day 1: 1 × 2000 meters (five laps of the track); 1 minute, 42 seconds per lap

Day 2: five miles

(continued)

TRAINING FOR A SIX-MINUTE MILE (CONTINUED)

Day 3:   five miles

Day 4:   4 × 400 meters (87 seconds each); 400 meters' rest;
          4 × 200 meters (40 seconds each); 400 meters' rest

Day 5:   rest

Day 6:   five miles

Day 7:   2 × 800 meters (three minutes, four seconds each);
          complete rest between efforts

busy or tired to get it all done in that time frame. A ten-day cycle allows more leeway and helps keep a person out of the 'compulsion trap.' "

Coghlan's schedule is designed to be undertaken only after a thorough level of fitness has been achieved (if you are not ready, follow the first 12 weeks of the program outlined in Chapter 3) and is geared specifically for a runner who may have been racing 10Ks or marathons and would like to attempt to break five minutes for the mile. A training program to attempt to break six minutes follows as well. To customize the program for your own racing goals at any other level, a calculator or a little math can help you easily adjust the workouts.

THE ARMORY TRACK AND FIELD CENTER

The current success of the Armory Track and Field Center is a result of the hard work and dreams of Armory Foundation president and past New York City Marathon winner Dr. Norbert Sander, who had run in the facility as a high school student. The Armory, which is situated in the Washington Heights neighborhood of Manhattan, was once a homeless shelter. Since its grand reopening in 1993, the Armory has hosted over 325,000 young people from around New York and the country who have come to train and compete on what is one of the fastest tracks in the nation.

Some of the most high-profile Armory events have been the USA Indoor Track & Field Championships in 2002, the Hispanic Games (5,000 entrants), and the New Balance Games, which has been the largest indoor high school meet ever held (6,250 entrants from 250 high schools in 2003).

The Armory is also host to NYRR youth programs, such as the New York Road Runners Foundation and its City Sports for Kids program.

But the Armory is more than a track. It is a place where thousands of high school students and adults from throughout New York City and the surrounding area come to exercise, to learn, and to aspire to improve their lives. In addition to athletics, the Armory has seen a tremendous growth in its community and school-based academic programs. The Armory sponsors programs in technology learning through its tech center, as well as programs for literacy, job training, teens at risk, immigrant services, teacher training, mentoring, and senior citizens' health.

The Armory is also dedicated to youth fitness. The PAL Center hosts over 400 daily participants, and there is a Sunday afternoon City Sports for Kids program for 6–13-year-olds. The Armory also hosts a City Track Program for grammar schools and, in close collaboration with NYRR and its Foundation, is set to address the growing problem of juvenile obesity in the city and the country.

The Armory inaugurates the National Track and Field Hall of Fame on January 24, 2004, at the annual New Balance Games. The Hall of Fame will attract visitors from around the world, educate youth about the sport of track and field, promote physical fitness through historical exhibits and artifacts, and feature hands-on exhibits to test physical fitness. Check out the Armory at www.armorytrack.com/

17
THE 5K

The 5K (five kilometers; 5000 meters; 3.1 miles) remains the most popular running distance in the United States. The distance accounts for 39 percent of the finishers and almost half of the courses certified by the USATF in 2002.

The 5K represents a challenge on every level—from simply completing the distance to catching the bug and training to run the distance well. In addition, the 5K offers a manageable alternative to thousands of runners—many of whom have run marathons—who are not able or willing to run longer distances on a continual basis. And the 5K provides racing experience at a less taxing, thus safer, distance than the 10K race or marathoning, especially in hot and humid summer months. Running the 5K also builds speed, an advantage for longer-distance races. A top track runner might do two or three 10Ks all season, preferring to race mostly distances in the 5K range.

A RACE OF STRENGTH AND SPEED

Like all good training and racing, doing well in the 5K requires balance. In this case, the balance is between strength and speed.

According to Eamonn Coghlan, the tactics for running the 5000 meters are exactly the same as for the mile. The key to running a smart 5000 is to relax, sit, and kick. For most average road runners, the 5K is a short distance. "It sometimes makes people panic," says Coghlan. "To do it well takes an ability to get into the proper pace and rhythm over the first quarter mile, then relax and settle down."

It's important then to concentrate on everything that's happening in the race. "Try not to focus on yourself, particularly on negative physical sensations," Coghlan advises. "Try to forget about yourself (that prevents panic), trust your instinctive ability, and focus on everything that's going on around you. Allow the environment to carry you along. Focus on other runners or spectators rather than worrying about your fatigue, a pain in your legs, or a stitch. Of course you're aware of yourself to a degree, but use your surroundings to help you through."

According to Coghlan, the 5K on the track allows you to focus easily because of the repetition—12 1/2 laps. He suggests starting in control, then moving into contention with 2 1/2 laps to go. "Because winning is almost always the objective (as opposed to running fast), I've always had a tendency to forget about the race, as long as I was being pulled along," Coghlan explains. "Then with those 2 1/2 laps remaining, I focus more on the task at hand. Concentration is also tiring, and saving that intense focus for a while assures you'll have it when you need it." The same can hold true of running on the roads. If you save something for that final half-mile, you'll probably pass a few people on your way to the finish.

It takes the strength of a marathoner and the speed of a miler to run a good 5K, Coghlan contends. A lot of milers moving up to the 5000m get caught up in doing too much speedwork. "I truly believe that you have to do an incredible amount of strength work to be able to get to the latter stages of the 5K and still have enough speed to be able to 'kick it in,'" he says. Strength work in this case means training that consists of repeat 800 meters and one- and even two-mile repeats.

Most milers concentrate on their 200-, 400-, and 800-meter speed to get their times down, while 5000-meter runners should concentrate on 800-meter through mile speed. As a result, Coghlan believes, those who do typ-

MEB KEFLEZIGHI'S RACE TIPS

I'm a big believer in hard work. Practice makes perfect. I train hard so that I know when it comes time to race, my body will be ready to deal with the stress. Psychologically, that's how I prepare myself to run hard races. It's the same for someone who wants to break 21:00 in the 5K. If you do some hard training, you'll grow accustomed to dealing with the pain factor. It's doing the workouts week in and week out that makes the difference on race day.

If you have the combination of strength and speed, you can go along with the flow and see how the race develops. If you're a strength runner, you should push it with about a mile to go, and use your power to make a really strong kick. If you rely more on speed, the last 600 meters you can really quicken the pace. Runners who have speed are dangerous when they smell the finish line.

—*Meb Keflezighi*

ical mile training often don't have the kind of strength it takes to get to the last 400 meters in a 5000 with the necessary speed. "If you do too much short speed training, you won't have the strength to be able to 'kick off' at the end. Whereas I believe if you have the strength to be able to get to the last quarter mile, you will have the speed. That final speed has to be saved, so it's essentially like icing on the cake. The mistake is to put too much icing on the cake by speeding up too early.

"I never had basic sprinter's speed. I was never a good quarter- or half-mile runner. My ability to run a quarter mile all-out is only 50 seconds, yet at the end of a 5000-meter race I can run 50 seconds for a quarter. At the end of a mile race, I can run 50 seconds; however, if I warmed up and ran only a quarter mile all-out, I'd still only run 50 seconds. What I did have was tremendous ability to 'kick off' the final turn and win my races."

TRAINING AND RACING

Here is the advice of American champion Meb Keflezighi. "The 5K is a combination of both strength and speed. You need speed to keep the turnover high, but also the endurance to maintain your desired pace. For my 5K training, I focus on longer intervals, including 1K and mile repeats. I'll also do five-mile tempo runs for the endurance, along with my weekly long runs, which are about 20 miles.

"The key to a 5K is you need patience to really run a smart race. You don't want to go out too fast, only to drop off. You need to be durable to hold on to your pace. You have to say to yourself, 'Well this hurts, but I'm going to keep at it.' If you go out too fast, you could be close to your PR in the mile at the first split, but then you'll likely fade. Remind yourself of all the challenging workouts you did to prepare for the 5K, which will help you keep up the pace even when it feels very challenging. In New York, when I won the U.S.A. Men's 8K Championship, I dropped in a 4:21 mile in the race, because I knew from all my hard training that I could hold on to that pace."

"I think the average runner focuses too much on mileage and not enough on speed," says PattiSue Plumer of training for the 5K. "To achieve maximum performance—no matter what the goal—you need some speed-work, or faster-paced running, whether it be fartlek or interval training. Either way, this training should be done at least once a week, at an effort quicker than race pace.

"To race a good 5K, run at least 40 miles per week. If you're currently running three to four miles per day at a comfortable pace and you're looking to improve your 5K, add some speedwork. For example, if your goal is a 20-minute 5K—a 6:30-per-mile average—you should run at least once a week at a six-minute pace—that is, 30 seconds faster than race pace—or as much under goal race pace as possible. Schedule at least one speed session per week; two or three faster-paced sessions are ideal."

GRETE WAITZ'S 5K PROGRAMS

Program I: Walk/Jog for 5K

This program is for people who have not been exercising for quite some time and might feel out of breath when walking up stairs. This program is also suitable for those over 50 and anyone who wants to get in shape so they can finish a 5K fitness walk/jog.

The program starts very conservatively, with just walking the first weeks. By doing this, you will slowly, and safely, improve your aerobic conditioning without risk of injury or burnout. After all, your muscles, joints, and ligaments need some time to get used to being active again.

Some may wonder if walking gives you the benefit of better aerobic conditioning. The answer is yes, it does, if you increasingly put more energy into your stride and pick up the pace. After a couple of weeks of walking, you may be tempted to try some jogging. If you do, start with no more than one minute at a time (see week 3). If you want to continue walking, do so, and walk faster when it is indicated in the program.

Be aware that you need more time to adjust to an exercise program if you are older. If you are in this category, take it easy on yourself. You may be better off with a slower progression than this program indicates. You have plenty of time on this journey of exercise and self-discovery, so don't rush it. Just keep in mind that a workout is not just a workout; it's a lifestyle that will make you stronger, healthier, and happier.

Walking Is the Way to Go!

- Almost everyone can do it.
- Walking is healthy.
- You can walk everywhere and anywhere.
- Walking is social.

Week	Workout 1	Workout 2	Workout 3
1	25–30 min. walking	30 min. brisk walking	35 min. brisk walking
2	35 min. brisk walking	35–40 min. brisk walking	40 min. brisk walking
3	10 min. walk, 5 × 1 min. fast walk or jog with 2 min. walk between, 10 min. walk.	40 min. walk or other aerobic activity like biking, swimming, aerobics, etc.	Same as day 1
4	10 min. walk, 5 × 2 min. fast walk or jog with 2 min. walk between, 5–10 min. walk	40 min. walk or other aerobic activity like biking, swimming, aerobics, etc.	Same as day 1
5	5–10 min. walk, 6 × 2 min. fast walk or jog with 1 min. walk between, 5–10 min. walk	40 min. walk or other aerobic activity like biking, swimming, aerobics, etc.	Same as day 1
6	5–10 min. walk, 4–5 × 3 min. fast walk or jog, with 1–2 min. walk between, 5–10 min. walk	40 min. walk or other aerobic activity like biking, swimming, aerobics, etc.	Same as day 1
7	5–10 min. walk, 4 × 4 min. fast walk or jog with 2 min. walk between, 5–10 min. walk	40 min. walk or other aerobic activity like biking, swimming, aerobics, etc.	Same as day 1
8	5–10 min. walk, 3 × 5 min. fast walk or jog with 2 min. walk between, 5–10 min. walk	Same as day 1	5 min. walk, 3 × 6 min. fast walk or jog with 2 min. walk between, 5 min. walk
9	5 min. walk, 2 × 7 min. fast walk or jog with 2 min. walk between, 5 min. walk	Same as day 1	5 min. walk, 2 × 7 min. fast walk or jog with 2 min. walk between, 5 min. fast walk or jog, 5 min. walk
10	5 min. walk, 2–3 × 8 –10 min. fast walk or jog with 2–3 min. walk between, 5 min. fast walk or jog	Same as day 1	5 min. walk, 2 × 10 min. fast walk or jog with 2 min. walk between, 5 min. fast walk or jog

*Spread the workouts through the week, allowing for recovery.

- Walking is inexpensive.
- Walking is good for losing weight.
- You can use walking as exercise and transportation.
- There is little risk of injury with walking.

Program II: Jog/Run 5K

The program on the following page is for those who exercise relatively regularly (two to three times per week). You may not have been running so much in the winter months, but as the weather improves, you are now ready and anxious to get fit for the spring and summer. Those under age 35 can make a quicker progression than others. This is the reason that very early on in Program II, the activity becomes one hundred percent running.

If you want to follow this program, you need to have some aerobic conditioning before starting out. The first four weeks are fairly easy, but from then on, you will need to put more effort in if your goal is to improve your running over the 5K distance.

You may feel that neither Program I or Program II is a good fit for you. I then suggest that you take a good look at both of them, and analyzing your current physical condition and your goals, blend them to best suit your needs. Take a little from each program and fashion one just right for you. If you need help, don't hesitate to ask an experienced runner or fitness expert.

PATTISUE PLUMER'S 5K TRAINING PROGRAM

"If I were to train a group of average athletes who want to maximize potential but who, like most people, have jobs and responsibilities and do not train full time, I would fashion a five-day-per-week training schedule, which I have done here. In my opinion, the truth is that most busy people cannot sustain a seven-day-a-week schedule. There are too many other stresses and responsibilities in their lives.

"The biggest mistake in this country is that we discount the stresses of outside life. A training program is no good if you are so beat you can't function in other aspects of your life. The mistake is that runners often don't modify their schedules when necessary. They don't take into account stresses such as staying up until all hours with a work project, or with a child who has the flu."

Week	Workout 1	Workout 2	Workout 3
1	5 min. fast walking, 10 min. jog, 5 min. walking 10 min. jog	30–40 min. other aerobic activity like biking, tennis, swimming, squash, aerobics, etc.	Same as day 1
2	5 min. fast walking, 12–15 min. jog, 3–5 min. walking, 12–15 min. jog	30–40 min. other aerobic activity like biking, tennis, swimming, squash, aerobics, etc.	Same as day 1
3	15 min. jog (start slowly) 3 min. walking, 15 min. jog	30–40 min. other aerobic activity like biking, tennis, swimming, squash, aerobics, etc.	20 min. jog (start slowly), 3–5 min. walking, 10 min. jog
4	30 min. jog (start slowly) include a walking period if you need it.	Same as day 1	35 min. jog (start slowly), comfortable pace (conversation pace)
5	35–40 min. jog (start slowly, try to increase the pace the last 10 min. without getting out of breath)	Same as day 1	40 min. run (make sure the pace is brisk, not too comfortable)
6	10 min. jog, 5 min. increased pace, 5 min. jog, 5 min. increased pace, 10 min. jog	35–40 min. easy run	Same as day 1
7	10 min. jog, 10 × 1 min. fast running with 1 min. jog between, 5–10 min. jog	35–40 min. easy run	45 min. easy run
8	10 min. jog, 5 × 2 min. fast running with 1 min. jog between, 5–10 min. jog	40–45 min. easy run	35 min. steady run
9	10 min. jog, 15 min. run (good steady pace), 10 min. jog	40–45 min. easy run	40 min. run with 8 "pick-ups" of 2 min. each enroute
10	10 min. jog, 4 × 3 mins. fast running with 2 min. jog between, 10 min. jog	45 min. easy run	35–40 min. steady run

*Spread the workouts through the week, allowing for recovery.

"I train with a group of people that includes runners from every walk of life—masters, parents, those with full-time jobs. That's why in prescribing a training program, I take into account all aspects of life. I've seen my coach do this with our group of runners as well.

"Often I am approached by athletes of various caliber who ask me whether to rest—to take a day off running. I take rest days. I tell them that an extra day of rest hurts a lot less than the risk of doing an extra day of training."

The Program

The following program includes parts of PattiSue Plumer's own training at one particular point in her season, which she adapted for this book. It is intended for those with some running experience who want to improve their times.

PattiSue Plumer's Weekly Schedule

MONDAY

- Ten-minute warmup, followed by drills and stretching.
- 4–6 × 1000 meters at approximately five seconds faster than your goal race pace. (If your goal is a 20-minute 5K, each 1000 meters should be run in 3:55.) You should take as much rest as you need between intervals in order to maintain your pace, but keep jogging. Maintain your pace over the course of the workout; stop the intervals when you are slowing. Accelerate over the last 50–100 meters of each 1000 meters.
- Ten-minute cool-down.

TUESDAY

- Easy 30–40 minute run, or cross training.

(continued)

PattiSue Plumer's Weekly Schedule (continued)

WEDNESDAY

- Thirty minutes of total running. Start with 10 minutes of easy running, then run one minute hard, one minute easy for a total of ten minutes, then run ten minutes easy.

THURSDAY

- Same warmup and cool-down as Monday.
- 8–12 accelerated 400 meters. Start the 400 at 5K race pace. Every 100 meters move a little faster, with the last 100 meters all out. Jog 400 meters between each 400. If needed, jog 800–1600 meters after each set of four.

FRIDAY

- Off or same as Tuesday.

SATURDAY

- Long run easy, 60–75 minutes.

SUNDAY

- OFF

Plumer's Comments on Her Program

There is nothing magical about one-minute or 200-meter repeats. They are just examples of one long-distance speed session and one short-distance speed session. I do the longer intervals in the first part of the week because, personally, faster speedwork breaks me down quicker than longer speedwork. And since I want to do speedwork at least twice a week, my program gives me a sufficient number of rest days between each session.

If, for some reason, you don't recover from these workouts—say, you are not ready to do a Saturday long run after a Thursday speed session—don't do it. Remember, I'm a believer in rest! Also, those with families or who want their weekends free may want to adapt the schedule to do the Saturday run on Friday.

18
THE 10K

The 10K (10 kilometers; 6.2 miles; 10,000 meters) is a road running standard. Even if you're a beginning runner, you've likely heard about the 10K. The popularity of this distance is indisputable and the number of participants nationwide continues to rise.

Do you want to become a versatile runner? Do you want to run a good marathon? Then take a cue from the elite. Alberto Salazar is the former American record holder in the 10,000 meters (27:25), the 5000 meters (13:11), and the marathon (2:08:13). He held those records simultaneously, and each performance contributed to the other. Says Salazar, "I believe that to run your fastest marathon you should be as close as possible to your fastest 10,000-meter shape a few months before."

Frank Shorter won the Olympic Marathon in the 1972 Games just a few days after running the Olympic 10,000 meters, coming in fifth in what was then an American record time of 27:51.

For the novice, a 10K is a good challenge. The distance is long enough to give the feeling of distance running, yet not as demanding as 10 miles or a half marathon. Running 45 to 60 minutes for a 10K will not require the extensive recovery a longer race does. Thus, you'll be able to resume regular training and racing fairly quickly after running a 10K; however, it is advisable not to run 10K races more than once every two to three weeks to allow for proper mental as well as physical recovery.

HOW FAST CAN YOU RUN?

You can factor your ability to run various distances by using the 10K as a gauge. The examples of two top runners' personal bests at 10K and the marathon, for instance, reveal that there is a pace variance of about 25 to 30 seconds per mile between 10K race pace and marathon race pace. Alberto Salazar's 10K record of 27:25 is 4:25 per mile, while his marathon record of 2:08:13 averages a 4:53 pace. The difference is 28 seconds. Frank Shorter's 10K best is 27:45, a 4:28 pace. His marathon best of 2:10:30 is a 4:59 pace—a 31-second difference.

Using about 30 seconds per mile as the average 10K–marathon differential, you can assess your 10K or marathon race time. If you want to run a 3:00 marathon, which is a 6:52 pace, using the above formula, you'd need to run a 10K at 40:00, or a 6:27 pace.

It is clear from the elite that quick 10K times can translate into marathon success. Almost every good runner will testify that performing successfully at various distances is related to the combination of strength and speed needed for 10K running. Therefore, the key to racing success at a range of running distances is based on 10K training. That's why many of the training programs and philosophies that appear in this book are based on performing well at 10K. The programs are then only slightly adapted for running the marathon.

RUNNING THE 10K

Grete Waitz offers the following series of tips for the 10K, from emotional preparation to physical training:

1. **First of all, don't panic.** Ten kilometers is about six miles, and most people can walk that distance comfortably at four miles per hour. Therefore, even walking all the way, you could do it in one and one-half hours. Think of it this way—any improvement on an hour and a half is progress!

2. **Make a commitment to train with a friend and perhaps do the race together.** When motivation is low and excuses are easy to find, that commitment will help get you through the rough times and to the race day.

3. **During your training, "hurry slowly," as we say in Norwegian.** Gradually and progressively increase your training, rather than try to cram it all into the last few days (as you might try to do for an exam).

4. **Take it easy.** If you can't handle the increase in training sessions, simply ease back a little and put in more walking sections.

5. **Don't let inclement weather keep you from training.** If the weather is hot, cut back a little or walk more often, and drink plenty of fluids. If it is cold, dress appropriately and be sure to warm up well.

6. **You should be able to talk to your partner when jogging.** So run at a conversational pace.

7. **In the event of illness or other health setbacks, let your body recover.** Be aware that you cannot make up lost time in training by pushing yourself hard the following week. Step back one week in your schedule and regroup. Change your goal if necessary.

TRAINING FOR THE 10K

Grete Waitz's 10K Program for Beginners

This program was developed by Grete Waitz for beginning runners—those who may have a base of fitness from another sport or who have been jogging and would like to participate in a 10K race.

Week 1
- Sunday: alternate walking and jogging in one-minute intervals for 12 minutes
- Tuesday: alternate walking and jogging in one-minute intervals for 14 to 15 minutes
- Thursday: alternate walking and jogging in two-minute intervals for 16 or 17 minutes
- Saturday: do alternate aerobic exercise (e.g., walking, cycling, swimming, aerobics, tennis)

At the end of this first week, you may experience more difficulty with your lungs than with your legs. Your legs are in use every day; however, your lungs probably haven't been worked so hard in a while. This discomfort will soon pass.

Week 2
- Sunday: alternate walking and jogging, one minute walking and two minutes jogging, for 20 minutes (if you have a regular training partner, one can check the jogging time interval, the other the walking interval)
- Tuesday: alternate walking and jogging at the same intervals as on Sunday

- Thursday: alternate walking and jogging at the same intervals as Sunday for 26 minutes
- Saturday: alternate exercise

The most difficult part of the program is over. You have survived the novelty of the activity as well as the first couple of training sessions and have likely adapted to the discipline of regular exercise. Most people who give up their training usually do so in the second or third week.

Week 3

- Sunday: jog for five minutes, walk for one minute. Repeat four times. Then jog for three minutes, walk for two minutes to finish. Total: approximately 29 minutes
- Tuesday: walk for two minutes. Jog for ten minutes. If the ten-minute jog is achieved, then repeat it after another two-minute walk. If it proved too difficult, then cut it down to five minutes and repeat twice more with a two-minute walk interval. Finish with a two-minute jog
- Thursday: five-minute jog, two-minute walk; ten-minute jog, two-minute walk; five-minute jog, two-minute walk; three-minute jog, two-minute walk
- Saturday: alternate exercise

Unless circumstances absolutely prevent it, try to vary your training venue. Footpaths in parks are probably the most pleasant, but playing fields, towpaths, country footpaths, and even the local track can all help to vary the scenery and maintain interest. All the training in this program is designed around time periods, not distances, so knowing the distance you have covered is not really important. Believe it or not, the hardest weeks are behind you. Disciplining yourself to go out training may have been difficult, the early stiffness may have been unpleasant—but you have made it. Keep some structure to your program, and don't become impatient.

Week 4

- Sunday: 12-minute jog, two-minute walk; five minutes running a little faster (but not racing); two-minute walk; 12-minute jog, two-minute walk; five-minute jog, two-minute walk
- Tuesday: 15-minute jog, two-minute walk; 15-minute jog, two-minute walk; five-minute jog, two-minute walk
- Wednesday: alternate exercise

- Thursday: 17-minute jog, three-minute walk; 15-minute jog, three-minute walk; ten-minute jog, three-minute walk
- Saturday: alternate exercise

Try to cut out, or at least cut down on, the walking stages in your training, and step up to four sessions per week.

Week 5

- Sunday: 25-minute jog; try not to walk if possible
- Monday: alternate exercise
- Tuesday: 25-minute jog; 6 × 100-meter strides, with walking breaks between each (striding means stretching out, but not flat-out sprinting)
- Wednesday: rest
- Thursday: 25-minute jog
- Friday: rest
- Saturday: 20- to 27-minute jog, including 3 × 1-minute run at a faster pace (not a racing pace); walk for one minute after each one-minute faster section; resume jogging; when you feel ready, pick up your jogging pace and go for another one minute of faster running

This fifth week is tough. Don't be despondent if you needed to walk a bit. Remember, the training needs to be progressive to keep raising your level of fitness.

Week 6

- Sunday: 30-minute jog, very easy—conversation pace!
- Monday: alternate exercise
- Tuesday: 30-minute jog, plus 6 × 100-meter strides (walking breaks between)
- Wednesday: alternate exercise or rest
- Thursday: ten-minute easy jog; 4 × 1-minute faster-pace runs with 2 minutes of rest/walk between; then five to ten minutes of easy jogging
- Friday: rest

- Saturday: five-minute very easy jog, then either do a 5K fun run, or approximately three-mile training run in which you push yourself a little; check your time

Think back to your condition eight weeks ago and be proud of yourself!

Week 7

- Sunday: 20-minute very easy recovery run

- Monday: alternate exercise

- Tuesday: 25- to 30-minute even-paced run (a little quicker than a jog)

- Wednesday: alternate exercise

- Thursday: 15-minute easy jog

- Friday: rest

- Saturday: 35-minute run

By now you should be enjoying the benefits of fitness—good sleeping pattern, healthy appetite, weight loss, etc.

Week 8

- Sunday: 35-minute run

- Monday: alternate exercise

- Tuesday: 30-minute run, plus 8×100-meter strides (with recovery)

- Wednesday: rest or 15-minute easy jog, if you're feeling really keen to do it

- Thursday: 15-minute jog, then 4×2-minute efforts, with 2-minute recovery; 10- to 15-minute easy jog to finish. Choose a nice circuit in your local park if you can.

- Friday: rest

- Saturday: ten-minute easy jog, then try out your 3-mile route again from two weeks ago; 5-minute easy jog to finish. Any improvement in time?

Only one more week of progressive training (the last week of the program is spent easing off to conserve energy for the race day).

Week 9

- Sunday: 45-minute jog; walk a little, but only if necessary
- Monday: alternate exercise
- Tuesday: 35-minute run, plus 6 × 100-meter strides
- Wednesday: rest, or 15-minute easy jog
- Thursday: 15-minute jog; 8 × 1-minute quicker runs, with a 3-minute walk or jog for recovery; 15-minute easy jog
- Friday: rest
- Saturday: 25-minute easy jog

You've made it. The next week is spent easing down so you are ready for your big day.

Week 10

- Sunday: one-hour jog, with walking intervals as necessary
- Tuesday: 20-minute jog
- Thursday: 15-minute jog
- Saturday: rest
- Sunday: 10K race

Nerves are a part of racing. The nervousness will not hurt you, and the adrenaline your body releases into your bloodstream will help your running; however, try not to get carried away and start too fast. And don't forget, it's okay to walk for short spells if you feel like it. Don't eat a large breakfast before the race, but do try to eat something light at least two and one-half hours before the start. Don't wear any new gear (including socks) for the first time in the race. Make sure it's all well worn and laundered a few times before the big day. Can you imagine ten weeks of hard work spoiled by a blister?

Week 11

You may be stiff the days after the event. Soaking in a hot bath may help ease the aches away—but so does exercise! Go for a short jog, 15 to 20 minutes, two to three days after the race, and maybe another one two days later. Or try alternative cross training. Keep at it—you have worked hard to get fit. Stay in shape. There are always other races and fun runs to enter.

10K FOR THE INTERMEDIATE AND ADVANCED RUNNER

I believe one of the keys to running a good 10K is to develop speed at shorter distances. The first time I ran 10K was in the Women's Mini Marathon in 1979 (31:15, then a world best). I did this coming from my track background, where the longest distance I ran was 3000 meters. (At that time, that was the longest race distance generally available to women.) The smartest way to do well at 10K is to develop ability at shorter distances, like 5K. In my case, after I did a good 3000 meters on the track, I knew I was ready for a good 10K.

The biggest mistake I think people make in running 10K is going out too fast. The 10Ks in which I haven't done particularly well are the ones in which I've started out too quickly—almost dying in the end. This is a particular risk when you're trying to run a good time. That's how it's usually been for me anyway, and why I eventually emphasized running for the victory rather than time. Although it's okay to try for a good time on selected occasions, that goal is just too draining to attempt all the time. As a beginner you may naturally experience continual improvement at first, but try not to put pressure on yourself to run a personal best every time out.

To avoid starting out too fast, you have to "have eyes in your stomach," as we say in Norway—a good gut instinct of control. You can hone that instinct by doing your homework. Know the course, take into account the impact of the weather, and have the self-control that comes from self-confidence and experience. Even if you see the split time at the first mile, and it's slower than what you expected, you can be confident you'll catch and pass people by the end.

On the other hand, because a 10K isn't really that long a distance, you can't let your competition get too far ahead of you, or stray too far from your time goal if you have one. Proper pacing is a balance. It's something you have to learn to judge. You do hear runners who have waited too long say that if the race had been a mile longer, they could have caught their competition or run their goal time. But they made their move too late.

Another thing to be diligent about is the warmup. You start a 10K much faster than, say, a marathon, and often, with the adrenaline and crowd effect, much quicker than you may have expected or are used to. Therefore, a warmup is crucial. I spend a good 30 minutes warming up for a 10K, unless, of course, it's

(continued)

10K FOR THE INTERMEDIATE AND ADVANCED RUNNER (CONTINUED)

in hot weather. Then I warm up less, and concentrate on staying cool but ready.

A 30-minute warmup may be too much for those not running competitively; however, some warmup is necessary. The point is to make sure your body is prepared to handle the initial quicker pace.

For a 10K, I taper my training the last five days before an event. If the race is on a Sunday, I'll do two easy days on Tuesday and Wednesday, a short interval workout on Thursday for sharpening, and take it easy again on Friday and Saturday. You may be "edgy" from tapering, but that's part of the process, and a sign you are ready to run.

—Grete Waitz

TEN MILES TO THE
HALF MARATHON

Some distance runners don't seem to be able to get going until about four or five miles into a 10K—when the race is nearly over. For these runners, ten miles to the half marathon is often an ideal race range. Besides, this distance is a good test of endurance—without the training investment and risks of a marathon. It is also good preparation for the marathoner. As practice for a marathon, races in this range allow runners extensive experience on the road, usually from one and a half to two hours on average. Runners are required to take water and learn patience in pacing.

> My favorite distances are ten miles to the half marathon. On the shorter end of the competition scale, the 10K has become such a speed event. On the longer end, the marathon takes too much out of you. The reason I've been successful in longer events like the marathon is because I don't do them often. The other reason is because I like aspects of the training. I get a lot of enjoyment from my weekend long runs, in which I go with a group of men, run hard, and feel good. I mostly stick to the relatively longer distances because the shorter races are more difficult for me to train for. I can't keep up with the necessary track work because of my mechanics. I tend to get injured.
> —*Joan Samuelson, Olympic gold medalist*

If you've run 5K and 10K races, you'll likely feel a measure of physical comfort in events in this range. You'll be running 10 to 20 seconds slower per mile than in the shorter distances (as long as you don't make the mistake of going out at your 10K race pace, that is). In addition, you'll also find that your next 10K will feel pleasantly short by comparison.

One drawback, however, is that there are fewer races of this distance available. It may be because there is a sizable participation gap. Of the top 20 largest road races in the United States in 2002, only one was a half

RACING TEN MILES TO THE HALF MARATHON

When I race a half marathon or 15K, I focus on getting into the pace I want to maintain. Right from the start you want to get into a groove. Your goal pace should feel comfortable. You shouldn't feel like you're taxing yourself at all through about the first eight miles. It should start getting hard at mile 10, and the last three are the toughest. I think of the half marathon as a ten-mile tempo run, followed by a hard 5K.

The 15K is shorter, so you should relax through five miles, then start working at it. The last two to three miles are tough. If you're hurting early, you've chosen a pace that is too fast.

—Marla Runyan

marathon (the Indianapolis Half Marathon). Runners seem to gravitate either to the shorter events or to the marathon.

I find the half marathon is one of the most popular events, and for good reason. Not everyone can gear up for a marathon, because of what's involved—the preparation, the recovery. But a half marathon is something most every runner can set their sights on, and people are. We're seeing this whether they are relatively slow, middle of the pack, or elite. It's also a guidepost for those who do want to run a marathon, because they can see where they are in their training—what their goal is, and what the next step is.

—Allan Steinfeld

NYRR has found the half marathon to be popular enough to include on its calendar a half-marathon series with prize money. About 20,000 runners participate in the series every year. The most well attended in the series is the NYRR Manhattan Half Marathon, run in August, which had 5,381 finishers in 2003.

TRAINING FOR THE 10K TO HALF MARATHON

For races that are just short of an hour, I think that the most important element is threshold training, which a lot of runners call tempo runs. I do two different types of workouts in this category, steady runs and tempo runs. Steady runs are between 10 and 14 miles. They are run at marathon pace. Tempo runs are shorter, usually around three to five miles. I run these at 15K to half-marathon pace. Improving these energy systems is really vital to racing well at these distances.

Racing these distances also has a speed and efficiency component. For this I do speedwork on the track. These workouts can be intervals of 400 to 600 meters, or any combination of these repeats. These workouts are important because you'll benefit from the efficiency, mechanics, and rhythm of running at a faster pace, so even when you go back to half marathon pace during a race, you will feel more comfortable.

When I am training for the 10K all the way up to the marathon, all the ingredients are the same. The program includes long runs, tempo runs, speedwork. If I'm working towards a 5K, I'll focus more on speedwork. If I have a half marathon coming up, I'll include more tempo runs. The marathon requires a lot of steady run training. Training is like a big bag, and you can reach in and select the type of workout that will best match your distance. Whatever you choose, the components should all be there.

—Marla Runyan

20

THE MARATHON

For the twenty-first century runner the marathon is no longer an esoteric Mount Everest. The marathon defines the goals of even the average distance runner. It's a sure bet that if you tell someone you're a runner, that person's immediate response will be, "Have you run a marathon?" Take Frank Shorter's word for it, "If you want to legitimize your running in the eyes of your peers, tell them you're training for a marathon."

> Running a marathon is a tremendous accomplishment. I never understood why people ran them until I did it. Crossing the finish line of my first marathon gave me that "first-time glow"—a sense of accomplishment that I have not felt since. I love the event. However, I don't think a person can indefinitely do the kind of training required to be competitive in the marathon. Then, again, everyone is different. Grete [Waitz] did it for ten years, a very long time.
>
> —*Francie Larrieu Smith*

Marathon participation is consistently on the rise. According to the USATF Road Running Information Center, 450,000 people ran a marathon in the United States in 2002. That's up from 390,000 in 1996. There are marathons everywhere—from the streets of the world's major cities, up and down mountains, to the Great Wall in China. The New York City Marathon is the prototype for big-city marathons around the world.

New York has been the inspiration and model for many of the world's other marathons. This is particularly the case for races that run through the streets of major cities. For many years, officials of NYRR have traveled the world advising on how to conduct a marathon. Some of the fledgling races they helped have grown to worldwide prominence. These include such events as the London, Berlin, Paris, Rotterdam, and Los Angeles Marathons, and scores of others.

Whether you prefer a small, quiet 26.2-miler in a rural area or the experience of the rush of running through a big city, the spirit of New York defines the meaning of the marathon race. In many respects, it is a symbol for the entire running movement.

I had the greatest experience in New York in 2002. It was a magical day. I really enjoyed having the elite women's start. I learned that in the marathon, unlike any distance in racing, individual mile splits mean absolutely nothing. You can't string a bunch of 5:30 miles together and get an end time. You can't break it down into 26 segments. It's about feeling comfortable at a given pace and staying relaxed and patient.

You focus on training to increase fitness, not necessarily pace. You focus on strengthening your legs and your lungs. You need to focus on improving your body physically. The marathon should feel like your long runs. Don't focus on hitting your mile splits. You should look at larger chunks of the race. Because of the length of the marathon, unbelievable things happen in that last three miles.

What I have learned is that the marathon is more about running the race. You need to focus on your competitors and running the race and how your body feels—not completely on mile splits. In New York in 2002, I ran the first half with the lead women, and some miles felt slow, some felt fast. I ran the second half over a minute faster. It really came down to just trying to run the race and react to what was happening at a given point.

—*Marla Runyan*

What is so compelling about running a marathon? That's hard to understand if you haven't done one, and sometimes the most difficult to comprehend when you're in the middle of one!

GEORGE SHEEHAN ON THE UNIQUE EXPERIENCE OF RUNNING A MARATHON (1992)

George Sheehan's philosophical musings on running have inspired people for decades. What he wrote for the original edition of this book applies just as well today.

When I ran my first Boston Marathon, the racers were little more than an informal club. Of the 225 of us who ran, many were present only on a dare or as a joke. Others were overweight, out of shape, and attired in gym suits and sneakers.

That first year, I finished 96th in 3:07 and, because of this, considered myself one of the top 100 marathoners in the United States. Fifteen years later, at age 61, I ran a slightly faster time in the New York City Marathon. I didn't crack the top 2,000. As one of only 126 starters in the first New York Marathon in 1970, I have seen its field grow to more than 25,000.

Someone on the outside of these events might well ask, "What is going on?" Back in 1970, America was already interested in getting fit. Dr. Kenneth Cooper's aerobics book, for instance, had already sold hundreds of thousands of copies. Although an emphasis on fitness was on the rise, only a handful of people—and few, if any of them, women—ran races. And only the hard core ran marathons.

My son, who is both a runner and an observer of this scene, had his own explanation for the marathoning boom: "Fitness is out, experience is in." Running has gone beyond fitness. The jogging movement, which began as a pursuit of health, has become an experiential quest. Runners are no longer content with fitness, but are seeking a new awareness of the self in the total experience of running—and more often than not they are culminating that quest by experiencing a marathon.

The desire to run comes from deep within us—from the unconscious, the instinctive, the intuitive—and the runner's progression to a marathon is a natural one—how to train, what to do before a race, what shoes to wear, what pace to set at the start, when to accelerate, how to achieve the proper attitude. I have become ready for the part of the marathon that is pure body.

The marathon, however, is more than that. It is, to use Yeats's description of poetry, "blood, imagination, and intellect brought together." The marathoner comes to be the total person running the total race.

When I run a marathon, I put myself at the center of my life, the center of my universe. For these hours, I move past ideas of food and shelter and sexual fulfillment and other basic drives. I bring my life and its meaning down to this struggle, this supreme effort that I must make.

The music of the marathon is a powerful martial strain, a tune of glory. It asks us to forsake pleasures, to discipline the body, to find courage, to renew faith, and to become one's own person utterly and completely.

The athletic experience can be divided into three parts: the preparation (training the body), the event (challenging the self), and the aftermath (creating in the mind). For the runner, the marathon is the ultimate athletic experience pushing training, challenge, and creativity to their absolute limits.

Running has been described as a "thinking person's sport." The reference is to the predominance of middle-class, highly educated people who have taken up this activity. But it also refers to the fact that it is a sport requiring considerable study of the workings of the body. Runners in training acquire detailed knowledge of how the body operates best. One must have a working knowledge of exercise physiology and nutrition to come to a peak.

Training is the science of running. The application of that science is sensual. Runners have an expression, "Listen to your body." They understand that biofeedback machines merely amplify messages that should be heard without technology. They develop what Maslow called "biological wisdom." They become experts in their own bodies. They become good animals.

This listening and learning are often done by working at the edge of self-inflicted pain. Training on hills and with speedwork means repeatedly pushing the limits of tolerance to oxygen debt. At other times, however, training can be a pleasure; there are days when I get tremendous enjoyment out of the effort and the sweat and the competence I feel. Like Thoreau, I occupy my body with delight.

In training for a marathon, I grow in physical wisdom. I learn how my body works best. I read the texts, of course, but then I take those lessons and test them on the road. I filter the theories on exercise through my exercising body and come up with my own truth. I remake my body to my own image. I prepare myself for an exploration of my outer limits.

The marathon is the focal point of all that has gone before and all that will come afterward. "The distance race," wrote Paul Weiss, "is a struggle that results in self-discovery. It is an adventure involving the limits of the self." It is William James's moral equivalent of war—that theater for heroism where the runner can do deeds not possible in day-to-day living.

"Life," said James, "is made in doing and suffering and creating." It is all there in the marathon—the doing in training and the suffering in the race and, finally, the creating that comes in the tranquillity of the aftermath.

James spoke of the peace and confidence that come from every muscle of a well-trained body. Taking that body through a grueling 26.2-mile race improves one's self-concept and self-esteem immeasurably. Even more, it provides the material for the creative acts to follow.

Robert Frost once said that to write a poem you first must have an experience. To do any creative act, you must have an experience. To make your life a work of art, you must have the material to work with. The race, any race, is just such an experience. The marathon is that experience raised to the nth degree. It fills the conscious and unconscious with the sights and sounds, the feelings and the emotions, the trials and accomplishments of the event.

All That Matters Is Going the Distance

After I had finished the New York City Marathon, my daughter asked me if I had relived my past while running through the familiar streets. Surely, she thought, those miles must have brought back memories of my early life in Brooklyn and New York City.

Other spectators thought I must have been inspired by the spectacle at the start of the race, the helicopters hovering like fish in a giant mobile. And hadn't I been filled with emotion, they asked, when we passed through the enormous crowds lining the route, shouting encouragement?

In truth, none of these things happened. A marathon is not a city, nor is it a crowd. It is not a sense of nostalgia or one of the wonders of the world, whether man-made or natural.

The vista during the marathon is of no consequence. Degree of difficulty is what inevitably concerns me. Weather and terrain are my considerations. Other athletes view their playing areas similarly, not by the aesthetics but by what controls and influences performance.

The golfer looks at a famous hole on a famous course and sees only where the pin lies and what the wind is up to. The baseball player cares nothing about the history of a ballpark or about the classic games played there; he wants to know the distance down the foul lines and what the infield does to a ground ball.

It is a matter of what is important. Yeats once wrote that the English had too many flowers in their poetry. "Scenery is fine but human nature finer" is the way Shelley put it. I try not to let the flowers or the scenery distract me from the task at hand.

To me, a marathon is a marathon is a marathon. There is nothing else, just the matter of taking my body—five-feet-nine, 136 pounds, nine percent body fat, and 60 percent slow-twitch fibers—a distance of 26 miles, 385 yards. Everything that affects this accomplishment is important; everything else, irrelevant. Worse than that, it is distracting and, therefore, ultimately defeating.

I will not deny, however, that each marathon imposes itself on my memory. The finish of every one I have run—more than 50 of them since that first one in Boston—will stay with me the rest of my life. Coming down the plaza at Boston's Prudential Center is not something easily forgotten, nor is the last mile through New York's Central Park.

There is nothing to compare to the feeling I get on completing a marathon. But I must not think of that until the end comes. There are, you see, only two concerns in a marathon: pace and form. Each step, each stride, must be made in a perfect form and at the perfect speed.

This sounds simple. Running is, after all, a reflex act. Nine-year-olds do it perfectly. There is no reason why an adult with sufficient discipline should not develop an effortless technique that requires no thought of the action. And since the body perceives exertion as efficiently as any instrument yet invented, it can be depended upon to pick that perfect tempo as soon as I settle down to serious running.

Unfortunately, once the marathon begins, what seems so simple becomes unbearably complex. The body loses the rhythm and harmony I know on the practice runs, and the messages that determine so accurately my pace in training are garbled and indistinct.

There are 26 miles, 385 yards to go, and I must focus not on scenery or on memories, but on the basics of marathon survival.

Why Run? Who Knows for Sure?

Near the 23-mile mark of the New York City Marathon, I ran along in the grip of the inexpressible fatigue that comes at this stage in the race. I once again engaged in a struggle between a completely exhausted body and a yet-undefeated will.

As I ran past a group of onlookers, one of them recognized me and called out, "Dr. Sheehan, what would Emerson have said now?" I had to laugh, even in that pain. It was a particularly deft shot at someone who had used other people's words to express his own truth—and I was now in a situation that clearly no one else could describe. But the question also went to the heart of why I ran marathons.

The case for distance running cannot be stated simply, even by its adherents. No matter how often I am asked—usually in more favorable circumstances than at the 23-mile mark of a marathon—my answer is always inadequate.

This inadequacy is not only mine. At one race, a New York Road Runners Club questionnaire was distributed to the entrants asking them why they ran. The list of suggested answers had been made by scientists of both the body and the mind, and there were 15 possible choices, the last one being, "Don't really know." The range of possible answers suggested that the researchers knew the runners would have trouble putting a finger on their personal motivations.

I think it suggestive, however, that only three of the answers—"Improving physical health," "Improving sexual capacity," and "Acquiring a youthful appearance"—had to do with the body. All the others (except the final disclaimer of not knowing at all) were about psychological benefits. Runners apparently take it as given that physical health is a by-product of, but not the real reason for, running,

I, too, am aware of that. I am my body. What I do begins there. But I am much more besides. What happens to my body has enormous effect on my heart and mind. When I run, I become, of necessity, a good animal. But I also become, for less obvious and more mysterious reasons, a good person. I become, in some uncanny way, complete. Perhaps it has something to do with a sense of success and mastery over this art of running.

The scientists tried to express this in their suggested answers. Do I run, they asked, to relax, to relieve boredom, or to improve my mental health? Is it possible, they inquired, that I do it to achieve recognition or to master a challenge or to find an additional purpose in life? Was running perhaps something I do for companionship and a sense of belonging, or because I am unhappy or unfulfilled without it?

What we were being asked was cast in the familiar "either/or" form. Is it process or product that pushes us? Is it what happens while we run, or what we achieve through running that motivates us? Is running for the body or the spirit?

Runners Are Different

My running is not an either/or activity. It is done for all these reasons and more. The product—the ability to run a marathon, the having done it—is indeed important, but so is the process. Training is not only a means, it is also an end in itself. The achievement is not the sole reason for running. There is also what goes on before the mastering of the challenge, what goes on while finding an additional purpose in life.

My running is both process and product. Sometimes it is all meaning and no purpose. Other times it is all purpose and no meaning. Sometimes it is work, other times play, and there are even times when it is an act of love.

We who run are different from those who merely study us. We are out experimenting what they are trying to put into words. We know what they are merely trying to know. They are seeking belief, while we already believe. Our difficulty is in expressing the whole truth of that experience, that knowledge, that belief.

So I wish Emerson had run that marathon, and that somewhere around the 23-mile mark a friend had asked him, "What's it all about, Waldo?"

Public Spectacle, Interior Drama

James Joyce took ten years of Homer's *Odyssey* and compressed it into a single Dublin day. He looked into the mind and heart and body of the hero Ulysses, and created Leopold Bloom, who is Everyman. Joyce took those inner and outer events that happen to everyone and put all of them into the waking-to-sleeping day of his Irish Jew. It takes 18 hours.

The marathon does it in three. Like many sports events, the marathon is a microcosm of life. The marathoner can experience the drama of everyday existence so evident to the artist and poet. All emotions are heightened. Agony and ecstasy become familiar feelings. The journey from start to finish reveals what happens to a person who faces up to the self and the world—and why he or she succeeds or fails.

The successful runner is the one who endures, taking life as it comes and saying yes to it. This trait is so commonly displayed in the marathon that it seems universal. I believe every human must have this endurance capacity.

The truth is that every runner in a marathon is a survivor or nothing, including the winner. Winning is, in fact, unimportant.

"Brief is the season of a man's delight," sang Pindar in his ode to an Olympic winner. Tomorrow is another race, another test, another challenge. And then there is another race, and another.

THE NEW YORK CITY MARATHON

Among the hundreds of races and programs created and conducted by NYRR, the New York City Marathon is the crown jewel. The marathon (and New York in particular) is more than just a footrace, it's an event. For a single Sunday every November, millions of people from all over the world come together for a challenge and a celebration in one of the most complex and grandest cities in the world. They call New York the Big Apple, and at least for a day, these people make it shine. And they make themselves shine—by running, or cheering, by volunteering to hand out water or put adhesive bandages on blisters. "I couldn't have picked a better race for my first marathon than New York in 2001," says American marathon record holder Deena Kastor. "All of my expectations were surpassed. The people, the history, just running on the streets of New York City—it was very special. After September 11, it was very patriotic, which made it more memorable. The atmosphere was even greater than I expected. How the race officials organize an event of this size in New York City is an amazement to me."

First off, the women's side of the race is so much more competitive now. It's amazing to see. The depth of competition, the pace—everything. The women's competition is now on par with the men, and it's exciting to see that.

For the race in general, the prize money development has helped the sport tremendously. It gives huge national media coverage to these amazing athletes. It enhances the race and gives it more visibility.

Even all the amenities like the pasta party, goody bag, and the expo—it's all an experience now. I see friends from all over the world when I show up at the expo; it brings the whole running community together.

—Bill Rodgers

What's more, the marathon represents a perfect human journey, a 26.2-mile odyssey through New York's neighborhoods. It is a journey that changes lives—from the disabled who prove something to themselves and others, to the dedicated yet, perhaps, unknown athletes who will cross the finish line first and, in so doing, change their lives forever.

The New York City Marathon is one of the largest races in the world. Next year it might not be. "It doesn't really matter," Fred Lebow once explained. "We're not reaching for the numbers—to be the biggest. We aspire only to be the best. In fact, we don't even want to be the fastest marathon. We want to have the most *competitive* marathon. What has always been most important above all, however, is to make sure that every single runner—not only the elite, but even the six- and seven-hour finisher—is treated with dignity and care."

I have been asked everywhere I go: Why do people run the marathon? Sure, there is a sense of status we gain among our peers. But I think the real reasons are more personal. I think it is because we need to test our physical, emotional, or creative abilities. After all, in practical life we cannot all "give it our all." We can't grow wings and fly. We can't sing without a great voice, or dance when we aren't dancers. Most of us won't perform on a stage. But whether a person is a world-class athlete or a four-hour runner, the marathon gives us a stage. In this case, it's the road, where we can perform and be proud, while millions of people applaud. It's like being on Broadway and getting a standing ovation!

For another thing, in an unequal world, in this one endeavor people of vastly differing abilities share something in common: the act of going the distance. Whether it's two hours or four or five, the effort and achievement are similar.

—Fred Lebow

Said Fred Lebow of the marathon, "It makes me feel good when people come up to me and say things about the marathon like, 'It changed my life.' Just to share the feeling of satisfaction people get is one of the reasons I always stand near the finish line to greet the four- and five-hour finishers. That's why I've always known that the marathon is more than just a 26.2-mile footrace; it's a life experience. It has always been that way for me, and over the years, I've seen that's true for the other runners who do it."

"This is not to downplay the vast importance of the world-class level of competition. Every winner of the race has thrilled and inspired millions of people, from television viewers to back-of-the-pack marathoners in the same race."

THE WHEELCHAIR DIVISION

While there have long been wheelchair entrants in the New York City Marathon, the Wheelchair Division did not become an official part of the marathon until the 2000 event.

Each year, many of the top wheelchair racers in the world compete in the New York City Marathon. Like the runners, wheelchair athletes who have completed a marathon within the past two years in under a specified qualifying time (as of 2003, 2:40 for men and 3:40 for women) are given automatic entry into the marathon. A number of international professional racers are given special invitations to compete in New York, which features over $13,000 in prize money. The result each year is one of the largest, most competitive fields of wheelchair racers of any marathon in the world.

The current course record for men of 1:32:19 was set in 2003 by Krige Schabort, originally from South Africa, who now lives and trains in Cedartown, Georgia. The women's record of 1:59:30 was set in 2003 by Chesi Blaumet of the United States.

The New York course is a particularly challenging one for wheelchair races, given its twists and turns as it winds through the five boroughs, and its many bridges with steep inclines. The difficulty of the course is perhaps best illustrated by the fact that the equivalent course records for the Boston Marathon, perhaps the granddaddy of wheelchair marathons and considered a fast wheelchair course, are 1:21:23 and 1:34:22, for men and women, respectively. Ernst Van Dyk, the three-time winner of the Boston Marathon, won that event in 2003, in a time of 1:28:32, but recorded a time of 1:35:36 in finishing second to Schabort in New York in 2003.

All Wheelchair Division athletes traverse the same Marathon course as the more than 34,000 runners. The wheelchair racers have their own special start, however, at 9:05 A.M., 30 minutes ahead of the elite women runners and one hour ahead of the elite men runners (and the rest of the field). The separate, early start—a practice followed in most major marathons—allows the wheelchair racers to avoid the runners and gives them a chance to showcase their talents at the front of the Marathon entourage.

New York City Marathon Wheelchair Race Coordinator Bob Laufer points out that the Boston Marathon has long treated wheelchair athletes on a par with all other participants, granting them equivalent television coverage and pre- and post-event promotion, as well as substantial prize money. Says Laufer, "We like to think that, while still in the early stages of our Wheelchair Division, we have made the New York City Marathon the Boston Marathon of the fall for wheelchair athletes—giving them media exposure, top-notch competition, and awards which will attract the best of the racers to New York City each year."

The cheers from the Marathon's over two million spectators for the wheelchair athletes are strong testimony for Laufer's contention and NYRR's efforts in creating a showcase for its wheelchair racers.

If I could change something about my marathon career, I would've required I be given an Olympic medal! No, seriously, there isn't much I would change. Although I would have loved to have won an Olympic medal, I am content with my accomplishments as a runner. During my career, I was the fourth fastest marathoner in the world, and New York City Marathon recordholder twice. The Olympic race wasn't in the cards for me; I didn't have the greatest day.

Would I have liked to have run faster during my career? Sure, but you have to compare yourself to the people in your era. People are running faster now because we know more about training for speed. But in my day, we did what we thought was best at the time. I have nothing but fond memories of my running career.

Today, I think there definitely have been advances in training. I always recommend massage and cross training; they are both beneficial to runners. I started getting massages in 1990. Even in the 1980s, we had picked up sports nutrition. I think there's more understanding now about weight training and running hills. There's more emphasis on timing. Workouts are now geared towards speed.

Before running was professionalized, when I was racing in the 1970s, some of the courses weren't accurately measured. Today it's an entirely different mindset. The standards have all come up. When the sport was professionalized, it raised the bar for everyone.

—Bill Rodgers

The New York City Marathon is truly grand. Exactly how big and how grand is it? Here are a few facts that shed light on the marathon's stature. The New York City Marathon is:

1. Among the largest marathons in the world, with over 34,000 participants from all 50 states and nearly 100 countries. (In 2003, over 73,000 runners applied to participate.) Amazingly, more than 98% of those who start finish.

2. The largest women's marathon field in the world, with over 11,000 in 2003. Beginning in 2002, New York has featured a unique elite women's race.

3.   The largest spectator sporting event in the world. (According to the New York City Police Department, more than 2 million people line the streets at various times during the race.)

4.   The site of three women's world records, one men's world record, and over 20 sub-2:10 times for men.

5.   The site of the 2001 USA Men's and Women's National Championships.

6.   The largest field of international runners of any marathon (approximately 10,000).

7.   Other "world records" include the world's longest urinal (328 feet) and the greatest number of volunteers for any mass sporting event (an estimated 12,000).

8.   As of 2003, New York offers $532,000 in guaranteed prize money (not including time bonuses), the most ever for the event.

MARATHON TRAINING AND RACING

There is no one program to prepare for a marathon and no single way to prepare on race day. We offer a variety of advice. Pick what suits you best.

Nina Kuscsik's Training Program for the Marathon

If you've been running for at least a year, have done some shorter races, or have been running 20 or more miles a week for the past three months, you may be ready to begin training to run the marathon. If you need to build up to 20 miles a week, remember to do so gradually; don't add more than 10 percent of your current mileage per week. You need to pick a race to work toward. The training program here allows for six months of preparation (or less, if you're a more advanced runner).

A successful training program follows the principle of adaptation to progressive stress. Research and experience show that all progress is made by stressing the body, allowing it recovery time, then stressing it again. Many helpful changes take place when the body is in a recovery period. For beginning runners, recovery means taking a day off. For those training for a marathon, recovery also takes place on easy running days. You will improve by respecting this cycle.

Marathon training must balance endurance and speed stress with recovery. The priority for first-time marathoners is to concentrate on endurance, because you need to increase your overall mileage and also the distance of your weekly long run. So the core part of your program will be building for the long runs. As you can see on the training schedule (see table on page 214), the stress levels are changed from day to day and from week to week.

> I had a great experience running the marathon in New York in 2002. Is it my best? No. But it was my first time at that distance, so I learned a tremendous amount about the last miles of the marathon. The final four or five miles were pretty rough, so I've learned what it feels like to push through to the end of a marathon. When I ran my first 10K at the Penn Relays back in 1995 during my freshman year at UCLA, I got lapped and said to myself, "I'm never going to run another 10K again. Stick to running the one-mile and two-mile races. That's what you're good at." Then I realized not every race is that way. Now I'm the fastest American in the 10,000 meters. You have to work to overcome struggles, both in racing and in life. The same goes for the marathon. It's not easy, but it's about learning a little bit each time you're out there.
>
> *—Meb Keflezighi*

Those who run 25 miles a week can join the schedule at week 5. Those who run 40 miles a week should adjust their program until they are doing a long run of 12 miles a week for three weeks and then move into marathon training for a minimum of three months.

How fast should you go on your everyday runs? Most people try to train at a pace that's too fast. Don't. Pushing it will promote injury and fatigue and will work against your completing your first marathon. Instead, put yourself at a cruise pace—don't push, yet don't go so slow you feel like you're not doing anything.

The mileage amounts on the training schedule are guidelines. The emphasis should be on gradually building the length of the long run and the total mileage per week. You need to build to 40 miles per week and hold that for eight to ten weeks, then taper down the last two to three weeks leading to race day. Remember, your overall increase in mileage

The tendency with marathon training is to overdo. The big mystery is how much mileage you can handle and still maintain a certain amount of intensity as well. For most top runners, I think that's about 105 miles per week. I've done more; I've done less. For my first marathon, I did much less. I've been trying to find the key mixture. I know what I need and what I like. I like long runs of 18 to 22 miles, and one 25-miler. I like one hard-paced run a week, 12 to 15 miles; one speed session of fartlek, 1 to 1 1/2 hours, or intervals of 1 to 3 1/2 minutes. (During marathon season, my coach and I formulate a buildup based on doing longer intervals.)

Now that I'm a marathoner I've realized that you've got to be careful with marathoning. It can kill you off quickly. It's a matter of being able to handle doing what you must to prepare properly for the event. While I enjoy the challenge of the marathon, I don't enjoy the feeling of being dead-legged all the time. It's not fun to be tired. My advice to other runners is to stay with the shorter races, and maybe do the marathon at most once a year.

—*Francie Larrieu Smith*

should not average more than ten percent a week, and it's beneficial if your mileage increases for several weeks, then levels off—or even decreases—for a week. This allows for recovery time to adapt to the new stresses.

If you have a running background of several years and have more time to prepare for your marathon, you may be able to raise your mileage up to 50 to 55 miles for eight to 12 weeks. This mileage gives you a different marathon experience. Your pace may be the same, but you seem to retain more flexibility in mind and body during the race. At 50 to 55 miles, many weeks can contain a ten-miler in addition to the long run. The training effect from handling more runs seems to make the difference.

Now check the training schedule against your work and social schedule for the next six months. Check the days in each week to schedule in your runs. You can write your schedule on a calendar or in a small book with blank pages. This will become your running log or diary. Plan time now for your five or six runs a week. Include time for stretching. Do you have a training partner? Coordinate schedules. Do you want to use a weekend morning for the long run, or would you be better off doing it during the week?

As you complete your runs, you can record them into the log. You can write in insights and feelings as you go. Document energy levels experienced on your long runs. Write down when you start breaking in new shoes.

You are embarking on a long-term goal. Any perks that keep you motivated are healthy. The diary is one of them and helps you build confidence when you look at it and see how far you have already come.

THE LONG RUN

In *The New Competitive Runner's Handbook,* author Bob Glover states that the long run of the week is "the single most important ingredient to marathon success." It is also the biggest challenge.

Before the marathon race itself, you will taper down your training for two to three weeks so you'll be rested. After the marathon, you have a recovery period without limits. But your long runs happen right in the middle of your training—with only a day or two of recovery. Respect the distance, as it will make you a marathon runner.

You don't need to run longer than 20 miles in training. Running too many miles at one time not only increases the chances of injury, but also produces a state of fatigue that lingers and interferes with training.

The long runs, done at a relaxed and even pace—for most people, a little slower than the everyday training pace—make you energy-efficient. They teach your body to utilize fat as well as glycogen as fuel to produce muscular energy. As exercise continues into hours, glycogen levels drop and a physiological fatigue sets in. This is known as "hitting the wall." But by doing these regular long runs, our bodies become efficient at utilizing more fat energy and less glycogen energy. This helps keep sufficient energy reserves for the latter stages of the run. Also, on your long runs you can practice taking water and energy replacement drinks; even energy bars and gels, on the second half of your run.

Usually you'll find your stride will shorten on longer runs. This is energy-efficient and will help you relax. You will take more steps per mile, but each step takes less energy. Monitor yourself as you tire. Try to keep up a regular rhythm in terms of the number of steps per minute you take. Your arms should not work harder. Your shoulders may begin to tighten, and that may give you a headache. Try dropping your jaw, arms, and shoulders at the same time for about twenty seconds. This will relax the shoulder and neck muscles.

Racing is completely based on your training. There are no illusions. Cheerleaders can't help you. The outcome is based on what you've done in the months before. Success results from months and months of consistent training, and then by honing it, such as with a series of races leading up to the big one. The key is to get to the starting line—after those months of training and several weeks of tapering and rest—in peak shape.

I think the number one mistake the average runner makes is overextensive training and racing, and racing beyond one's training. I know people out there who are doing four-hour runs on weekends and they've got regular, full-time jobs. Those of us who run for a living spend a lot of time running, but those with other full-time jobs may do just as much.

The main problem is that most people simply don't know how to train properly and, therefore, they're breaking down with injuries left and right. They don't know what shoe is right, either. Let's face it, a lot of places that sell running shoes still don't know how to advise the running customer properly.

—Bill Rodgers

SPEEDWORK

Speedwork is any running done faster than your everyday training pace. It helps improve your running form and leg strength. Through this work, you and your body learn how to pace yourself while in the discomfort of oxygen debt, how to recover from it, and then how to go back into it. From speed training, you gain the ability and confidence to push yourself a little harder in workouts and in races.

If you haven't done much speedwork in the past, you may need to wait until you've gotten used to the stress of higher mileage. If you try speedwork and it tires you so badly that your mileage suffers, hold it off longer. Even without speedwork, if you follow the training schedule, with its built-in stress/rest cycle, you may find your pace picking up.

After you've adapted to the higher mileage, though—as tolerated—you can give speedwork a try. Increase the pace of some of your runs. You can run over hillier courses or pick up the pace near the end of a run, even on your longer runs.

Speedwork for first-time marathon training does not need to be run faster than 10K pace—and even work at this pace should be limited to once a week and should not total more than 7 to 10 percent of your total weekly mileage.

Some sample speed workouts you can do on a track are eight to twelve 440s (a 440 is 440 yards, or once around the track), with slow jogs, lasting 220 to 440 yards, between each fast run for recovery; and four one-mile runs (a mile is four times around the track) with 440- to 660-yard recoveries. The warmup, the cool-downs, the fast runs, and the recovery jogs are added together to make the day's mileage total.

Races are part of the larger training picture and can be goals in themselves. They can be fun and can help you mark your progress. Even if you haven't done speedwork, you are likely to see improvement at a race because of your added mileage.

Shorter races can be handled as a speedwork day; longer races—10 miles to 25K—can double as long runs, but limit them to one a month. In the long races you'll learn the importance of starting slow enough, you can practice drinking water on the run, and you get great feedback on your pace because the elapsed time is usually called out or displayed at each mile marker.

You are unique, and your training program should reflect your individuality. Your age, weight, athletic background, and biomechanical, physiological, and psychological processes are special to you and coordinate best when your training plan is designed to meet your needs. The following tips may help.

- **Compare sensibly.** When you admire the performance of another runner, don't think that if you follow the same training program you can run like her or him. Consider age, build, lifestyle, and running experience. Then learn how the runner trained when she or he was at your level and adapt that information into your training program.

- **Don't overlook running with others.** This can add variety and fun to your training. It's good to agree on pace and distance in advance; however, sometimes you still end up running harder or longer than you planned. If so, run easier than planned the next day or so. Doing speedwork with others is a powerful way to train and is very different from doing it alone. Be sure that you don't get caught up in racing on each repetition.

- **Be consistent but flexible.** Having a long-term schedule really helps here. If you miss a few days or a week because of illness, injury, vacation, or unexpected events, there is time to get back on schedule. But gradually ease back into it; it may take several weeks to catch up, and that is okay.

Flexibility pays off, but use caution. You can miss sleep occasionally and get away with it, for instance, but if cutting sleep to get in planned mileage becomes a habit and the result is a lower energy level, you may need to re-examine your goals.

- **Beware of overtraining.** This problem—and it's a concrete physical and mental problem—comes from too much mileage, too much intensity, or just too much too soon. The results are chronic fatigue, working harder to stay on your usual training pace, a loss of interest, restless sleep, possible cold symptoms, and possible injury.

  What to do? Cut back mileage by at least a third, and cut down the intensity. Sleep late, enjoy a dinner out or a movie. It's truly the only solution. When you're feeling more yourself, resume training gradually—and train easier!

- **Stretch.** And do it on your rest days as well as your running days. After a long or hard run, cool down, stretch, then gently stretch again about an hour later. (It's good to stretch warm muscles.)

- **Watch your running shoes.** You may be thrilled by how comfortable your shoes are midway through your training program. But will they still be in good condition 12 weeks later? The midway point may be a good time to buy and break in a new pair. *Do* buy good shoes.

- **Respect the weather.** In winter weather, stay off icy surfaces. Running on them increases your chances of injury by slipping or by altering your running style. Also, head into the wind when first going out on those cold days so you'll have it at your back on the way home. This is especially important on your long runs, because in the latter stages as you tire, you produce less heat and can get chilled too easily. Always bring a hat and mittens or gloves on the long runs. Tuck them away in your pockets or waistband, if you find you don't need them.

  Hot weather slows the pace and dehydrates the body. Drink lots of liquids during the day and during your runs. Try to run early in the morning or in the evening, when it's usually cooler and you're out of the sun's most intense rays. Training classes for the Honolulu Marathon teach that you must drink enough so that your urine is clear of noticeable color at least once a day.

- **Don't change your habits the days before the race.** Don't eat strange foods or stuff yourself. You can carbohydrate-load just by changing the proportions of your diet; eat less protein and more complex carbohydrates. The day before your marathon, run a few miles and stretch. Then try not to do a lot of standing around. Don't go shopping or to exhibits. Eat a simple early dinner the night before.

MARATHON DAY

Eat a light breakfast at least three hours before the race. Don't wear any new clothes to run in. You need proven comfort more than appearance. Pin your number on your race shirt before you leave home. Drink liquids and put petroleum jelly on your friction areas. Warm up just a little and stretch gently before the race.

During the race itself, you want to run as effortlessly as possible for the first ten kilometers (6.2 miles) at least. It should feel as if you're holding back some; if you're pushing the pace to reach a projected mile time, you're going too fast too early. Slow *down*. Burn your fat, not your glycogen. If it's an unusually warm or cold day, readjust your time to a slower pace.

In terms of psychological and energy reserves, the first half of the race is 16 miles and the last half ten. Remember form and rhythm. Keep your stride economical. Don't push hard up or down the hills. Just run.

If you have to run an uneven stride because of any pain that develops and persists, seriously think about dropping out; otherwise, you risk greater injury. Slow down or walk if you have cramps or a stitch or just feel that you have to. Every step counts.

Drink liquids as prescribed (see Chapter 27). If you've learned to drink a diluted carbohydrate drink or eat orange slices or energy bars or gels in practice races or on training runs, this will help you, especially in the last half. Try to drink some every 20 minutes. The carbohydrates really help keep you alert, and research shows that they help performance when running over 1 1/2 hours.

You are well prepared for this event. That makes it possible, if not easy, to finish. Sometimes it's not so easy: In the last ten kilometers you may be going along okay, then suddenly be uncertain if you can run two more steps. This is where you begin to dig deep and find reasons for going on. Spectators help with words of encouragement. Watch how little children will look at you in wonder.

You *are* a wonder. Just keep up your form and rhythm. The choice in every step is yours and becomes a big decision. You can go faster, slower, shuffle, walk, or stop. And you trained for six months for this? Yes, it really is a glorious journey. Congratulations.

The table on page 214 is Nina Kuscsik's sample schedule for a first-time marathoner who has made a long-term commitment to training for the

Anyone who runs more than two marathons a year, given the physical stress, has to be doing it mainly for some psychological reason—one that's even beyond the reason I run. It must have to do with a reinforcement of accomplishment, rather than a reinforcement of performance.

Anybody who runs more than two marathons a year is not going to run his or her best marathon in that year, unless it's the first or second one. If they say they ran harder in their third, my answer to that is: "You must have been holding back because you knew you were going to run another one."

The point is the recovery aspect. I ran the Honolulu Marathon easy, just as a training run, and three weeks later I was just getting back to the point where I could train again. And my recovery is pretty good. So I can't understand the people who run many marathons. Perhaps they have a talent for running more, easier—and that's how they get their reinforcement.

—Frank Shorter

event. Remember, these are guidelines and can be adjusted according to how you feel.

FRED LEBOW'S MARATHON CHECKLIST

Fred Lebow was a master race director who advised runners all over the world. He also saw, ran, and tested scores of marathons and other races. Here are his tips.

1. A pretty course is nice, but it's meaningless if efficiency is not an event's top priority. Make sure the course is properly measured. (It should be advertised that the course is "certified.") Also, the event should have frequent mile or kilometer markers, or both, and clocks or split timers.

2. Water, water everywhere. The race should include lots of fluid stations—at the start, along most every mile or kilometer, and at the finish.

3. Location of the start and finish. It is best that either of these are close to the place you are staying. Check for important amenities.

For example, since 1991, the New York City Marathon buses that take runners to the start are equipped with rest rooms. And although it's about a 30-minute trip to the start, when the runners get there, rest rooms and a light breakfast, including hot drinks, are provided.

FIRST MARATHON: THE SIX-MONTH TRAINING SCHEDULE

Week	Mon.	Tues.	Wed.	Thurs.	Fri.	Sat.	Sun.	Total Miles
1	—	4	5	3	—	3	7	22
2	—	4	5	4	—	3	7	23
3	—	4	5	4	—	3	9	25
4	—	4	5	4	—	3	7	23
5	—	4	6	3	—	3	9	25
6	—	4	6	4	—	3	10	27
7	—	4	6	4	2	4	10	30
8	—	4	6	4	3	3	12	32
9	—	4	6	4	—	4	12	30
10	—	4	7	5	3	4	10	33
11	—	4	7	3	4	3	12	33
12	—	5	8	5	3	4	10	35
13	—	4	7	4	6	4	12	37
14	—	5	7	4	5	4	15	40
15	—	4	6	4	6	4	12	36
16	—	4	8	4	6	4	15	41
17	—	4	8	4	7	5	12	40
18	—	4	10	4	6	4	15	43
19	—	3	8	0	7	3	18	39
20	—	6	10	5	7	3	12	43
21	—	4	8	0	7	4	20	43
22	—	3	7	5	9	4	12	40
23	—	5	10	5	—	4	20	44
24	—	3	6	3	8	3	15	38
25	—	4	8	4	—	4	12	32
26	—	4	6	4	—	2	MARATHON	

4. It's preferable that race registration include an expo (exposition)—a type of fair—with exhibits, demonstrations, and services relevant to runners. This is an important part of the ambience, and part of the social aspect of the event. In that vein, it's also nice if the race includes a pasta party and/or reception. It doesn't have to be a big race to feature these things.

5. If you're going to travel to the race, it should be a place to which you can fly directly. If getting to a race is a chore, it drains a lot of mental and physical energy better used to run.

6. Speak to friends and other runners for advice and useful tips on races they have run, preferably the one you are about to undertake.

NEW YORK RUNNER'S RACE DAY ADVICE

Take care of pre-race details as early as possible in order to free yourself to focus on physical tapering and mental preparation. Make a checklist of what must be done before the race and do it. The following tips for marathon races appeared in *New York Runner,* but many of them can generally apply to any other race.

Pre-Race

- For a marathon, be sure to get plenty of sleep, carbo-load effectively, and keep hydrated during the marathon countdown.

- Double check how you'll get to the starting line and home after finishing. Have a back-up plan in place for anything that could go wrong: the car doesn't start, you miss the bus to the start, and so on.

- Avoid introducing anything new into your life during the final weeks, such as starting a new job or work project, moving, or remodeling. Some runners tend to do something counterproductive at the last minute out of nervousness. Whether it's trying out a different workout, switching to fast-looking new shoes, or stuffing yourself with a magical food or supplement, if you're not used to it, don't do it.

- At least a month in advance, pick out the shoes and clothing you'll wear. This gives you plenty of time to break them in. Because you won't know the race day weather forecast, select a variety of potential outfits.

- Use your last long run and race as a full dress rehearsal. Practice carbo-loading, drink the same sports drinks that will be available on the course, and eat the same sports gels or other fuels you'll consume during the marathon. Run at the same time of day you will for the marathon. Wear the same clothes and shoes.

- Carbo-load and hydrate properly, but taper off caloric intake slightly as you cut back mileage to avoid unnecessary weight gain. About 100 calories equals a mile of running.

- Try to avoid catching a last-minute cold or flu. You should taper early, get enough sleep, wash your hands often, and keep away from as many potentially germ-carrying people as possible.

- Cut out cross training and weight training over the final two weeks to better rest your muscles.

- Relax, rest. Stick to less physical ways to spend your time—read a book or go to the movies—and save every ounce of extra physical energy for the marathon. Avoid tasks requiring prolonged heavy thinking or that produce stress.

- Stay off your feet as much as possible the last three days and on marathon morning. Use walking tours as part of post-race recovery. Enjoy sightseeing once the stress of the marathon is out of the way.

- Avoid the pre-marathon hoopla. Don't spend hours at pre-race clinics, exhibits, and so forth. By all means go for a few minutes to enjoy the atmosphere, but don't spend a lot of time on your feet.

- Get the weather report and adjust clothing and race strategy accordingly. Avoid being out in the sun as much as possible the last few days before the race.

- Organize your support crew. Encourage lots of people to be on the course to give you a cheer. Review how you will meet running partners at the start, and friends and family at the finish area.

- If you want the crowd along the way to give you an extra boost, wear something distinctive. Print or write a name or slogan on your singlet to give spectators something to cheer about.

- Throughout the marathon countdown, think "calm." Focus on staying relaxed. Expect to feel edgy as the big day approaches. This is normal and happens to all marathoners.

Race Day

- For a morning race, wake up at least three hours before starting time to give yourself plenty of time to fuel up, dress, recheck your bag, etc. Arrive at the race at least two hours early (one hour for a lower-key and shorter distance event), in time to take care of pre-race concerns without feeling rushed.

- Be prepared as much as possible for changes in the weather. A good choice is to position your support crew along the course with extra clothing. You may start the race with an extra shirt you can toss away after you've warmed up, but don't overdress since you'll heat up during the race.

- Don't waste energy with a running warmup on marathon morning, but don't get stiff by standing or sitting too long either. Move around every 15 minutes or so.

- Know where the starting line is, and in a big event, as start time gets close, position yourself so as not to get caught in a crowd and not be able to make it to your planned starting spot.

GRETE WAITZ'S MARATHON ADVICE

Before the Race

1. Be truly motivated to train for a marathon. Do it for yourself—not on a bet or a dare or because "everyone else does."

2. Be well trained. Maybe some people will feel this is unfair, but I personally do not feel that a normal, healthy younger person needs six hours to finish a marathon. Others must agree, as there is a time cutoff in some marathons.

3. To begin the racing experience with the marathon is to start at the wrong end. Take a couple of years to build a running base and try shorter distance races. You may even discover that 26.2 miles is not your ideal distance.

4. Be sensible about your expectations. If you want to run three or four hours and just enjoy the scenery, fine. If you are running competitively (even on a relative level), however, be prepared not only for the physical rigors but also for the effort of enormous concentration.

5. Marathon training is no great mystery. Don't throw your current training out the window in search of that "magic" marathon program. My marathon training is fundamentally the same as my

training for shorter distances, except the mileage is higher. I still do speedwork, but add a long run once a week leading up to the race, about 15 to 18 miles. The importance of maintaining quality training for a marathon is illustrated by the fact that most of today's top marathoners have also been top track runners.

6.   You should build up your long run slowly, the same way you build all mileage, and make sure to get used to running on asphalt if you aren't already.

7.   The hard/easy rule still applies for marathon training. Intersperse rest/recovery after hard efforts. If you're running fairly low mileage, allow for some days off. At 40 miles a week, you might try taking off the day before the long run. It's often not how many miles you run, but how they're distributed that counts.

8.   Do some shorter races leading up to the marathon. They are important as intermediate goals, for achievement and confidence, and to prepare you for the big day.

9.   Be especially careful to avoid overtraining and injury. The bigger the event, the more we tend to push ourselves in training. For marathon training, the basic warnings still apply—when in doubt, do less rather than more. Be even more conservative as you approach the race. First and foremost, get to the starting line healthy.

10.   Practice drinking fluids in training. If you plan to drink anything other than water, such as a sports drink, try it in training as well.

11.   Eat a balanced diet, including the foods that best supplement training and racing efforts. I already eat a high-carbohydrate diet, so I don't deliberately change what I eat before a marathon. I just add more food according to my hunger. I never eat a big meal the night before any race, as it usually just gives me trouble the next day. I find it better to eat a bigger lunch and lighter dinner the day before a marathon.

12.   If medical services are located at the start of a race, do not hesitate to ask questions. If complimentary pre-event massage is provided, the New York City Marathon Medical Committee suggests a five-minute session to help loosen you up. This, however, does not replace your warmup and stretching before the race. Massage therapists at the start of the New York City Marathon use no creams or oils that might clog pores needed for sweating.

During the Race

1. Respect the distance. Think ahead, past the great feeling in the early miles. Twenty miles is where the race really begins.

2. Take the race one mile at a time, being flexible enough to adapt to the unknown and the unexpected, including weather and/or course conditions and your personal biorhythms on race day.

3. The last half hour of the marathon is always difficult for me. I often use relaxation techniques at this point. I tell myself to relax each specific part of my body—neck, shoulders, arms. Then I may repeat some words like "steady, push" to keep up the pace and my confidence.

4. Drop out if you have to. I believe in sticking with an effort, and I have never dropped out of any road race other than a marathon. When I did drop out of those two marathons, I knew I had to. Because of the length of the race, there's a much greater potential for serious problems. The race is not worth risking illness or injury. There's a difference between difficulty and danger, and you will have to learn to judge for yourself what would necessitate stopping. Major marathons have aid stations at each mile, so if in doubt, consult a medical expert.

Finishing Tips

During the race, blood has been redirected to your legs, away from your internal organs. This is "normal" physiology that you should know about. You must continue to walk after finishing your race; move for at least 20 minutes. If you don't walk and stop or sit down, the blood flow to your internal organs will not redirect quickly to the pre-race state. You would then feel nauseous (not enough blood flow to the stomach) and vomit, as well as feel very dizzy and weak. Walking helps to redirect your blood and bring you back to your "everyday" physiology. Drink fluids slowly at the finish and certainly not until you have adequately "walked it off."

After the Race

1. A full and careful recovery from a marathon is extremely important. Recovery measures should begin the moment you finish. Keep moving, get warm, and drink water. The days following the

race I maintain a state of "active rest." I walk or jog and get a massage within a day or two if my legs aren't too painful to be touched. Most runners are concerned about loading up with carbohydrates before the race but fail to replenish afterward. I eat the same diet after the race as I do before the race. More people probably get injured from insufficient recovery measures than from the marathon itself. My own motto is, it's a waste of time to train to be a better runner for at least a couple of weeks after a marathon.

2. No matter how the run goes, remember that every marathon is a learning experience; you can never learn too much about the event.

3. While massage therapists are used at the finish of the marathon to assist in relieving cramps, post-event massage has been shown by medical studies to be contraindicated within the first two hours after running; it does not prevent post-event muscle soreness. Research has shown that from two hours post-finish on is the most effective time for post-event massage.

21

ULTRAMARATHON

RUNNING AN ULTRA—
CAN YOU GO THE DISTANCE?

There is a "beyond" for a distance runner. It's called the ultramarathon, which is any run farther than the 26-mile, 385-yard marathon. What does it take to run an ultramarathon? Ted Corbitt, one of the most renowned and accomplished pioneers of the sport of long-distance running, was also a master at ultramarathon distances. He set national records at 25, 40, 50, and 100 miles and was inducted into the National Distance Running Hall of Fame in its inaugural class of 1998. The Ted Corbitt Award is presented annually by USATF to outstanding American ultramarathoners. Corbitt has written extensively on the subject and offers the following advice:

"If the thoroughly trained marathoner has courage, patience, and a willingness to keep moving in the presence of deep, monotonous fatigue, that person can run up to 50 miles based on marathon training. Sergey Popov of Russia, and later Abebe Bikila of Ethiopia, world record holders in the marathon, both expressed the feeling that they could have run for another 10 kilometers.

"The biggest mistake to avoid when running ultras—and all races, for that matter—is to run too many. When you are running well, there is a temptation to do too much. You feel invincible. Even if you don't verbalize it, it's there subconsciously. But especially in the long distances, it can truly shorten your career.

"Beyond 50 miles puts a runner into another world. Longer training runs—up to 30 miles at a time—and weekly distances of 100 to 200 miles for extended periods of time, integrated with judicious rest periods, prepare a runner for any ultramarathon challenge. Not all runners, however, thrive on this level of training.

"In addition to patience, to run ultramarathons one must possess the ability to suffer, both physically and mentally. Ultras last for hours! Another ultra runner once called it "monotonous agony." Ultramarathoning, however, can give you the same sense of achievement and self-esteem that all running provides. With ultras, you don't have to be a champion; it is gratifying just to finish. But like all running endeavors, you have to keep going

Ted Corbitt, who at the age of 81 set an age-group record of 240 miles at the Six Day Race on Wards Island in New York, went on to smash his own record by 63 miles in the same event a year later, at age 82. He continues to walk in ultras, stresses the importance of hydration, and recommends weight training—which he endorses for everyone.

when it gets rough. You've got to be a fighter—seeking to overcome a new form of fatigue."

Stu Mittleman, a multi-time American and world record holder in ultra distances from 100 miles to six days, is also an exercise physiologist. It sheds light on the magnitude of his achievements to consider that for his 1000-mile record, he ran 85 miles a day for nearly two weeks. And on the way to completing his 100-mile run in a time of 12:56, he averaged 7:40 per mile and went through the marathon distance in 2:56. Mittleman is also an accomplished triathlete, having competed in the Ironman World Triathlon Championship. He finished second overall in the Ultraman Triathlon, a double Ironman distance.

Mittleman reveres the act of running for long distances, and well he should. For him, long, endurance running is a natural extension of the human condition. "I put it in historical perspective," he says. "This is our heritage, our evolutionary gift, dating back to our days as hunters and gatherers." Mittleman contends that while our anaerobic "fight or flight" capabilities always existed, they were not enough to challenge a world that was generally bigger, stronger, faster, and capable of greater individual violence. "Humans," Mittleman maintains, "could act in groups and had the capacity for tremendous feats of endurance." In fact, he believes, "If done intelligently, the human body may derive more healthful benefits from a moderately paced six- to 12-hour run than by trying to hammer a hard marathon."

And in fact, so immersed did Mittleman become in his ultra running that he claims the difficulty was not so much to perform his achievements, but to adjust to a world where he didn't run. "I used to joke that 'it only hurt when I stopped,' and to some extent I really meant it. My training was based on the belief that I could condition myself to the point where my main objective was to move. When the race ended and moving forward was no longer the primary objective, I felt the most uncomfortable."

On paper, Mittleman's achievements would seem to exact grueling and debilitating outcomes. Yet he approached his races with a unique philosophy. "An ultra is not something to be conquered, or to emerge from victorious. It cannot be viewed as something to overcome by gritting your teeth and bearing it." In fact, while Mittleman claims to have watched a number of his competitors grind to a hobbling finish, he says, "If I planned it right, and was optimally healthy and fit, I would actually get stronger as the race went on."

STU MITTLEMAN'S TRAINING PHILOSOPHY FOR THE ULTRAMARATHON

Ultra training should be based on achieving optimal health and fitness. The initial part of training, Phase I, focuses on establishing fundamentally sound health practices (nutrition and rest), ensuring proper equipment selection (most important, shoes that fit and provide support), and achieving a good level of fitness (a balance of flexibility, strength, low body fat, and aerobic base training).

Most important, to be a successful ultra runner, you must learn to listen to your body and discover how to move comfortably and efficiently. A heart rate monitor can help you accomplish this.

The key to using the heart rate monitor effectively is setting your target zones correctly. There are three target zones to consider:

1. **The Most Efficient Pace Zone (MEP)** represents the highest level of effort that can be maintained without feeling strain or undue discomfort. This is the most important zone for the endurance athlete to master. It should be set first. A simple formula for determining the upper limit of your starting MEP target zone starts by subtracting your age from 180. This number represents the midpoint of your MEP target zone. Your initial MEP zone is determined by adding and subtracting five from this number, to give you a narrow ten-beat target heart rate zone. For instance, if you are 30, subtract 30 from 180 to get 150, and then add and subtract five to create an MEP zone of 145 to 155. You may have to increase or decrease the zone by five beats up or down if the feeling is too easy or too difficult. (As a guideline, running pace in the MEP usually ends up at about your current marathon pace. Thus, the MEP is a good predictor of marathon pace.)

   Training in the MEP zone will increase your body's ability to utilize fat, which is the key to maximizing ultra endurance. When running in the MEP, you should develop body awareness and concentrate on how your body is feeling. Make sure the pace is not too hard and not too easy. The feeling is one of balance. You want to be efficient and productive. MEP workouts start out at about 20–30 minutes in length and can be extended to 30 to 45 minutes after a few months of training. Once you can handle up to 45 minutes comfortably, extend the duration of your weekend MEP by 20 minutes every other week. Once you reach this point, you should be able to maintain this pace for more extended periods of time.

2. **The Mostly Aerobic Pace Zone (MAP)** represents a very comfortable, easy, recovery zone. The MAP starts about 20 beats below the midpoint of the MEP. Run in the MAP on the days after most MEP workouts, races, or SAP interval workouts (described below).

3. **The Speedy Anaerobic Pace Zone (SAP)** is faster than the MEP. For most people, this zone will extend from the midpoint of the MEP to 20 heartbeats faster. This is a challenging zone, and, unlike the MEP and MAP target zones, it should elicit an anaerobic (sugar burning) response. You will know you are burning sugar once you begin to hear the forced expulsion of air (initial stages of hyperventilation) and the movement starts demanding all of your attention (no daydreaming is possible).

The best way to organize your fat-burning workout is to allow plenty of time to warm up. This should be accomplished by doing "preliminary exercise." This is simply a very low intensity of the mode of exercising in which you'll be training. If you're running, then walk first or run very slowly.

Preliminary exercise should ideally be done for ten to 15 minutes. This enables you to mobilize fat and put it into the blood for use as energy when you are training. Without this "mobilization," your body will be less likely to burn fat and more likely to burn glycogen (which is stored in the working muscles) or blood sugar. Fat is not stored in the muscles and must first be mobilized, put into the blood, and finally pumped to the working muscles before it can be burned.

Finally, what you eat affects how well you burn fat. For the most part, you should avoid refined sugars (candies, cakes, ice cream) and hydrogenated fats. Your body does need high-quality sources of fat to burn fat effectively (physiologists call this the law of mass action—your body needs fat to burn fat). High-quality sources of fat include extra-virgin olive oil; flaxseed oil; avocados; seeds; nuts; fish and fish oils; and various blended oils that are available at health food markets.

Ideally, as you progress, the pace you are able to maintain while staying in the target zone will begin to increase. At some point, generally after four to six weeks, your progress will begin to level off. At this point, changes may be made in training that may include some out-of-target zone training (anaerobic work); however, it is very important that aerobic efficiency is maximized by improving fat metabolism prior to the onset of anaerobic training. If you begin to focus on anaerobic work prior to these improvements, you will gain anaerobic benefits at the expense of your endurance potential.

Sample Training Program for an Ultra of Six Hours or Longer

Phase I, First 8–12 weeks

1. Focus on basic fitness and health.
2. Establish sound nutritional practices (eat a balanced diet and avoid simple sugars).
3. Develop an aerobic base by alternating MEP (20–30 minutes) and MAP (30–90 minutes) training days, not including 10 to 15 minutes warmup and cool-down.

Phase II, Weeks 8–24

1. Do three 20- to 30-minute MEP workouts each week; for example, Tuesday, Thursday, and Saturday. MEP workouts may be extended to a length of 30–45 minutes during this phase of the training program.
2. Every other week, add ten minutes to the Saturday MEP workout. Substitute a road race if desired.
3. On alternate weekends, do long, slow distance runs of approximately two to three hours in length.
4. End Phase II with a ten-mile run on the track in the target zone. Take note of each mile split time. Compare consistency of pace.

Phase III, Weeks 24–36

1. Do two 30- to 45-minute MEP workouts each week; for example, Thursday and Saturday.

2. Every other week, add 20 minutes to the Saturday MEP workout. Substitute a road race if desired.

3. On alternate weekends, do long, slow distance runs of approximately three to four hours in length.

4. Add one SAP interval workout each week, preferably on Tuesdays. Plan a total of 15 to 20 minutes of SAP zone training, not including recovery periods and ten to 15 minutes of warmup and cool-down. This can be 15 one-minute SAP runs, followed by 15 one-minute MAP recoveries. Or, another sequence can be five three-minute SAP runs, followed by five three-minute MAP recoveries. Any SAP run over five minutes should be followed by a MAP recovery of no less than two to three minutes. On days prior to, and following, each SAP workout, run easily in the MAP for 30 to 60 minutes.

5. Phase III ends the week prior to the ultra race. Skip long runs for two weeks before the race.

FRED LEBOW ON ULTRAMARATHONING

When I first got involved in the running scene, I didn't quite understand marathoning, let alone ultras. But particularly after conducting ultra events at the club, the ability to run such long distances fascinates me.

For years, the NYRRC conducted a 100-mile race, and then we put on a six-day run. I had read about a six-day run held in the early 1900s in Madison Square Garden. People used to pay to watch the runners. I began to read old archives on the subject, and about ultras in Ted Corbitt's book. We put on the first six-day run in 1983 on the track at Randalls Island. We got tremendous press coverage. ABC television's *Nightline* came out every day to focus on Stu Mittleman. What most captivated people, I think, was exploring the unknown. How could people run 100 miles every day? We brought in the best ultra runners in the world for the event. In 1984, Yiannis Kouros of Greece broke a decades-old six-day world record with 635 miles.

Ultramarathoners are very special people. As a rule, they are different from other runners. This kind of running is very total and very meditative. They are often very intelligent, introspective people. Many ultra runners are loners; several are authors or poets.

Ultras put other distances into perspective, like the marathon. To many people, the marathon is the ultimate distance. But that's not really true. There is the 100-mile, the 1000-mile, and the six-day runs. Those are the ultimate distances.

22

CROSS-COUNTRY

Cross-country is the original and most challenging form of distance running. Many of the world's most accomplished distance runners, past and present, have a strong base in cross-country running. They stress the quality and variety of this form of running—for all levels of ability.

Some of the best and most famous cross-country running is done in New York City, in Van Cortlandt Park in the Bronx—one of the nation's oldest and most venerated courses. NYRR conducts cross-country races for all ages and abilities there. Many national cross-country championship races are also held at Van Cortlandt Park.

NYRR has long recognized both the value and the excitement of cross-country running. In the early 1980s, NYRR began a campaign to host one of the most prestigious events in the sport: the annual World Cross-Country Championships. It took four years of hard work and extensive lobbying to be granted that meet by the International Amateur Athletic Federation (IAAF), the world governing body of the sport. When the race took place in New York in 1984, it marked the first time the event had ever been held outside of Europe or North Africa.

> I absolutely love cross-country. I've been running cross-country since 1984. I am drawn to the naturalness of running along trails and in the woods; it's being close to the outdoors that I enjoy most.
>
> When I'm marathon training, there is so much road running involved. And when I train for the track, I spend a lot of time doing workouts on the track. But when I train for cross-country, I never get bored. The trails are always changing.
>
> —*Deena Kastor*

Fred Lebow felt that one of the purposes of bringing the World Championships to the United States was to popularize cross-country among the masses, much in the way road running has blossomed. Although that did not happen on a large scale after staging the Championships, NYRR continues to endorse and promote the sport. To this end, not only does New York Road Runners conduct events, but also for many years officials have attended National and World Cross-Country Championship events.

Says cross-country standout Deena Kastor, "I started running cross-country when I was 11 years old, during the sixth grade. I love using the terrain and the elements as part of racing cross-country. Whether it's surging down a hill, escaping around a corner, or stampeding through a puddle, there are tactics involved in cross-country that make racing so exciting. I am a strong hill runner, so I attack the hills during a race. Really, there is so much that goes into a cross-country race.

"I think cross-country makes you very strong. When I was in high school, most coaches made their athletes run cross-country in the fall. We had basketball players out on the trails; it helped their endurance and taught them the discipline of doing challenging workouts."

Cross-country is the root of everything. Cross-country is the basics of running, and of our human heritage. In the distant past, we were hunting, gathering, and foraging. You really get to commune with nature when you run cross-country. It's a very different experience than the roads, or the track. Cross-country marks the change of season, which is sort of symbolic, since we go through this emotionally and mentally. You go through the change of seasons in your life.

Cross-country is a great equalizer, because the middle distance, long distance, and even the sprinters run it. In most college and high school programs, everybody runs cross-country, because unlike track, teams can have unlimited numbers of participants. So everybody gets an opportunity.

—*Allan Steinfeld*

The varying running surfaces in cross-country help develop various muscles and save the legs by absorbing some of the shock that harder surfaces don't. The change of running venue and style also adds important variety to training, making running more seasonal. It can allow you to go into different running events with strength advantages and added enthusiasm.

For example, Deena Kastor sees the connection between cross-country and marathon running. "All cross-country workouts revolve around improving your strength, which translates into all disciplines of running, including the marathon. Cross-country is perfect marathon preparation. It simply makes you very strong. All the hills and intensity—mile repeats—they build a strong base that pays off in the marathon."

In terms of racing strategy, cross-country is basically the same as any race but for the terrain. Competitors might make a move going up a hill, or create a gap after leaping over a log or turning a corner. If you want to try cross-country, head to one of the all-comers meets. If you feel intimidated by racing, try cross-country by training on trails and through woods to get the feeling, and gain the benefits.

TRAINING FOR CROSS-COUNTRY

British cross-country expert Cliff Temple believes that training on the ground, as opposed to the roads, is a good investment, even if you never plan to race cross-country. Its gains are similar to resistance training, with the degree of that resistance created by mud or thick grass. This often serves to build strength in the same fashion as hill running or running on sand dunes. Therefore, while the going might be slower than on the road, the strength developed may result in faster times on the roads.

The reason, Temple explains, is that the changing ground composition gives you less in return for the effort expended. You don't get the same slight "bounce" you normally feel when road running in well-cushioned shoes. To compensate, you are forced to work harder with the lifting muscles of the thighs (quadriceps), to traverse the thick grass or heavy mud.

CLIFF TEMPLE'S TRAINING TIPS

In order to acclimate to cross-country, run casually for about 30 to 40 minutes your first few times out. Then alter your sessions to include speedwork.

In a typical speed session, cover two to three miles in warmup, then run a series of eight 60-second efforts at faster than race pace, with a steady, two-minute recovery jog in between. These 60-second bursts should be run over anything (within reason) that comes in your path, whatever the terrain. The faster runs may even seem easier than running steadily through long grass—and they will certainly produce a higher pulse rate and greater mobility than running on the road!

Alternatively, devise a loop of between 600 meters and 800 meters using natural paths and obstacles, and run a series of four to six repetitions of the

To avoid injury, I have corrected some mistakes I used to make. For example, after my first two years in triathlon competition, which I spent on the verge of being injured, I began running on trails instead of roads. At first I thought it would throw my legs off, all the twisting and wobbling from the uneven surface. But the opposite is true. It has strengthened and protected my legs. Road running works just certain muscles. Negotiating the trails—with the rocks, stones, and tree roots—seems to work the entire leg, and in addition, gives relief from the pounding. If you get on the trails, you'll experience quicker recovery and not get so torn down. That's why I now do 70 percent of my running on trails. When you read about an athlete running 110-mile weeks, what you often don't read is that the person is doing 90 percent of that running on trails.

—Mark Allen

full distances, with a four-minute recovery. If you prefer, break the loop up as naturally as possible into, say, four sections of about 200 meters; run the first and third sections comfortably. Run continuously, lapping the circuit for a predetermined time—say, eight minutes. Then, after a five-minute rest, repeat it.

This is, in essence, interval training in a cross-country form and set-ting. You can fashion any form of distances, repetitions, or recovery. "But somehow, when executed in a pleasant setting (such as loops of a quiet lake), it never seems such a soul-destroying business as it is on a track," offers Temple.

When running cross-country, don't expect

1. To feel quite as comfortable or rhythmic in your running as on the road.

2. To set a personal best, whatever the distance. Don't compare cross-country times with road times.

3. To keep your shoes clean. Wear old shoes, but preferably shoes that have a bit of grip on mud. Unless you are racing seriously, spiked shoes are not essential, but they are a great help on exceptionally muddy courses.

Expect

1. To enjoy a change of running environment, and a new running experience.

2. A physical benefit from the effort you expend. You may ache a little the day after your first race because your running action will probably have been different on the uneven ground.

3. An initial feeling of relief when you've finished, then a lasting feeling of satisfaction, and, finally, the desire to try it again.

PART 4
THE PSYCHOLOGY OF RUNNING

23

MOTIVATION

The running boom produced abundant testimony to the physical and mental benefits of the sport, testimony that motivated people of all ages and circumstances to pursue running for health and well-being. New runners today find motivation in the achievements of dedicated runners, not only the elite, but also the social runners who've literally gone the extra mile in their lives. But how and where do the old guard find motivation?

> Sustained motivation is essential to achieving your potential. To keep your motivation high, use mental stimuli. Find what gets you psyched and surround yourself with it—posters, sayings, photos, running magazines, videos. The more you see it, the more you remember it. For example, you might put up either a sign on your wall or a note on your mirror or desk reminding you of your goal time. One runner I know uses his goal marathon time as his access number for an automatic bank machine.
>
> —*Grete Waitz*

Two decades after the running boom began, nearly 10.5 million Americans ran 100 days or more in 2002, while an impressive 11,161,000 people have been in the sport for ten or more years, according to American Sports Data, Inc. The organization concludes that while some sports come and go, running remains strong and popular across a wide demographic. At NYRR, longtime participation is also documented. In the early 1980s, most New York City Marathoners were going the distance for the first time. Twenty years later, nearly 70 percent of the over 34,000 participants had previously run a marathon.

But after long years of hard work and challenges met, running can get a little stale. If anyone understands the need to keep running fresh, it's Amby Burfoot, for whom running has been both vocation and avocation for more than three decades.

Overracing makes people stale. I've found that overracing is particularly common when people start to improve and they don't want to miss the feeling of doing well. But they find they can't race every week, either the mind or the body will tell them that. Runners have to adjust their training to accommodate life stress. Running should be a relief from stress, a way to help cope with it, not another added stress.

Another cause of running staleness is setting unrealistic goals, or not accounting for external factors like weather conditions and how they affect performance. I spend half my time reminding disappointed runners they have to consider factors like heat and humidity. Often these people will go out and run hard the day following a disappointing race out of anger and frustration. They want something so badly that they don't want to pay attention to all the variables.

—Bob Glover

AMBY BURFOOT'S MOTIVATION TRAINING

During the 40 years that I've been running, as both a Boston Marathon winner and a midpack recreational runner, I've had plenty of time to think about the key ingredients of a training program. I've thought about long runs and hills, speedwork and tempo training, stretching and strengthening, cross training and circuit training, nutrition and psychology. And the more I've weighed and analyzed the contributions of each of these, the more I've leaned toward a conclusion that might surprise you: None of them is important.

The only thing that's important in your training program is motivation. And yet every year most runners spend hundreds of hard, sweaty hours planning, executing, and improving their training elements. The same runners spend almost no time planning, executing, and improving their motivation—despite the fact that motivation is the foundation on which all training is built. Without motivation, the benefits of a couple of great track workouts slip away faster than the high tide. Without motivation, the best stretching program grows boring, boredom leads to quitting, quitting stretching leads to injury, and the injury leads to unfulfilled dreams.

All successful runners have recognized the critical role of motivation. What they haven't recognized, however, is that motivation is a skill. It can be learned and practiced. You may not be very good at motivating yourself right now, but you can get better at it. All it takes is a little bit of time and a lot of creativity.

I succeed based on my own personal motivation, dedication, and commitment. I know a lot of women want to beat me. I'm not going to let them. My mind-set is, if I'm not out there training, someone else is. I train to race. I love to train, but I love to race even more.

Can you build the motivation to be competitive, or is it something to which you're predisposed? I don't know. But I believe it's okay just to race for the social aspect. I found that out after attending a race to cheer for a friend, a recreational runner. "Kick, kick!" I yelled to her at the end. "You should feel the adrenaline," I told her when it was over. I felt she shouldn't want to let people pass her, but she didn't care. That lack of interest in being competitive isn't just the case for women; I've known men that way, too. They just want to be fit, maybe run against the clock.

—*Lynn Jennings, former USA National and World Cross-Country Champion*

Thirty years ago, while training for Boston, I motivated myself in the most primitive manner—with thoughts of my opponents. On those mornings when I was tempted to roll over and fall asleep again, I imagined my racing rivals leaping out of bed and roaring out the front door on a ten-mile workout. The thought so terrified me that I was generally lacing up my shoelaces within five minutes. All other elite runners, I'm sure, have used more or less the same tactic to get themselves going. For the elite, fear of losing a race is often the most powerful motivator.

It doesn't work, however, for everyone else. Midpack runners know that they will never win a race, that no one will ever hand them a $10,000 check for their weekend road-race performance. They have to find other less material motivations to help them stay the course. I learned this eight years after I finally did win the Boston Marathon in 1968. In 1976 I decided I no longer wanted to run for the laurel wreath. Other things in my life—family or job—had grown more important. At the same time, I did want to continue running. The fitness, the friends, the stress relief, even the occasional race—these were still important to me. Since I would no longer be winning anything, I would have to find new ways to keep myself motivated.

I now measure my running career by a far more significant milestone than my 1968 Boston Marathon win. On each of the past 40 Thanksgiving days, I have completed the annual five-mile race in Manchester, Connecticut. I have won Manchester nine times, but I'm much prouder that I'm still running it every year even though I now finish far back in the pack. My Manchester "streak" has become one of the most sacred things in my life. It's an annual celebration at which I renew my membership in the human race and my involvement in healthy, vigorous sport.

As I have aged, my running times and goals have changed, and so have my inspirations. I used to idolize the Olympic greats—the Paavo Nurmis, the Emil Zatopeks, the Abebe Bikilas, the Frank Shorters. Now I have a different hero—"Old John" Kelley, who has run the Boston Marathon 60 times. I have had the good fortune to know Kelley since I first started running 40 years ago, and I have always been struck by the high energy and good spirit that seem to infuse every pore of his body. Kelley has been able to keep running, I believe, by treating each mile as the best and most important he has ever run. He could idly reminisce over the years when he won Boston and other great races, but he doesn't. Kelley concentrates on the mile he's running right now. And perhaps the next one. He keeps shuffling forward, and the wind seems always at his back, the road always rising up to meet him—not because he's Irish, but because he treats every mile as the most challenging and exciting of his life.

In many ways I now try to model myself after Kelley. I've developed a set of motivational tricks that I'm constantly reviewing and redefining. They have only one purpose: to keep me running. They've worked for 29 years, and I think they'll work for another 29. I present them here with brief explanations and an advisory note. One man's (or woman's) motivation is another's black hole. These ideas will work best if you adapt them to your own needs and personality.

Don't Lock Yourself In

In fact, you don't have to *do* anything. You don't have to run long every Sunday. You don't have to run speedwork twice a week. You don't have to run hills. You don't have to run the same course every day, and to run it faster today than yesterday. Running is not an all-or-nothing proposition.

Success does not come to the most righteous and rigorously disciplined runners but to those who continue running. And the surest way to keep running is to maintain a high level of motivation by refusing to see running as a series of rigid rules. To get to the finish line, you'll have to try lots of different paths.

> Don't strive for perfection. Most running programs are full of all the do's you have to follow to achieve success, and there is some truth to all these lists. Surely, improved running and racing do not occur haphazardly. But beyond a certain point, many of these do's become jailers. They prevent you from experiencing the full variety that running has to offer. They become dead ends rather than open doors, paths you follow blindly and without seeing all the opportunities to change and try something new. The result is burnout.

Be Spontaneous

Fitness takes many forms. Running happens to be one of the best and most efficient, but there are many other activities that can increase your strength, flexibility, and aerobic conditioning.

While running was the first exercise to make a dent on America's fitness consciousness, many others have since followed. With bicycling and swimming came the triathlon boom, the father of cross training. This mixing together of many forms of training is the healthiest trend to hit runners in two decades. Cross training now includes everything from in-line roller skating to mountain biking to hiking to weight training to Nordic skiing.

In its well-known advertisements, Nike has caught the spirit of cross training: Just do it. This should also be a slogan for all runners. Don't think too much about some new activity. Don't try to analyze whether it will improve your 10K time. If it's fun and sweaty, just go out and do it. In the long run, you'll be much better off for having a wide variety of aerobic activities in your repertoire. Everyone should do more than just run. (See Chapter 10 for more information about cross training.)

Break the Rules

Once upon a time, Dr. Ken Cooper, the Sir Isaac Newton of fitness, established the first law of aerobics, which reads: you must do at least 30 minutes

I didn't realize this as a youngster, but the most important factor for motivation is goal setting. You should always have a goal. For some people, that's staying fit and healthy, running a few times a week for 30 minutes. For me, it's competition and having time goals.

I made a conscious decision well into my career to shift from concentrating on track running to road running. I used that new focus in 1984 when I sustained an injury. I set my sights on the Women's Mini Marathon in New York, because it is the largest women's road race in the country. It was like a cookie I held out for myself.

My goals are both intermediate and long range. An example of a long-range goal is the marathon. As far back as 1974, I had a goal to run a marathon. I did one 12 years later. I will continue to pick my races carefully in order to give my best possible effort.

What's kept me motivated is not having reached the goal I have always had: to win an Olympic medal. But I'm realistic enough to know there are other goals.

The average runner can sustain long-term interest by keeping running fun. There are all kinds of possibilities. I do a workout every Friday that's one of my favorites. I jog a mile and a half to the local high school track. I take off my shoes and do eight to ten strides barefoot on the grass. Then I put my shoes back on and I jog home. That's the entire day's running. I love it. You don't have to be a slave to a particular program. A lot of people think that even if they stop during a workout, it's not a workout. But every session is different. Just because you slow down, or even walk, it's still a workout.

—Francie Larrieu Smith

of aerobic exercise at least three times a week. Millions of Americans lived and breathed by this rule, and their lives improved because of it.

Naturally, running soon developed other major rules. For example, when doing intervals, always run 400s on a track, always follow a hard day of training with an easy day, and never run in a snowstorm. Millions of American runners followed these rules, and in general they prospered. But along the way, some things were lost—things such as creativity and inspiration and spontaneity, the very things that inevitably lead to the best runs that life has to offer.

The best run of my life took place on a beautiful spring day 12 years ago. I decided to spend the whole day running. My brother and I boarded an early-morning train and rode 55 miles to the west. When we got off, we started the long run home. I use "run" loosely. What we did that day, traipsing along the balmy Connecticut shoreline, was to run for 15 minutes, walk for 5 minutes, run for 15 minutes, and stop at every McDonald's along the way (there were plenty).

I had never run that far before. Or walked during a run. Or stopped at McDonald's for Cokes and apple pies. I had never taken a whole day off from work to do nothing but run. Having broken so many rules, I felt completely liberated and I never enjoyed a run more.

A final caveat on rule-breaking—despite what I've written above, there is one rule you should never, ever break. Follow this rule at all times: Always run during a total eclipse of the sun!

Simplify

Don't measure your pace or the miles you've covered. Too many runners have become slaves to their training logs. It can also help to take a less-is-more approach to your running. When you quantify every part of your running, you steal much of the magic.

If you still want to keep a record of your running, do everything in minutes. You can even set yourself daily or weekly goals in terms of minutes run. But don't burden yourself with the need to run five miles at an eight-minute pace on a 100°F-day in July, or force yourself to run ten miles in January when the mercury is hiding below zero.

You can even construct a slimmed-down but effective training program I call the "20-20-60 plan" by logging your minutes of running. Every week, take one or more easy runs of 20 minutes. On another day, do a "tempo" run: a warmup and cool-down with 20 minutes of hard, sustained running sandwiched between. Also include a weekly long run of 60 minutes. You can get into reasonably good shape—or maintain your present condition—with this simple 20-20-60 approach.

Set Completion Goals, Not Time Goals

You can't beat the clock, at least not for long. Eventually, all runners reach the point where they can't and won't get any faster. Unless these runners begin to cultivate other reasons for running, they'll soon grow discouraged with the sport and quit.

Because of the opportunities in age-group competition, many runners challenge themselves against others of the same age. And I know at least one runner who has figured out a way to compete with himself and nearly always win. George Hirsch, publisher emeritus of *Runner's World* magazine, wipes the slate clean at the beginning of each year. He pretends every race is his first effort at the distance, so he sets a "PR for the year" with each race early in the season. Then he spends the rest of the year trying to improve on his PR, or personal record. This is but one of the dozens of mental tricks veteran runners often play to keep their running fresh, challenging, and new.

Midpack runners often envy those up front, but they shouldn't. Elite runners, by definition, have no choice but to try to get ever faster. When they don't, they lose. Racing has no meaning for them outside of winning. Midpackers, on the other hand, can invent dozens of different ways to have fun and succeed during a race. I have seen runners dance at every band along the course, sit down on the sidewalk to enjoy a fluid stop, and run in big, chatty social groups. And why not? All these options seem fun to me.

Find New Challenges

After a while, merely finishing 10K road races, no matter how much you allow yourself to play along the way, becomes old hat. Every runner needs new challenges. So concentrate on the marathon one year, the mile the next. Then return to the marathon, only this time with a whole new training program. In recent years, increasing numbers of runners have been leaving the roads and taking to the trails. Here, they say, they get back in touch with what they liked most about running in the first place—the outdoor environment, smaller crowds, and a new adventure. While some trail races cover 100 miles or ascend rocky mountaintops, many are much more accessible. The average runner can manage them with just small amounts of special preparation—investing in a slightly sturdier pair of shoes or taking a refresher course in reading topographical maps.

Road relays are another fast-growing alternative to the weekend ho-hums. Many of the best road relays cover fascinating parts of the world—Mount Hood to the coast in Oregon, Jasper International Park in British Columbia, the lakes region of New Hampshire, the beaches of Long

Island—and allow groups of runners to cover distances they could never do as individuals. Teams may include only men over 50, mixed men and women, and women only, and nowhere else does running's famous sense of camaraderie shine through so brightly. Every member must truly help every other member, and when the team finally reaches the finish line, you know you wouldn't have gotten there without everyone's contributions.

Remember, Running Is a State of Mind

This is the most important of all my motivation guidelines. If you can train your mind for running, everything else will be easy. Always remember that how long you stick with your conditioning program is much more important than how long and how hard you train today. It used to be said of baseball pitchers that the legs always go first. This is rarely the case with runners. With us, the mind always goes first, and then everything else falls to pieces. So stretch your mind before your hamstrings, and strengthen your creativity before your stomach muscles.

"THE RUT"

Author and coach Cliff Temple calls running staleness "The Rut." He says part of the problem is being torn between two conflicting feelings: not wanting to stop running, but feeling like a record stuck in a groove. Here are suggestions adapted from his writings for getting out of "The Rut."

Find new pastures.   Most people run from the same place, on the same route. Once or twice a week, you might consider driving (or taking public transportation) to a different area and running from there. Just remember to pack the necessities, like a change of dry clothing and a drink. If you're normally a city runner, try the suburbs or country—and vice versa. If you're in unfamiliar territory, don't forget to take or make a map if necessary, or make the course an easy one so you won't get lost.

Bare your wrist.   Running a new course can help break the often self-imposed pressure of timing every run, a habit that can also lead to "The Rut." Try just running how you feel, and don't compare it to other workouts. That means leaving your watch at home and letting the sunshine get to that thin strip of unexposed skin around your wrist.

Find a new direction.   Direction in this case is not north or south, but where your running career is heading. You may have started out to lose weight, to complete a fun run or even a marathon, and once achieved, those goals were suddenly behind you rather than in front of you. Perhaps aiming to better your race times or participate in a specific event some months ahead may help spark your motivation.

Change the time of day you run.   Is there a reason you always run at the same time or day, or is it just habit? This may be another potential cause of "The Rut." In the same way that you may try different routes, trying a different time of day on certain occasions may help. You may, in fact, discover that you are more of a morning (or an evening) person.

Don't become a running bore.   If every conversation seems to revolve around your personal best times or your various aches and pains—particularly among nonrunning family and friends—then chances are you've become a running bore. This may be alienating you from others. Balance is important in every aspect of your running, including avoiding "The Rut." So try to mix normal domestic and work life with the demands and desires of running.

Find some company.   If you do most, or all, of your running on your own, then running in company can sometimes help you out of "The Rut." It may be only once a week when you can meet with one particular running partner or a group, but it can be a great help. Is there one particular session or day on which you feel more vulnerable to "The Rut" than others? If so, that is the day on which to find company.

24

THE MENTAL EDGE

How much of what runners achieve is determined by the mind? Some say it's as much as half mind and half body, and that you can't maximize one without the other.

> Who knows what percent of athletic success is mental ability? We hear everything. A well-known sports psychologist, Keith Henschen, once said to me, "Ability is 90 percent physical and 10 percent mental, but let me talk to you about that 10 percent." Some people are driven harder than others. I think the good ones are different, maybe because of self-confidence. Fundamentally, they see themselves as successful people.
>
> —*Tom Fleming*

Good running psychology, or "mental edge," comes from, among other things, focus, confidence, and concentration. Unlike physical ability—determined more or less by birth—mental edge can be learned, then honed through experience and sheer will. To exercise the body, then, is only part of the formula for success. You can exercise your mind, perhaps your most underdeveloped muscle. Consider the following techniques to help you achieve peak mental edge:

- **Relax.** When you're too uptight for a race, no matter how well trained you are, you won't run your best. To run well, you've got to be relaxed. Tension causes your muscles to contract. Proper relaxation allows your body to perform. And when you're relaxed, you can concentrate on the mental aspects of running. So before a race or hard effort, relax. Take slow, rhythmic breaths. Jog slowly. Shake out your limbs. Roll your head. Practice your own personal form of meditation and centering.

- **Think positively.** To succeed, you must believe you can succeed. So think positively. When you train, visualize yourself achieving a goal, whether it be losing weight or running a good time in a race. Close your eyes and see yourself through each step on the way to your goal. Focus on details. The more you think positively, the more confidence you'll possess and the better prepared you'll be to succeed.

Deep down I always believe I can win. That's hard with road racing, because everyone is in a different peak cycle, so you might not know exactly who your competition is. It's terrible to say, but even when I go up against Liz McColgan or Ingrid Kristiansen—true superstars—I always feel deep down that I can beat them. But the best thing that ever happened to me was when I learned not to worry about them. I learned to be proud of my performances, and the fact that I did the best I could do. It was very difficult when I started getting beaten on the track on a regular basis, and my American records got broken. At least I used to be able to say I was the best in the United States; suddenly, that wasn't so. But I learned I could still run well, even if I did not win every race.

—*Francie Larrieu Smith*

Some running should be different mentally just the way it is different physically. On my easy runs, I may use the time to relax and let my mind wander, but I never do that in hard workouts or races. At those times, I always focus on the task at hand. Spend at least some of your training time, and other parts of your day, concentrating on what you are doing in training and visualizing your running success.

—*Grete Waitz*

- **Concentrate.** Block out distracting details when you run. Training and racing are not times to contemplate shopping lists or tomorrow's appointments. Great competitors are able to concentrate precisely on the task at hand, to block out distractions, and to focus on their goals.

When I was a running coach in NYRR classes, I worked on helping students develop the toughness needed to be competitive and meet their goals. I emphasized focusing in a race, and not losing consciousness of what you are doing. Concentration is part of the discipline of racing. So, for example, saying hello to someone in the middle of a serious race is against the rules. You can say hello before or after, but during the event, you should be mentally focused on your goal. That doesn't mean it's not perfectly acceptable to run a race for the social aspect. That's why my first question to someone who is planning to race is always, "Exactly what do you want to achieve?"

—*Cliff Held*

- **Get the feeling.** The feeling is that sense of being "on" or of being completely ready. While running, it is a sense of ease or invincibility. Being "on" is part of what many call "runner's high." Try to recapture the feeling from a good race or workout. Then you can re-create it for future events. Who knows the feeling? Watch runners finish a race. Those who have won, excelled, or achieved their goals raise their arms, punch the air, or even shout with joy, triumphant with the feeling.

- **Plan and study.** As you condition your body, strive also to understand your running—from training principles to competition. Read books, keep a training diary, and attend clinics to learn how to understand your running. Experience itself—running and racing—will best help you determine your individual needs and goals.

THE PSYCHING TEAM

The New York City Marathon Psyching Team, which began its work in 1983, is composed of a group of 80 to 100 volunteer psychiatrists, psychologists, and social workers who are on hand at the Marathon to deal with the many entrants who suffer psychologically-oriented problems, such as anxiety over finishing the race or suffering too much pain. And according to Michael Simon, Ph.D., former captain of the Psyching Team, the purpose is also to

If you want to achieve a high goal, you're going to have to take some chances. Going into the 1992 Olympic Trials marathon, when I decided to give it one last push, people like my college coach Bill Dellinger asked me how much I was going to train. I answered: 100 miles a week, and that I'd try to work on my quality. That was all I needed at that stage, I said. Then all of a sudden I realized, who am I kidding? When I looked at what all the top marathoners are doing, and what I used to do, I knew that my commitment wasn't enough. I used to do 120 miles a week with tremendous quality. After a long layoff and running poorly, how could I possibly think that with much less volume and less quality, I was going to be able to come close to what I did before, or close to what the best are currently doing?

I reasoned I could run 100 miles a week, and not get injured, but there's no way I could be competitive. The only chance I had of making that Olympic team was to be running 120 miles a week. If I got injured, so be it. Dellinger would then say to me, "I told you so." And I'd say, "You're right, Bill. But if I'd have run 100 miles a week I would have gone in there and gotten killed. I would have run 2:15, and I wasn't going to do that." *[In that race, Salazar was one of nearly half in the field who dropped out due to hot and humid weather.]*

There's also a mental risk. A lot of people don't do everything possible they can in terms of fine-tuning their training, really making their training quality—no matter how much or little it is—because they are constrained psychologically. I believe that a lot of the time it's because of the fear of really giving it everything they've got. They are constrained by the fear of failure, of coming up even a little short. If they don't give it everything, they've always got an excuse. It's frightening for a lot of people to make the maximum effort and then fail.

Is taking the risk worth it? That depends on your philosophy of life. You realize that striving and giving it your all, but falling a bit short, is going to help you more than never having taken that risk.

—Alberto Salazar

assist runners to allow themselves to be the best they can be physically, and to increase their sense of enjoyment and accomplishment. Because these anxieties are exacerbated by the long wait at the race start and the extreme fatigue at the race finish, the volunteers staff both these locations. The psyching team is a unique feature of the New York City Marathon.

The following tips, composed by Dr. Harold Selman and Maryellyn Duane, Ph.D. and amended by Michael Simon, are intended for runners before the marathon, but are relevant for all running and racing:

1. **Don't worry about worrying.** Concern over an upcoming event such as the marathon is perfectly normal and desirable. If not out of hand, it can even enhance your performance. Yet if you experience nervous feelings, such as butterflies in the stomach, shoulder tightness, dry mouth, or frequent urination, think of the nervousness that causes them as excitement, readiness, eagerness, and an adrenaline surge. After all, your body is getting ready for a major task.

2. **Say all your fears out loud.** To help bring your unconscious worries into your conscious awareness, say them out loud. Once they become conscious, you can begin to exert control over them and even use them to your benefit.

3. **Go over all pre-race and race details in your head.** Control what you can, and make sure there are no big surprises on race day. Keep a sense of humor about your obsessing—if nothing else, it will help you stay busy when there is nothing else to do.

4. **Body scan.** Imagine your body as being a finely tuned machine. Think of your senses as the gauges, with the rest of your physical being as the well-oiled part. Check the gauges from head to toe often. See how well the machine runs.

5. **Decide what to wear in advance.** Make sure you look marvelous, but be comfortable at all costs. Plan to bring different outfits with you to the race to suit changeable weather. For those who can stand the attention, your name strategically placed on your outfit will undoubtedly bring extra attention and cheering from the crowd.

6. **Get in touch with your inner resources.** Use positive self-talk for affirmation. To help you overcome problems or challenges (such as "hitting the wall," feeling pain, or breaking a shoelace) problem-solve by thinking how you might handle the situation. Imagine positive resolutions to anticipated challenges and think of the sense of accomplishment you will feel.

7. **What you see is what you get.** Imagery is also useful for relaxation, distraction, coping with pain, and dealing with any potential obstacle. For example, you can visualize yourself as a strong, graceful animal; see your tight muscles melting like snow on a warm day; or connect yourself to the runner in front of you, visualizing a rope or fishing line, and let that person carry you with him/her.

8. **Imagine yourself having a great run.** Use all your senses to visualize yourself in vivid detail enjoying every minute of the race. Go to sleep dreaming of what a thrill it is to run the race.

9. **Plan to take music breaks during the race.** Play a few of your favorite tunes the night before, and you'll be sure to get a music lift when you remember them during the race.

10. **Do some relaxation exercises at the start.** Make use of your time while you are waiting to begin the race. Close your eyes and direct yourself inward. Regulate your breathing. Imagine a scene that is pleasant to you, and relax all your muscles.

11. **Plan to affirm yourself during the race.** Negative thoughts creep into every marathoner's mind. Combat them by consciously telling yourself that you are doing a great job. Be your own cheering team.

12. **Enjoy fellow runners' company at the start and during the race.** There is nothing like a sense of camaraderie to move you along. Be friendly and share this great experience with others. Don't be afraid to speak to your cohorts.

THE ABUSE OF RUNNING

The physical benefits of running are well known, and the psychological benefits are touted as well. This fact is confirmed by those who study the sport, as well as those who engage in it; however, running can change from a positive pursuit to a negative one. And for many runners, this is a common shift, at least to some degree.

Running abuse shares characteristics of other obsessive-compulsive disorders, including alcoholism and drug abuse, and is defined as running at the expense of health, relationships, and work performance.

HOW TO HANDLE EATING DISORDERS

ADVICE FOR COACHES, FRIENDS, PARENTS

If you think that an athlete is struggling with food issues, speak up! Anorexia and bulimia are self-destructive eating behaviors that may signal severe underlying depression and can be life-threatening. Here are some tips from Nancy Clark M.S., R.D. for approaching this delicate subject.

- **Heed the signs.** Anorexic behavior includes extreme weight loss (often emaciation), obsessive dieting, compulsive exercise, Spartan food intake despite significant energy expenditure, and distorted body perception (i.e., frequent comments about feeling fat despite obvious thinness). Anorexics commonly wear layers of baggy clothing to hide their thinness and may complain about feeling cold.

  Bulimic behavior can be more subtle. The athlete may eat a great deal of food and then rush to the bathroom; you may hear water running to cover up the sound of vomiting. The person may hide laxatives and display other secretive behavior. The bulimic may have bloodshot eyes, swollen glands, and bruised fingers (from inducing vomiting). Some even speak about a magic method of eating without gaining weight.

- **Approach the athlete gently.** Be persistent, saying that you're worried about his or her health. Share your concerns about the athlete's lack of concentration, light-headedness, or chronic fatigue. These health changes are more likely to be steppingstones for accepting help, since the athlete undoubtedly clings to food and exercise for feelings of control and stability.

- **Don't discuss weight or eating habits.** The athlete takes great pride in being "perfectly thin" and may dismiss your concern as jealousy. The starving or binging is not the important issue, but rather a smoke screen over the larger problem. Problems with *life* are the real issue.

(continued)

- **Focus on unhappiness as the reason for seeking help.** Point out how anxious, tired, or irritable the athlete has been lately. Emphasize that he or she doesn't have to be that way.

- **Be supportive and listen sympathetically.** Don't expect the athlete to admit he or she has a problem right away. Give it time. Remind the athlete that you believe in him or her. This will make a difference in the recovery.

- **Provide a list of sources for professional help.** Although the athlete may deny there's a problem to your face, he or she may admit despair at another moment. If you don't know of local resources, some organizations are included in the Resources at the back of this book.

- **Don't deal with it alone.** If you feel you're making no headway and the athlete is becoming more self-destructive, seek help from a trusted family member, medical professional, or health service. Make an appointment with a mental health counselor and bring the athlete there yourself. Tell the athlete that you have to involve other people because you care about him or her. If you're overreacting and there really is no problem, the health professional will simply be able to ease your mind.

- **Talk to someone about your own emotions.** Remember that you are not responsible and can only try to help. Your power comes from using community resources and health professionals, such as a guidance counselor, a registered dietitian, a therapist, or an eating disorders clinic.

—*Nancy Clark M.S., R.D.*

HOW TO SPOT RUNNING ABUSE

Answer the following questions composed by Harold Selman and Maryellyn Duane. They say, "If you answer 'yes' to five or more, you need to examine your running closely. It would be a good idea to discuss your situation with a friend, coach, or counselor."

1. Do you weigh yourself before and after your runs?

2. Do you repeat the same running routine regardless of physical condition or weather conditions?

3. Do you keep running until you "round off" miles, even if you are tired or late for another activity?

4. Are you enjoying your runs less than previously?

5. Do you have running injuries?

6. Do you continue to "run through" your injuries?

7. Are you disappointed if you don't better your race performances or training runs?

8. Do you binge or eat junk or fatty foods, then increase your mileage to work off weight gain?

9. Do your friends and family tell you that you run too much?

10. Is running your only social outlet?

11. Do you get especially depressed when you are injured?

12. Do you often feel exhausted before you begin your runs?

13. Does your running schedule interfere with your work life?

14. Do you run marathons or ultras "back-to-back"?

15. Do you actually run more than what you tell others?

16. Do you think about running when your mind should be on other issues?

17. Is recording your running in a log or diary a central part of your day?

18. Would you consider injuring yourself to continue a running "streak"?

19. Do you continue to run despite your doctor's recommendations to the contrary?

20. Do you sometimes run in isolated or dangerous areas?

RUNNING AND RECOVERY: THE DON IMUS STORY

As his millions of listeners nationwide can testify, Don Imus spares no one. United States senators, governors, and prominent newspaper columnists (even a president) have been regulars on *Imus in the Morning*.

Despite his usual venom, on one subject Imus speaks with complete reverence: running. Exercise and a healthy lifestyle are the crux of his life—a life that was once governed by alcohol, drugs, and cigarettes. In the 1980s, Don Imus succeeded in rerouting his extreme and destructive addictions to positive, disciplined exercise and diet.

"Before I started running in 1978, I didn't do any kind of exercise," Imus explains. "I rode my motorcycle. I had run track in high school—the 100 and the 220 yards—and played football. But I was never a star athlete.

"For some reason, I wanted to start running," he continues. "It was in Cleveland, where I had returned for a year from New York to work doing radio. There weren't many people running in Cleveland then. I remember that I had trouble finding a store to get running shoes. The first pair of shoes I had was Adidas Country, the ones made of leather.

"When I first started running, I had arthritis, and both my ankles swelled up. I used to have to take a cane out running every night. If it was snowing in Cleveland, I'd be out there running in the snow with that cane. Finally, after a couple of months, the swelling went down. Then I gradually increased the running; I'd jog a quarter-mile and walk a quarter-mile. Eventually, I got to the point where I could run for three miles, then five miles. I continued to run on and off. But I didn't really start seriously running until some years later."

Imus started drinking when he was about 30 years old. He went through periods when he would drink and take drugs, then forgo the drugs and switch from hard liquor to wine or beer. "I considered drinking wine or beer not drinking. When I began running, I was drinking, but I wasn't doing any drugs," he says.

"I had been smoking all my life—a couple of packs a day. When I came back to New York in 1979, I stopped smoking. I continued to run and drink. Then I started doing a little cocaine, and I started smoking again. I smoked and ran for years. I got into cocaine heavily in 1980 to 1981. I wasn't into it that long, but I did a lot in those couple of years. I still ran, but not while I was on cocaine; it's a debilitating drug. I would go through periods when I would run, then I'd go for a month without running. By this time, I was doing cocaine, drinking, and smoking.

"Because of all the stuff I was doing, I never progressed to running much below an 11-minute-mile pace," Imus continues. "The first three or four minutes of running were horrible, because I couldn't catch my breath. My chest was so tight. Then after those few minutes, I was fine. I could run for quite a while. Then, of course, when I stopped running I would start coughing. I used to run a lot in Riverside Park in Manhattan. Lots of times when I'd stop, and start coughing, other people would stop to ask me if I was okay.

"By 1987, I was in pretty bad shape. I went to rehab, because I thought I had no other choice. I wasn't going to make it. In Alcoholics Anonymous, they talk about high bottoms and low bottoms. Physically, I was in as bad shape as you can possibly get and still be alive.

"I stopped drinking on July 17, 1987. Quitting drinking made a huge difference, emotionally and physically. I stopped doing cocaine in June 1983. I stopped smoking in the middle of 1989. After I stopped smoking, I started running a little faster. Before, I couldn't talk when I ran. I had difficulty breathing. I quit smoking because it started to be a pain."

During all the years of doing alcohol and drugs, Imus ran on average three days a week. While in rehab, he started running every day. "It replaced the drugs and alcohol," he explains, "plus I just liked it. I liked the way I felt after I'd run for 45 minutes or an hour every day.

"When I got out of rehab, I went to the Sports Training Institute in Manhattan. That's where I first started running on treadmills. In 1986 I bought two treadmills. I also did some weights back then, but I didn't have a serious program."

Is Imus addicted to exercise? "Actually, I do the running even more intensely than I did drinking and drugs," he says. "I was an episodic drinker and drug user. I wasn't a daily drinker or drug user. I can't imagine not running, though. In fact, I once wanted to see how long I could do it without taking a break. In 1990 I decided to see if I could run every day for a year. I ran every day for 375 days, averaging four miles a day. My streak ended in August 1991. There are days in a year—this is true for any person—you're not going to feel well. So there were obviously days throughout that year that I felt horrible. I had a couple of colds. I was on the road and I still ran—in Boston, in Texas. That streak gave me a great sense of accomplishment."

When asked to compare the addictions—drugs and alcohol versus running—Imus says, "I guess the difference is that running makes me feel good, and the other stuff kept me from feeling bad."

As of 2003, Imus, a married father with a young son, still works out at least three times a week, running and lifting weights at a gym. As he recently told his listeners, "I do it because I have to. I've learned not to set unrealistic goals—because it's better to do something than nothing."

PERSPECTIVE

Successful running—like most all endeavors—is about balance. This is true mentally (psychologically and emotionally) as well as physically. The downside in running is caused by a loss of perspective.

"One can't be too one-sided," says triathlete Mark Allen. "Athletics should reduce stress, not increase it. Obviously there is the stress before races or in serious training. That's part of the challenge, and challenge is okay. But if your training is like pulling teeth, or you fight with your spouse before heading out the door, you need to evaluate your athletic goals within the framework of the reality of your life."

Alberto Salazar believes that "struggling with my running for the past six or seven years has been the greatest thing that ever could have happened to me. It's made me a much tougher and more resilient person, one who is more ready for whatever life might throw at me in the future. I'm just so much better equipped for adversity, for not having things turn out the way I want them to."

What is the source of my success? I think it's a combination of consistency and balance. I know I haven't succeeded as an athlete merely because of my physical gifts. I found that out as a competitive swimmer. I think it is my mental ability. The key has been to strike a balance between training and the rest of life. Most people see my racing success, but they don't see what is really behind it. The only reason I have gotten here is because of the balance I have kept—with my wife, friends, healthy lifestyle—all the aspects of life.

—*Mark Allen*

"I think my attitude is key," explains Eamonn Coghlan. "I try not to get caught up thinking about the task ahead. I just do what has to be done. I have the belief in myself that what I am doing is right. Then I let the rest happen. A lot of athletes get caught up. They focus so much on the goal, the end result, rather than the process of getting to that point. As a result, they waste an awful lot of nervous energy. They get so caught up that, as the event nears, they crack up from nerves. They can't handle it; they lose all their self-confidence.

"Sure I get nervous about competition. But I differentiate between being nervous and being uncontrollably nervous," Coghlan continues. "I try to eliminate obsessing over the goal while I'm training for months on end. I know what my goals are. I know what I have to do. I visualize my race, then I forget about it when I'm not running. I don't become a hermit because of my running. I socialize with my friends.

"Of course I had those times of thinking about an event and feeling the butterflies in my stomach. On the day of a race I'd wake up with my stomach in knots. But rather than get sick from that, I learned to love that feeling. I'd be nervous but happy. That was the adrenaline working for me. What I try to do is harness the nervous energy, not allow it to worry me, and try to preserve it until the gun goes off. Then that energy goes into my race."

PART 5
NUTRITION

25

PHYSICAL FUEL

A car can't run without gas, and a runner can't run without fuel. Like any other machine, the higher the quality of fuel used, the better the performance that will result. Unfortunately, runners don't come with owner's manuals, outlining optimal fuel choices. So what should a runner eat? What vitamins and minerals promote peak performance? And when should runners load up and on what types of foods?

Runners tend to be very health-conscious, more aware perhaps than the general public of the importance of a healthy diet and good nutrition in maintaining fitness. Yet every runner—from beginner to elite—seems to have a question about optimal eating.

> According to scientists at the Gatorade® Exercise Physiology Lab, runners typically burn between 100 and 150 calories per mile, or 2,600 to 3,500 calories per marathon. To replace those calories— basic nutritional needs aside—a runner would need to eat about ten bagels, or 35 to 47 peaches, or 11 to 15 servings of regular yogurt with fruit, or about two pounds of plain cooked pasta. At 100 calories burned per mile, about 91 million calories were burned by the 34,729 runners in the 2003 New York City Marathon.

WHAT ARE HEALTHY FOODS?

Sports nutritionist Nancy Clark knows what runners need—a sound diet based on healthy foods. "When you're training hard—juggling work, exercise, and family—and eating on the run, you may have little time or opportunity to eat the proverbial three square meals a day. Yet, you can maintain a healthful diet," says Clark. "The trick is to eat a variety of wholesome foods that will protect your health, invest in your muscular strength, and contribute to your exercise program."

HEALTHY EATING TIPS

1. Eat as much raw food as possible.

2. Use nonfat or low-fat dairy products, like ricotta, cottage, or farmer's cheese, instead of cream cheese or full-fat hard cheese. Or cut the heavier variety with the lighter, using a mixture of the two in sandwiches and cooking.

3. Cut mayonnaise, sour cream, or other such dressings or sauces with yogurt, broth, milk, or lemon juice (in tuna fish or potato salad, for example). Change the proportions gradually if you need to acquire a taste for the lighter version. Eventually, you may be able to do without the heavy stuff entirely. If the dish seems too dry, add more of the liquids.

4. Add lemon or vinegar to cut salad dressing or try eating salad with only lemon or vinegar, emphasizing herbs and other seasonings for taste.

5. Use soy products in place of conventional protein sources. Soy products can be used instead of meat or cheese in such dishes as casseroles, spaghetti sauce, lasagna, Mexican food, and stew. Tofu goes nicely with noodle or rice dishes, or whipped in the blender with lemon juice, yogurt or water, and herbs as salad dressing.

6. Avoid oil by using a small amount of water to cook vegetables in recipes that call for them to be sautéed or fried. Use a steamer for other cooked vegetables, and bake rather than fry such vegetables as eggplant and potatoes.

7. Use the water in which potatoes or vegetables have been cooked or steamed for making sauces, baking bread, cooking rice, or in any other recipe that calls for liquid. If there is no immediate use for this water, refrigerate or freeze it (in premeasured proportions if desired).

8. If you use white flour, add some bran or wheat germ to it.

9. Rinse or drain canned tuna fish and canned vegetables and fruits, even if packed in water, to reduce the salt or sugar in the water. Don't hesitate to rinse any food (even prepared) that contains excess salt or fat.

10. Dilute juice or soda with as much water as possible.

11. Cut out up to half the sugar called for in baking recipes, or replace sugar with frozen fruit juice or mashed ripe fruit, like bananas or pears. Make desserts with a fruit base rather than with such things as chocolate, cream cheese, or whipped cream.

12. For healthy snacks, keep raw vegetables on hand or freeze berries, orange slices, or juice in ice-cube trays. Freeze flavored yogurt to satisfy ice cream cravings.

—Grete Waitz

GENERAL GUIDELINES FOR EATING OUT

In today's hectic world, it's difficult enough to fit running into a busy schedule, let alone find time to prepare good, healthy meals. More and more people save time by eating out, or by ordering in food from a neighborhood restaurant. You can maintain a nutritious diet for a healthy active lifestyle by adhering to a few key guidelines.

Lauren Wallack Antonucci, M.S., R.D., C.D.E., has created the following checklist and chart to assist you in maintaining good nutrition on the go.

1. Try to include as many different colored foods as possible on your plate at each meal (sweet potatoes, brown rice, colorful vegetables, salmon).

2. Be proactive. In a restaurant, ask how dishes are prepared and request that added fats/sauces be omitted.

3. Look for menu items that are baked, broiled, steamed, poached, or grilled.

4. Ask for dressings/sauces on the side...and use them sparingly! Dab them on with your fork, rather than pouring them on.

5. If you really crave something you know is not the healthiest choice, order an appetizer-size portion, or split it with a friend.

6. Trim visible fat and skin off all meats (including fish).

7. Start with a clear or vegetable-based soup or a salad with a small amount of light dressing.

8. Beware of empty calorie drinks. Alcohol is not only dehydrating, but sugary drinks like margaritas and piña coladas can easily contain 300–500 calories each.

9. Ask for an extra side order of vegetables, baked potato, or noodles and hold the butter and cream sauces.

10. Enjoy new cuisines. Keeping these guidelines in mind, you can surely find delicious and nutritious foods almost anywhere.

GUIDE TO MENU SELECTION ON THE GO

Foods to Include:	Foods to Limit:
Breakfast:	
Whole-grain cereal	Sugary/Processed cereals
Low-fat milk/yogurt	Whole milk/yogurt
Hot cereal (oatmeal, farina)	Croissants, pastries, doughnuts
Whole-wheat English muffins, breads, and bagels	Sausage, bacon, ham, Cheese and meat omelets
Pancakes	
Fruit and fruit juice	
Eggs/vegetable omelets (with egg or egg substitutes)	
Deli/Diner:	
Lean turkey, ham, grilled chicken (ask for extra veggies on sandwich)	Other cold cuts (bologna, salami) Grilled cheese sandwich
Whole-grain breads/rolls	Creamed soups
Broth-based soups	Pastries/muffins
Broiled chicken or fish	Mashed potatoes, French fries
Salads (with olive oil–based dressing not creamy)	Sodas
Baked potato	
Fruit	
Juice, sports drinks, seltzer	
Fast-Food Restaurants:	
Grilled chicken sandwich (no mayo)	Fried chicken/fish sandwiches
Plain regular hamburger (no cheese, no mayo)	"Supersized" anything, or extra cheese/meats
Baked potato	Big special sandwich

(continued)

GUIDE TO MENU SELECTION ON THE GO (CONT.)

Foods to Include:	Foods to Limit:
Salad with low-fat dressing	BBQ ribs
Low-fat or nonfat milk	Chicken nuggets
Low-fat yogurt fruit parfait	French fries/onion rings
	Biscuits

Pizza Parlor:

Thick crust pizza	Extra cheese
Whole-wheat pizza	Cheese stuffed crust pizzas
Veggie toppings	Meat toppings

Snack/Vending Machines:

Pretzels	Snack cakes
Peanuts	Ice cream
Dried fruit	Candy bars
Granola bars/fig bars	Regular chips
Baked chips	

Restaurants:

Italian:

Veggies grilled in olive oil	Antipasto
Grilled fish/chicken	Fried calamari, other fried, breaded fish
Marinara and Marsala dishes	Parmigiana dishes
Red or white clam sauce	Alfredo/cream sauces
Chicken cacciatore	Stuffed shells/manicotti
Fruit/fruit ice/sorbet	Cheesecake, cannoli

Chinese:

Won ton soup	Fried egg rolls
Steamed dumplings	Fried dumplings
Steamed spring rolls	Egg dishes
Noodles and rice (preferably brown)	Sweet and sour/battered dishes
Vegetarian/tofu dishes	Duck

Mexican:

Fajitas	Nachos with cheese/meat
Plain, soft tortillas (preferably whole-wheat)	Quesadillas

(continued)

GUIDE TO MENU SELECTION ON THE GO (CONT.)

Foods to Include:	Foods to Limit:
Vegetable and chicken based dishes	Refried beans
Burritos	Tostadas
Bean soup, chili, rice and beans	Taco salad
Enchiladas	Sour cream
Seviche	
Guacamole (small portion)	

Indian:

Tandoori	Malai (coconut sauce)
Vegetable curries	Samosas (stuffed fritters)
Naan, roti (breads)	Poori (bread)
Dahl	Fried dishes
Seekh kabob	Mughlai

Japanese:

Sushi, sashimi	Tempura
Miso soup	Tonkatsu
Green salad with carrot/ginger dressing	Fried tofu
Teriyaki, yakitori	
Tofu (not fried)	
Edamame (soybeans)	

Quick Home Meal Essentials:

Fresh/frozen vegetables
Bagged salads and pre-cut veggies
Tuna in water (or bagged tuna)
Potatoes/sweet potatoes (to bake or microwave)
Frozen breakfast burritos
Frozen entrées with word "healthy" in title
Pre-cooked chicken
Veggie burgers
Pasta and tomato sauce
Lean beef/lean turkey meat
Low-sodium soup
Salsa (for use on potatoes, salads, veggies)
Fresh or canned fruits (in light syrup or in its own juice)

FELICIA STOLER'S NUTRITION TIPS

As part of the medical team for the New York City Marathon, I am asked a lot of questions at the pre-race expo. The most common one is, "What do I eat before and during the race?" I'll reply, "What do you usually eat before you run?" or "What do you typically eat or drink while doing a long run?" And my next line is, "Don't do anything different on race day."

Runners can be meticulous about their physical training regimen but forget to practice their eating and drinking. When you run, do you run on an empty stomach? If you've ever made a conscious effort to eat two to three hours before you run, have you noticed a difference? Many runners I've counseled have found that eating before they exercise helps them to run better.

For many of us, our bodies can utilize what we already have in storage for fuel, but having glucose (from carbohydrates) and fatty acids circulating in our blood stream means that our muscles can use those fuels immediately rather than having to pull them out of storage or create them. Our liver can produce glucose through a process called gluconeogenesis, but it is not the best way to refuel during running.

Eating in the Morning

Some runners get up in the morning and run on an empty stomach. First thing in the morning, you probably haven't eaten for at least eight hours. I recommend getting up 15 minutes early and having at least a glass of juice (whatever your personal preference may be). The key in the morning—especially if you do not have a lot of time to spare—is consuming something in liquid form. It will pass through the digestive system quicker, allowing immediate fuel availability. The risk for gastrointestinal discomfort will also be lower.

Eating During the Day

If you exercise during the day, or in the evening, when should you eat? First, you need to determine how much time you have to eat before you run. If you have two hours, then you can eat a full meal that includes carbohydrates. Remember to stay away from greasy, fried, or heavily seasoned foods. Make sure you have a full glass (8 oz.) of water half an hour before you run, and then you are good to go.

If you have only an hour before you run, then have a light snack of a carbohydrate-rich food. It can be whole-grain bread, a bagel, a cereal bar, a piece of fruit, pretzels, yogurt, cottage cheese, or a fruit smoothie. You may consume a sports bar, but make sure it is one that contains carbohydrates (not just protein). In this case, have the eight ounces of water 20 minutes before you begin your run.

If you eat something and it doesn't agree with you, try eating something different. If you feel uncomfortable eating one hour before, try eating 90 minutes before you run. Eventually, you will find a pre-run food strategy that makes you feel good when you run.

The question of carbohydrate loading often arises. The famous Ronzoni pasta party is held the night before the New York City Marathon. Gorging on pasta the night before the race is not true carbohydrate loading. There is a more comprehensive diet for carbohydrate loading. Some runners do not feel comfortable over-indulging on carbohydrates because they feel bloated (glucose is stored in the body with water). Once again, try out a meal like this before a long run and see how you feel.

When a runner travels to run a marathon, there's the temptation to try new foods. Again—don't try something you've never had the night before the race. Save it as a reward for finishing the race. Another great thing about running a marathon like New York City is that there's food available from every country in the world so there is something for everyone to eat.

Eating During the Race

Eating during a race is another skill that must be practiced. The general rule of sports nutrition is that exercise less than an hour in duration does not require refueling in progress. Over an hour, you need carbohydrates and electrolytes (in addition to fluids). Sports supplements come in many forms—bars, gels, and liquids—and with different proportions of nutrients. Real food works well, but may be too bulky to carry.

Try various products and rate how you feel. Keep a little journal for yourself. Did you feel good after eating the product? Did it cause any cramping or discomfort? Did you feel like you had more energy to keep on running?

When eating and drinking during running, do not wait for physical cues to signal the need for replenishment. It can take time for the body to absorb the nutrients and have them readily available for your muscles to use—so plan to replenish before you are "empty." One of my clients worked it out with her neighbors that she would put water bottles with sports drinks on their porches along her running route.

Eating After Running

After your run, it is important to replenish what was used during exercise. A combination of nutrients is necessary, the most important ingredient being fluids. The next most important nutrient is carbohydrate, followed by protein. Some would argue that consuming protein beforehand would be better for post-race repair. Again, it is a matter of comfort and what works best for you. Fats are important in addition to the other nutrients—many of us get them from food preparation methods, or from protein foods.

Vitamins and Minerals

You should ask your physician or a nutritionist about your particular nutritional needs. Vitamin and mineral needs change throughout the life cycle.

Calcium is an important nutrient for men and women. We hit peak bone density into our 30s and it depletes from there. In addition to providing the body with a skeletal frame, calcium is a neurotransmitter and is essential for muscle contraction. Folic acid is important because it helps to lower homocysteine levels in the blood (high blood homocysteine levels are highly correlated to heart disease). Potassium is also important for maintaining heart health. Vitamin C helps maintain collagen in the body, so for Masters runners, adequate intake is essential. Vitamin E, a fat-soluble vitamin, is considered to be a powerful antioxidant.

There is another category of nutrients called phytochemicals—found in the pigments of plants—which are thought to have anticancer and possible cardio-protective properties. Some great choices for phytonutrients include flax seed oil, olive oil, avocados, soy, green peas, wheat germ, whole grains, tomatoes, red peppers, broccoli, spinach, carrots, cantaloupe, tangerines, oranges, strawberries, grapes, green tea, wine (moderately), garlic, and onions.

Eating fiber is also important, not just because of the nutrients contained in the food, but because it helps to maintain the health of the colon. Eating a balanced diet can usually meet one's nutrient needs, but taking a multivitamin and mineral supplement can fill in any gaps in the diet.

Here are some suggestions for food sources of nutrients:

Nutrient	Food Sources
Protein	Meat, fish, poultry, pork, legumes, dairy

Fat-Soluble Vitamins

Vitamin A	Dark green, yellow, and orange fruits and vegetables, fortified dairy products
Vitamin D	Fortified dairy products, egg yolks, fish oil
Vitamin E	Vegetable oils, nuts, seeds, leafy vegetables, wheat germ
Vitamin K	Green vegetables, dairy products, egg yolks, green tea, soybeans

Water-Soluble Vitamins

Vitamin C	Citrus fruits, tomatoes, green leafy vegetables, berries, peppers, cantaloupe
Thiamine	Enriched grains, pork, wheat germ, legumes, fish, seeds
Riboflavin	Meat, nuts, green leafy vegetables, chicken, fish, grains, fortified dairy products
Niacin	Meat, nuts, legumes, fish, poultry
Vitamin B-6	Poultry, fish, eggs, meat, beans, nuts, bananas, legumes, whole grains
Folate/Folic Acid	Green leafy vegetables, citrus fruits, legumes, nuts, wheat germ
Vitamin B-12	Animal proteins

Minerals

Calcium	Dairy products, leafy green vegetables, canned salmon and sardines, with bones
Phosphorus	Meat
Magnesium	Seafood, fish, nuts, legumes, grains, wheat germ
Iron	Meat, eggs, grains, legumes, nuts, seeds
Zinc	Meat, seafood, fish, poultry, seeds, legumes, egg, pork
Iodine	Iodized salt, seafood, fish
Selenium	Seafood, meat, poultry, whole grains, egg yolk, mushrooms, wheat germ, onion family, dairy products

SOME SPECIAL CONCERNS

In addition to questions about good nutrition and healthful eating, Nancy Clark provides answers and advice to runners with common concerns.

What If You Constantly Crave Sweets?

First, assess your meal patterns. Among many runners, breakfast and lunch are either nonexistent or insufficient because of lack of time, the desire to have eating not interfere with training, and just plain habit. Once you build up a calorie deficit during the day, you get too hungry. Sweets cravings may simply be a sign that you're physiologically ravenous. To prevent these cravings, as well as filling up on nutritionally empty sweets, eat more calories at breakfast and/or lunch (depending on when you train) and plan a second, small lunch or keep a snack handy in the afternoon if you eat a late dinner.

Many women know all about premenstrual sweets cravings. According to the research, a complex interplay of hormonal changes seems to influence women's food choices. High levels of estrogen may be linked with premenstrual carbohydrate cravings. Women may, in fact, be hungrier. During the week before menstruation, a woman's metabolic rate may increase by 200 to 500 calories daily. That's the equivalent of another meal. But in an attempt to fight off the extra eating and the threat of weight gain, women commonly get too hungry and succumb to sweets. If you feel hungry, give yourself permission to eat an extra 200 to 500 wholesome calories a day the week before your period. That ought to tame the cookie monster, yet won't contribute to weight gain.

Exercise speeds up the pace at which food passes through the stomach, so if you feel uncomfortably full after every meal, you may be able to walk off the discomfort rather than resort to medication. Doctors quoted in *Food and Nutrition Letter* (Rodale Press) studied the digestive systems of those who either stood around or walked for an hour after eating. Food went through the stomach nearly 40 percent faster for those walking than for those standing still.

If you crave a sugar fix before exercise, you may be hypoglycemic (have low blood sugar) and consequently be fatigued. Sugar taken during exercise, however, can actually enhance performance if you're performing for longer than 60 to 90 minutes. Again, the safest way to avoid sweets cravings is to eat adequate calories earlier in the day. If you haven't done that, and you are hungry and craving sweets, eat them within ten minutes of exercise to avoid hypoglycemia. Be aware, however, that you may experience an upset stomach.

Finally, there's nothing wrong with a moderate amount of sweets if desired as part of your weekly intake. But keep sugar to a minimum—that is, less than 10 percent of your daily calories. If you crave cookies, eat one or two small ones slowly, savoring each mouthful, and if candy is your weakness, have a small piece as a dessert after lunch rather than as a dinner substitute.

How Can You Lose Weight and Still Have Energy to Train?

The overwhelming concern among sports-active dieters is how to lose weight and yet maintain energy for training. High-energy, low-calorie reducing is possible. The trick is to choose wisely what and when you eat.

Remember, anything eaten in excess can be fattening. Excess calories, particularly those from fats, are the dietary demon. For example, one teaspoon of carbohydrates has only 16 calories; that same amount of fat has 36 calories. Your body can very easily store excess dietary fat as body fat. You're more likely to burn off excess carbohydrates. So don't trade a fat-free baked potato for fat-rich cottage cheese, or eat spoonfuls of peanut butter from the jar, thinking that's better than a handful of crackers.

Prebreakfast aerobic exercise may burn fat faster than exercise at any other time of day. Some studies have indicated that although you burn the same amount of calories no matter what time of day you run, two-thirds of the calories burned in a prebreakfast run will come from fat, when in the afternoon, fat will account for less than half the calories burned. The other half comes from burning carbohydrates—glycogen and glucose.

Does it matter when you eat? It seems to. If you feast at night—a common habit among some runners—you may gain weight more easily than if you eat the same amount of calories earlier in the day. You can also easily overeat at night. The bottom line for dieters is that you should eat at least two-thirds of your calories during the day, particularly a good breakfast, and then the balance at night. You'll not only burn off the calories when you exercise and have more energy for training, but you'll also prevent yourself from getting too hungry and overeating. Remember, when you get too hungry, you may lack the energy to care about how much you eat.

Evaluate when, why, and what you eat—and correct any poor patterns. Eat slowly. Overweight people tend to eat faster than their normal-weight counterparts. Practice moderation rather than heavy denial. You're less likely to binge. Avoid temptations by limiting time in the kitchen and the supermarket cookie aisle. Post a list of nonfood activities to do instead of eating when you're bored, lonely, tired, or nervous: read a book, play the piano, write in a journal, call a friend. Finally, think lean and fit. Being positive about yourself is important for successful weight loss and your well-being.

What About Vitamins?

Approximately 40 percent of Americans take supplements, and an even higher percentage of athletes take them. Among the nation's top female runners, 91 percent have reported taking supplements on a regular basis. But too many people believe that a vitamin supplement can replace a meal

It's not just women who have to be good to their bones. Men also get osteoporosis, a condition that weakens the bones. According to *Runner's World* magazine, researchers studied the effects of calcium and vitamin D supplementation on the bone mineral densities of men. They hoped to find that an extra 1,000 milligrams of calcium a day would slow the rate of bone loss. What they found, however, was that the men in their study, ages 30 to 67, experienced bone loss in both their arms and back despite the extra calcium intake. To reduce their risk of developing premature osteoporosis, men should do as many women already do—engage in regular weight-bearing exercise (which strengthens bones) and eat calcium-rich foods.

and fulfill 100 percent of their nutritional needs. They're wrong. It's food that supplies protein, energy, fiber, and phtyochemicals (health-protective compounds found in plant foods). No vitamin provides energy (calories) or compensates for a meal of junk food.

True, you need adequate vitamins to function optimally, but an excess offers no competitive edge. No scientific evidence to date proves that extra vitamins enhance performance. You can get the fundamental nutrients required by the body to maintain good health by eating a variety of foods from the four food groups (two exceptions are iron and zinc).

To clear up another commonly held misconception, exercise does not increase vitamin needs. Exercise doesn't burn vitamins, just as a car doesn't burn spark plugs. Vitamins are catalysts that are needed for metabolic processes to occur.

If you usually eat a well-balanced diet, a supplement is unnecessary for the occasional off day. Most athletes with a hearty appetite get plenty of vitamins from wholesome foods, making multivitamin supplementation necessary only for some individuals at risk of nutritional deficiencies. Supplements may be appropriate for the following: dieters who are restricting calories, chronic undereaters, food-allergic people, lactose-intolerant people, and pregnant women. All these cases, however, should be verified by consultation with nutrition or medical experts.

In general, get vitamins from food first, but if you wish to get psychological health insurance by supplementing your diet, take a single one-a-day-type multivitamin. Rather than taking megadoses of vitamins, which may cause toxic reactions, have your diet evaluated by a registered dietitian who specializes in sports nutrition and learn what nutrients you are actually getting, which you may be missing, and what are the best food sources from which to gain them. You can find a local sports dietitian by using the referral network at www.eatright.org.

How Do You Eat Well as a Vegetarian Athlete?

You can do fine as a vegetarian if you know your nutrition. Many athletes proudly declare they are vegetarians, believing that vegetarian means being health-conscious; however, many of these vegetarian athletes consume inadequate protein to support their athletic program. They are simply non-meat-eaters who have not subsequently adjusted their diets.

Believing carbohydrates are the key to endurance success, some non-meat-eaters fuel up on them and forget the protein. Adequate protein is essential to build, repair, and maintain your muscles. Long-distance runners

Even low levels, two days a week, of aerobic activity can significantly compromise iron levels. But eating iron-rich foods is better than taking supplements to offset a deficiency, according to a study by Roseann M. Lyle, Ph.D., at Purdue University in Indiana. According to *Self* magazine, after 12 weeks, women who had ingested 12 mg. of "muscle" foods—meat, fish, and poultry—had equal if not higher iron levels than those who had ingested a 50 mg. supplement.

can burn some protein for energy. The other mistake some people make is to replace red meat with eggs and cheese for protein, unaware that these foods have far more fat and cholesterol than lean meats. In this respect, a grilled cheese or egg salad sandwich is worse than a lean roast beef sandwich without mayonnaise.

You need not be an expert in nutrition, nor spend hours in the kitchen preparing vegetarian specialties, to meet your nutritional needs adequately. Following are some meatless but protein-packed eat-and-run choices:

Grains + milk products: multi-grain bagel with yogurt, cereal and milk, pasta and low-fat cheese

Grains + beans and legumes (such as peanuts, lentils, kidney beans, pinto beans, etc.): whole-wheat toast with peanut butter, pasta and tomato sauce with canned kidney beans

Legumes + seeds: hummus (ground chick peas with sesame paste)

Milk products + any food: milk, yogurt, or cheese (preferably nonfat or low-fat) added to any meal or snack

By eating a variety of different kinds of foods throughout the day, you'll get the most complete nutritional value. In addition, to boost iron intake, which may be lacking in nonmeat diets, cook in a cast-iron skillet, buy iron-enriched breakfast cereals, eat lots of dark green vegetables, and have some vitamin C–rich fruit or vegetable with each meal.

What Should You Eat Before, During, and After Running?

Pre-running or racing food has several functions: to help prevent hypoglycemia (low blood sugar), to stave off hunger feelings, to fuel your muscles and your brain, and to give mental assurance that your body is well fueled. Each person has food preferences and aversions, so no one pre-run food fits the bill for everyone. To determine what food is best for you, experiment with the following guidelines:

1. Eat carbohydrate-based meals daily to keep your muscles fueled.

2. Choose quality carbs that are low in fat—whole-wheat bread, sesame crackers, brown rice—as they tend to digest easily.

3. Avoid sugary foods, such as soda and candy, within an hour before hard exercise. If you must have sweets, enjoy them five to 15 minutes before you exercise.

4. Allow adequate time for food to digest. The general rule is to allow three to four hours for a large meal; two to three hours for a smaller meal, and less than an hour for a small snack, according to personal tolerance.

5. Allow more digestion time before intense exercise than before low-key activity.

6. If digestion is a problem, choose liquid foods (a smoothie, instant breakfast, yogurt) because they leave the stomach faster than solid foods do.

7. If eating before a race makes you nervous, don't do it, but be sure to eat extra the night before.

8. If traveling, take along some nonperishable foods to make sure you have something to eat. For example, bring oranges, dried fruit, and bagels.

9. Always eat familiar foods before a race. Don't try anything new.

10. Drink plenty of fluids.

Nourishment during running is recommended for workouts lasting 60 to 90 minutes or more. In this case, it is always best to experiment in training with anything you intend to try in a race. Best choices are carbohydrates—most conveniently in the form of sports drinks. Hard candy, gummy bears, gels, diluted juice, and defizzed cola are some other choices that runners report using to maintain their blood sugar.

Most fitness runners recover at their own pace because they don't deplete their muscles' glycogen, or fuel stores, with a typical 20- to 30-minute workout. Hardcore endurance athletes, however, should monitor their diets carefully to ensure proper refueling.

What you eat after a hard workout or race can affect your recovery. One priority is to replace the fluids lost by sweating as well as the carbohydrates you deplete. Initially, right after exercise, a glass of juice or other small carbohydrate-rich food and water will do the job. Adding a little protein can further enhance recovery. Preferably, within two hours you should have consumed 300 calories of high-carbohydrate foods. Examples are one cup of orange juice and a bagel, a fruit smoothie made with yogurt, or a bowl of cereal with milk and a banana.

High-carbohydrate sports drinks can also refuel your muscles. But be aware that these types of fluids generally lack the vitamins and minerals found in wholesome foods. Use them to supplement a healthy diet, not as a food replacement.

What If You Feel Tired All the Time?

Since there are both nutritional and nonnutritional causes of fatigue, here are some possible reasons to help determine why you may be feeling chronically rundown or ill.

- **Mental Fatigue Due to Low Blood Sugar.** If you are among those breakfast- and lunch-skippers, the low blood sugar that results from this habit could have you feeling fatigued. If your reason for skipping meals is lack of time, it's worth it to take even a few minutes to eat something easy. If you don't feel hungry, try eating less at night and distributing your calories more evenly throughout the day.

- **Muscular Fatigue Due to Lack of Carbohydrates or Lack of Protein.** If you eat high-fat meals, try making some of the following switches with these popular foods: use more bread dough and less cheese in thick-crust pizza; more rice with Chinese food instead of egg rolls; and carbohydrate-rich snacks, such as whole-wheat pretzels, juice, fig bars, and dried fruit, to supplement your meals—particularly if those meals are irregular or unbalanced. Fatigue can also relate to lack of protein, common in nonmeat-eaters and runners who eat too many carbohydrates.

- **Fatigue Due to Iron Deficiency Anemia.** The real key to getting enough iron is absorption. You can enhance absorption by drinking orange juice or ingesting other vitamin C–rich foods with iron-rich foods, and limiting caffeinated drinks, particularly tea, with iron-rich foods.

- **Fatigue Due to Lack of Sleep.** You can be tired mentally, from an intense job or other pressures, or physically, from strenuous exercise. In addition, if you eat a large or late dinner, you may have trouble falling asleep. Again, try reversing eating habits—more during the day, less at night.

- **Fatigue Due to Overtraining.** Rest or recovery days are essential parts of a training program; they allow the muscles to replenish their depleted muscle glycogen. There is a difference between being a "compulsive runner," proud of long streaks of running or hard workouts, and a "serious athlete," who trains wisely.

- **Fatigue Due to Stress and Depression.** Work or life stress can cause depression and the feeling of lack of control. But you can control one aspect of your life: your diet. This can make you feel better both physically and mentally.

Although chronic fatigue can be a symptom of a medical problem, fatigue caused by habits outlined above can be resolved with better eating, sleeping, and training habits. If you're concerned about lack of energy, your best bet is to get a nutrition checkup with a registered dietitian and a medical checkup from your doctor.

Should You Consume Beverages with Alcohol or Caffeine Before or After Running?

It seems the alcoholic drink of choice among runners is beer. Perhaps you've heard the myth that beer is a good sports drink because it contains carbohydrates and other vitamins and minerals. In truth, *beer—or any alcohol—is a poor sports drink for many reasons*. First of all, alcohol has a dehydrating effect that gets you running to the toilet, rather than replacing valuable fluids. Drinking beer before an event increases your chances of becoming dehydrated during the event. As for carbohydrates or other nutrition, beer is a poor source. The truth is that most of its calories are from alcohol, which your muscles don't store, so with beer you're more likely to get loaded than carbo-loaded.

A major problem with postexercise drinking is that runners are dehydrated and they drink on empty stomachs. Drinking quickly to quench thirst and drinking on a empty stomach cause one to be affected by alcohol's depressant effect quickly. Instead of consuming beer immediately after exercise, first quench your thirst with two to three glasses of water. Have a high-carbohydrate food, then stretch and shower. Then have a beer at mealtime, if desired.

Will caffeine help you run better? For some runners, yes; for others, no. One reason drinking caffeinated beverages before exercise seems to help some people is perhaps because it stimulates the nervous system. But in some people, caffeine can cause the jitters or an acidic coffee stomach and have a dehydrating effect. So when considering caffeinated beverages, be sure to evaluate your personal sensitivity to this stimulant. Experiment during training to determine the right amount, if any, that works for you.

What About Eating Junk Food?

Rather than looking at foods as either good food or junk food, it is better to consider the entire diet. After all, you could limit your diet to several good foods, excluding all others, and actually end up with a poor and unbalanced diet. Any food in moderation can fit into an overall wholesome diet. Gaining understanding of certain foods may help you gain a perspective on their place in your diet.

TIPS TO LOWER YOUR FAT INTAKE

- Combine equal amounts of ground beef with shredded raw vegetables like carrots or zucchini.
- Blot the oil on pizza and burgers with a paper napkin.
- When eating chicken, stick to the white meat and remove the skin *before* you cook to eliminate the temptation to eat it.
- Use jelly or jam on toast instead of butter or margarine.
- Use mustard instead of mayonnaise.
- Put one slice of cheese instead of two on your sandwich.
- Order mushroom pizza instead of pepperoni.
- Use fat-free dressing instead of regular, or cut regular dressing with vinegar or lemon.

Here are other fat facts:
- The softer the cookie the higher the fat.
- The moister the cake the higher the fat.
- The cheaper the food the higher the fat.

Sugar.   Although sugar is reputed to be an evil that causes sugar highs and sugar lows, only some people are truly sensitive to its hypoglycemic effect. Most tolerate sugar just fine. Although refined sugar is a nutritional zero, a sweet treat can appropriately fit into a meal plan without sabotaging a healthful diet.

Fat.   Of all the nutritional culprits, fat is the most harmful. Low-fat diets, though, don't mean no-fat diets. Generally, athletes should consume 20 to 35 percent of their calories from fat in their diet. For example, for an active woman who eats 2,000 calories per day, a 25 percent fat diet equals 500 calories, or 55 grams of fat per day (the equivalent of about four tablespoons of olive oil or, less desirably, a cup and a half of premium ice cream). Learning to read food labels will help you determine the fat content of various foods and, thus, compute your daily total. Preferably you will select the more heart-healthy fats, such as olive oil, peanut butter, nuts, and other vegetable fats.

Salt.   Many athletes mistakenly think that salt causes high blood pressure. They go to great extremes to limit their salt intake without understanding that salt does not cause high blood pressure. In fact, most runners have low blood pressure, and since you lose salt during hard workouts, salt replacement can be an appropriate part of a sports diet. If you and your family members have no history of hypertension, go ahead and enjoy some pretzels, salty peanuts, or canned soups.

When considering junk food, remember that there is a fundamental difference between poor dietary habits and a moderate amount of nutritionally questionable foods. Instead of categorizing good or junk, simply make sure you're eating an overall well-balanced diet that includes nutrient-rich powerhouse foods. These include whole-grain breads and cereals, oranges and orange juice, cantaloupe and bananas (which are nutritionally preferable to apples and grapes), dark-colored vegetables (spinach, tomatoes, and green peppers, superior to paler iceberg lettuce and cucumbers), and low- or non-fat milk and yogurt or soy milk or soy yogurt. By eating more of the best, you can include a few treats without sabotaging your health with one snack.

26

RECIPES AND EATING TIPS

Here are some recipes and healthy eating tips.

LAUREN WALLACK ANTONUCCI'S
HEALTHY EATING TIPS

- Drink a minimum of 8–10 glasses of (non-alcoholic) fluids daily.

- Increase your fruit, vegetable, and salad intake. Aim for 2–3 servings of fruits and 3–5 servings of vegetables each day.

- Avoid creamy dressings. Use olive oil–based dressings.

- Buy and store healthy snacks you enjoy (fruits, veggies, low-fat yogurt, granola or energy bars) in individual serving sizes.

- Snack on light popcorn, pretzels, dried fruit, and nuts.

- Choose pre-packaged veggies with salsa or cup up fruits with flavored low-fat or nonfat yogurt for a great treat.

- Watch portion sizes of high-fat or fried foods. Eat a small amount of these foods, and increase portions of healthier choices (veggies, pasta, potatoes, rice, fruits, lean protein).

- Start meals with broth or vegetable-based soups/salad with low-fat dressing if watching your weight.

- Keep busy with running and other activities you enjoy daily.

- Ask yourself, "Am I hungry?" before eating.

- Prepare meals/snacks in advance as often as possible to avoid poor last-minute food choices when extremely hungry.

- Use whole-grain breads/cereals. Try oatmeal or ready-to-eat cereals for a quick and healthy breakfast/snack.

- Drink juices or sports drinks rather than soda (or skip caloric beverages altogether if watching your weight).

Honey Chicken

From the kitchen of Joan Samuelson, 1984 Olympic marathon champion.

3 lb. chicken, cut up

3 tbsp. butter or margarine, optional

1/2 cup honey

1/4 cup prepared mustard

1/2 tsp. salt

1 tsp. curry powder

Remove skin from chicken pieces, wash, and pat dry. Melt margarine, add other ingredients. Roll chicken in mixture, coating both sides. Arrange meaty side up in pan. Bake in 375°F oven for 45 minutes to one hour, or until chicken is tender and golden. Delicious with rice. Serves 4–6.

Nutritional analysis (with butter or margarine)
Good source of protein.

Calories: 3,000, or 500–750 per serving

Protein: 280 gm., or 46–70 gm. per serving

Fat: 75 gm., or 12.5–19 gm. per serving

Carbohydrates: 171 gm., or 28.5–43 gm. per serving

Forester's Casserole

From the kitchen of Lisa Ondieki, 1992 New York City Marathon champion and a former New York Mini 10K champion.

1 lb. boneless chicken breasts

3 tbsp. olive oil

1 large onion, chopped

8 oz. mushrooms

2 tbsp. flour

10 oz. unsweetened apple juice

4 oz. chicken stock

LAUREN WALLACK ANTONUCCI'S
HEALTHY SNACK IDEAS

SWEET SNACKS

8 oz. (1 cup) low-fat or nonfat yogurt with 1/2 cup Jello
1 frozen whole-wheat or bran waffle with sliced fruit and syrup
1 cup low-fat or nonfat milk and 1/2–1 cup sliced fruit, 4–6 oz.
   juice, and ice blended into a shake
1 cup sweetened, fortified cereal and 1/2–1 cup low-fat or nonfat
   milk
1/2 cup canned fruit in water or in its own juice
1 fudge bar
1/2 cup low-fat ice cream or 1/2 cup low-fat frozen yogurt with
   chopped nuts
1 oz. dark chocolate

SAVORY SNACKS

3–6 graham cracker squares (with natural peanut butter if desired)
3–5 cups of air-popped popcorn
1/2 bag of microwave light popcorn
1 granola bar or energy bar
Pretzels (1–2 oz.), with 1/4 cup nuts or dried fruit
1 small bag of baked chips or soy chips

COMBINATION SNACKS

1/2–1 sandwich with whole-grain bread, natural peanut butter,
   tuna, or turkey
1 whole-wheat pita or tortilla, with veggies and 1–2 oz. turkey or
   low-fat cheese
1 cup of vegetable/tomato soup with 4–6 crackers
1 piece of fresh fruit, such as an apple or banana, with peanut butter
1 whole-wheat English muffin with 1–2 slices low-fat cheese and
   tomato (or tomato sauce)
5–8 whole-wheat crackers with 1 tbsp. low-fat cream cheese
8 oz. (1 cup) low-fat or nonfat yogurt with 2 tbsp. chopped nuts or
   3/4 cup dry cereal
10–15 baby carrots with 2 Tbs. hummus spread and 8 oz. low-fat
   or nonfat milk
1/2 cup low-fat cottage cheese and 1/2–1 cup sliced fruit

Salt and pepper, to taste

Parsley, chopped

Stir-fry chicken pieces in skillet with 2 tbsp. hot oil until golden brown. Remove from pan. Place mushrooms, onions, and 1 tbsp. oil in pan, cooking until tender. Add flour and gradually blend in apple juice and stock. Stir over gentle heat, add chicken, and continue simmering until sauce thickens, about 10 minutes. Serve with chopped parsley. Serves 4.

Nutritional analysis

Good source of protein, potassium, and A and B vitamins.

Calories: 1,200, or 300 per serving

Protein: 140 gm., or 35 gm. per serving

Fat: 41 gm., or 10 gm. per serving

Carbohydrates: 61 gm., or 15 gm. per serving

Chicken with Mushroom Sauce

From the kitchen of Mary Slaney, Olympian who at one time held every American record from 800 meters to 10,000 meters.

1 1/2 lb. boneless chicken breasts

1/2 cup evaporated skim milk

1 cup fine, dry, whole-wheat bread crumbs

2 cups fresh sliced mushrooms

2 tbsp. sliced green onion

1/2 cup dry white wine

1 tsp. lemon juice

1/8 tsp. dried thyme, crushed

1/8 tsp. dried marjoram, crushed

Flatten chicken breasts. Dip in milk, then in bread crumbs. Roll up jelly-roll style. Place in 8 × 8 × 2-inch baking pan. Bake covered in 350°F oven for 20 minutes. Meanwhile, for sauce combine in skillet mushrooms, onion, wine, lemon juice, thyme, and marjoram. Cook until vegetables are tender. Spoon sauce into dish with chicken. Bake uncovered for 5 minutes more or until chicken is done. To serve, spoon sauce over chicken. Serves 4.

Nutritional analysis

Low in fat; good source of protein and potassium.

Calories: 1,000, or 250 per serving

Protein: 31 gm., or 8 gm. per serving

Fat: 4 gm., or 1 gm. per serving

Carbohydrates: 15 gm., or 4 gm. per serving

Curried Chicken Salad

From the kitchen of Marcus O'Sullivan, former Irish Olympian and top miler.

$1/2$ cup yogurt

$1/2$ cup light or nonfat mayonnaise

1 tsp. curry powder

1 large onion, chopped

2 lb. cooked chicken, skinned, boned, and diced

1 cup chopped walnuts

1 cup raisins

Chopped parsley

Combine yogurt, mayonnaise, and curry in large bowl. Add onion, chicken, walnuts, and raisins. Toss. Refrigerate 2 hours. Serve on lettuce with sprinkled parsley. Serves 4.

Nutritional analysis

Good source of protein, iron, and potassium.

Calories: 2,300, or 575 per serving

Protein: 150 gm., or 37 gm. per serving

Fat: 128 gm., or 32 gm. per serving (mostly healthful fats from walnuts)

Carbohydrates: 160 gm., or 40 gm. per serving

Vegetable Curry

From the kitchen of Priscilla Welch, 1987 New York City Marathon winner and former Masters world record holder.

2 carrots, about 1 cup, sliced to preference and partially cooked

Assorted other vegetables (about 2 cups), such as:

$\frac{1}{2}$ bunch broccoli flowers, about 1 cup

1 scallion, sliced

1 cup baby corn

1 cup water

1 tbsp. cornstarch

1 cube or packet chicken broth

Curry powder, to taste

Partially steam carrots and broccoli for about 5–10 minutes. Sauté vegetables about 3 minutes. Add curry, to taste. Mix cornstarch with approximately 3 tbsp. water and stir until smooth. Pour water into saucepan, add cornstarch and broth cube or packet. Heat until thickened. (Crumbled-up rice cakes can also be used for thickening.) Pour over rice or noodles. Serves 3–4.

Nutritional analysis

Low in fat and an excellent source of vitamins A and C (vitamin content will vary with vegetables used).

Calories: 260, or 65–86 per serving

Protein: 13 gm.

Fat: 1 gm.

Carbohydrates: 39 gm.

The interesting aspect of the runner's diet is that it has become everyone's diet. What people in general are eating is not far removed from the Ronzoni Pasta Party before the New York City Marathon. We've gotten to the point that eating like a marathoner ready to race (and when you're training hard, you eat that way all the time) has become the prescribed diet for everyone.

—*Frank Shorter*

Pasta with Vegetables

From the kitchen of Bill Rodgers, four-time champion of both the New York City and Boston Marathons.

  2 oz. thin spaghetti

  $1/2$ clove garlic, minced

  2 tsp. olive or salad oil

  $1/2$ small zucchini, cut into thin strips

  $1/2$ small carrot, sliced thin

  $1/4$ cup frozen peas, thawed

  $1/4$ cup low-fat or non-fat cottage cheese

  Parmesan cheese, grated, to taste

Cook pasta as directed. Sauté garlic in oil until tender. Add zucchini and carrots and cook 1–2 minutes. Add drained pasta to vegetables. Add peas and cottage cheese. Toss well with pasta. Serve with grated cheese. Serves 1.

Nutritional analysis
Excellent source of complex carbohydrates with vitamin A and protein.

  Calories: 430

  Protein: 21 gm.

  Fat: 14 gm.

  Carbohydrates: 100 gm.

Pasta Primavera

From the kitchen of Eamonn Coghlan, former world champion and Olympian.

  1 lb. dry pasta or 2 lb. fresh

  $1/4$ cup olive oil, or less, according to taste

  $1/2$ cup chicken broth

  4 tbsp. fresh basil or chives, minced

  2 cloves garlic, minced (optional)

  Salt and pepper, to taste

3 cups vegetables, about ½ cup each; choose from the following:

Asparagus, cut in 3-in. pieces

Red peppers, cut in strips

Green peppers, cut in strips

Carrots, sliced

Zucchini, cut in julienne slices

Broccoli florets

Cherry tomatoes

Cook pasta until al dente. While pasta is cooking, plunge the vegetables in boiling water for 15 seconds. Rinse in cold water. Sauté garlic in olive oil, add broth, and heat through. Add all vegetables and herbs, season with salt and pepper. Toss pasta with vegetable mixture in large bowl. Add grated cheese if desired. Serves 4.

Here's some news about vegetables. Some real nutrition stars are broccoli, spinach, kale, potatoes, and yams. Starchy vegetables like potatoes and lima beans are also good sources of vitamins and minerals. All dried beans and peas are equally nutritious and high in fiber. Ironically, claims *Environmental Nutrition* newsletter, the lowest fiber counts are for salad vegetables—cucumbers, lettuce, mushrooms, and radishes. Salad is often consumed for fiber intake, yet an average salad has less fiber than one-half cup serving of cooked carrots.

Not all fruits and vegetables are created equal. In general, the deeper the color, the more nutrients they contain. Think red and green for the best nutrition. According to *Prevention* magazine, pink grapefruit has more than 30 times the vitamin A of white grapefruit, and anything that's red like a tomato, or orange like a carrot, has a lot of beta-carotene, which the body uses to manufacture vitamin A. It appears that a diet high in beta-carotene helps protect against most types of cancer. And the greener the greens, the better. Romaine lettuce, for example, has twice the calcium and iron, eight times the vitamin C, and more than ten times the vitamin A of the paler-green iceberg lettuce.

Nutritional analysis

Excellent source of complex carbohydrates while relatively low in fat. Good source of vitamins A and C, depending on choice of vegetables.

Calories: 2,300, or 575 per serving

Protein: 77 gm., or 19 gm. per serving

Fat: 66 gm., or 17 gm. per serving

Carbohydrates: 357 gm., or 89 gm. per serving

Japanese Noodles with Ginger

From the kitchen of Patti Catalano Dillon, former American record holder at a variety of road race distances.

1 lb. udon noodles (Japanese whole-wheat noodles) or other noodles

2 to 4 cloves garlic

1 2-inch piece fresh ginger (about 1 square inch)

1/4 cup tamari sauce or soy sauce

1/4 cup honey or 1/2 cup brown rice syrup

1/4 cup oil, preferably sesame

Cook the pasta according to the package directions. In a blender or food processor combine the remaining ingredients. Process for 1 to 2 minutes, until smooth. In a serving bowl toss the ginger mixture with the warm noodles. Serve hot or cold. Serves 4.

Nutritional analysis

Calories: 1,600, or 400 per serving

Protein: 48 gm., or 12 gm. per serving

Fat: 48 gm., or 12 gm. per serving

Carbohydrates: 244 gm., or 61 gm. per serving

Tofu Lasagna

From the kitchen of Judi St. Hilaire, former winner of the New York Mini 10K.

2 8-oz. pkgs. tofu, herb-flavored, soft-curd

1 tbsp. olive oil

1 medium onion, chopped

1 clove garlic, chopped

1 cup mushrooms, sliced

4 cups spaghetti sauce

12 lasagna noodles

8 oz. low-fat grated or sliced mozzarella cheese

1/2 cup grated Parmesan cheese

Boil noodles until just tender, and rinse in cold water. Heat oil in skillet and sauté onions, garlic, and mushrooms. Crumble tofu and add to skillet mixture; stir until steaming stops, about 5–10 minutes. Add 1 cup spaghetti sauce and simmer about 5 minutes. Spread 1/4 cup spaghetti sauce on bottom of 9 × 13-in. baking pan. Layer 4 noodles, 1 cup spaghetti sauce, then 1/2 of tofu mixture. Repeat and top with 4 more noodles, 1 cup spaghetti sauce, and cheeses. Bake at 350°F for 15 minutes or until cheese melts, browns, and bubbles. Serves 8.

Nutritional analysis

Excellent source of complex carbohydrates and protein; relatively low in fat.

Calories: 2,700, or 340 per serving

Protein: 165 gm., or 20 gm. per serving

Fat: 91 gm., or 11.5 gm. per serving

Carbohydrates: 290 gm., or 36 gm. per serving

Tuna Pasta Salad

From the kitchen of Gillian Beschloss, former age group NYRR Runner of the Year.

1 lb. tricolored pasta twists

3 tbsp. vinegar

3/4 cup olive oil

1/4 cup lemon juice

Pepper, to taste

1 head broccoli, cut into florets

2 yellow squash, sliced

2 zucchini, sliced

1 green pepper, diced

1 red pepper, diced

1 medium Bermuda onion, diced

16 1/2-oz. can tuna, drained (or shrimp or crabmeat)

Cook pasta, rinse in cold water, and drain well. With whisk, mix oil, vinegar, lemon juice, and pepper. In large bowl combine vegetables, pasta, and dressing, and toss gently. Add tuna and toss gently again. Place in refrigerator and chill for 1 hour. Quick and easy to make. Can be stored in refrigerator for a few days and is ready to eat at any time. Especially great for runners on the go. Serves 4–6.

Nutritional analysis

Plenty of complex carbohydrates; good source of vitamins A and C, calcium, protein, and fiber.

Calories: 3,600, or 600–900 per serving

Protein: 100 gm., or 17–25 gm. per serving

Fat: 360 gm., or 30–45 gm. per serving

Carbohydrates: 800 gm., or 133–200 gm. per serving

Pasta with Beans

From the kitchen of Orlando Pizzolato, two-time New York City Marathon champion, and Ilaria Pizzolato.

1 lb. potatoes, pared and cut into 1-in. chunks

2 large onions, cut into eighths

1 28-oz. can tomatoes

2 stalks celery, sliced

3 cloves garlic, minced

1 tbsp. sage

1/4 cup chopped parsley

2 1/2 qt. water

1 1/2 cups short tubular pasta, uncooked

1/2 tbsp. cinnamon

1 large can cannellini beans (19 oz.), drained and rinsed

Salt and pepper, to taste

Parmesan cheese, to taste

Combine potatoes, onions, tomatoes, celery, garlic, sage, parsley, cinnamon, and water in large pot. Cook very slowly over low flame for about 2 hours. Add beans, salt, and pasta. Cook until pasta is al dente—about 20 minutes, stirring often so pasta doesn't stick to bottom. Pour soup into bowls and sprinkle with pepper and Parmesan cheese. Wait at least 5 minutes before serving. Great time-saver when cooked ahead and reheated at mealtime. Serves 6.

Nutritional analysis
Rich in carbohydrates while low in fat; good source of potassium, protein, iron, and B vitamins.

Calories: 1,450, or 240 per serving

Protein: 44 gm., or 7 gm. per serving

Fat: 12 gm., or 2 gm. per serving

Carbohydrates: 251 gm., or 42 gm. per serving

Sesame Pasta with Broccoli

From the kitchen of Paul Friedman, former NYRR Runner of the Year.

8 oz. uncooked pasta

1 head broccoli (or other vegetable)

1 cup plain yogurt

1 tbsp. soy sauce

2 to 3 tbsp. tahini

Optional:

1 to 2 cloves garlic, minced

Dash Tabasco

1/2 tsp. cumin

Diced red and green bell peppers

Snow peas

Shredded carrots

Cook the pasta according to the package directions. Drain. While the pasta is cooking, steam the broccoli until tender (but still crisp). In a small bowl mix the yogurt, soy sauce, tahini, garlic, Tabasco, and cumin. Add the pasta and toss to coat. Add the bell peppers, snow peas, and carrots. Serves 2.

Nutritional analysis

Excellent source of calcium.

Calories: 1,100, or 550 per serving

Protein: 38 gm., or 19 gm. per serving

Fat: 20 gm., or 10 gm. per serving

Carbohydrates: 192 gm., or 96 gm. per serving

Fat: 66 gm., or 17 gm. per serving

Carbohydrates: 357 gm., or 89 gm. per serving

To get the most vitamins out of steamed and boiled vegetables, cooking time is critical. Vegetables that tend to cook unevenly, such as asparagus and broccoli, will cook uniformly and much more quickly when the stalks are lightly peeled. Use a vegetable peeler rather than a paring knife so you remove only the top layer. Also, according to *Glamour* magazine, root vegetables, such as potatoes, beets, and turnips, will not cook faster if peeled and will lose vitamins if they are.

Yummy Granola

From the kitchen of Lynn Williams, Olympic medalist and former New York Mini 10K winner.

1/2 cup margarine (can be reduced to 1/4–1/3 cup)

2 heaping tsp. honey

2/3 cup brown sugar

2 tsp. almond or vanilla extract

5–6 cups oatmeal flakes

1 cup shredded coconut (optional)

1/2 cup wheat germ

1/2 cup bran

3/4 cup slivered almonds (or chopped walnuts)

Melt margarine, honey, brown sugar, and extract in large pot. Add remainder of ingredients and stir thoroughly. Spread mixture on cookie sheets and place in a 350°F oven for about 8 minutes, or until toasted light brown. Remove from oven and allow to cool on cookie sheets. When cool, break it up into chunks and store in cool place. It keeps a long time. (*Note*: Dry ingredients can be added in any combination you prefer). Makes 16 1/2-cup servings. For a lower-fat variety, experiment by replacing some or all margarine with fruit juice concentrate (apple, orange, or a combination). Eliminate or reduce the amount of sugar (sweeten to taste).

Nutritional analysis:

Good source of fiber, vitamin A, potassium, and iron.

Calories: 3,520, or 220 per serving

Protein: 135 gm., or 8.5 gm. per serving

Fat: 192 gm., or 12 gm. per serving

Carbohydrates: 384 gm., or 24 gm. per serving

Carrot-Pineapple Cake

From the kitchen of Kathy Pfiefer, former national-class road racer.

1 3/4 cups sugar

1 stick margarine, or try substituting 1/2 of the margarine with 1/4 cup of applesauce

4 eggs, or egg substitute

1 tsp. vanilla

2 cups all-purpose flour

2 tsp. baking powder

2–4 tsp. baking soda

1 1/2 tsp. baking soda

2 cups lightly packed shredded carrots

1 8-oz. can crushed pineapple (drained)

$1/2$ cup raisins

Cream cheese frosting:

$1/2$ stick margarine

4 oz. low-fat cream cheese, softened

1 tsp. vanilla

1 $1/2$ cups powdered sugar

1 tbsp. milk (to desired consistency)

Preheat oven to 350°F. Spray bottom of 9×13-in. baking pan with a nonstick vegetable oil spray; set aside. Let margarine soften at room temperature, then cream with sugar. Beat in eggs, then stir in vanilla. Stir in flour, baking powder, cinnamon, and baking soda. Add carrots, pineapple, and raisins; stir just to blend, and pour into pan. Bake for about 45 minutes. For frosting, let margarine and cream cheese soften at room temperature; then cream together. Add vanilla and powdered sugar. Stir well. Add milk to desired consistency. Allow cake to cool before frosting. Kathy says, "A few calories, but well worth it." Serves 12–15.

Nutritional analysis

Lots of carbohydrates, some vitamin A, potassium.

Calories iced: 4,350, or 290–362 per serving

Calories plain: 3,000, or 200–250 per serving

Protein: 90 gm., or 6–7.5 gm. per serving (iced)

Carbohydrates: 660 gm., or 44–55 gm. per serving (iced)

Fat: 180 gm., or 12–15 gm. per serving (iced)

Honey Bran Muffins

From the kitchen of Pat Porter, eight-time national cross-country champion.

1 $1/4$ cups all-purpose flour

3 tsp. baking powder

$1/4$ tsp. baking soda

$1/2$ tsp. salt

1 $1/2$ cups all-bran cereal

1 cup skim milk

$1/3$ cup canola oil

$1/2$ cup honey

1 egg

1 cup raisins

Sift together flour, baking powder, baking soda, and salt, and set aside. In mixing bowl, pour milk over bran cereal, add oil and honey, and let stand a few minutes. Add beaten egg and mix well. Add dry ingredients to cereal mixture, then add raisins. Stir well to combine. Grease 2 $1/2$-inch muffin pans (coated with vegetable oil spray) and pour batter until each cup is three-quarters full. Bake at 375°F for 20–25 minutes, or until firm to the touch. Serves 12.

Nutritional analysis

Low in saturated fat; good source of dietary fiber.

Calories: 2,400, or 200 per muffin

Protein: 48 gm., or 4 gm per muffin

Fat: 96 gm., or 8 gm. per muffin

Carbohydrates: 420 gm., or 35 gm. per muffin

PART 6
FITNESS AND
SAFETY

27

HYDRATION

THE RULES ABOUT FLUIDS

When the weather is steamy or your body is down a quart and the workout is far from over, it's a bad time to begin wondering if you've had enough to drink. You need to drink. On a hot day, runners are at risk for dehydration if they don't drink as described below. Not drinking may lead to early fatigue or heat illness. The key is: *Drink not too much and not too little.* Either way you can get into trouble in the heat.

For simple rehydration on an average day, water does the job; however, sports drinks have made the issue more complicated than that. Research shows that the sugar and salt in those drinks form an "active pump" that gets more water into the body faster than the unassisted process (simple diffusion of water). The additional salt is advantageous to help hold onto water and maintain proper blood sodium levels.

Runners should practice with fluid replacement drinks. Don't try something on race day you haven't used in training. Here are some practical tips for deciding how much to drink, both during training periods and on a race day.

FLUIDS ON RACE DAY

Water and sports drinks provide you with fluid, by far the most important nutrient your body needs to finish a running event healthy! Follow these recommendations and you will prevent dehydration.

- Drink at least 16 ounces of fluid one to two hours before the race.
- Drink another 16 ounces of fluid in the hour before the race.
- Check your urine a half hour before the race. If it is clear, you are well prehydrated. If it is dark and concentrated, drink more fluids.
- During the race, drink no more than one cup (8–10 ounces) of fluid every 15–20 minutes along the way. This does not mean a cup at EVERY water station.

- DO NOT take any product with ephedra in it. Ephedra increases your risk of "heat illness."

TOO MUCH FLUID CAN BE HARMFUL

Most athletes understand the importance of drinking fluids, but some don't understand that drinking too much can be harmful as well. According to NYRR Medical Director Lewis Maharam, M.D., by far and away the most common mistake novice runners make is drinking too much water. Over-hydrating can lead to a dangerous condition known as hyponatremia (low blood sodium). During a race, at every water station they see, they'll drink one or two cups, and that leaves them hyponatremic. This condition can lead to nausea, fatigue, vomiting, weakness, sleepiness, disorientation, and in the most severe instances, seizures, coma, and death. Dr. Maharam says the newest research shows that much of what we think about dehydration is really a myth. We've gone too far in the campaign to educate people on preventing dehydration.

According to Dr. Maharam, "The medical community, and everyone else that was worried about hydration for performance, really wanted to make sure there was enough fluid in the body to perform better. But people went too far. They were told, 'It's hot, you want to drink more and more.' But people get sick being out there for long periods of time, drinking that much."

> According to medical guidelines, endurance athletes should consume 12 to 16 ounces of fluid prior to a race. Along the marathon course, runners should drink no more than eight ounces of fluid every 15 to 20 minutes.

To avoid hyponatremia follow these easy guidelines:

- Follow the fluid recommendations.
- Try not to drink more than you sweat.
- In the days before the race, add salt to your foods (provided you don't have high blood pressure or your doctor has restricted your salt intake).

- Stop taking nonsteroidal anti-inflammatories 24 hours before your race, and do not start again until a minimum of six hours after finishing the race.

- Include pretzels or a salted bagel in your pre-race meal and eat salted pretzels during the last half of the race.

- Favor a sports drink that has some sodium in it over water, which has none.

- Carry a small salt packet with you, and during the last half of the race, if you feel that you have been sweating a lot or if it's a warm/hot day, consume that single packet.

- After the race, drink a sports drink that contains sodium and eat some pretzels or a salted bagel.

WEIGH IN DAILY

Step out of bed every morning and onto the scale. If you're anywhere from one to three percent lighter than the day before, rehydrate by drinking eight ounces of fluid for each pound lost before training again; between three and six percent lighter, rehydrate and back off that day's training intensity; over seven percent, get to the doctor.

DRINK DURING WORKOUTS

Two hours before your workout, drink about a pint (16 oz.). Drink again as early as 15 minutes into the session, but keep the doses small—four to seven ounces.

AFTER WORKOUTS

Weigh yourself right before and after workouts. For every pound you lost, drink a pint of electrolyte replacement fluid, like Gatorade, watered down to whatever strength you like.

Heat Cramps

Loss of water and salt from sweating that is not replaced, especially during exercise or physical labor outdoors during hot, humid weather, can cause

I think the average runner now makes a much greater effort to stay properly hydrated and fueled. Back when I was racing, a lot of the races, including the Boston Marathon, didn't have staffed water stations. I remember running along the course and having to ask people for water. Now there is a much greater awareness about hydration. Sports bars, gel, and other energy supplements help the beginning runner because, at a slower pace, these runners are out on the course longer and therefore need to keep their energy stores up. Even elite runners are using them, so they enable everyone to run better.

—*Bill Rodgers*

FITNESS WATER

Fitness waters are lightly flavored, sometimes colored, often vitamin- and mineral-enhanced alternatives to plain water. They were created in response to research showing that many exercisers don't drink enough fluids before, during and after workouts.

Are fitness waters better for you than plain water? According to Marathon Doc Lewis Maharam, M.D., the added vitamins may help with post-exercise muscle soreness. Other than that, the main reason to choose a fitness water is if you are more likely to drink it than plain water.

Fitness waters are different from sports drinks, however. They contain only about 10 calories per 8-ounce serving—compared to 50 or more per serving in a sports drink—and thus are not optimal for fuel replacement during a long workout or race or on a hot day when you lose electrolytes through sweat.

Drink fitness water when you would typically drink plain water, such as in a workout of an hour or less, or a 5K to 10K race on a cool day. Stick to sports drinks when you need to rehydrate and refuel for longer workouts and races, or on warm days when you sweat profusely.

(Adapted from "Ask Marathon Doc,"
New York Runner, Sept./Oct. 2002.)

muscle spasms or heat cramps. Usually in abdominal or leg muscles, heat cramps are often accompanied by weakness and nausea and are the first warning signs of dehydration.

To relieve heat cramps, massage cramped muscles and cool the body with cold tap water and wet towels. Slowly sip plain, cool water. If left untreated, heat cramps may lead to more serious heat illnesses.

Heat Exhaustion

Heat exhaustion is a more serious, systemic condition, often building up slowly over several days or weeks. It may appear after vigorous exercise or come on gradually from dehydration. Symptoms include cool, pale, and moist skin; profuse sweating; dilated pupils; headaches; nausea; dizziness; and vomiting. Body temperature will be elevated.

Medical attention is necessary to treat heat exhaustion. First move the person to a cooler location and place in a shock position, lying on the back with feet up. Loosen or remove excess clothing and rehydrate with water or an electrolyte solution.

Heat Stroke

Heat stroke is a more severe and advanced form of heat exhaustion. It is a potentially fatal condition requiring immediate medical aid.

Experts estimate that approximately 200 deaths occur each year from heat stroke, but actual numbers are probably higher due to the number of incidents attributed to other conditions, such as heart attacks.

Heat stroke is triggered by profuse, prolonged sweating, leading to the eventual inability to sweat. Heat stroke can also lead to hypothermia (high body temperature), hyponatremia (decreased concentration of sodium in the blood), and hypovolemia (low blood volume).

The most telltale heat stroke symptoms include cessation of sweating, hot and reddened skin, confusion, agitation and bizarre behavior, rapid pulse, seizures, and unconsciousness.

While waiting for medical assistance to arrive, move the individual to a cool, shaded area and loosen or remove excess clothing. Next, cool the body by fanning and immersing in a cool—not cold—bath or wrapping in wet sheets. Provide small amounts of fluids.

Heat illness is a serious medical condition resulting from inadequate fluid intake to replace fluid loss through sweat, and actually due to asking your body to work metabolically harder than it has been trained to do in the heat. To prevent heat illness you should back off on the speed and intensity of your workouts on hot days. Drink appropriately. And stop if you start to feel "off" and cool down. If you're competing in a hot weather event, consider using that extra water that you aren't going to drink at the water stations to wet your head. This allows your body to cool through evaporation through your head. Also, take advantage of water spray stations along the course. To prevent dehydration, the main cause of heat illness, it is important to drink fluids before, during, and after physical activity in hot weather.

SKIN CARE

Have you ever noticed a great paradox of many a seasoned runner—a fit athlete with the body of a teenager, but the face of an ancient? Fred Lebow was discussing this phenomenon years ago with New York plastic surgeon and avid runner Dr. Dan Weiner, whom he met on a flight from Boston to New York. Lebow told Weiner that some runners believed that their excess facial lines and sagging were due to the "bouncing" action of running. Now people know better. Weiner explained the physiological reason—sun and weather exposure.

RUNNERS SAVE FACE

Runners and other exercisers once avoided sunscreens or other creams because sweat caused them to drip into the eyes, creating an annoying stinging sensation. Today, several companies make products specifically for use during exercise that do not run or drip. And sunscreen and sunblock products are constantly being improved and refined.

> Exercise is good for your skin. According to information from *Vitality* magazine, it boosts production of collagen, which keeps skin supple—plus, sweating increases the flow of nutrients to the skin's surface.

Dan Weiner believes runners no longer advance the "bouncing" theory as to why their skin does not "go the distance" as well as the rest of their bodies. He feels they are currently aware of their high-risk status regarding degenerative skin changes and the possibility of skin cancer; however, Mickey Lawrence, who also takes an interest in this area and works with NYRR, has her doubts about this raised consciousness regarding the problem. To emphasize the need for conscientious skin care, here's a review of the facts from Weiner, Lawrence, and other experts.

1. One major fallacy is that skin damage is caused only by the sun. While sun is the primary destructive agent, wind, cold, and dryness also contribute. What's more, sun is potent during unsuspected times. For example, sunlight gets through on cloudy days, as do up to 80 percent of the sun's damaging rays. In addition, temperature is not a gauge of sun danger. It is solar radiation that causes harm, and there's as much of that on a nice spring day in New York City as there is in the middle of summer in Florida.

2. Although millions of people will develop skin cancer in the next decade, many times that number of people will develop degenerative changes and experience premature aging of the skin. These changes include an initial dryness, scaling, and abnormal pigmentation, followed by premature aging with lines and wrinkles. Finally, in some cases, skin cancer develops. This is why year-round protection against all the elements is necessary. Runners are obviously at high risk as they engage in an outdoor activity on a regular basis.

3. Note the sun protection factor (SPF) of a sun care product. This is a guide to the length of protection, not to the amount of protection. Dan Weiner feels that, in general, sunscreens with an SPF of 12 to 15 are sufficient. Products are made as high as SPF 45 for those people with sun-sensitive skin, those exposed to the sun all day, and those who live in more intense sun areas.

4. Dan Weiner stresses the need for runners to apply skin care protection diligently all year long. Remember to apply skin care cream or sunscreen at least 20–30 minutes before going out to allow it to be effectively absorbed. Reapply as needed. Don't forget the traditionally neglected parts of the body, such as the ears, around the hair line, under the eyebrows, the area between the nose and mouth, the lips (use lip balm with an SPF), exposed scalp, and the back of the hands. Use a sun block that contains zinc oxide or titanium dioxide, as these ingredients will afford the broadest UV radiation coverage. Sunscreen should be used even if a person already has a tan, and using sun-block year-round can help retard aging of the skin.

5. Summer running sense includes running at low peak sun hours—particularly avoiding the hours between 10 A.M. and 2 P.M. (3 P.M. if possible)—and wearing protective clothing, such as T-shirts and hats or visors.

6. While some protection is better than none, don't assume that a singlet or T-shirt can shield you from the sun. The sun's UV rays can penetrate clothing, contributing to long-term sun damage. It's a good idea to apply sunscreen under your running shirts. Clothing with UV protection is also available from outdoor gear stores, athletic clothing stores, and online, as well as laundry additives with an ultraviolet protection factor that "washes in" protection to normal clothing.

7. Skin cancer is the most common cancer in the U.S. Approximately half of all cancers in this country are skin cancers. In fact, more people contract skin cancer than all other types of cancer combined. Due to an increase in outdoor activity and a depletion of the ozone layer, cases of skin cancer are rapidly rising.

   Who gets skin cancer? Ask some of those most vulnerable—runners who hit the road during the noonday sun, many of whom enjoy the freedom of going shirtless. In fact, according to the Centers for Disease Control, more men are dying of skin cancer (malignant melanoma) than of any other cancer. Maybe that's because it seems men have a greater difficulty maintaining diligent skin care. Their rationale is often that women have a history of applying creams and cosmetics, while it is harder for men to become accustomed to the habit. In addition to advising diligence about skin protection while outdoors, Weiner recommends regular moisturizing and conditioning of the skin. Professional facials are good, he adds, even for men.

8. Know the signs of skin cancer—a skin growth that increases in size and appears pearly, translucent, or any shade of brown, black, or multicolored; any change in a mole or birthmark, or one that is irregular in outline; a spot or growth that continually itches, hurts, scabs, erodes, or bleeds; and an open sore that does not heal for more than one month, or heals and then reopens. Any suspicious signs should be checked by a physician immediately.

29

MASSAGE

Since 1980, NYRR has been providing massage to runners, administered by volunteer massage therapists. Major events such as the New York City Marathon, the USA 8K National Championships, and the New York Mini 10K feature massage.

The biggest job by far is at the Marathon, where 100 massage therapists serve the field of 34,000 runners, at both the race start and finish. They are overseen by Marisa D'Adamo, M.S., P.T., S.C.S., the physical therapy captain of the New York City Marathon, who reviewed this chapter.

Massage for athletes has also been part of the worldwide sporting scene for many years. Most professional and amateur runners are aware of or are using sports massage as a regular part of their training program. In fact, many teams or clubs retain a massage therapist to aid their athletes.

BENEFITS OF MASSAGE

According to NYRR massage experts, a runner can run better, longer, and more easily with a massage. It raises the level of performance and, at the same time, lowers the level of stress that running can cause to the body. Massage can serve as a warmup—and warming up is a vital part of any athlete's training program. Warming up involves the gradual and coordinated preparation of the muscles, along with the joints, lungs, and heart, for the increased stress of exercise. Massage literally increases the blood circulation—in essence, it heats the blood. The blood then carries that heat throughout the body, just as any other warmup would do.

Massage also serves as a cool-down activity. It slows down the breathing and pumping of the heart, cools the muscles, and then soothes and relaxes those muscles, relieving cramps and any other post-running physiological stress. In reducing muscle tension, spasms, and cramping, massage greatly promotes general relaxation and rapid recovery.

Although a post-event massage is similar to a pre-event massage, the state of the body is entirely different. After a race or hard workout, the muscles are in a state of fatigue and congestion; the tissues are filled with waste products. Massage increases the blood circulation and assists the blood in eliminating these waste products.

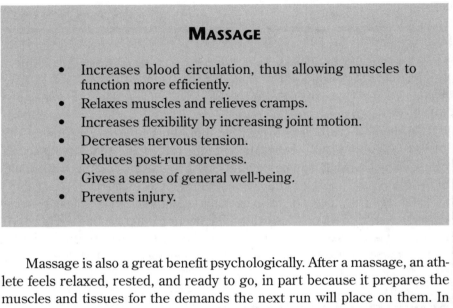

MASSAGE

- Increases blood circulation, thus allowing muscles to function more efficiently.
- Relaxes muscles and relieves cramps.
- Increases flexibility by increasing joint motion.
- Decreases nervous tension.
- Reduces post-run soreness.
- Gives a sense of general well-being.
- Prevents injury.

Massage is also a great benefit psychologically. After a massage, an athlete feels relaxed, rested, and ready to go, in part because it prepares the muscles and tissues for the demands the next run will place on them. In doing so, massage decreases the likelihood of further injury. As a result, athletes benefit from the knowledge that they are better prepared and protected because of being massaged. The bottom line for most athletes is that massage serves as a reward for their discipline and hard effort.

MASSAGING RUNNERS

The NYRR massage experts deal with a large number of people on a short-term basis, most of whom they do not know. Their job is to provide short but effective pre- and post-race massage. The following explains their massage philosophy and approach:

> A runner's feet and legs are probably the most important part of the body to be massaged. However, paying some attention to the lower back, shoulders, even the neck muscles and the jaw, can be a great help. For example, a 15- to 20-minute uptempo light massage over the entire body acts to stimulate, rather than sedate, the runner. They do not use ice, nor do they do any deep, specific, or trigger-point work. This avoids the need for the athlete to go through any period of muscle breakdown and recovery. Incidentally, oil is usually not used in

this type of sports massage because it can clog the pores, thereby preventing the body's normal cooling system through sweat.

Although massage is an excellent post-event treatment, a runner must be thoroughly cooled down first. However, for races of half-marathon and longer, massage is contraindicated for at least two hours after the event. Massage therapists at NYRR events do not use heat; however, if an athlete is cold, that person will be wrapped in a blanket. NYRR massage therapists also do not work on sprains, cuts, bruises, or blisters, or on those with thermal problems (hypo- or hyperthermia) or dehydration. NYRR is fortunate to have on hand a highly skilled medical staff to which these runners are referred.

All things considered, there is no more effective way to prepare an athlete's body for total commitment than by giving that person the added opportunity for freer motion. Regular massage keeps the body in better physical condition, helps prevent injuries, and reduces pain. It also helps heal and restore mobility in injured muscles. Sports massage gives runners extra protection and betters their performance—at each event and for the length of their careers.

HOW TO FIND A MASSAGE THERAPIST

Although you can look in the yellow pages of the telephone book or call a massage school for referrals, word of mouth is the most effective way to find a good massage therapist. Most massage therapists are able to do sports massage, but some have special training or even certificates in sports massage. In addition, many physical therapists specializing in sports medicine offer sports massage along with rehabilitating of injured athletes. For general information, you can contact the American Massage Therapy Association (see Resources).

The cost of a massage varies widely, depending on the experience and reputation of the therapist and in what part of the country that person works. Average rates are $60 to $100 per hour. Most therapists also have half-hour rates.

PARTNER AND SELF-MASSAGE

Massage is not new, nor is it the exclusive practice of professionals. It is part of the theory of the healing and calming power of touch. A runner's muscles can derive enormous benefit from regular, properly administered self-

or partner-massage. You can safely and effectively massage your feet, ankles, legs, buttocks, shoulders, and neck—or have a partner do it. The following is taken from an article by Marilyn Frender on self-massage, which can also be done by a partner. It previously appeared in *New York Running News*.

Self-massage is most effective if done regularly—after every run (or at least every speed workout) or at some other time during the day when you can relax. It's crucial to know that while massage can help relieve fatigue and soreness, it cannot cure an injury. If you feel persistent pain in your muscles or joints, see a medical specialist. Here are some guidelines to self-massaging various parts of the body.

Foot Massage

This is the most important, and often neglected, area to massage. Start by soaking your feet in warm-to-hot sudsy water for about 30 minutes. Towel dry. Sitting up, massage one foot at a time. Work the toes, too, since stiff, unrelaxed toes can cause pain on the run. And don't neglect the arches. You may want to use creams or petroleum jelly, especially if you tend to develop calluses or blisters. After massaging the feet, keep them elevated for about 20 minutes.

More on Massage

How does massage work? Massage can "jump start" a body by increasing the blood's ability to carry oxygen by 10–15 percent. It can accelerate muscle recovery after exercise by providing a gentle stretching action to the muscles and connective tissues that support and surround them.

Massage helps prevent cramps both during and after running by removing lactic acid. There are many different types of massage available. How to choose? When looking for a massage professional, marathon legend Bill Rodgers, who has received weekly massages since 1980, suggests finding therapists who are specifically familiar with runners and their special needs. Says massage therapist Liz Hartshorn in an article in *New York Runner* magazine, "Massage therapists who specifically do sports massage are oftentimes the best bet for the runner because they are trained in the kinesiology/physiology requirements of each particular sport."

Heel Massage

Running's constant pounding may produce low-level pain here, known as jogger's heel. Use your thumbs to apply direct pressure to the tender area, pushing hard for up to 15 seconds at a time. You might also want to try deep friction massage. Move your thumbs back and forth with strong pressure across the heel in the sore spots. Again, if pain is severe, or lasts, see a doctor.

Achilles Tendon Massage

It is easiest to massage this area if you sit up with your legs crossed. Work one leg at a time, feeling with fingers and thumbs around and behind the ankle bone. Apply direct pressure up and down the length of the tendon.

Calf Massage

It's common to feel tightness and soreness in the calves and behind the knees. For relief, sit down and cross your legs so you can comfortably reach the sore areas. Massage with kneading or compression, probing for sore areas.

Kneecap Massage

To soothe minor pain in the front of the knee, apply pressure with thumbs around the kneecap, rubbing gently anywhere you feel a tender spot. Circle the kneecap with your thumbs, with legs outstretched.

Thigh Massage

Both the hamstring and the quadriceps muscles (back and front of thigh) can benefit from self-massage. Apply firm pressure up and down the leg, working tender spots with thumb and fingers, using deep friction to increase circulation.

Lower Back and Buttocks Massage

You should be able to reach these areas comfortably either standing up or lying down. Standing, place your hands on the hip bones and move in small circles with your thumbs. Run your fingers and thumbs firmly down the gluteus medius muscles on the sides of the buttocks and across the gluteus maximus muscles on the cheeks.

Neck and Shoulder Massage

Use finger and thumb pressure and light friction up and down the muscles in the back of your neck and across the shoulders to relieve tension and stiffness. Move your head from side to side and shrug your shoulders to work out the kinks. A word on determining pressure; for most self/partner massage, in which there is no injury present, the amount of pressure given is left to the discretion of the receiver. Deeper pressure can relieve tight areas more effectively, but soreness the day of a race is a high price to pay. When in doubt, leave adequate time to recover. Practice makes perfect!

30

HOT AND COLD WEATHER RUNNING

The beauty of running is that you can do it year round. Temperature extremes are no reason to halt your routine. You should, however, follow certain guidelines and precautions, and be aware that it takes about two weeks to adjust to climatic extremes. You may want to go easy at first if you are not accustomed to the weather conditions.

COLD WEATHER RUNNING TIPS

Here are some cold weather running tips adapted from a NYRR brochure written by Bob Glover. These tips should help you prevent injuries and get through the doldrums of the long, dark winter.

Poor Footing

During winter months, the main weather-related cause of injuries is poor footing. These injuries most often come from being tight when trying to guard against slipping on snow- or ice-covered running surfaces. Tense muscles, whether consciously or unconsciously tightened, are more prone to strains and other overuse injuries. Runners usually alter their running form to increase traction, which leads to further problems. Lateral foot slippage often occurs on icy spots, causing a pulled muscle or tendon. The most common winter running injuries are groin and hamstring pulls caused by slipping and sliding through the snow. These nagging injuries often require rest, or they will still be with you when the snow has melted. Of course, you may also slip and fall. If you do, try to land lightly and then immediately stop your run and ice the injured area to reduce swelling. Running in a few inches of snow forces you to work muscles normally not taxed. If your quadriceps become fatigued, knee injury could result. Limit your running in snow and slippery conditions to 30–45 minutes at a time to minimize injuries.

Training must go on with or without dry surfaces if you intend to keep reasonably fit. The best prevention against injuries in the winter is to make sure you warm up well (start with brisk walking or a slow jog), maintain good flexibility (cold weather runners are less flexible) with regular stretching exercises, and run relaxed (don't allow yourself to tense up out of fear of falling). When running on slippery surfaces, shorten your stride slightly and shuffle along, maintaining good balance. Be especially careful on downhills and turns and when running in the dark. Don't attempt fast running under slippery conditions. Studded shoes that aren't overly worn are the best in the snow—just like the snow tires you put on your car for better traction. Adjust your pace. It takes more effort to run with extra clothing and with difficult footing, so don't be obsessed with trying to maintain the same training pace you hold in warmer, drier conditions.

Frostbite

To prevent frostbite, keep covered, keep dry, and keep moving. Frostbite usually occurs to ears, face, fingers, and toes. It can result in the loss of fingers or toes and has even caused deaths. Frostbitten skin is cold, pale, and firm to hard to the touch. The first step in treatment is to warm rapidly without excessive heat. It is recommended that immediate medical attention be given. Prevent frostbite by keeping the extremities and face well-protected in extremely cold weather.

The danger of frostbite greatly increases with wind, which when combined with air temperature produces the "windchill factor." Running into the wind intensifies the windchill factor and makes you colder, while running with the wind may speed you along and produce a sweat. Therefore, begin your runs into the wind on out-and-back courses; otherwise, you'll build up a good sweat with the wind at your back and then turn into a biting wind for the return, which may cause frostbite or at least extreme discomfort.

Hypothermia

Hypothermia is the lowering below normal of the central, or core, temperature. As the temperature falls, the body responds by shivering, which is the muscles' attempt to produce heat. If not attended to, hypothermia can cause you to become incoherent and then lapse into a coma, even die. Hypothermia usually strikes when you are wearing wet clothing. If your clothes are soaked from getting splashed with slush, or if you sweat too much from overdressing, you should stop running and change your clothing right away.

Take your wet clothing off immediately after running, or hypothermia may strike.

Clothing

The key to running in the cold is wearing the right clothes in the right combination. The secret to maximum comfort is layering—an inner wicking layer, an insulating middle layer, and an outer windbreaker layer. You may not always need three layers, especially if racing—and because newer performance fabrics can be warm, wick away persperation, and are lightweight.

An efficient layering system keeps you warm by trapping body heat between layers. You can always adjust for heat build-up by unzipping or removing the outer layer or more. Or, if you cool off, you can put it back on. Not only do layers trap and regulate body heat more effectively than one thick layer, but perspiration also moves more readily through thin layers than one thick one.

By wearing the right fabrics in the right order, moisture will be wicked away from your skin (by the inner layer) and transferred to the second or third layer for evaporation. If one piece of the clothing in the system fails in its function, you will not keep as dry and, thus, as warm. Wet clothes can't keep you warm.

The Inner Layer.   This clothing is against your skin and should consist of a breathable fabric, such as polypropylene, which allows water vapor to pass through and wicks perspiration from the skin to help keep you dry. This layer should be lightweight and fit fairly tight to your skin. Don't wear an absorbent fabric such as cotton next to your skin. It will get wet, soggy and make you feel uncomfortable and cold.

The Middle Layer.   This layer may not be needed in mild weather, but for cold days it is essential to add additional space to trap heat—just like the insulation in your attic. This layer is usually heavier than the inner layer, but it also needs to be breathable and to wick moisture away. It should fit more loosely and be easy to remove so you can adjust if you get too warm. Go with fabrics that will keep you warm and dry such as fleece and wool. Some runners prefer to use cotton for this layer, as it absorbs moisture.

The Outer Layer.   The key function here is to protect you from the wind and at least repel rain and wet snow. It must be breathable to allow the moisture and excessive heat that have been transferred from the inner layers to escape to the environment. Your biggest enemy in keeping warm isn't the air temperature, but strong winds, which can blow away your body heat. This layer should fit loosely and be zippered to allow for more efficient temperature adjustment. Ideally, this outer layer will also be waterproof to protect you in cold, heavy rain or snow. Nylon windbreakers will help protect against the wind, but since nylon isn't breathable, you may find them too warm if you are running hard or for more than 30 minutes. Newer jackets made from performance fabrics solve that problem.

Your legs generate a lot of heat and need less protection than the upper body. One layer is usually enough. The most common choices are tights or a pair of nylon pants such as Coolmax® or GoreTex® over a pair of shorts. On really cold or windy days wear tights covered by pants. (A word of caution: When exercising in winter, a man's private area can get wet with sweat and then suffer discomfort or frostbite as a result of strong wind and cold. A good preventive choice is special windbriefs that wick away moisture and have a windproof panel in front).

Running feet usually keep plenty warm as long as they stay dry. Steer clear of puddles! If your feet get wet, get indoors and dry and warm yourself immediately. One layer of wicking socks made of acrylic or polypropylene is usually enough, but in very cold weather you may choose to go with an inner, thin sock made of a wicking fabric covered by an insulating outer sock.

As much as 50 percent of body heat is lost through the head so it is critical to keep it covered. The hat is also the first piece to remove if you need to cool off. It is important to protect the ears from frostbite—choose a hat that covers them. Runners with plenty of hair may get by with just a headband over the ears or ear muffs. In very cold weather you might need a headband covered by a fleece or polypropylene hat. Strong winds may require you to wear the hood from your jacket as well. In extreme cold protect the face too—either wear a facemask or a balaclava, or slather your exposed skin with petroleum jelly.

Fingers and hands are very vulnerable to frostbite. Mittens are warmer than gloves, but many runners still prefer gloves. A good bet is an inner glove liner, made of a fabric such as Thermax® or polypropylene, that wicks moisture covered by a windproof glove.

Should You Overdress or Underdress?

While there is far more danger in underdressing than in overdressing, both can lead to discomfort and danger. Overdressing can lead to dehydration and heat illnesses. Beginner runners are more likely to overdress as are many novice racers. With experience you'll learn what works best for you. The key is knowing what to wear and to wear as little as possible without underdressing. A good rule of thumb is to dress as though it were 20 degrees warmer outside than it really is. You should feel a little chilly when you first step out, but soon your body heat will warm you. Be flexible, too. On a single run the conditions may change several times. Don't toss away any articles of clothing when you are running or racing unless you are positive you won't need them again. If you get hot when running or racing, first remove your hat and tuck it in your shorts, then your gloves or mittens, then unzip your outer layer, and then remove it and tie it around your waist. It is still important to drink fluids when racing or doing long runs since you will dehydrate due to sweating. As you cool, replace your clothing in opposite order. It is also important to have warm, dry clothing available to put on immediately after finishing your run or race.

Cross Training

You don't have to run every day all winter through inclement and unwelcoming conditions. On the other hand, don't just hibernate, quit, and get out of shape. A good method for maintaining your fitness during the winter is to cut back on your outdoor mileage and replace some of it—especially on bad weather days—with alternative training. Basically, 30 minutes of biking or swimming indoors is an aerobic training equivalent to a 30-minute run. So, too, is an aerobics class, using a rowing machine, and other forms of alternative exercise. The most natural way to exercise when snow clogs your running paths is to ski cross-country. Of course, running indoors on a treadmill is also a great option.

Keep Running Enjoyable

As much as possible, run during the daytime rather than at night. Daylight running is much more cheerful in the winter, and it is warmer when the sun is out. Make a date a few times a week with other runners to keep winter running from becoming too dreary. Run in events like NYRR weekly races to keep fit and enjoy the warm hospitality of others.

Here are some more cold weather tips.

- Although some people fear that running in cold weather can damage their lungs, this is not possible. That's because the lungs warm air sufficiently as it enters. If the cold air is uncomfortable to breathe, a face mask or hat that covers the nose and surrounds the mouth may help.

- Several parts of the body are more vulnerable to frostbite, such as toes, fingers, the nose, and ears. Bring a handkerchief or tissue to dab your eyes and nose often. If you feel pain or numbness in these areas, wiggle and move them, but don't rub. This can damage the blood vessels if the skin is in fact frozen. Don't blow warm breath on the skin either. The best way to warm these areas is with other parts of your body, such as putting your hands in your armpits.

- If the thought of that initial hit of biting cold makes it hard to get outside, try warming up indoors first to get the blood flowing. If the thought of going out at all is just too chilling, but you don't have access to equipment for alternative training, work out by repeatedly climbing or running up flights of stairs, jumping rope, or running in place.

- While icy surfaces can be treacherous for running, snow is usually no problem. If you are worried about the quality of your training, remember that a slower pace in more difficult conditions can equal a tougher workout under more ideal conditions.

- In extreme cold, coat your face (or at least your nose and cheeks) with a layer of petroleum jelly. Don't forget year-round skin care. (See Chapter 28, Skin Care.)

- If your hands are especially sensitive to cold, wear two layers. Combine a pair of gloves with mittens. The same goes for the ears—another spot likely to suffer most from cold. Try a headband covered with a hat for double protection.

Runner and one-time *New York Running News* contributor Kay Denmark has come up with some tried-and-true tips on surviving the winter season.

- Dry, awful winter claws, be gone! Let the cold weather work for your hands by giving them a hot mitt treatment while running. Glob on the petroleum jelly, then tuck those fingers into mittens or cotton socks. No matter how hot your hands get while running, try not to take off their coverings. The heat helps the jelly soften your skin.

- For those too macho to wear gloves in the winter, an old washerwoman trick can help. Before going out, briefly soak your hands in vinegar, and let them thoroughly air-dry. This helps to keep your hands warmer. It doesn't last forever, so it's best for short runs—or hanging out the laundry to dry, as originally intended.

- I don't know about you, but I can't run with my mouth shut. After enduring bone-chilling weather outdoors, when my teeth reach the warm air of my apartment, I experience a painful sensation. If you can relate, never fear, because there is a solution. Try placing a dry towel or washcloth in your mouth upon crossing the threshold. It works. It also proves delightfully entertaining to any eyewitnesses!

- Winter is not especially kind to hair. Those precious locks need some protection from the drying effects of wind and cold. Before running, pour some conditioner into the palms of your hands and work it through your hair.

- Ginger tea is great for warming up after a run. I learned about this magical liquid from an elderly woman in the tropical rain forest of Dominica, and it's the best winter brew of which I know. It helps break up congestion, and the subtle, hot kick of ginger warms a cold winter body. Simply place four or five thin slices of fresh ginger in a cup and add boiling water. Allow the brew to steep a while.

- Winter noses are often frozen, chapped, and unattractive. Rather than walking around with greasy-looking, petroleum-jellied nostrils, a simple solution is to apply some lip balm. Hey, it works on your lips, so why not?

- Here's a tip you'll likely associate with summer, but it applies equally to winter. Sunblock protects against winter sun and wind, which can be extremely destructive to your skin. (For more information on this important subject, see Chapter 28, Skin Care.)

- Wind can propel every bit of available dust into your eyes. By the time your run is over, your eyes may be red, irritated, and even puffy. Try a remedy often attributed to Ethel Merman. Put a small amount of witch hazel on cotton balls, close your eyes, and put the cotton on your eyelids. This soothes abused and tired eyes.

HOT WEATHER RUNNING TIPS

Running during the summer months can be quite enjoyable with extended daylight hours and the warmer weather. But running in hot weather can be trouble, and racing in it can be dangerous. Summer heat and humidity can cause muscle cramps, blisters, fatigue, heat exhaustion, and heat stroke. Symptoms that you should be aware of include headache; dizziness; disorientation; decrease in perspiration; and pale, cold skin. At the first sign of any of these symptoms, stop, walk, or rest. A precautionary plan to ensure safe, healthy running is outlined in a NYRR brochure written by Bob Glover:

1. **Wear breathable, light-colored, loose clothing.** Choose a fabric such as Coolmax® that wicks off the sweat. Loose singlets are best unless you'll be out for a long time in hot sun. If running in direct sunlight, protect your body with a light-colored loose shirt that covers your shoulders and upper arms. Wear a lightweight, light-colored hat that shades your head. Sunglasses will protect your eyes and help you keep relaxed. Don't overdress on a warm day—a singlet or short-sleeved shirt and shorts is all you'll need. It is important to minimize clothing to provide an optimal skin surface area from which evaporation can occur.

2. **Pour water in and on you.** On a very hot, humid day, you may lose between 6 and 12 ounces of fluid for every 20 minutes of running. Drink before you run, during your run, and before you get thirsty. Make frequent stops—at least one every two or three miles. Pour water on you to cool you off and drink plenty of water or sports drinks. Continue to drink after your runs.

3. **Avoid the heat. Run during the cool of the early morning or late evening.** Or, on very hot days, just stay indoors and exercise where it is air-conditioned. Run in the shade as much as possible. Hot pavement burns the feet and reflects heat upwards. Try running on the dirt shoulders and trails or on grass.

4. **Adjust your pace.** Start slowly and run a steady slower pace in both training runs and races. You may need to slow down by as much as a minute per mile or more and be prepared to make further reductions along the way. Check your pulse frequently to see how your heart is responding to the heat. Take walk breaks if needed to keep your temperature down.

5. **Adjust your distance.** In hot weather shorten your running distance. Cut your 30-minute run to 20 minutes or your ten-mile run to six to eight miles. Postpone long marathon training runs for a cooler day or at least shift it to a cooler time of day.

6. **Give yourself time to acclimatize.** If the weather suddenly turns hot, or you have arrived in a hot climate, pull back. Ease into running in the heat. Slow down your pace; shorten your runs. During your first workout in the heat, cut your intensity by a minute or more per mile. Give yourself seven to ten days to slowly adjust to the heat.

7. **Heat train for races.** If you plan to race in hot weather, train in hot weather. Give yourself ten to 14 days of progressive heat train-

ing. A few times a week, run at the hottest time of day—but go easy. Remember to adjust your time goals. No matter how well you heat train, you can't run as fast on a hot day as you can on a cool day.

8. **Be in shape.** An unconditioned runner places an extra burden on the body by running in the heat. The same is true of an overweight runner. Running in the heat to get in shape is a bad and perhaps dangerous idea.

9. **Remember to warm up and cool down.** You still need to prepare the body for a run even in hot weather. After a few minutes of limbering exercises, start your workout with a walk and then a slow jog to adjust to the heat outdoors. Then bring the pace up to a comfortable level. After running in the heat, your body temperature will remain high. Blood vessels are dilated in your skin and your arm and leg muscles. Stopping suddenly may stress your heart as it continues to pump blood through these dilated vessels. Walk slowly for five to ten minutes as part of your cool down. Then stretch thoroughly.

10. **Most important—use common sense.** If you feel dizzy, overheated, or cold, stop and walk. Get out of the sun and get fluids on you and in you. Don't race or train hard in very hot or humid weather. Heat disorders can affect any level of runner, seasoned competitor and novice alike.

31

SAFETY

In April 1989, Trisha Mieli, a young woman runner who came to be known as the "Central Park jogger," was brutally beaten, raped, and left for dead in New York City's Central Park. This incident brought the issue of running safety into international focus.

For years, NYRR has held educational forums on safety for runners and lobbied to improve safety conditions in Central Park and other areas.

In response to the jogger attack, the NYRR Community Services department was instituted, which is overseen by a full-time staff member. The NYRR also finances gatekeepers in a kiosk in Central Park and works with the Central Park police precinct in a crime watch effort.

Contrary to what people often believe about big cities, and New York in particular, this city—which has the largest concentration of runners anywhere—happens to be one of the safest places in which to run. It's a little-known fact, but the Central Park precinct has long had the lowest crime rate in the city. That's in part because various organizations, including NYRR, have lobbied to provide better safety services.

The following runners' safety information is adapted from a brochure once distributed by NYRR, as well as NYRR safety clinics given by now retired detective Lucille Burrascano of the New York City Police Department.

SAFETY TIPS

1. There's safety in numbers, so don't run alone. Although this is the cardinal rule of running safety, a majority of runners do their running solo. Find a partner or a group to run with. A local runners' club is a good place to start. If you must run alone, go where there are other people.

2. Whenever possible, run during daylight hours. If you must run in the dark, wear light-reflecting or light-colored clothing, and avoid running in deserted areas. Whenever possible, choose routes that enable you to avoid running in the street.

3. Be thoroughly familiar with your route. Know the location of phones, call boxes, police stations, fire houses, hospitals, and 24-hour businesses.

4. Listen to your instincts and be willing to vary your route if you sense that you are in danger. If you are alone, wait for another runner if possible.

5. Avoid running in deserted or poorly lighted areas, or adjacent to dense foliage or places from which you can be set upon without warning. Be especially alert at blind corners or when you are crossing intersections.

6. Run against traffic whenever possible. Move first when a vehicle is coming toward you. Do not expect vehicles to move for you.

7. Run relaxed and confident, yet be aware of your surroundings and who is around you at all times. Run defensively—watching for and avoiding cars, bikes, and dogs.

8. Don't acknowledge or respond to verbal harassment.

9. Carry a whistle or alarm device to summon emergency assistance.

10. Don't wear jewelry, such as chains, medallions, rings, and expensive watches.

11. Tune into your surroundings, not out.

12. Avoid wearing headphones. It has become common practice among many people to run with headsets. Generally, it is considered unsafe, as the runner is usually unaware of his or her surroundings and cannot hear outside noise well. In 1991, NYRR attempted to ban the use of headphones in its races. So many loyal runners/headphone users complained that the ban was rescinded. However, NYRR policy states that wearing headphones while running is an unsafe practice. For runners who still insist on using them, the NYRR recommends they pay careful attention to their surroundings, keep the volume as low as possible, and perhaps use only one of the earphones.

13. Always carry some form of personal identification while running (including medic alert ID if applicable) in case of emergency. It's also a good idea to carry a small amount of paper money. Consider bringing a cell phone. Write personal information and blood type on the inside of your shoes.

14. Before heading out, tell a friend where you are running, and when you expect to return.

> The Road Runners Club of America (RRCA) is a strong safety advocate and has published an extensive number of safety bulletins. For further tips and information on organizing community safety, check on the Web at www.rrca.org.

WHEN DOGS ARE NOT RUNNERS' BEST FRIENDS

Like long-hounded mail carriers, it is not uncommon for runners to be plagued by dogs. What should you do if you're confronted by a dog during a run? A lot of times the animal will just come up and smell you, and then it will go away; however, some dogs are inherently aggressive. The best thing to do is just to stop and be nonthreatening. If you run away, they usually will chase you. If you try to throw something at them or hit at them, they'll try to bite. Just be as nonthreatening as you can. And if you can't, you should yell, "No! Go away!" or "Down!" or "Sit!"

If you have a squirt bottle of water, use it, but spraying mace in a dog's face is not recommended because the dog may then chase you. What you don't want to do is get into a chase with a dog because almost every dog in the world is faster than every person.

If you do get bitten by a dog, go to a hospital immediately. If possible, find the owner of the dog to determine whether the dog has been vaccinated against rabies.

PART 7
HEALTH AND MEDICINE

RUN HEALTHY

To run healthy means to run using common sense. So if you have been in-active for more than a few months, or have any health problems, consult a qualified physician for a thorough medical examination before undertaking a running program. Lewis Maharam, M.D., also advises that you do the fol-lowing:

- **Avoid the "invincibility syndrome."** Don't take the "must go on" or "must win" attitude to extremes. If you're not feeling well, espe-cially during an acute viral infection or when suffering from a sys-temic disease, stay off your feet.

What kept me relatively injury-free throughout my career was sound training and racing. My career had a sensible sequence—from shorter distances on the track to longer distances on the roads. Nothing I have done was on an impulse. Admittedly, my first marathon in 1978 was sort of run on a whim, but to a degree I was well prepared by having a strong running background. In those days, however, the amount of marathon training knowl-edge and widely available information wasn't even a fraction of what it is today.

This doesn't mean I didn't make mistakes along the way in my career. Looking back, I regret that very often I didn't cut back on my training when I felt something was wrong. I made the com-mon mistake of thinking I could run through it, that it wasn't as bad as it was. I think this sense of invincibility is what all we run-ners have in common. And we learn the lesson the hard way, be-lieving we are the exception. Much of the time, we're good at giving advice to others, but when it comes to ourselves, we don't follow the rules.

So don't be afraid to take a day off. Don't be afraid to use al-ternative training. I think that's why so many people get injured, because they don't cut back when they hear a message from the body.

—Grete Waitz

- **Get a good night's sleep before a race.** Do not take any sedatives. Have a light meal three or four hours before a race. Carbohydrates such as toast, crackers, and fruit are best. Avoid heavy meals containing fats, proteins, and sweets. Avoid all alcoholic beverages before a race, and definitely do *not* take any drugs that serve as stimulants.

- **Watch the weather.** Adjust your race or training goal if it's hotter or more humid than usual. Do not overdress. Clothing should feel comfortable and should be loose-fitting. Wear clothes you've worn before while running. New clothes could chafe or cause other discomfort. Light-colored clothes will help reflect heat. Remember that you heat up as you run. If you feel comfortably dressed at the start of a race or training session, you are probably overdressed.

- **Wear proper running shoes.** Shoes should fit well and should feel comfortable. New or badly worn-out shoes could cause discomfort and injury. Use the rule of thumb when fitting shoes—you should be able to feel a gap about as deep as your thumb between your longest toe and the end of the shoe.

- **Do warmup exercises.** Proper warmup before a race or training session and cool-down exercises after are essential. Follow your normal stretching routine after these exercises.

- **Be alert and safe.** Watch the condition of the road as you run to avoid accidents. Gravel, curbs, grates, and potholes can be dangerous if you don't see them.

- **Run at your own pace.** Do not push too hard too soon. This will invariably lead to early exhaustion. If you develop a leg or other cramp, slow down or stop running. Massage and slowly stretch and relax the involved muscle. If the cramp continues, ask for assistance.

- **When racing, avoid all sudden sprinting.** This is important to keep in mind, especially at the end of a race. If you've been regularly practicing speedwork, your body will be used to accelerating. But even in trained runners, sudden sprints may lead to leg muscle injuries.

- **Don't run through illness.** It is imperative that you withdraw from a race if you have a fever, chills, generalized malaise, cold or flu, nausea, vomiting, or diarrhea. If there is the slightest doubt, stop at a first-aid station or ask advice from medical personnel at the race. You should also avoid running and training when you're ill.

What I've learned over the years is that you really have to tune into your "denial mechanism" quickly if you want to stay active. In other words, everybody gets to a point where they start to overdo it, and break down or get hurt. And almost everybody denies it when it first hits.

Staying healthy is a question of how quickly you can get beyond the denial and deal with the reality. You then have an opportunity to back off that little bit you need to recover. And it doesn't take much adjustment, because what I've also found is that you don't have to back off a lot if you can recognize the potential problem soon enough.

It's really very simple to recognize. It's accepting that you're limping. My test is, any time you get to the point where something is truly interfering with your running gait, back off and let it heal. Don't keep going simply because you can keep going.

—*Frank Shorter*

Lewis G. Maharam, M.D., recommends using the "Concept of Relative Rest" to aid runners in managing running injuries. Simply put, if an athlete has pain while running, he or she must stop running.

Pain is not the same as discomfort. Running pain may be defined as enough distress to require the shortening of a workout (i.e., decreased distance or time), distress to the point that a runner must change or alter running form, or distress to the point that the athlete is concerned about continuing the activity.

Most running injuries do not cause pain while running, but they may cause discomfort afterward. If that is the case, a runner has a second decision to make. When post-running discomfort is severe enough to cause limping, or it lasts from one day to the next, the runner may still run, but should cut the workout in half until the pain falls into a manageable category, i.e., it is tolerable.

Pain is subjective, so the real test is whether the person can run with normal form. Post-running discomfort should then diminish within the first couple of minutes to hours after running and should not be severe enough to cause a limp. In this case, the runner can continue to do the normal workout, but should not increase until the post-running discomfort subsides more rapidly.

Dr. Maharam prepared these tips for New York City marathoners, but they can also apply to runners doing any serious event.

"As you get ready for any long-distance race, it's crucial to avoid common mistakes that can keep you from starting, or jeopardize your effort on race day. The ten tips below are based on guidelines written by my predecessor, the late Andres Rodriguez, M.D. Over many years as medical director of the New York City Marathon, Andy saw a lot of talented, experienced runners wind up in the medical tent, and many others fail to even start the race. He complied a list he called *The 10 Commandments of Healthy Running.* I've adapted them, incorporating the latest medical information and advice":

1. Get checked out. A thorough exam by a sports medicine physician can pinpoint physical characteristics—e.g., over-pronation (feet with an excessive inward roll), high arches, bowed legs, leg-length discrepancies—that may increase your susceptibility to injury. You can still run with these conditions, but you may have to make adjustments in footwear, training, and supplemental activities.

2. Go at your own pace. If you struggle through races and workouts, you will eventually break down. Remember to train, not strain.

3. Don't be a slave to your training schedule. No one hands out trophies for having a perfect running log. Your body will tell you when you need to back off to avoid an injury. It's your job to listen to it.

4. Warm up, stretch, run, cool down, and stretch again. At the end of a workout or race, your muscles are full of micro-tears. If you don't stretch again after some easy jogging or walking, they will heal at a shorter length, and you will risk pulling a muscle the next time you work it hard.

5. Listen to your body. Do not run if pain is altering your form. If you feel sick, you probably are. Stop and get help if you need it.

6. Pay attention to your diet. Carbohydrate is the body's main fuel for endurance exercise. You also need some protein for muscle recovery and fat for essential body functions. Read up on the basics of sensible, healthy eating.

7. Stay hydrated. Aim to take in one cup of fluid (8 ounces) for every 20 minutes of running. Sports drinks work best, but don't try something in a race if you haven't used it in training.

8. Wear proper, comfortable shoes. Do *not* try new shoes on race day! Rather, break them in with at least three or four runs, even if

you're wearing a model you've used before. Proper fit is crucial, so buy new shoes in the afternoon or evening when your feet are slightly larger than in the morning. Shoe length should be a thumb's width longer than your longest toe.

9. Dress for the weather. Layers allow you to adjust to changing conditions. On race day, bring warm throw-away clothes to the start; you can toss them to the sidelines once you get moving. Consider tying a lightweight top around your waist in case it cools off later.

10. Watch road surface conditions. Beware of potholes, bumps, debris, oil slicks, and other potential hazards.

Remember, there are no guarantees in the marathon, or in any race or run. By controlling the things you can, you increase your chances of success.

INJURY PREVENTION AND CURE

As every athlete, coach, and medical professional can verify, if you've been running long, hard, or far enough, you've likely experienced some type of injury at one time or another. In fact, witnessing the medical care network for just one event, the New York City Marathon, is proof. From runners eagerly seeking guidance on injuries at the Marathon Expo and clinics, to those being cared for on race day by 1,500 medical volunteers, no single subject seems to concern—and often obsess—a runner more than injury.

Injury seems to have little relevance until it hits you personally. Then, no matter what level of runner you are, it can be devastating. For the elite athlete, it represents the loss not only of personal identity, but of a job and a livelihood. For the serious athlete, being forced to take off from running is like losing a dear friend. Even for a beginner, it can be like having a (new) rug pulled out from under. You will never realize how much you cherish your running until—even temporarily—it is no longer yours.

That's the bad news. The good news is that injuries heal, and with the injury experience comes wisdom. Coping with injury (or illness) is one of the many aspects of running that, as George Sheehan has articulated so well over the years, shows us that running is often a metaphor for life, including personal adversity.

Why all the heavy philosophy? Because putting things in perspective is not always one of the great skills of the injured runner. Over the years, a great number of telephone calls to NYRR (often characterized by desperate pleas for help) have been from injured runners. Through its Medical Committee, NYRR has an extensive network of health care professionals. And to illustrate the yin and yang of the sport, other than participation in NYRR's major races, the best-attended functions are the injury clinics.

RUNNING SURFACES

Believe it or not, the surfaces on which you run have a great deal to do with your body's health. In fact, marathon legend Bill Rodgers claims that the two most important factors in avoiding injury are to vary training surfaces and to build gradually.

Physiology expert David Martin, Ph.D., says that when choosing a running surface, the most important things to consider are first, the firmness of the surface (the softer the surface, the more shock it will absorb), second, the symmetry (when one part of the body is imbalanced, such as the feet, the rest follows), and third, the smoothness of the running surface. Since three to four times a person's weight pounds into the foot and ankle as he or she runs, consider these surfaces: concrete (the hardest), asphalt, cinder or rubber tracks, sand (packed and loose), grass, or a treadmill.

Although sand seems to make sense, running on it should be limited. Packed sand is usually on a slant and soft sand causes your heels to sink, creating strain on the Achilles tendons. So if you do enjoy sand running, limit your time, and make sure to change directions.

The most highly recommended surface? That would be a dirt or a cinder trail that is not cambered (slanted downward from the center). While asphalt is a better choice than concrete (i.e., sidewalks), make sure that if the asphalt surface is slanted, you regularly change directions on which you run the slants, especially on long runs. This will reduce your chance of injury.

As always, make sure to listen to your body, the best clue to proper and well-balanced running surfaces for you. (Adapted from "Running Surfaces," *New York Runner,* May/June 1998.)

(Podiatrist Dr. John Pagliano, quoted in an article in the June 2002 issue of *Men's Fitness* magazine, counsels against running on concrete, saying, "If you switch to softer surfaces, you can cut your injury risk by 50 percent." In rating ten running surfaces, *Men's Fitness* concluded that concrete is the worst; grass is the best.)

An Ounce of Prevention

Certified sports chiropractor Dr. G. Thomas Kovacs notes that overuse injuries are obviously due to factors such as running on hard, nonshock-absorbing surfaces, overstriding, downhill running, and improper shoe selection. But other factors, he explains below, will also affect your musculoskeletal system.

- **Flexibility and stretching.** Be sure you are flexible enough and that your stretching routine concentrates on the muscles used for running, such as lower back, hamstrings, and calves.
- **Strength.** Do you have adequate strength in your quadriceps, shins, and abdominal muscles to make it through your workout, or do you ignore strengthening those "opposing" running muscles?

Most sprains and strains should be treated with ice until the swelling is gone. Ice, best applied in a plastic bag or wrapped in a towel, dulls the pain as well as decreases the blood flow, lessening internal bleeding and swelling. After icing, wrap an elastic bandage snugly but not tightly around the sore area, and elevate it above the heart. Stop ice treatments as soon as the skin is numb, usually after 15 or 20 minutes. Ice is not the remedy for blisters or open wounds, or if you have circulatory problems.

Here's a first-aid idea for pulls and sprains that need cold applied to them immediately to keep swelling down. Instead of fumbling with ice cubes, use a bag or two of frozen vegetables—corn, peas, or other small items. They're handy, and can be easily shaped to fit around whatever it is you've damaged. Or you could fill balloons with various amounts of water and freeze them. This way you can make custom-fitted cold packs.

- **Diet.** Does your diet consist of candy bars, or vegetables and whole grains? Sixty to 65 percent of your diet should be in the form of complex carbohydrates, while proteins should be 15 to 20 percent and fats should be 20 to 25 percent. Remember, you are what you eat.
- **Rest.** Do you allow your body adequate time to rest and recuperate?

- **Vigilance.**   Do you monitor key factors of overtraining, such as resting heart rate, body weight, and number of hours slept per night? Did you know that an increase in resting heart rate of ten beats has a high correlation to injury within three days? An unexpected weight drop of three pounds will also have the same effect.

- **Equipment.**   Running shoes should be selected to fit the runner's foot type (e.g., high arched, low arched, etc.) and running characteristics (mileage, surface, type of running, etc.).   In the opinion of medical experts, shoes should be changed every three to six months regardless of wear. If a runner is unsure of the type of shoe, he or she should err toward a more stable shoe rather than a more cushioned one. Lightweight shoes are not considered adequate for most runners to train in on a day-to-day basis and should be reserved for racing or time trials only.

- **Warmup.**   Do you make the same mistake as numerous runners by assuming that warming up is the same as stretching, or do you warm up properly by first running slowly so you can stretch farther and perform better? A one-degree increase in muscle temperature during warmup will make your muscles 13 percent more efficient. This translates into more power!

- **Program planning.**   Do you suddenly increase your weekly mileage by as much as 50 percent, or do you increase properly by 10 percent per week? Do you end your workouts by racing someone to the finish line, or do you cool down properly so that your heart can relax slowly?

- **Hydration.**   Are you the type of person who has a beer or two before you go out for a run, rather than hydrate yourself with water?

WHAT TO DO WHEN YOU CAN'T RUN

Athlete and doctor Norbert Sander, winner of the 1974 New York City Marathon, advises that you avoid the pitfall of giving up entirely—not exercising, overeating, and getting into a general depression—when sidelined by an injury. "As the years and injuries come and go, the experienced runner usually begins to appreciate the personal benefits and positive feelings derived from good fitness and day-to-day running," he explains. "The temptation to push close to the injury edge in the hopes of greater performance

If you exercise to the point that your muscles hurt the next day, you might think the best way to ease this discomfort is to work through the ache. But research outlined in *Vogue* magazine indicates that exercise slows, not speeds, muscle recovery, and may even lead to injury. A Massachusetts research team had a group work their arm muscles to exhaustion, then put one arm in a sling for three days. Although both arms stayed sore for the same number of days, the immobilized arm regained its strength more quickly. Another group of researchers tested whether exercising with sore muscles increased the risk of injury. They found muscle soreness in runners caused them to stiffen their lower bodies, thus making them poorer at absorbing shock, causing a greater risk of injury. Researchers have this advice for the sore: Give your muscles a rest, at least for a day or two. Cross training is a good option.

becomes less appealing, and, thus, the amount of downtime usually decreases."

Sander writes that most world-class marathoners have relatively short periods of extraordinary performances due to the tightrope walk necessary between record-breaking runs and physical breakdown. The risk at the top is quite high, although worth it at least for short periods. "I myself had two periods of high-level running—one for four months after I graduated from college and won 14 of 15 races, culminating in a time of 61:40 for a 20-kilometer race. Predictably, my penultimate run was followed by a year-long ankle injury that effectively killed off any chance of progressing on to the next level, which I thought, at that time, would be national class. Ten years later I had a resurgence, but without my former speed, going up in distance to the marathon. I won Yonkers in 1973, New Orleans and New York in 1974, and placed second, fourth, and fifth in three other international marathons," Sander explains.

According to Sander, getting back to high-level competition after injury can take a very long time—mentally and physically—especially in terms of the spiritual resolve to press deeper and deeper into oneself. Today there are a good number of conditioners to help keep you in shape when running is impossible—stationary or outdoor cycling, in-line skating, cross-country ski machines, and deep water running all can help to maintain a level of fitness and avoid the depression that often accompanies an injury.

If you can't work out the standard minimum of 20 to 30 minutes, don't give up on working out at all. Studies have found that multiple short bouts (three ten-minute sessions, for example) of moderate-intensity exercise resulted in significant training effects—nearly the same as those produced by a single 30-minute bout. This just proves how simple achieving fitness can be.

33

SPORTS MEDICINE

NYRR Medical Director Lewis Maharam, M.D., has accumulated years of experience overseeing runners' health in his role as medical director of some of the largest and most prestigious running events; in his various positions with sports medicine organizations; and in his private sports medicine practice in New York. In this chapter, Dr. Maharam takes you through a comprehensive variety of possible problems and their cures and offers a prescription for prevention.

BLISTERED, BRUISED, AND SMELLY FEET

Running creates friction: either because of side to side motion or front to back; or between the foot and the shoe, or the foot and the ground. As a result, the skin of the foot is often prone to injury.

Friction, together with sweat and abrasion, can cause skin irritation on the top or bottom of the foot. The result can be hardened skin (**corns** or **calluses**) or **blisters** as the body tries to protect itself. Other problems include **dry skin**, **athlete's foot** (fungal infections), and **warts** because of the environment in the shoe.

Blisters are fluid-filled sacs that occur due to skin irritation. Initially, blisters should be drained using a sterile pin or lancet. The skin should not be peeled away from the blister; this leaves a raw, open painful sore and can lead to infection. There are many over-the-counter products that can be used to protect the skin after the blister is lanced. These products include Spenco® Second Skin, Dr. Scholl's® Blister Treatment, and moleskin, all of which are easily found. These items can be put over the blister after application of any antibiotic cream.

To prevent blisters, one must find their cause. Most often it is a bony protrusion on the foot (like **bunions** or **hammer toes**), a poorly fitted shoe (a shoe that is too tight or too short), or increased foot perspiration. The means of blister prevention include the padding of the bony projections, wearing properly fitting shoes, and using sports socks when running long distances. Other aids include foot powders (Zeasorb® or Tinactin®) to keep the feet dry, and friction-reducing insoles from companies like Spenco®, Dr. Scholl's®, or Langer PPT®.

A callus or corn is hardened skin that occurs in high friction areas (the bottom of the foot, or over bony projections). They are often painful. Treatment includes foot soaks (Johnson's Foot Soap® or Dr. Scholl's Sit and Soak®) to soften the skin, followed by abrasion by a pumice stone or corn and callus file, each of which is commercially available. Properly fitted shoes, sports socks, and friction-reducing insoles are also helpful.

Warts are a viral skin infection. They are usually seen as small, round, callus-like skin lesions and are often painful. They are commonly mistaken for corns or calluses. When scraped or abraded, a wart bleeds, while a callus does not. Foot soaks and abrasion of the wart are accompanied by the use of over-the-counter wart medication (Trans-Ver-Sal®, Clear Away Plantar®). Be sure to follow all the directions on the package of medicine.

Athlete's foot is a fungal infection that often occurs on the bottom of the foot or between the toes. The skin of the foot may itch; be blistered, red, scaly, or peeling; or be soft and mushy; and the foot may smell bad. If you suspect athlete's foot, use an athlete's foot powder daily, spray your shoes with Lysol®, keep your feet dry, and change socks and shoes frequently. In addition, an over-the-counter athlete's foot cream like Lamisil®, Lotrimin®, or Tinactin® should be applied to the affected area twice daily for at least one month (even if the symptoms subside).

Items like Certain-Dri® or Dri-Sol® can be combined with foot powders for runners whose feet sweat excessively or smell bad. For excessively dry skin, Am-Lactin®, Eucerin®, or Lac-Hydrin® skin creams applied to the foot nightly and covered with a Baggie® or Saran Wrap® are recommended.

THE SPORTS PODIATRIST

Podiatry is the diagnosis and treatment of disorders of the foot. Sports podiatry is the application of this science to treatment of foot maladies in the athlete. A good sports podiatrist must have a strong background in foot biomechanics (the study of the laws of locomotion).

Thirty to 40 percent of all running injuries are foot-related. When these injuries are added to those in the lower leg that involve faulty foot biomechanics (shin splints, knee pain, etc.), this number grows to 60–70 percent.

The ability to run injury-free requires healthy feet and foot structure. In running, the foot must adapt to terrain, absorb shock, and act to stabilize and propel the body. These functions are a result of proper foot biomechanics. Failure of the foot to perform any of these functions, improper timing of these functions, or increased or decreased magnitude of these functions can lead to foot or lower leg injuries. When you consider that the running foot can receive loads of two to three times the body weight in each stride, it is a marvel that we can run at all!

When there is an injury to the foot or lower leg that is related to foot structure or foot biomechanics, runners should consult a sports podiatrist or see a reputable sports medicine–certified physician or orthopedist for a referral. In some cases, a "team" approach to an injury is the best option. The athlete is treated simultaneously by a physician or orthopedist, a podiatrist, and a physical therapist or chiropractor trained in sports medicine. This approach helps to get the athlete better faster since each member of the "team" contributes in his or her specialized area.

The sports podiatrist evaluates foot structure, biomechanics, and gait abnormalities and may prescribe corrective support or orthotics (foot inserts) to restore normal mechanics. In addition, the podiatrist may suggest shoe gear changes, urge rehabilitation (strength and stretching programs), take X-rays, prescribe medication, or recommend surgery as needed.

INSOLES, ARCH SUPPORTS, AND ORTHOTICS

Shock-reducing insoles, arch support insoles, and foot orthotics are often used to prevent or control running-related foot or lower leg injuries. Unfortunately, the lay public and even members of the medical community are often confused about these devices, so they are commonly misused or abused. A runner must understand the difference between an insole, arch support, and an orthotic.

The first task is defining the term *orthotic*. The medical community views an orthotic as any device, appliance, or apparatus used to support, align, prevent deformities, or improve the function of the foot. According to this definition, many devices may be considered orthotics, including over-the-counter arch supports, shoe inlays, shock reducing insoles, heel cushions or cups, and even felt or silicone pads. When sports podiatrists use the term *orthotic,* they are referring to a very specific type of foot support. It is important to recognize that all types of foot supports have their place, but they must be used properly if they are to prevent injury.

Shoe inlays or shock-absorbing insoles are devices placed into the shoe to absorb shock or alter the load pattern on certain areas of the foot. Spenco®, PPT®, and Dr. Scholl's Pillow Insoles® are examples. They are flat (with little or no arch), cut to the length of the shoe, and made of soft, flexible materials. Insoles are most often over-the-counter devices, but in some cases may be custom-made. Even when custom-fitted they are NOT considered orthotics by most podiatrists. Regardless, they are often all that is required for a bruised or irritated foot. In some cases, an insole is combined with an arch support and can accomplish two tasks.

Most runners are familiar with the vast array of over-the-counter arch supportive insole devices available at running stores or pharmacies. These "generic" supports are usually flexible and made to the size of the foot over a common form or "last" with increased support on the inside of the arch. Arch supports act similar to a "truss" by placing bulk under the arch, providing a physical barrier to arch collapse. If enough support is placed under the arch, the amount of arch drop, or pronation (inward rolling of the feet), is reduced. Even custom-made arch supports are not considered orthotics by most podiatrists. Certainly, runners with mild foot deformity who are experiencing foot or lower leg problems may benefit greatly by using arch supports.

An orthotic is a foot support that is custom-made over a cast or impression of the foot that is then "corrected" so that foot and lower leg alignment is consistently maintained. Orthotics are often required when there is a significant misalignment of the foot or lower leg leading to injury. The design of an orthotic determines its effectiveness. There are two major design factors: the material used in the construction and the length and shape of the orthotic.

Materials that are used to construct orthotics can be flexible, semi-flexible, semi-rigid, or rigid. For running, it is the opinion of sports medicine doctors that flexible or semi-flexible materials work the best. Some practitioners prefer to use more rigid materials. Experience has taught us that more flexible materials are generally superior. It is true that flexible or semi-flexible materials are less durable, but this minor concern is far outweighed by better performance. Materials like leather, cork, moldable rubbers, foams, or lightweight aerated plastics make excellent orthotics for runners. With minimal maintenance, orthotics made from these materials should last for three to five years.

The length and shape of the orthotic is a primary concern. Runners should understand the demands of running on the foot to understand why this is the case. The job of an orthotic starts with the initiation of the running cycle as the heel of one foot contacts the ground. The orthotic needs to guide the foot and lower leg into the proper angle of contact to allow shock attenuation and slow leg rotation. This is accomplished by heel posting (angulation) on the inside of the orthotic, and the heel cup of the device. This phase of running lasts for only a split second, so orthotics that are "heel control" based are somewhat inefficient for runners.

Next, the running foot pronates (rolls inwardly) to absorb shock. Orthotics are designed to allow normal pronation, but limit abnormal or "over" pronation. The entire orthotic is involved in limiting pronation. To accomplish this, the orthotic must perfectly contour to the runner's foot. Any gap between the orthotic and the foot may allow foot deformation and "over" pronation. Finally, during the push-off phase of running, the orthotic must guide the running foot up onto the metatarsals (the forefoot) and allow normal supination (outward roll) to occur. Orthotics that end behind the metatarsal heads (i.e., short of the ball of the foot) do not accomplish this task as well as full-length orthotics (those that are posted/angulated through the ball of the foot). This last point is extremely important. Orthotics that end behind the metatarsals are 30–40 percent less efficient in runners.

The last concern about orthotics is that often when they are working poorly, the reason is traced to improper usage. The only time an orthotic can work is when it is worn.

Some types of running problems in certain runners require the devices to be used any time the athlete bears weight. Other problems may require only sporadic use. A good rule of thumb is to start using your orthotics at all times until the problem subsides. Then, gradually ease off the wearing time until you are comfortable with the amount of wear time or until your symptoms return. Always, the best way to wear orthotics is as much as possible. Foot and leg-related running problems are like high blood pressure; there may be no symptoms until something goes very wrong, very rapidly.

These facts may explain why arch supports, insoles, or poorly-made orthotics may not perform up to the expectations of a runner. First, arch supports or insoles may be prescribed when orthotics are required. Second, devices termed orthotics may be called so improperly. Third, even when properly named, orthotics may be improperly designed or constructed. Lastly, to be useful, orthotics must be used.

If you think you need orthotics, are unsure about their efficiency, have running problems that persist, or if your orthotics are uncomfortable, see a sports-oriented podiatrist or physician. He or she may have an easy answer to your problem.

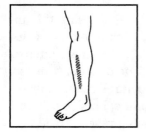

SHIN SPLINTS

"Shin Splints" is a generic term used to describe any lower leg pain. The most distinguishing feature is pain that occurs on the inside of the shin bone along the course of the posterior tibial (shin)

or soleus muscle (calf) or tendon. Generally graded from I to IV based on symptoms, shin splints are caused by injury to the muscle, tendon, soft tissue lining of the bone, or the shin bone itself. The front and outside of the shin bone are less frequently involved. The two most painful grades, III and IV, are commonly termed tibial stress syndrome (III) and stress fracture (IV).

A stress fracture in a runner can be a serious problem, and may require specialized testing and cessation of running until healed. Most other grades of shin pain can be managed while the runner continues to run.

POSSIBLE CAUSES

- Abnormal biomechanics of the lower leg and foot (over- or under-pronation, leg length discrepancy)
- Muscular imbalance between the calf and shin muscles (tight calves)
- Poor choice of shoes (shoes are not supportive, too light, or too highly cushioned)
- Poor running form (over- or under-striding or crossover running)
- Overtraining (too much, too fast, too soon, too often)
- Nutritional disorders (poor diet)

TREATMENT

Initial treatment includes controlling the biomechanics by changing to a more supportive training shoe and/or the use of arch supports or custom-made running orthotics. Aggressive calf stretching (multiple times per day), ice, relative rest, and correction of training errors or running form when indicated may also be recommended.

STRESS FRACTURES

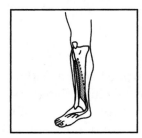

Commonly termed a grade IV shin splint, this injury represents a "hairline" crack in either of the lower leg bones (tibia or fibula). The pain is intense and pinpointed on the bone. The onset of pain can be gradual or rapid. Stress fractures can usually be distinguished from other "shin splints" by the intensity of pain, since it usually prevents running.

The lower leg may even be achy or painful when standing or walking or even sitting. Diagnosis is made primarily by symptoms, although X-rays, a bone scan, or an MRI may confirm the diagnosis.

POSSIBLE CAUSES

The same as shin splints. Repetitive stress fractures that respond poorly to treatment require more extensive investigation into nutritional disorders or other metabolic causes.

TREATMENT

This is one of the few running injuries that requires absolute rest. A runner should avoid running on a stress fracture until the bone is healed. Depending on the severity of the injury, this can be from four to 12 weeks or longer. In most cases, there is no necessity for immobilization (cast or splint). Crutches, air casts, or splints are sometimes helpful to allow increased mobility and lessen pain.

Cross training, using non–weight-bearing activities like swimming, flotation vest running, and cycling, can help to maintain cardiovascular fitness.

It has been shown that 40–50 percent of all lower leg stress fractures have a biomechanical cause. Custom-fitted running orthotics are essential to prevent re-injury in this case. Other treatment includes aggressive calf stretching, shoe change, controlled return to running, and nutritional counseling when needed.

CALF MUSCLE STRAINS/ACHILLES TENDINITIS

Calf muscle and achilles tendon strains or tears are quite common, but need not be disastrous if treated quickly and properly. This injury presents as a mild ache to a sharp or burning pain in the back of the leg or above the heel

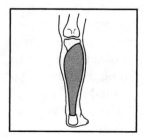 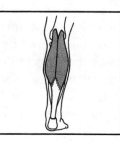 bone. Pulling the foot up or running or walking on the toes may reduce the pain. At times a "bump" or "knot" may be felt or seen in the muscle or on the tendon.

POSSIBLE CAUSES

- A tight or inflexible calf muscle
- Improper training (too much speed training, fartlek, bounding work, or hill training)
- Poor shoes (not enough pronation control, too lightweight, too cushioned, or extreme cut away under the arch)
- Abnormal biomechanics (leg length discrepancy, over pronation)
- Improper warmup or cool-down
- Overtraining

TREATMENT

Calf flexibility is imperative. Until proper flexibility is regained the calf and achilles remain prone to re-injury. Strength training for the calf should cease until proper flexibility is regained.

Physical therapy may help to achieve the goal of increased flexibility more rapidly. Switching to more supportive shoes (especially for those runners wearing sprint shoes or lightweight training shoes), and moderating workouts (less speed and hill training and more long, slow distance running) is helpful. Other treatments include proper warmup and cool-down, ice, relative rest, anti-inflammatory medication, and massage therapy.

KNEE INJURIES

Forty percent of all running injuries are said to involve the knee. The cause of running knee pain can be intrinsic to the knee (i.e., caused by imperfections in the knee such as torn cartilage, injured ligaments, etc.) or extrinsic to the knee (i.e., caused by imperfections outside the knee such as knock-knee, bow-leg, flat foot, etc.).

A common type of extrinsic knee pain is called **patello-femoral syndrome** and is due to a mal-tracking of the kneecap. This type of knee pain is transient, aggravated by activity, relieved by rest, increased when going up or down hills or stairs, intensified in a seated position, and often due to extrinsic causes. The area of involvement is most often on the inside and front of the kneecap, although it can occur anywhere around the kneecap. This syndrome is said to account for more than half of all running knee injuries. The vast majority of patello-femoral knee pain is caused by abnormal biomechanics of the lower extremity and is generally controlled before radical treatment or surgery is necessary.

Intrinsic knee pain generally occurs inside the knee or near the joint line and is not commonly seen around the kneecap. It is more intense, not always alleviated by rest, and may be combined with a severe weakness or "giving way" of the knee. Often the runner can point to an actual injury to the knee as the cause of the initial pain.

Any running knee injury that is repetitive or consistent should be evaluated by a sports-oriented physician or orthopedist.

POSSIBLE CAUSES

- Imbalance or weakness of quadriceps muscle (especially the inside quad or vastus medialis obliquus)
- Abnormal lower leg biomechanics (abnormal foot pronation, knock-knee, bow-legs, leg length discrepancy, etc.)
- Poor choice of running surface (hilly, rocky, uneven, hard, etc.)
- Tight or imbalanced hamstrings
- Training errors (too much, too fast, too soon)
- Poorly constructed shoes (too light, highly cushioned, or under-supportive)

TREATMENT

Treatment of extrinsic knee pain revolves around finding the cause. Rest, ice, and anti-inflammatories are sometimes helpful. In most cases, exercises to strengthen and balance the quadriceps muscles are beneficial. Terminal extension quadriceps lifts are the most productive exercise (lifting through the last 30 degrees of the extension arc of the lower leg). These exercises can be done at home, but physical therapy is more reliable.

Changing to more supportive shoes and using store-bought arch supports is also helpful. Most runners with knee pain require custom molded running orthotics to align the lower extremity. Runners should also reduce the amount of running and cease hill or speed work until the pain subsides enough for them to run with normal form; running with a change of form due to pain will always cause problems somewhere else on the body.

My worst cycle of injuries started off with a stress fracture in my shinbone in 1982. After being out for six weeks and missing the indoor season that year, the very first step I took—literally—I got an Achilles tendon strain. From February to September I was out of action. I went to scores of doctors in an attempt to have my problems remedied—physical therapists and chiropractors among them.

I had two stress fractures in 1983, one in each shin. I missed the 1984 Olympic Games as a result. In 1986 I didn't run well because I went on a special diet and inadvertently lost a lot of weight. Then I had another stress fracture in 1987 and again in 1988.

It was terrible, particularly missing the Olympics. Years later, you look back on the times of injury and the intensity of it has dimmed. But when you realize what you actually went through, it seems overwhelming. It's difficult to describe the frustration, day after day. My wife, Yvonne, had to live through this with me—a pain in my shin, a pain in my Achilles, not being able to do the thing I wanted to do. The only thing on your mind 24 hours a day is, "How do I get rid of it?" And 24 hours a day, in an attempt to calm me down, Yvonne is saying, "Leave it alone. Don't be touching your shin and your Achilles. Forget about it."

I'd get out of bed in the morning and I'd put my foot on the floor and I'd feel the pain. It started and ended my day. It was as if it would never, ever go away. I used all sorts of electronic devices. At one point, I wrapped my shin in one device for 14 hours a day. It was a cast that sent electronic waves to the bones to try to speed the healing process.

That's why I say you can't forget about it. It's there all the time and it just won't go away. But all of a sudden, it seems, the injury is gone. How does it seem to go away overnight? I don't know.

Eventually, I became very philosophical about injury, because what else could I do? I'm not bitter that I missed the 1984 Olympics. I'm not bitter that I missed running in the outdoor European Championships, even though I should have been a favorite to win. A negative attitude is not going to help you overcome the frustration. But a positive attitude will. It will also help you to enjoy other things during that 24-hour daily cycle of obsession, as opposed to letting the injury dominate your life.

If I had it to do over again, would I change anything in my career? Yes, I'd be more careful about injuries. I think there's a very fine line—most runners know about it—between staying healthy while maintaining top shape and getting injured. The intensity of

(continued)

some of the training I did was too much, particularly in 1980 before the Moscow Olympics, and even in 1983, my good year. I did some incredible sessions day after day. There was probably no need to do that. I didn't practice what I preach. I think all runners fall victim to that.

—*Eamonn Coghlan*

Lateral Knee Pain

Pain on the outside of a knee that does not swell or lock and that comes on after intense races or increased training is usually inflammation of the iliotibial band (a band of tissue that begins high on the side of the leg and extends to the outside part of the knee). Pain results when this band becomes too tight and rubs either at the hip or right by the knee where it crosses a bone called Gerdy's tubercle (named, incidentally, for a 19th-century French surgeon). People with iliotibial band syndrome will say that they typically get the pain not with the first step of running, but rather, a mile or two into the run.

Possible Causes

This pain is due to a tight iliotibial band that you can blame your parents for. People typically have tight iliotibial bands if they have a body that tightens easily, or is inflexible. Some people are inherently more flexible than others.

Treatment

The treatment is very simple. The runner should undergo an intense stretching program using these stretches:

Iliotibial Band (ITB) Stretches

Cross leg over thigh and place elbow over outside of knee. Gently stretch by pushing bent knee across body.

With arm against wall or pole, slowly stretch toward wall or pole with the other arm supporting the trunk.

If you can't do a stretch on your own, you should go to a physical therapist.

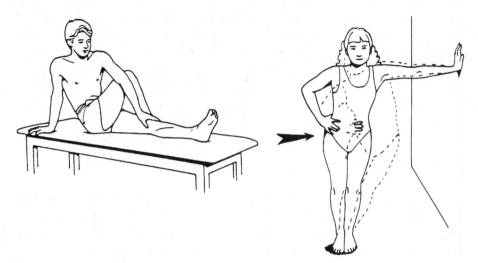

Many runners are sore at one time or another, notes Ann Rugh, a physical therapist and former longtime coach with NYRR running classes. Sore quadriceps (the muscles in the front of the thigh) and hamstrings (back of the thigh) are especially common. "Soreness doesn't necessarily mean you're injured, but it can make running uncomfortable, slow you down, and may increase the risk of injury," says Rugh. Fortunately, there are several things you can do to combat or avoid the problem.

Doing as much of your running as possible on soft surfaces, such as grass or dirt, can be a big help. It's worth it to walk, bike, or drive to a suitable area. No matter where you run, you should warm up your legs with a few minutes of walking or light jogging, then thoroughly stretch, holding each move for at least ten seconds. Stretch after you run, too, when you can often get a fuller extension because the muscles are warm and loose. Rugh also recommends icing the legs immediately after a run, concentrating on spots that feel sore. "I advise people to freeze water in a paper cup, then peel the top of the cup away and stroke the entire area of both legs up and down. Spend five to eight minutes on each leg." This can help reduce the inflammation that leads to soreness. Keep the legs elevated to prevent pooling of blood, which can aggravate inflammation. You can also try ice baths (see page 152).

Another post-run strategy is implementing weighted knee extensions, which are best done with a weight machine or a light weight bound to the front of the lower leg. "This is not a strength exercise," Rugh stresses. "You should use less than half the maximum weight you can lift, and move each leg smoothly for just a few minutes to gently stretch it out." As with any running-related exercise, the decisions of whether, when, and how much to do should depend on your body's response. If these strategies don't work, or if severe pain or joint discomfort develops, consider cutting back your mileage and seeking professional attention, perhaps from a physical therapist or doctor familiar with sports medicine.

MRI'S: A CAUTIONARY TALE

Runners should never allow themselves to be treated and have surgery based on an MRI result alone. The rule is: Never treat the MRI; treat the patient. MRI's can be misleading. Find a running doctor who can tell you whether the cause of your pain is due to the cartilage that is seen on the MRI.

Dr. Maharam relates this incident, "A patient with knee pain can go to a doctor who isn't knowledgeable. That person sends you over for an MRI, gets a picture with a cartilage tear, and says, 'You need surgery.' You have the surgery, but you still have the knee pain, because it wasn't caused by the tear. You may not have needed surgery. You need to get an evaluation from a doctor who understands knee pain in a runner.

"Not all tears cause pain. It depends on where they are, and how severe they are. I've seen a good number of people who have come to me for second opinions, having been told they need surgery for their cartilage. Lo and behold, they have patella femoral disorder. I ended up treating the "runner's knee" (with exercise and an orthotic) and the pain was gone. The MRI still showed the small cartilage tear, but the runner never needed surgery."

Internal Knee Injuries

These injuries are marked by a more subtle, deep pain that continues over a long time, despite such conservative measures as rest and reduction in training. They may result in swelling, locking, or giving way of the knee, and an inability to extend the leg.

The most common in this category of running injuries are tears of either the medial or lateral cartilages. While the act of running itself rarely produces these tears, the constant pounding, or even a misplaced step, can turn a small defect into a complete tear that passes from the cartilage out into the joint space and produces characteristic swelling, locking, and instability. These are potentially quite serious injuries and may require surgery to heal properly.

Possible Causes

Unlikely from running itself. This category of injury is often caused by prior contact sports knee injuries or skiing accidents. Often forgotten, the residual effects of these injuries may set the stage for cartilage tearing while running years later. If a runner continues to train on a torn cartilage, the resulting friction between the unprotected femoral and tibial bones may lead to early irreversible osteoarthritis of the joint.

HAMSTRING INJURIES

Hamstring injuries can become chronic if not taken seriously immediately. Stretching from the ischiotuberosity (the point we sit on) in the

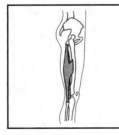 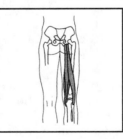

pelvis, the hamstring passes down the back of the leg and inserts just across the back surface of the knee. Running parallel to the hamstring is the sciatic nerve; thus, many chronic hamstring strains are mistaken for sciatic nerve damage.

A tight hamstring can cause lower back pain or a calf strain because it is a connecting site. It is important to remember that when working hamstrings you should also work the opposing muscle, the quadriceps in the front of the leg. Both the quadriceps and the hamstrings need to be strong and flexible for successful running.

POSSIBLE CAUSES

- Asking your hamstrings to do more than they are capable of doing, either because they are too short or not strong enough.
- Overuse
- Speed training
- Poor warmup
- Inflexibility
- Running when injured

TREATMENT

Stretching and strengthening are the keys to good hamstring health. Stretching alone after a hamstring injury is not enough. The runner has to rebuild muscle, and maintain it, so that when he or she goes back to running full-speed, the hamstring is ready and prepared to do that.

Dr. Maharam recommends doing hamstring curls lying down, one leg at a time, five sets of ten, with as much weight as it takes so that on the fifth set you reach muscular failure (you can't do more) by the fifth or sixth repetition. If you get to ten on that fifth set, you have too little weight; if you get to only one, you have too much weight. You should do this a minimum of three to four times per week, in addition to stretching after warmup in the morning and after doing these strengthening exercises.

Warmup is either a light run with a short stride length or working out on a bike until you break a sweat. And then, stretch, because muscles are like taffy, and they stretch better when they are warm. If the hamstring situation does not improve, you may want to see a qualified sports medicine physician to determine that the hamstring problem has not become chronic, because if it has, it requires physical therapy using modalities to help decrease inflammation and speed the healing process.

SCIATICA

Leg pain that passes down the back part of the upper part of the leg, sometimes extending to the foot is a sign of sciatica. (Note: This is a symptom, not a diagnosis.) True sciatica is usually due to pressure on lumbar nerves from the spine. The pressure may be caused by slippage of a cartilage disk out onto the nerve, a spasm muscle, or by the effects of degenerative arthritis of the lumbar spine.

POSSIBLE CAUSES

There are hundreds of diagnoses that may create a sciatic symptom. If you are having a symptom and see a doctor who tells you that the diagnosis is sciatica, you need to get to another doctor. Finding out which cause will lead to a treatment plan that can speed recovery. Without a diagnosis, and only knowing your symptom of sciatica, it's like shooting in the dark.

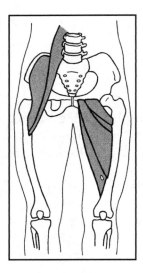

INJURIES TO THE GROIN

Muscle injuries to this area are due to strains of the adductor muscle (right side of figure: groin muscle located on the inside of the leg extending to the knee) or the iliopsoas muscle (left side of figure: higher groin muscle that extends from the lower part of the pelvis to the upper part of the groin), or sometimes both. Hernia needs to be ruled out by a proper examination. Strains of these muscles can result in months and even years of decreased running.

POSSIBLE CAUSES

Usually overuse (excessive long runs or speedwork). A groin strain can also be caused by a slip or a fall. Often the injury is made worse by continuing to run despite growing pain, until virtually all training is impossible. A significant amount of damage is done during the period of continued running, especially if races are run. If you can't run with normal form, it's time to stop and see a sports doctor.

TREATMENT

Physical therapy, as well as stretching and strengthening these muscles, is the key to rapid recovery.

In runners, the possibility of a pelvic stress fracture or an inflammation of the pubic bone should be considered when groin pain is severe, made worse on standing, and remains despite proper therapy. A good sports medicine doctor will help you make that diagnosis.

MEDICAL PROBLEMS IN RUNNERS

While runners are generally healthy, any persistent complaint should be investigated thoroughly, since exercise does not make one immune to general disease. Since the well-trained are used to a level of well-being generally above the sedentary, real disease may surface in many subtle ways early in its course.

Most commonly seen are the following:

Abdominal Pain

Kidney stones create abdominal pain as they begin in the outside abdomen and in some cases move to the front of the pelvis.

Possible Causes

Kidney stones are slightly more common in runners due to the dehydrating effects of training.

No one is absolutely sure what causes stitches or cramps, but they are most likely an abnormal contraction or cramp in the diaphragm, the large muscle used in breathing that separates the lung and abdominal cavities and is attached along the bottom of the rib cage. *Runner's World* advises that the treatment of any acute muscle cramp is stretching the muscle. To stretch the diaphragm during exercise, take a big breath, hold it as long as possible, and then force the air out against puckered lips.

Treatment

Copious post-training hydration, especially with water and juices, is necessary. In general, colicky flank and/or back pain and bloody urine are hallmarks of a stone.

Exertional Hematuria

Bloody urine that occurs during or just after running and that clears rapidly (exertional hematuria) is generally benign. It is seen more in summer months and occasionally is accompanied by a very slight burning. If the dark, bloody urine continues or remains unchanged even after training and throughout the day, a medical consultation should be undertaken to rule out more serious problems. Urinary infections are not more common in runners.

Blood in the urine, known as hematuria, sometimes results from physical trauma of the urine hitting against the walls of the urinary bladder caused by strenuous exercise, such as running. It's been known to occur in some people after a particularly hard workout or race (such as a marathon). A contusion to the kidney area can likewise cause blood to appear in the urine.

Hematuria caused by physical trauma usually clears up by itself within a few days. There is nothing you can do to prevent it or speed its passing. (Staying hydrated while you work out or race and drinking plenty of fluids afterward, however, do prevent dehydration and help keep your kidneys functioning normally.)

The only time to be concerned about hematuria is if it lasts longer than three or four days, or is accompanied by pain or difficulty in urinating. If either of these things happens, you should see a urologist immediately. The doctor will examine you, test a sample of your urine, and order further necessary tests before prescribing a treatment.

Chances are, however, that the problem will pass quickly—and, after giving your body time to rest, you will be ready for your next challenge on the road.

All runners who run farther than 5K will show blood in the urine in a urinalysis. Therefore, it is recommended that if you are going for a physical exam that you do not run just before you go.

—*Lewis Maharam, M.D.*

Possible Causes

Thought to be related to physical trauma to the bladder while running.

Treatment

Hydration (two to three quarts of fluid throughout the day it appears). One is safe if the condition clears by the next day. If it persists, seek medical attention.

Diarrhea

Abdominal pain and cramping with diarrhea are sometimes seen during or just after running.

Possible Causes

If the symptoms persist, stool analysis for parasites should be done as well as an examination of the bowel for various types of colitis. Occasionally, runners with gluten (wheat products) sensitivity may experience abdominal pain, especially if there is a family history of adult celiac disease (chronic diarrhea secondary to poor absorption of nutrients). Simple dietary changes can in some of these cases be very helpful.

Treatment

Eliminating all caffeine (coffee, tea, chocolate, and colas) and milk products (in the case of possible lactose sensitivity) from the diet may help. Do not take medications such as Imodium® or Lomotil® prior to running. They may cause dehydration.

Chest Pain

Pain in the chest, during running or otherwise, is one symptom that should not be ignored. Chest pain occurring during exercise is a serious medical signal and should be attended to immediately by a physician.

Treadmill stress testing, eco stress testing, thallium stress testing, and cardiac angiography, when appropriate, can pinpoint the area of heart involvement and direct the physician toward a solution. According to Dr. Maharam, "Running through chest pain is dangerous until the cause of it is found; however, not all chest pain is cardiac. There have been several cases of pulmonary embolism caused by pooling of the blood in the calves during long trips, either in a car or an airplane, or just following a long run or a training session. Taking birth control pills is a risk factor for getting these blood clots. If you have a pulmonary embolism or blood clots in your legs, a lung scan, vinegram, or immediate use of anticoagulants in a hospital setting are necessary.

"Most often, chest pain is simply muscular, either from lifting, sprinting, hyperventilating, or even coughing. Tenderness over the muscles of the chest wall is a hallmark, and the use of anti-inflammatories over a few days alleviates the pain."

Chronic Fatigue Syndrome (CFS)

One of the most common medical problems in endurance runners is periodic fatigue, Norbert Sander has pointed out. In over 90 percent of cases of chronic tiredness and lackluster running, however, a direct organic medical cause cannot be found. Despite this, there is almost always an overuse syndrome involved, both physical and mental. This may result from simple overload in professional, home, personal, or athletic life that insidiously wears down a runner who continues to train at a high level. Often in these cases there is a fair degree of denial with runners, disappointed that no clear medical problem is present. With patience, time, and reduction of overload, however, normal levels of energy slowly return.

This is not to discount the other 10 percent of cases where true depression may be present as well as a host of disorders ranging from anemias, chronic viral syndromes, and mononucleosis to more subtle hormonal im-

During my years of not running well, I had biomechanical problems, blood problems, and I knew that if I could solve those problems, I should run well again. I never believed in this mystical "burnout syndrome," or chronic fatigue syndrome. I believe there's a specific physiological reason, and that you can always break it down to an actual deficiency or biomechanical problem.

You can be so overworked that your system doesn't work well, if you want to call that burnout. But then, you figure out how to get your system to work well again, and you're not burned out. It's like a car overheating. What do you do to fix it? You fill it up with water, change the oil, so it runs normally again.

A lot of my problems were that I had surgeries that laid me up for a long time. I had nerve damage after one of those surgeries. That took 2 1/2 years to heal. That brought me up to 1988, and physically, since then, I really haven't had any major biomechanical problems.

Then it was a matter of trying to come back slowly and surely. I started at a young age and did something very successfully for ten years. Then I didn't do it at all well for six years. You think that in a couple of years you'll be right back where you were. But it doesn't work that way. I had a long, gradual buildup. All of a sudden to jump back in, it's hard.

—Alberto Salazar

balances. The search for causes may lead one to a diagnosis such as Epstein-Barre virus, which still has not been proven to cause any specific disorder. In fact, over 80 percent of the normal population tests positive for Epstein-Barre virus; however, the presence of this virus does not mean it is the cause of fatigue.

The proper approach to fatigue syndrome is to take it seriously, seeing a physician for a complete medical history, physical examination, and laboratory screening, including a complete blood count, a survey of all electrolytes, liver function tests, a kidney function and glucose test, a mononucleosis screening, a Lyme screening, and even in some cases an HIV test. Thinking over one's daily routine and training schedule is also very important in coming to grips with the cause of chronic fatigue syndrome when no organic cause is found.

Increasing amounts of research is indicating that some people who believed they had CFS actually had either Lyme disease or depression. Another small sub-set of those people complaining of chronic fatigue turned out to have a low serum ferritin (a protein that stores iron) level that responded very quickly to taking an iron supplement.

Ozone gas in our breathing space is especially a problem in the summer months. There's more sunshine, less wind, and trees hold pollutants underneath their leafy canopies. As a result, there are more frequent summertime air-quality warnings—essentially ozone alerts. According to *Longevity* magazine, studies show that people who exercise vigorously for more than an hour when the ozone level is high can experience lung irritation; shortness of breath; shallow, rapid breathing; and coughing. It is, therefore, best to pick cloudy over sunny days, and to exercise in the early morning before pollution accumulates. The hours of 11 A.M. to 4 P.M. are particularly hazardous. Runners should opt for park paths instead of highways.

Also, a study from Penn State quoted by the American Running Association showed that a change from nose to mouth breathing during exercise increased the dose of ozone absorbed in the lungs. That's because the nose acts as a filter. So, if you have to be in smog, breathe through your nose, and avoid activity at an intensity that forces you to switch to mouth breathing.

EXERCISE-INDUCED ASTHMA AND YOUR WORKOUT

Doctors now believe exercise-induced asthma (EIA) affects many more active people than was once thought, says Dr. Maharam. Too many athletes wrongly assume they have breathing problems because they're out of shape and grow discouraged with their workouts. Exercise-induced asthma may not be life-threatening but it is uncomfortable, inconvenient, and holds you back from doing your best. The good new is, it's manageable.

Diagnosis

Only a doctor can tell you whether your symptoms are exercise-induced asthma, or just the normal experience of vigorous exercise with which it's often confused because the symptoms of EIA are similar to being out of shape: shortness of breath during or after exercise, chest tightness, coughing, and wheezing. The doctor makes a diagnosis by measuring the amount of air you breathe in and out at rest, then during the beginning of an exercise session, and again several minutes into that session.

EIA does not strike immediately, usually taking six to 12 minutes of vigorous exercise to trigger an attack, and symptoms don't reach their peak until anywhere from five to 15 minutes *after* you've stopped your workout. Then, in somewhere from a half-hour to an hour-and-a-half, the symptoms are gone completely.

The Probable Cause—And What To Do

Exactly what triggers an EIA attack is not yet completely known. The consensus is that it starts with the sudden cooling of your body's airways. Exercise makes you breathe harder—usually suddenly—and your bronchial tubes must quickly warm and humidify a lot more air to ready it for the lungs. In the process, the airways can cool down and dry out, which can irritate sensitive tissues. So to protect themselves, the tissues contract into a state of bronchospasm.

That suggests a couple of possible strategies for managing the condition if it's not severe enough to warrant medication. Breathing through your nose to warm and moisten the air before it reaches the bronchial tubes is one common suggestion, though it's not very easy during anything but a mild workout. Wearing a face mask is probably more practical since it helps enrich inhaled air with heat and moisture from your skin. But just staying out of cold, dry air in the first place may be the best course. Use an indoor track or treadmill on crisp days, or consider a different sport.

The warm, moist atmosphere of an indoor swimming pool is far less likely to set off an EIA episode than the cold air of an outdoor track. It's also known that in general, so-called "high ventilation" sports that require continual exertion at a fairly high intensity, like long-distance running, cross-country skiing, and cycling, are more likely to bring on an EIA episode than "lower ventilation," intermittent sports like golf, baseball, tennis, and weightlifting. And since EIA usually holds off for at least six minutes into your workout, the alternating work-and-rest periods of interval training keep some athletes symptom-free. Warming up 45 minutes to an hour before your actual workout can mean a detour past the EIA episode.

What you *shouldn't* do is avoid exercise. Just the opposite, in fact. Aerobically fitter athletes don't breathe as heavily during their workouts, so while their EIA might kick up at the same breathing rate, they're less likely to reach that rate in the first place.

And no matter what your sport, if high concentrations of airborne irritants like pollen or pollutants increase your chance of an attack, it is a good idea to exercise indoors on days when those pollutants are abundant.

Though some athletes can keep their exercise-induced asthma under control with simple workout strategies, most need the additional help of a medication. This option can be discussed with a qualified physician.

MEDICATIONS, PROCEDURES, AND MEDICAL MODALITIES

Along with the running boom of the 1970–1980s came the field of sports medicine. Many of the treatments runners commonly undergo today were, not long ago, considered new and radical.

The medical modalities described below are fairly common today, and many runners (and other athletes and exercisers as well) benefit from them. Although they represent a wide range of treatments being used by today's runners, there are likely many others that fall into this category.

Anti-Inflammatory Medication

Anti-inflammatory medications are nonsteroidal agents that diminish pain and reduce microswelling around injured tissues. Minor inflammation due to injury should respond with the use of these medications in three to four days. More serious inflammation will not sufficiently respond. Any prolonged use (longer than one week) of these medications should be monitored by a physician.

These medications are available over-the-counter, and stronger doses are available by prescription. Dr. Maharam generally recommends the new anti-inflammatories like Celebrex® (available by prescription) that cause less stomach irritation. Aspirin or ibuprofen can cause stomach irritation. It takes a much greater number of aspirin to be effective, and aspirin seems to irritate the stomach more frequently.

"The short-term use of anti-inflammatories is generally safe as long as there is no allergy to them and one is without a history of gastritis or stomach ulcer. They are best taken with foods. Recent medical research has shown that nonsteroidal anti-inflammatories (NSAIDs) like Advil®, Motrin®, Aleve®, ibuprofen, naproxen, etc. may be harmful to runners' kidney function if taken within 24 hours of running. Acetaminophen (Tylenol®) has been shown to be safe.

NSAIDs are thought to increase the possibility of hyponatremia (see Chapter 27) while running long distances because they decrease blood flow to the kidneys and interfere with a hormone that helps the body retain salt. Therefore, it is recommended that on race day (specifically beginning at midnight before you run) you do not use anything but acetaminophen (Tylenol®) if needed until six hours after you have finished the race, are able to drink without any nausea or vomiting, have urinated once, and feel physically and mentally back to normal. Then, an NSAID would be of benefit in preventing post-event muscle soreness.

Arthroscopic Surgery

Arthroscopic surgery is reserved only for those infrequent cases of cartilage tear inside the knee that are the cause of the runner's pain, and for repair of the anterior cruciate ligament (ACL) when needed. Surgery is usually a one-day procedure, for which you go in the morning and go home the same day. Nowadays, this procedure may even be done under local anesthetic. During this surgery, a small incision is made below the kneecap and a scope is pushed inside to effect the repair.

Aggressive physical therapy under the guidance of a sports medicine physician is essential to ensure an excellent result and rapid return to full training.

Physical Therapy

Running injuries that are especially receptive to physical therapy treatments are strains of the calf muscle, hamstrings, and gluteal muscles of the hips and buttocks as well as low-back syndromes. What does physical therapy and one of its modalities, deep muscle massage, actually do? Since the time of the ancient Greeks, athletes have treated their muscles by deep stimulation and stretching and strengthening. This has been an important step in preventing muscle injuries. Muscles are especially well vascularized (have a good blood supply), while cartilage, ligaments, and tendons have a relatively poor blood supply. By increasing blood supply to muscles while breaking up microscar tissue, the injured areas heal faster.

Ultrasound, electrical stimulation, massage, range of motion stretching exercises, specific strengthening exercises, and newer techniques such as ionophoresis (absorption of cortisone applied across the skin locally to muscles) are all tools that are very effective in the hands of a certified physical therapist.

Physical therapy is an important medical modality with runners. The treatment is best undertaken with a sports medicine physician where he or she can guide the physical therapist in treatment. Physical therapy is both preventive and rehabilitative—a system of working with muscles, soft tissue, and joints.

Some of the physical therapy techniques include manual mobilization to increase range of motion; several types of massage, for example, friction (particularly used for injuries such as tendonitis); regular sports massage (to increase circulation and flexibility); and muscle energy, a manual technique that strengthens and stretches the soft tissue. Strengthening exercises are done with free weights or machines such as isokinetic machines. Other modalities include electrical stimulation and ultrasound.

Tzvi Barak, P.T., Ph.D., O.C.S., points out that various specialties in the field of physical therapy have been established. He recommends that runners seek out either orthopedic or sports clinical specialists.

Chiropractic

The word *chiropractic* comes from the Greek *cherios* (hand) and *practos* (done by). Chiropractic work includes joint mobilization or adjusting procedures to reestablish normal ranges of joint movement by correcting misaligned or subluxated vertebrae. Chiropractors adjust vertebrae to reestablish normal nerve supply to organs, glands, muscles, joints, and skin by relieving pinched or compressed nerves. Since every function of the body depends on the brain's and spinal cord's normal functioning, ensuring proper nerve flow via the spinal nerves is of utmost importance to chiropractors.

Dr. G. Thomas Kovacs evaluates runners statically and dynamically, sometimes watching them run on a treadmill or even outdoors. Work with athletes is not confined to evaluating one particular area of injury. "We must realize that structure determines function and we must look at the body as a whole," says Kovacs, "from the feet all the way up to the head."

Dr. Maharam (a medical doctor) believes that chiropractic has a role when used as an interventional therapy. "My chiropractic friends who teach agree that a chiropractor who tells you that you need to come for an adjustment weekly for the rest of your life is making a mistake. Chiropractic should be used as an interventional consult from your sports medicine physician. He or she will know when it is appropriate and when another modality might be better."

PART 8
AGING AND EXERCISE

34

AGING AND EXERCISE

As Dr. Margaret Dessau and an increasing number of experts see it, aging need not be an inexorable path to disability and dependence. Older people can continue to lead active, productive, and independent lives, provided they maintain proper diet and exercise programs. Dr. Dessau knows this from the example of her active octogenarian parents, who have inspired her ideas. And in the running community, examples abound. One is NYRR founder Ted Corbitt, who at 85 continues to walk in ultramarathons and spends a few days a week in a gym.

"Although the incidences of cardiovascular disease and cancer increase with age, individuals can minimize their risks by getting regular exercise and following prudent diets. A healthy lifestyle can prevent atherosclerotic heart disease and even reverse the damage done by fatty deposits already narrowing coronary arteries," says Dr. Dessau. There is increasing scientific evidence that good diet and exercise can lessen the risk of various types of cancer.

There are many physiologic changes in all the organ systems that occur with aging; however, significant declines are not inevitable. That's because these changes result more from physical inactivity and disuse than from the aging process itself. In fact, many of the declines in function can be prevented, or greatly minimized, by moderate—and even mild—regular exercise.

Not only can the cardiovascular system be protected from atherosclerotic disease, but also from the typical signs of aging, such as excess fatigue (loss of stamina) and breathlessness. Contrary to previous thought that deconditioning results from aging itself, studies show that aerobic capacity can be maintained with age if moderate exercise is continued (moderate meaning in intensity and duration). This requires doing physical activity for a minimum of half an hour at an intensity that raises the heart rate to 70 percent of its maximum rate (see Chapter 4, "Heart Rate Monitor Training," for the formula to determine this figure) at least five days a week.

The American Heart Association has now added "lack of exercise" to the list of major risk factors for heart disease—joining such other risk factors as smoking and high blood pressure and high blood cholesterol. Although there are still varying opinions on how much exercise is enough,

I can't run a 51-second quarter anymore; I can't run it in 60, nor should I try, because I'd surely get injured. But it's important in your own visualization and mentality not to defeat yourself. A lot of people think, "Oh, this is what I used to do." In my own case, what I used to do is almost 40 years ago. Just deal with the realities. You want to stay healthy and fit, not get injured, because it takes too long to recover as you get older. It's different when you're younger, but my view comes from learning to deal with these issues at age 57. It's an entire mind-set. Now, when I go out to run, and complete two or three miles at ten-minute pace, I accept that and say: This is great. Three weeks ago I couldn't do this. Just setting new and different goals, and not dwelling on the past, is important. As long as I stay healthy and fit, that's what counts. The way I look at it, your body is the only one you've got, and you want it to last.

—*Allan Steinfeld*

and how vigorous, various studies have endorsed even a moderate amount of exercise for improving heart health and losing and/or maintaining weight. A September 2003 study quoted in the *Journal of the American Medical Association* found that together with diet modifications (i.e., cutting calories), even walking 40 minutes a day resulted in significant weight loss, as well as a significant improvement in cardiovascular fitness.

Musculoskeletal fragility (bone weakening) and osteoarthritis (joint stiffness) are the common degenerative changes found in joints, cartilage, and bone. They can be prevented by appropriate exercises and stretching. Bone density can actually be increased, resulting in fewer fractures. Frequently with age, muscles need longer periods of slow stretching to warm up before exercise to prevent muscle strains or tendinitis.

Obesity and depression, often associated with aging, also are not inevitable, but again, are primarily results of inactivity. The loss of muscle bulk and power, together with increased percentage of body fat, can be minimized by continued exercise, while improving overall mood and vigor.

Another benefit of exercise is its versatility. As one ages, exercise may be modified according to specific needs. If arthritis is causing pain in the weight-bearing joints, such as the knees or hips, an exercise such as running can be replaced by brisk walking, biking, or swimming. Exercise in a pool is helpful, where the buoyancy alleviates stress. Exercising in a

As you get older, the physical changes are real. But the most interesting parts of aging are the mental aspects of coping with how your body changes. I still like to compete, so it's a matter of redefining how you measure your performances. I make my living through my running, so it's easier to train. But I admire the people who have stressful jobs and are able to continue their running. Races give you a focus to train, and staying fit gives you perspective to deal with the rest of the things in life. I think these are some of the biggest lessons I've learned about running in my later years.

What I've done as part of growing older is run with people my age. Age group running is terrific. We've all adapted; there's a mutual understanding among the Masters and veteran runners. When you turn 40, you still want to compete. The Open Division is still exciting, but you start to rethink in terms of competing among the Masters.

When you're younger, you don't think about the injury aspect of running. When you're older, running isn't the "be all and end all." There's more to life. But you still want to be able to get out there on an ongoing basis.

I think we're going through a revolution for Masters running like there was in women's running. We've seen what a terrific plus women's running has been for the sport. There are times we can all say "Wow, maybe I can learn something from the older runner." I was at the Boilermaker race this year and a 72-year-old was in front of me for the first three miles! I didn't have a great day, but I couldn't believe it. Seeing successful older runners gives us all a perspective on how we can stay fit, healthy, and active for so many years.

—*Bill Rodgers*

warm pool is helpful in specific cases, especially in alleviating spinal disk problems. Exercise is adaptable on many levels. If vision or hearing is a problem, for example, indoor exercise with a companion is a safeguard.

If aging is viewed negatively, we will only fulfill our low expectations of quality and length of life. For inspiration, we can look to other societies in which people remain healthy and vital into later years, like the Huriza in Pakistan, who often live over 100 years. Significantly, their lifestyle is grounded in physical activity and good diet.

Whether we live longer or not by exercising is yet to be confirmed conclusively in studies; however, the mental and physical benefits of exercising are clearly evident and widely acknowledged. Life is a cycle, and as such, goes through various predictable biological changes. Some we can avoid; some, which are natural, we cannot. Overall, exercise can reward us with a fuller, more vital, and more spirited life—no matter what the length of that life.

RUNNING ADVICE FOR YOUR 40s AND 50s

Flexibility and joint range of motion commonly decrease with aging, explains Lewis Maharam, M.D., "I tell my patients that they will be inclined to have fewer injuries if they follow this formula: warm up, stretch, work out, stretch, cool down, stretch."

- Middle-aged runners should also drink plenty of water to keep their muscles, tendons, and ligaments hydrated and thus help prevent pulling and tearing.

- Weight gain is common during middle age, and running can help keep weight within desirable ranges. It is also a proven risk-reducer for blood pressure and cholesterol levels—important indicators of heart disease risk—which becomes increasingly significant after age 40.

- Now more than ever, be sure to warm up, cool down, and stretch the muscles and tendons. A strength-training program is another hedge against injury.

- Don't suddenly change your routine or introduce something new, such as racing a half marathon, without proper preparation, or injury may well result.

- Prepare your body for running by staying hydrated and eating a healthy, balanced diet.

- If you are competitive, adjust to the fact you may no longer set PR's (personal records), but you can still place in your age group, rate well in age-graded tables, and reap the health and fitness benefits that come with running.

- If you are new to running, adapt it to meet your needs and lifestyle. Don't worry about the "right" pace, schedule, or outfit.

- Fit running into a time slot that works best for you. Be flexible, but exercise control over your time in ways you may not have been able to in the past.

(Adapted from "The Forties and Fifties: Running Through Years of Fulfillment," by Gail Waesche Kislevitz, *New York Runner,* July/August 2002.)

ROLE MODELS

Sid Howard

Although he is 65 years old, "Super Sid" Howard's "running age" is 26, an age that more accurately reflects his physical appearance and his attitude. Howard can be considered such a youngster because he took up serious running only at the age of 39. Told by his high school coach that he was too small for football, he ran cross-country in high school, but quit school at 17 and joined the Air Force. He tried running again 22 years later, when his son told him, "Dad, they've got an old man's race at the high school." It was an age 35-and-over mile that Howard covered in 5:05. Three months later, he ran the New York City Marathon in 3:02.

Super Sid, father of six, grandfather of 18, and great-grandfather of three, didn't stop there. The Plainfield, New Jersey, resident and Manhattan business owner achieved his ultimate fame at age 60, when he ran an indoor 800 meters in an age-group world record of 2:14.75. Howard has called that race, "The second biggest thrill of my life. The first was when my first son was born." The record stood for four years, until it was broken by three-hundredths of a second.

Howard also holds age records for 800 meters outdoors (age 63, 2:18.5). In 2003, he won the 1500 meters at the World Veterans Games for ages 60–64 in 5:04.6, and set a single-age record for 800 meters for age 64 at those same Games, recording a time of 2:18.6. He also holds the American age-group record for age 60+ in the outdoor 800m with a time of 2:12.71, and he has been a four-time NYRR age-group Runner of the Year. Howard is the only runner to participate in every Masters Fifth Avenue Mile, winning his age group twice, in what he calls "one of my favorite races." He has run six New York City Marathons, recording his best time of 2:46:27 in 1981.

"I have learned to adjust my running with my age," says Howard. "As I continue to turn the pages of the calendar, I find I need more time to recover." He now runs 25 to 30 miles per week, "very low mileage, but more quality." He swears by the recovery aid of his regular ice baths—20 minutes in water covered with ice—which he takes after every hard workout or race.

Howard maintains his twice-weekly speed workouts with the Central Park Track Club, of which he's been a member since 1978. He lifts weights, and tries to do 400 sit-ups after every run. "If you can do sit-ups and push-ups, these are the two most important exercises for runners," advises Howard, who focuses on core body conditioning to help avoid injuries and to contribute to maximum performance.

Sid Howard's future goals? "I'd love to be the person there when someone says, 'Guys over 95 get on the line.' I want to be able to run—and not just jog—when I'm 100. That's my ultimate goal."

Al Gordon

Al Gordon, still going strong in 2003 at age 102, is the official starter of the NYRR's annual Al Gordon 15K race. He tells how his athleticism began:

"My father never drove an automobile, and we took many long walks together. He lived until age 87. I was always athletic. In high school, I was on three or four teams. I was an average college runner, competing in the quarter-mile (in 51 to 52 seconds) and the low hurdles. I was a long way from setting the world on fire, but I got a lot of third places."

Although running was something Gordon always did, he didn't start pounding out the longer distances until he was 40 years old. Still, he was far ahead of his time. Gordon recalls, "This was in 1955, and people thought I was nuts. But in those days, the people weren't the problem. The greatest danger was the dogs!"

His first road race was a 10K in Central Park in 1976. After his wife—who was also very athletic—died, he started running even longer distances, and decided to do a marathon. In 1983, he ran his first marathon in London, and was the oldest finisher in that race. He ran the 26.2-mile race one other time.

Gordon, who together with his three sons is a graduate of Harvard University, is known for having paid for the building of that school's indoor track, one of the most heralded state-of-the-art facilities in the country. He is also a NYRR board member and NYRR benefactor. The Al Gordon Library at the club is named for him.

But Al Gordon's success story only begins with his own athletic achievements and philanthropy. He has five children, whom he inducted into the exercise and fitness ranks when they were young. At each child's 16th birthday, for example, their father took them to Holland for a four-day walk totaling 100 miles, in which 15,000 people participated. He also took each one of them mountain climbing.

Running is in the family, too. His oldest son sought to make the U.S.

Olympic team in the 400 meters, and all three of his boys still run. His oldest daughter, a bank vice president, ran the Boston Marathon—her first—at age 35 in 2:57. His other daughter was a professional dancer.

"I have always believed in physical fitness," says Gordon, who has also played tennis and skied. "If people are physically fit, they are better adjusted for life. Running is the greatest anodyne. It's mental therapy. While running, one develops a rhythm—the mind becomes detached.

"Let's face it, exercise is an addiction. The body wants to do it. It's just like having a dog who gets excited when he senses it's time to go out for a walk and run. Since having a knee operation, I do certain exercises. Now they're an addiction. It's as if I wake up and I'm compelled to do these damn exercises!"

Gordon's prescription for a long and healthy life is obviously one to which his experience attests. "Short of abusing your body, I think genetics has a great deal to do with it, no matter what you do. But I think if you do reasonable physical exercise, eat less, and you're conscious of your health, you'll feel better." It doesn't come without effort, he adds. "You have to push yourself."

Al Gordon is still inspiring runners. In 2003, he again sounded the starting horn for the annual Al Gordon 15K race in Central Park. While he's done with golf, he still does his calisthenics at home and maintains his active (and daily) working life, centered on philanthropic causes, at an office he uses in his son's company.

A grandfather of ten and great-grandfather of two, he also travels, most recently to Montana and to England. A great honor was conferred on Gordon in 2001, when he was awarded the O.B.E. (Order of the British Empire). He received his medal at a ceremony at the British Embassy in Washington.

Al Gordon's philosophy is summed up in a statement from a Kidder, Peabody & Co. tribute dinner in his honor: "If I had my life to do it over again, I would do it even more vigorously. My philosophy is to enjoy each day and thank God when you wake up each morning that you have got another day. As long as you can do it, you do it."

Anna Thornhill

Artist Anna Thornhill did not grow up athletic—in fact, far from it. Raised in various locations around the world, but mostly in Malaysia and England, Thornhill spent her youth trying to avoid the two things she hated most: math and physical education.

One thing she knew she loved, however, was art, which has been her calling since she was a young child. In fact, it was her art that got her running, and led to the discovery of her athletic talent.

"I used to devote my entire life to art," she relates. Her success culminated in a sold-out show in 1975. By then, however, her skin had turned yellow and her health began to suffer. "What we didn't realize then is that the art materials were toxic. Twenty-five years later, of course, there are warning labels, but, meanwhile, a lot of artists are dead."

Thornhill sensed that she had to get outdoors and get moving somehow. Her husband, Simon, had grown up playing soccer but hated running; however, she had a running neighbor who one day took her along. His loop was four miles, and on her first try, she ran that extraordinary distance. "I took to it like a duck to water," she says.

She began running in May 1977, at age 37, and entered her first race in October—the New York City Marathon! Since then she has run over 30 marathons, with a best of 2:57:00, and one 100-miler, while logging 80 to an astounding 155 miles a week in training. She also ran a world road best for her age (50) in the one mile, with a time of 5:24. Thornhill regularly goes head to head with women 20 and 30 years her junior. She also frequently trains with her husband, who eventually got hooked on running as well.

To see Anna Thornhill, with the compact, muscular body of a 20-year-old, is to understand why she believes that there is not necessarily a lessening of speed and strength with age. "I ran my best times in my early 40s, and they are still the same times I run now. I don't believe in erosion. Invariably, the loss is due to a lessening of training."

Perhaps the most inspiring of her experiences, however, is Thornhill's two-year battle with menopause. "Some women breeze through menopause," she says. But Thornhill was not one of them. Of her troubles she says, "Initially I was in shock. Deep down, you believe if you're in good shape, it can't be happening to you." Once she was over the crisis, however, she was overcome by new feelings of joyousness. Says Thornhill, "I believe that being in good physical and mental shape helped pull me out of the trouble. And now, to feel so great is quite a surprise. On reflection, I am astonished, considering what I had read about menopause—that you're depressed. I find the reverse is true.

"Running has enormous psychological and physical benefits, especially for women in the older age categories. It celebrates your age and your ability. As you get older, you set new goals.

"Some women pretend; they try to hide their age. I say nonsense. Why hide it? Celebrate it!"

Anna's Thornhill's 2003 updated story is best told in her own words:

"It has been 13 years since I walked/jogged through the menopause door, and for me it has been a liberating and empowering experience. I feel stronger, wiser and have a better perspective on life. Time, however, seems to be speeding up while my running times are slowing down. After 60, this is supposed to happen to all runners and is considered normal. Paradoxically, I enjoy racing more, somewhat in the way I did when I first started at 37 years old and was a newcomer to the sport.

"I don't pay much attention to my competition, but am very aware of doing my best. For me, racing is a unique experience—very intense, focused, and complete." At age 50, Thornhill ran the Fifth Avenue Mile in 5:24. At 56, she became the oldest person to win the Yonkers (New York) Marathon. One month later, she ran the Hartford Marathon in 3:16:17. She still trains and races exactly as she did 15 years ago, and wins awards and age-graded prize money, but now listens to her body more.

"I have been fortunate in not having any serious running injuries as I have gotten older," Thornhill says. "However, I do have some aging health problems. Apart from these stumbles, getting older has been an enjoyable experience. Right now, I want to live forever as I am having such a good time."

Toshika D'Elia

Toshika D'Elia began running at age 41. At 50 years old, she covered the marathon distance in 2:57:20, a world record at that time for her age. Perhaps it is no wonder that even though D'Elia still appears to compete with the athleticism of a woman four decades younger, her coach says initially she had a difficult time accepting that her running times were slowing.

"I think you begin to truly accept the aging process more gracefully when you are over 55 or 60," she says. "At age 50, you still have a lot of energy. I think that it's actually life goals, or what you emphasize, that change slightly. I am very involved with my grandchildren now, which means so much to my pleasure. I am happy to adjust my training regime to spend time with them. This has helped me to accept my aging as it relates to my running.

"I run a half hour slower for the marathon than I did at age 50, and three to four minutes slower for the 10K. I can accept that I am slower, as long as I'm in good shape."

Now 74, Toshika D'Elia still gets joy and satisfaction out of her running, not to mention accolades. She has won her age group as NYRR Runner of the Year 21 times, and since 2000, has set American records for 70+ in the one mile (7:03), 5K on the road, and also on the track (24:09); for 10K (48:53), the half marathon (1:50:28), and two indoor world records (800m in 3:28 and 3000m in 14:07).

A sensible runner, she supplements her mileage with deep water running, which constitutes one-third of all her distance—essentially, her easy days. This three-day-a-week water routine is rounded out with a bit of weight-lifting and swimming. She also maintains her career by working part-time at the New York School for the Deaf, in White Plains, New York, where she taught for 36 years.

D'Elia can also take pride in the fact that her running seems to have spawned a dynasty. "How lucky can I get? My daughter helped me; now my grandchildren are taking it up. We share the commonality of sports." Her oldest grandson, Ben Diestle, has inherited his grandmother's winning ways. In 2003, he was the first Bergen County freshman in the county's cross-country championships.

D'Elia's goal is to preserve herself and her running. "I owe it to myself not to become a health nuisance," she says. To that end, she would like to concentrate on distances up to the half marathon, as opposed to the full 26.2-mile marathon.

For now, she will continue to gain support from her grandchildren, and in turn, to inspire them. After all, they have been there to watch her every year she runs the Fifth Avenue Mile, including her 7:03 American-record run.

Dr. Dan Hamner

Dr. Dan Hamner not only practices what he preaches, he also does both at a superlative level. A top Masters runner, who at age 57 ran a 1:20 half marathon and has run 15 marathons with a best of 2:51, he also heads a Manhattan sports medicine practice and is the author of a book on the subject of health and exercise.

As a high school senior in his native Kentucky, Dan Hamner competed in the quarter-mile and long jump, winning the AAU long jump title. He hung up his running shoes after that though, until he put them on again 30 years later, in 1986. At age 47 1/2 he began by running laps around the track at Emory University in Atlanta, where he was doing his professional training in cardiac rehabilitation. But it wasn't like the old days. After all, he had never run over two laps, even as a youthful competitor.

But something immediately clicked for him. "It hit me how much I used to like to run. I remembered that instant gratification you get from sprinting." Hamner began to get serious, reading up on exercise physiology to educate himself on his running.

By November 1986, Hamner had moved to New York. That's when a friend took him on a three-mile run. Four weeks later he ran his first race, a five-miler, in a time of 37:40. From a couple of training runs to a five-mile race is a huge leap, but, Hamner admits, he's a "type A runner."

"I was hooked, crazed. I started beefing up my mileage. After that first race, I raced every weekend." He joined the NYRR running class, and nine months later ran a 1:20 half marathon. He went on to rediscover track, of which he says, "I love it more than I ever did." He has since participated in the half-mile at the World Veterans Games.

A heavy drinker who quit the habit in the early 1980s, Hamner has reason to be thankful for rediscovering running. "It's like a gift from a higher power," concludes the Alcoholics Anonymous adherent. "I had wrecked myself with alcohol. Now I am rejuvenated. I feel young for my age, like a 25-year-old. I work 12 hours every day."

Hamner has a definite belief in one's ability to improve with age. "I don't see any limits," he has said. "We can all break the rules. I believe the only thing we can't escape are those illnesses that seem to lurk behind the bushes, like prostate cancer and lymphoma."

In 1997, Hamner underwent a heart valve replacement. "I didn't know I had a congenital heart defect," he relates in 2003. "I'd been a good athlete all my life, so nobody paid much attention to the possibility of something like that." That was until Hamner ran the Fifth Avenue Mile at age 55, recording a speedy 4:49. "I felt a tingling in my hand and lips. I thought I was having a heart attack," he says.

On July 15, 1997, he had his surgery. Six years later he says, "I can do anything. And although I'm the same speed in a quarter-mile and the mile, I'm just not as fast in long-distance running. But maybe that's age."

Hamner still places in his age group in track events on a national class level. In January 2002, he was part of a Masters 4 × 800-meter quartet (which included Sid Howard, NYRR Board member Norman Goluskin, and Jim Aneshansley) that set the world age record at the Armory Track and Field Center in Manhattan. A month later, the foursome broke their own record.

Hamner has made some changes, though. He has lowered his weekly running mileage to 30, but kept his two track sessions. He uses swimming and an elliptical trainer and Jacuzzi more often ("Every runner should have access to a Jacuzzi," he says), and he gets more sleep.

But one thing that has not changed is his strong passion for what he does. "I've talked to a lot of people with heart problems like mine. It's surprising how many older people have it. The fact is that with this condition, the more exercise you do, the less medication you need. Maybe one day we'll even find a way to do without medication altogether."

In the meantime, Dan Hamner runs on, accompanied by his longtime girlfriend, Rae Baymiller, in whom he takes great pride as one of the top female Masters runners in the world.

Norb Sander, M.D.

Norb Sander, who is 61, and the driving force of the Armory Track and Field Center, has always been in it for the long run—literally and figuratively. He is driven by the legacy he strives to create: a future for youth—to bring them into the world of his sport.

Sander began running in his native Yonkers, New York. At age 10, he took up cross-country and went on to compete in high school races, eventually placing third in New York's Catholic High School Cross-Country Championships. Sander ran in the famed Penn Relays in college and eventually moved up to the marathon, winning the Yonkers Marathon and New Orleans Marathon in 1973, and the New York City Marathon in 1974. In those early days, when the race circled Central Park, Sander says he had to "jump over baby carriages" to make his way to the finish.

It was Sander's early running days at the Armory, when the track consisted of a flat hardwood floor, that eventually convinced him of the necessity to "really build a shrine, a place we could say was as good as anything." His obsession has created the miracle of the Armory, where in the winter of 2003 alone, 200,000 people of all ages and locations ran. Today, he is president of The Armory Foundation. His advocacy extends to his position on the board of directors of NYRR, and the organization's dedication to children's running and fitness.

Sander still puts in 20 to 35 running miles a week, and managed in his early fifties to run a 2:47 marathon in New York. April 2003 saw the 40th anniversary celebration of Fordham University's 4×1 mile relay team at the Penn Relays when Sander ran his best ever on the second leg in a stunning upset over a Villanova team that included two Olympians.

But his running achievements do not rival Sander's commitment to youth. "It's nice if I'm 61 years old and I run around the park, God bless, but it's more important that we get behind kids growing up, because running can so much affect the direction life takes."

(Adapted from "Dr. Norbert Sander," by Peter Gambaccini, *New York Runner,* Summer 2003.)

FRED LEBOW ON AGING (1992)

"You change perspective as you age. I've had to realize that I probably won't break seven minutes a mile anymore. I have to be satisfied with breaking nine minutes a mile. Not only am I older, I'm less healthy, so I have to accept that I cannot run as fast as I once did. But I get the same pleasure, if not more so, from what I can do. In fact, I'm delighted by what I can do.

"You can come to believe that when you reach 60, you're not old. Even when you reach 70 and 80, there's no limit. Your body has more power, more resources, than you can imagine. You don't have to sit in a rocking chair, you can be out running.

"I remember a runner in her eighties from Florida who ran some of our races—Ruth Rothfarb. She used to run down a major avenue and pass people sitting on the porch in their rocking chairs. This woman was a tremendous revelation and insight to those people. 'Do you know how many people I got out of those rocking chairs—going for a walk, maybe someday going for a run?' she said to me. It's encouraging to realize that the older you are, the more others will benefit just by seeing you run.

"There are a couple of people over age 90 in the New York City Marathon. They're so energetic; they've got great life stories. They've been successful professionally. One's a doctor who still practices part-time. There are some amazing 'older' people in the New York City Marathon.

"Since I got cancer, this has taken on even added meaning. I was never depressed much in my life, but every once in a while at the club, there is a setback. We lose a sponsor, an event doesn't come off right. I don't get dragged down by this like I used to. Why bother? I've been through a lot, and now is the time to enjoy myself. Besides, what are these little setbacks compared to the troubles of the rest of the world?

"Frankly, I used to fudge my age—lie about it to state it more directly. I'd make myself a few years younger than I actually was. Now I never do. I'm proud to be exactly who and what I am.

"Aging has taught me about all of these things. And I have learned to watch, and be inspired, by the spirit of the older runners who participate in NYRRC events. They are true role models for us all."

35

MASTERS RUNNING

Dr. Margaret Dessau gently reminds us of an unalterable fact: from the moment of birth, we age. Nevertheless, the effects of exercise and physical fitness on the aging process are less certain than the fact of aging itself. And what is still yet to come is a thorough examination of competitive athletes and the aging process.

A handful of prominent pioneers in various sports have prompted society to question its assumptions about aging and competitive athletes. Yet, very few sports have provided an arena of competition for both athletes and all-comers over age 40. Running has, and it's called masters running.

Masters running is not only for running superstars, but also for anyone else who is ambitious and has a bit of latent talent to aspire to succeed in age-group competition, or just wants to test him or herself in age-graded results. Even for those of us not on, or even near, the world-class level, role models such as Bill Rodgers and ultra-marathoner Stu Mittleman, both still competing in their fifties and Toshika D'Elia in her seventies inspire us to maximize our athletic potential and to enjoy it far longer than was previously believed possible. And this is just by sticking with training. Who is to say how far we can go when the science and technology that have been devoted to general sports psychology are focused on those over 40? Older athletes face an unknown world, one filled with both challenges and social barriers, which are now gradually being questioned and tested.

Top NYRR and world performer Rae Baymiller is testing those limits. The world age-group marathon record holder (age 50–59, 2:52:12) wants to be the oldest woman to qualify for the Olympic marathon trials by running 2:48 for the distance. She told *Runner's World,* "I believe people need to repackage themselves as they go through life a little bit, and take what they've learned and apply it to something else. I'm fascinated by aging and longevity and our unfit population. A comment was made to me years ago that you move through life with one vehicle, and if you don't take care of that, what have you got?"

MASTERS ATHLETES—SOME FINDINGS

Dr. Lewis Maharam has co-authored an article on masters athletes that highlights major findings of interest. Studies show that athletic participation has, in fact, a significantly positive impact on the health profile of those who undertake it. The areas of scientific research and findings include:

- **Muscle function.** There is a loss of strength related to aging, resulting in a 40 percent reduction in muscle mass from the age of 20 to 80. Ten percent of that loss occurs between the ages of 25 and 50. However, strength training, begun at any age, has been shown to reverse this muscle loss. It has been shown that strength differences between masters runners and younger runners are not due to age-related change, but to a lower training volume and intensity.

- **Heart Rate.** One study found that male masters athletes (62 years old on average) who engaged in regular vigorous endurance exercise eliminated the usual decline in maximum heart rate associated with aging. The study found that the participants substantially maintained their cardiovascular function as they aged because they maintained a reasonably consistent training program. Based on this study, it appears that a hard training program continued into the masters years should reduce the loss of maximum heart rate by a significant amount.

- **Maximum Aerobic Capacity.** The rate of decrease for masters athletes is approximately half that of their sedentary peers.

- **Flexibility.** Flexibility and joint range of motion commonly decrease with aging. While a decrease in flexibility is usually viewed as negative, this lack of flexibility in masters middle-distance runners actually contributed to the fact that they were found to have increased efficiency of running. However, to maintain and/or increase flexibility, make sure to maintain a regular program of stretching.

- **Degenerative Joint Disease (DJD).** DJD or osteoarthrosis occurs more frequently with aging. It is commonly believed that DJD is caused by wear and tear of the joints. However, DJD may actually be the result of a lack of movement of a joint. Studies have also shown that there is no correlation between long-distance running and the later development of DJD, and that regular activity may, in fact, reduce the pain and/or disability caused by DJD.

NUTRITIONAL NEEDS

It appears that we may need greater amounts of protein as we age. Although there has been research that found that excessive iron intakes were associated with heart disease, runners of both genders may have increased iron losses, and research suggests than an intake of 18 mg. of iron per day is appropriate. (For those who have been warned off iron supplements, a blood test would be indicated to determine iron need.)

For ensuring proper amounts of this and other nutrients, taking a low-dose multivitamin and multimineral supplement (of RDA levels) appears to be a low-risk solution. With age, the thirst mechanism becomes even less sensitive and the kidneys' water output is greater. So masters athletes are advised to create a careful hydration strategy, ensuring enough fluids, and being on the lookout for signs of (and taking care to avoid) dehydration. (Adapted from "Masters Athletes—Factors Affecting Performance," by Lewis G. Maharam, et al., *Sports Medicine,* October 1999.)

MARATHON RECORDS

The New York City Marathon is an example of how untested the limits of masters performances are. While the age records in this race leveled off years ago and remain static for ages 16 to 38, dramatic improvements were seen in the decade between 1987 and 1997 from those in the masters (and near masters) ranks, ages 38 through 44. Greater participation, encouragement, and incentives (including financial) for older runners undoubtedly account for this improvement. When one considers that running times are measured in seconds, and that a minute in a marathon is significant, the contrasting times on page 386 (showing improvement by as much as 12 minutes) take on even greater meaning.

While these times have generally leveled off since 1997, overall participation in the marathon in this age group has increased. What's more, runners in older age groups are setting records and changing expectations of what we can do as we age.

THE THREE A's

Acceptance. Accommodation. Adjustment. These are "the three A's" of masters running—and of aging in general. Coach Bob Glover says he tries to get masters to do two important things. The first is to adjust running times to the aging process. He says that although you can still improve to a point,

1987 Age Records		Age Records, 1997 (unless indicated)	
Men			
39	2:28:09	39	2:15:06 (2001)
40	2:17:30	40	2:16:15
41	2:21:04	41	2:14:34
42	2:19:09	42	2:15:54
43	2:22:44	43	2:18:18
44	2:27:39	44	2:18:16 (1998)
Women			
39	2:40:34	39	2:30:03 (2001)
40	2:35:30	40	2:35:30
41	2:39:11	41	2:39:11
42	2:43:10	42	2:30:17
43	2:40:50	43	2:40:50
44	2:48:13	44	2:36:15

it is better to compare yourself to your peers than to performances you achieved when you were younger. Obviously, improvement will be more dramatic if you are just taking up the sport, but at some point that improvement levels off.

The second adaptation for a master, Glover suggests, is to allow for more recovery time. If you normally did two speed sessions per week, it might be better to adjust to aging by doing just one and allow more days after a hard training run or race to recover. For beginners in this age bracket, Glover—who teaches all beginners regardless of age to intersperse running and walking—prescribes even more walking.

Aging also helps a person to fully savor the activity. As 12-time national 1500-meter champion Regina Jacobs said in a 2003 *USA Today* article, "In my 20s, I considered myself a racer. I hadn't yet fallen in love with running." By age 40, she had. "Without love of the process of running, training, and everything else that goes into the details of becoming a great athlete, you're never going to achieve the goals you want."

GERARD HARTMANN ON PEAKING PAST FORTY

There are ways and means to stay fast and strong into middle-age, as athlete and physical therapist Gerard Hartmann explains.

"I am excited about entering the category known as 'vets' or 'masters.'

Forty-seven-year-old Alan Ruben has run the last 17 New York City Marathons and is a four-time age-group NYRR Runner of the Year, most recently in 2002. Ruben set his personal best for the marathon—2:29:54—in Boston in 1988. His goal is to be "running for a lifetime," and this goal affects his approach to his running. "I always look long-term. Patience is the key word. I don't have to do it all at once." At the same time, Ruben maintains high expectations for himself. "I try not to expect to run slower. I still measure myself against my best times."

What also keeps Ruben going is the health and fitness his running provides. "I feel the sense of well-being running gives me, but having come late to the sport, I have a point of comparison. I can still recall the days of feeling sluggish, and the results of having a poorer diet."

Despite changes in his routine, such as having a family with two young children, Ruben has kept up the pace. Here is some of what he has done to achieve his success, and what he continues to do to realize his goal of "lifelong running."

- **Consistency and regular scheduling**. Ruben runs the same time and distance every morning before work. The same two evenings a week, he does harder training with his team. "Being consistent means doing it day in and day out, and the same is true of weekly, monthly, and yearly schedules."

- **Keeping company**. While he does his morning runs alone, Ruben relies on company for the harder workouts. "As you get older, it's harder to drag yourself out for the hard runs. It makes a big difference to have company."

- **Being conservative**. "If I feel something is not quite right, I'll take a day off." Ruben doesn't schedule days off, but he remains flexible, and takes them as needed.

- **Taking it easy**. "It's important for the hard running to be hard, and the easy running to be easy, so it allows for recovery. In the same way you don't want to be tired for races, you don't want to be tired for your hard training."

I know from my experience as a sports injury therapist that veterans must be in tune with their bodies. A slight niggle can sideline a veteran for weeks (recovery takes much longer than with younger athletes). The vet must continually monitor telltale signs and be willing to take rest days and adapt as problems arise.

"I have also learned that no matter how well we eat or how carefully we exercise, there are no guarantees; we can do little about the genetic factor. The sudden deaths of Jim Fixx and, more recently, my good friend Noel Carroll testify to that. I believe that stress is the silent killer. Everyone has a different tolerance to stress. My personal approach if I have a very stressful day in the clinic is to adapt—do a shorter run at a more relaxed pace or even take a complete rest day and de-stress in a hot bath. Many athletes squeeze their training into hectic workdays; I question the wisdom of this.

"There are four main changes typical of the veteran runner: increase in body fat, decrease in muscle mass/strength, decrease in flexibility/range of joint motion, and decrease in variety of running."

INCREASED BODY FAT

The accumulation of fat is the most prevalent age-associated physiological change. With age, the average individual loses six percent of lean mass (muscle) per decade, but maintains or increases total body mass by gaining fat. Simply put, many runners are carrying nearly 30 pounds of dead weight (fat) on a skeletal structure that is shedding muscle, which is why so many get injured.

Aside from increasing strength and preventing injury, the obvious benefit of greater muscle mass is that muscle is metabolically active; an increase in muscle raises basal metabolic rate, which means the body burns more energy.

The best way to limit weight gain is to exercise more while eating less and limiting alcohol consumption.

There are many reasons why veterans should watch their diets—injury prevention, better performance, a healthy immune system, and shorter recovery time, to name but a few.

There are also those dreaded "free radicals." While the oxygen we breathe is vital for life, it is also incorporated into these very reactive substances (free radicals), which are harmful. A runner uses up to 30 times more oxygen than a "couch potato," and that extra oxygen makes for extra free radicals. It is therefore vital to include antioxidants in the diet to prevent and repair the damage caused by free radicals. The best known antioxidants are vitamins A, C, and E. A balanced diet rich in fruit, vegetables, cereals, nuts, seeds, legumes, fish, and dairy products will meet your requirements.

Many veteran runners take the supplement glucosamine to inhibit wear and tear on joints, ligaments, cartilage, and connective tissue. Glucosamine is nontoxic and has no known side effects.

DECREASED STRENGTH

Muscle strength and mass tend to decrease 30 to 50 percent between the ages of 30 and 70. As we age we weaken, because bundles of muscles and nerves called "motor units" deteriorate.

Between the ages of 30 and 70 the average person loses 20 percent of the motor units in all the large muscles. Regular exercise counteracts or delays the detrimental effects of aging. Muscular adaptation depends on the intensity, duration, frequency, and pattern of the stimulus.

Many veterans get stuck in a rut—running at the same pace all the time. Regular running quite obviously has cardiovascular benefit, but is likely stimulating only one level of fitness potential.

Running at low intensity increases the oxidative capacity primarily of "type one" (slow oxidative) fibers, whereas strength training tends to be more effective in producing hypertrophy in "type two" (fast glycolytic) fibers.

I recommend a program that focuses on the core muscles of the upper and lower back as well as the abdominals, gluteals, adductors, quadriceps, and hamstrings. When any of these core muscles weaken, imbalances can occur, and that is when the stress of running shifts to vulnerable joints— ankles, knees, hips—and shins. That is when you get injured.

The muscular system is, like a chain, only as strong as its weakest link. The goal is to build muscle mass that can absorb shock, protecting the skeleton from overload.

Remember that strength training is not just for younger runners. A strength program will help you maintain muscle as you age. Strength training also maintains bone density, which, like muscle mass, declines with age.

DECREASED FLEXIBILITY

It is true that flexibility decreases with age, and for clear physiological reasons.

Collagen and elastin, the primary structural components of muscle, undergo specific physical and biochemical changes. Collagen reflects a loss of the minimal extensibility that existed earlier and reflects an increased rigidity. Elastin likewise changes with age. Elastic fibers lose their resilience and undergo various alterations, including fragmentation, fraying, clarification, and other mineralizations.

Nonetheless, evidence indicates that flexibility can be developed at any age. The rate of improvement will vary with age, as will the potential for improvement. In general, the longer you wait after adolescence to start on a flexibility program, the less are the chances of absolute improvement.

Clearly, the main reason many veteran runners are stiff is that they spend too little time stretching. I recommend at least ten minutes of stretching per day. Flexibility is an integral part of training, and the only way to improve flexibility is to stretch regularly.

DECREASED VARIETY

Many runners lapse into the same old leisurely pace. Although steady running does have its place, one-paced training promotes only one aspect of fitness.

This means that the training elements that preserve speed should never be neglected—even during the off-season. In addition to incorporating varying intensities of running into the schedule, it is also beneficial to do form drills along with strength work and flexibility exercises to keep snap in the legs and maintain a speedy mind-set even when not racing. Lost leg speed is difficult to regain—especially as the runner ages.

FORM DRILLS

Three basic drills can be done at least three times a week either at the start or end of running.

The first drill focuses on a high knee action. Stand tall, relax arms and shoulders, and lift one knee to waist level, thigh parallel to the ground, while keeping the other leg straight as your foot strikes the ground. Quickly alternate knees, keeping one foot off the ground at all times as you move forward for about 30 meters. Perform three times.

This will teach you to run tall and use the basic sprinting technique: extending the support leg while lifting the opposite knee. So many veterans run low to the ground because they seldom train to develop form and proper carriage.

Once you master this technique, incorporate the arms. Each time you raise your thigh parallel to the ground, bring the opposite hand up to forehead level without allowing the arm to cross the midway point of the body. Again, do this drill for 30 meters three times.

Once you master the exaggerated arm and knee action, your body will begin to use this technique when you run fast.

In the final drill, which I call "quick feet," you simply move your feet as fast as you can across the ground, as if you were walking on hot coals. Perform the drill three times, again moving forward 30 meters each time.

VARYING INTENSITY

Many runners never achieve their potential. Because they run slowly, their intensity is low and demands are confined to the aerobic pathway.

You need to incorporate faster distance runs. This entails doing, say, an eight-miler at a faster than usual pace. This will demand a higher oxygen supply, enlarge the heart, and improve perfusion of blood to the muscles.

Another strategy is to run three to five miles very fast, at or near anaerobic threshold. This boosts tolerance to such intensity and improves muscular capacity for glycogen.

The fast run should be preceded by a ten-minute warmup run and followed by ten to 15 minutes of easy running. Stimulating the various energy pathways and getting accustomed to varying speeds is a sure way to improve performance.

The competitive veteran will benefit from various forms of interval running. An example would be: ten minutes warmup and $6 \times 800m$ with two minutes jog recovery between each; or $10 \times 400m$, jogging 200m between each. Always jog ten to 15 minutes to cool down.

Some runners feel they must have access to a track to do interval training or speed work. But sessions can be done on parkland, riverbank, trail, playing field, and several other surfaces (though for hard sessions avoid roads).

With running, the focus is on mechanics and leg speed, lifting the feet off the ground as quickly as possible. Keeping speed intact is a year-round enterprise that entails a consistent training pattern with a variety of workouts. Rather than just grinding out the miles, stay focused on form and make leg speed a part of the daily routine. (For more information, visit the Hartmann Web site, www.hartmann-international.com.)

MASTERS TRAINING

Can you improve as a master? Yes, you can, says Olympic gold medalist Frank Shorter, but you have to keep personal records so you can judge your relative performance. "The way I gauge it is that I know what training intensity is, and I know the feeling of competition. I've developed a sense of how close I've been able to come now to my maximum. What I've found is, I can reach about 95 percent of 'all out.' The last 5 percent is very hard for me because I know that no matter how much I get out of myself, I'll never run a 2:10 marathon again; I'll never run under 28 minutes for 10,000 meters; I'll never run under 13:20 for 5K. There's just something about realizing that which makes it hard to go absolutely all out in a competitive situation. The way I view it, you just have to get the satisfaction somewhere else.

"But people don't need to perform well in order to be able to run," Shorter continues. "I run because I like the motion. I like being out there. In that way I'm like any average runner."

Frank Shorter believes there are specific adaptations to training as a master that will help maintain conditioning. One thing you can do is maintain a weight training routine. He points out that we lose a certain amount of muscle mass and strength with age, and while it's only a percentage, it's enough that if you've been very active as a younger person, it has a significant impact on your performance. That's why he does a 30-minute weight routine several times a week, to build and maintain muscle.

Shorter also stresses the aspect of recovery. "As you get older, you still maintain the same daily goal as to how much training you'll do. You lock into a certain amount that you feel is a day's exercise. If you maintain that amount from age 30 to 45, and you've been losing muscle mass, in essence

---

I went to Cooper's aerobic center in the summer of 1991, when I was 43. I had all the tests done. They showed I had pretty much maintained all of my fitness. My VO_2 max had gone down very little. They predict about 1 1/2 percent drop after age 30, which would total about 18 percent for me; however, mine went down only 7 percent. I went in at the same weight I was in 1975—134 pounds.

I think that athletes believe that if they maintain the same body weight, they maintain the same conditioning. But although my weight hadn't changed, my body fat had gone up 4 percent. It doesn't take a rocket scientist to figure out that if your body fat goes up 4 percent and you weigh the same, there are that many pounds of muscle that are no longer there. Based on that alone, I think logic would indicate that the more of that muscle one can maintain, or get back in my case, the more it will help.

—*Frank Shorter*

you've been slightly overtraining as you age. You're aiming to reach your daily quota, but you've had less strength to do it. You're going to be taxed more, and obviously it will take you more time to recover."

RUNNING ADVICE FOR YOUR 60s AND 70s

Runners in this age group run for the love of it, pure and simple. Though many took up the activity to lose weight or improve their health, they've stuck with it through the years for relaxation, stress-relief, and social reasons.

- Take advantage of a flexible schedule and run when your energy levels and motivation are highest.

- Avoid retirement isolation by making your runs social. Introduce your friends, children, and grandchildren to the joys of running.

- Warm up the muscles with light exercise before a run, and cool down afterward.

- Stretch diligently. Muscles, tendons, and ligaments lose elasticity over time due to decreased water retention and need stretching to stay flexible.

- Don't ignore pain or try to play doctor. Dealing with an injury isn't just about making the pain go away; prevention and recovery are just as important.

- Try cross training activities to add a new dimension to your running and spare your joints.

- If you can't run, walk. Most participants in NYRR Healthwalking classes, for example, are age 60 and over.

(Adapted from "The Sixties and Seventies: Stepping into the Golden Years," by Gail Waesche Kislevitz, *New York Runner,* Sept./Oct. 2002.)

MASTERS COMPETITION

Bill Rodgers says, "I retired from competitive marathoning in 1992. In 1996, I ran the 100th Anniversary of the Boston Marathon, and I have even thought about running New York again. I almost ran in 2001 in memory of September 11.

"I'm still running 50–80 miles/week. I train with my friend a few days a week, and we still do speed work and workouts. I used to run 120 to 130 miles a week. Now I have two kids. Priorities change, but I still love the sport. It's more about the enjoyment of running that gets me out there.

"I still compete in 25 races a year. I just raced my 24th Bix 7 Miler, and now I am focusing on being a competitive veteran runner. I'm undefeated in my age group this year, except for one track race. I'm trying to be the number one in the 55–59 age class."

The number of masters athletes (40 years and over) in road racing events is much higher than ten years ago, with the estimated number of masters finishers in 2002 rising to 3,160,000, up from 2,040,000 in 1993. That's proof you don't have to be a "world-beater" to be a masters competitor.

With innovations like age-graded race results, and just being out among your peers, there's plenty of incentive. Besides, age changes a person's perspective on competing. Sure, it's great just to run, but there is something even more special about doing it in a race. You become part of a community of those who are forever young at heart, literally and figuratively! You realize you are unique; what a privilege it is to be able to put yourself "on the line." And for those few minutes or even hours you race, there is just you against yourself, your peers, or the clock. There are none of the usual distractions—the typical daily challenges, worries, or responsibilities that come with adult life.

Of course, I felt some of this as a younger competitor, but it intensifies with time. When I'm in a race now, I feel especially powerful. I marvel at the fact I can, and am, still doing this at age 52. I keep my eye on the 20-somethings around me, and when I begin to pass some of them, with great satisfaction, I remark to myself: "Sweetheart, I could be your mother."

Here I am, still at it, I'd tell those kids, if I had the breath. Road running is a marvel, because it means we can still have this experience, feel the feelings of being an athlete, a racer. How special that is, I realize. How proud I am to be here. How important it is to show my friends, my family, and especially my children that I don't just sit and watch the world from the sidelines; I "go for it."

One of my favorite "masters memories" was nearing the end of a 10K, when a young girl from the sidelines shouted at me: "You're one of the top girls." Even in the pain of my race effort, I smiled. I was 46 years old, but she had defined exactly the way I feel—like a girl.

—Gloria Averbuch

ING New York City Marathon 2003 winners Margaret Okayo and Martin Lel, both from Kenya, wear the traditional laurel wreaths.
Photo © Victah Sailer

The 2003 USA Men's 8K Championship, contested in Central Park. Meb Keflezighi (center) won the event.
Photo © Victah Sailer

In addition to races at a variety of running and walking distances, New York Road Runners also conducts novelty events—like the annual Backwards Mile.
Photo © Sarah Lyman Kravits

**The New York Mini 10K, the original and most prestigious
all-women's road race.**
Photo © Scott McDermott

**Runners ascend 86 flights of stairs in the Empire State
Building Run-Up, an event that spawned races in major
buildings in various other parts of the world.**
Photo © Ed Haas

**Dr. Norbert Sander, now the head of the Armory,
a premier track and field center, won the
1974 New York City Marathon.**
Photo: © Michael Tighe

A record 34,729 participants finished from the over 73,000 who applied to the New York City Marathon. They were cheered on by the 2.5 million spectators who lined the marathon course.
Photo © Ed Lederman

The foursome (left to right, Dan Hamner, Norman Goluskin, Jim Aneshansley, and Sid Howard) set the 4 x 800-meter Masters world record in January 2002 in the Armory Track and Field Center. Standing behind them is Allan Steinfeld, President and CEO of New York Road Runners.
Photo © Ed Haas

**Kathrine Switzer (left) and Nina Kuscsik holding relics from
the early days of the New York Mini 10K.**
Photo © Nancy Coplon

American marathon record holder Deena Kastor has run the New York City Marathon and the New York Mini 10K.
Photo © Victah Sailer

A New Year's tradition since 1979, this race begins at the stroke of midnight.
Photo © Ed Haas

(From left to right) Olympic champion Frank Shorter, *Runner's World* **publisher emeritus George Hirsch, four-time New York City and Boston Marathon winner Bill Rodgers, and the legendary Fred Lebow.**
Photo © Nancy Coplon

Over 10,000 women are set to take off in the annual Race for the Cure to benefit breast cancer research.
Photo © Jack Gescheidt

**Some of the over 12,000 New York City Marathon
volunteers that help the participants to hydrate.**
Photo © David M. Everard

The wheelchair division of the New York City Marathon features an international field that competed in 2003 for over $13,000 in total prize money.
Photo © Scott McDermott

The New York Road Runners Foundation gets kids fit. Pictured here are children running under the guidance of Foundation chairwoman Grete Waitz.
Photo © Scott McDermott

PART 9
CHILDREN'S RUNNING AND FITNESS

36

CHILDREN'S RUNNING AND FITNESS

As road running and the fitness movement have blossomed over the years, NYRR staff, as well as other experts in the field of sports and fitness, noticed that something was missing. While adults are striving—and succeeding—to improve their health and fitness, the nation's children are falling behind. From one decade to the next, those who measure children's fitness have found that it has been declining steadily.

Even more children in this country are overweight than ever before, about double the number who were heavy in the late 1970s. By 2003, the situation has become a crisis, with studies confirming and vast publicity decrying the rising rate of obesity in children, and strong recommendations by experts to keep children active. Yet action lags far behind. Only 32.2 percent of students nationwide attended P.E. class in 2002, down ten percent from 1991. Perception of the problem lags as well. In a recent study of 5,500 children between the ages of two and 11, researchers at the Centers for Disease Control and Prevention discovered that 32 percent of the mothers thought their overweight children were "about the right weight." Forty percent of children ages five to eight show at least one risk factor for heart disease, such as obesity, high blood pressure, or elevated cholesterol. These early risk factors make them more likely to develop heart disease later in life. From ages six to 17, only 32 percent of children meet minimum standard recommendations for cardiovascular fitness, flexibility, and upper body strength.

The National Association for Sports and Physical Education (NASPE) recommends that students should have a *minimum* of 60 minutes of moderate to vigorous activity every day.

Unfortunately, at this time we can't look to schools to get the job done. Only one state in the country, Illinois, requires daily physical education instruction in its schools. Even then, most school P.E. includes a significant amount of nonphysical activity (i.e. waiting, sitting, standing), and statistics show that in all grade levels, girls do even less than boys.

The poor state of children's fitness in the United States, as well as a shift in the demographics of NYRR's membership, led NYRR to develop children's programs. The majority of NYRR's members—as well as others in the running movement—who had previously been single and in their 20s, are now parents in their 30s and 40s. Their lifestyles have changed, as have their needs and interests. Running is not merely a solitary activity, but something they want to share with their families. To serve the changing needs of these people, it has become a NYRR priority to expand fitness, making it a family affair. An equal priority is to reach out to the population of underserved youth through the NYRR Foundation.

In honor of the late "Coach" Joe Kleinerman, New York Road Runners has established its first scholarship. The Joe Kleinerman Scholarships, created in 2003, are awarded annually to one male and one female scholastic runner who are graduating from New York City public high schools and continuing on to college, with selection based on athletic and academic achievement.

Kleinerman was an accomplished runner, coach, and administrator. He distinguished himself with hundreds of top finishes in races on the roads, track, and in cross-country. A co-founder and board member emeritus of NYRR, he helped professionalize running and make it accessible to all ages and levels of runners. Kleinerman was particularly instrumental with his early support of women's running.

The third factor in the move to develop children's fitness is community involvement. NYRR has always sought to be a vehicle for improvement in the quality of life of the community, particularly of the inner-city population. As part of this effort, NYRR conducts an extensive running and fitness program for children and youth, which began on Father's Day in 1981 with the first Pee Wee Run.

Today, through its affiliated foundation, NYRR conducts two highly successful children's running and fitness programs: Running Partners and City Sports For Kids.

City Sports For Kids seeks to enhance physical fitness for youth, to develop self-esteem through success-oriented sports, and to build bridges of understanding through play for boys and girls of various races and religions. The program provides instruction for children ages six to 13 in a variety of sports skills, including basketball and such track and field activities as high jump, sprinting, long jump, and shot put.

DISTANCE RUNNING FOR CHILDREN

A statement from the Committee on Sports Medicine of the American Academy of Pediatrics recommends that if your children enjoy running and have no adverse symptoms, there is no reason why they shouldn't train for and compete in running events. The committee noted that there are risks connected with training and racing including overuse injuries and a delay in a girl's first menstrual period. In addition, children have a less efficient temperature control system than adults which means they may be more likely to experience heat- or cold-related problems, and take longer to acclimatize in hot and humid climates.

With these exceptions, it is not known that children are more likely than adults to experience problems arising from running. Running is a natural activity, the committee concluded, and it fosters healthy physical and psychological growth.

There are approximately six noncompetitive races held per year as part of the NYRR program. The races, for two- to 12-year-olds, are of distances from 25 yards to one-half mile. These runs are extremely popular, with over 300 participants per event. The significance of these runs is that they are held in conjunction with adult races, which achieves two of NYRR's major goals: to bring out all generations, and to make running and fitness a fun family affair.

The goal of NYRR programs is to create a lifelong pattern of fitness among families by encouraging everyone to share the experience of getting fit and healthy together. Together, mom, dad, and the kids—grandparents, too—create the best support for maintaining a healthy diet and regular aerobic exercise. This, in turn, fosters a closeness and harmony that strengthen the family. Healthy eating and making family exercise part of your weekly schedule are essential ingredients for a successful family fitness program.

NEW YORK ROAD RUNNERS FOUNDATION

The New York Road Runners Foundation was founded by New York Road Runners in 1998. Its mission is to establish community-based running programs that enhance physical health, emotional well-being, and personal achievement within underserved populations throughout New York City, and to disseminate its program expertise to interested parties across the United States and around the world.

In response to the critical lack of physical education programming in New York City public schools and the crisis in overweight- and obesity-related illnesses among youth, the Foundation's focus is on serving children. Running Partners Teams, the Foundation's cornerstone initiative, is a youth development program for children ages six to 18 of all athletic abilities that links the sport of running to success in school and life. Combining training for running one to five miles, workshops on health and nutrition, and academic lessons related to their program experiences, Running Partners Teams uplifts participant's bodies, minds, and spirits.

As of Fall 2003, the Foundation has established Running Partners Teams in more than 50 schools and community centers throughout New York City, serving over 2,000 predominantly at-risk youth a week, but recognizes the need to serve tens of thousands more. Through its affiliation with New York Road Runners, benefits include participation in New York Road Runner races and special events and the involvement of Olympic and champion athletes such as the Foundation's chairwoman, nine-time New York City Marathon winner Grete Waitz.

The value of Running Partners Teams is best expressed by the participants themselves. A 13-year-old boy said, "I love to be in Running Partners because it's not just about winning awards, it's about doing your best to become your best." A 12-year-old girl said, "What I learned from running was to never give up. You don't know what you can do until you try."

The Foundation continues to grow, expanding its provision of Running Partners and running clinics. Its newest initiative, Fitness Partners, sends expert instructors into schools without physical education classes to present a series of workshops on running and fitness-related issues.

Contact the Foundation at foundation@nyrrc.org, and visit its Web site at www.nyrrc.org/divisions/foundation.

When it comes to children and sports, there is often a fine line between parental pressure and support. This is especially the case when the parents themselves are very interested and/or active in the sport. Without the proper guidance, children often get discouraged for a variety of reasons, and eventually lose interest.

Adults very often direct sport for their children based on adult models. This isn't necessarily the wrong approach, but it happens quite often that the child's needs and wishes are not exactly the same as the adult's. Neither the coach's nor the parents' ambition should be the basis for a child's sports program.

Teenage years are crucial in maintaining a sports program. This is the time during which youth tend to drop out of sports participation. To help your child stick with it, consider what I have learned in my experience as a teacher working with young people. The following is a list of reasons I have found as to why youth quit sports participation. You can use some of the positive steps outlined in this chapter to keep these things from happening.

- Boring and/or monotonous training
- The perception that the expectation for good performance and results is too great
- Lack of parental interest in the child's activity
- Too little encouragement
- Too great a feeling of defeat
- Lack of a sense of security in training
- Failure of adults to realize and/or be sympathetic to what children want from the sport
- Adults' inability to distinguish children's varying capabilities
- Neglecting and/or failing to develop the social aspect of the sport

—Grete Waitz

THE STATE OF YOUTH FITNESS

The following information is adapted from an NYRR brochure on children's fitness written by Bob Glover.

Studies by the President's Council on Physical Fitness and Sports and the National Association for Sports and Physical Education (NASPE) demonstrate that the youth in this country need to improve their fitness levels.

Do physically fit children have more efficient immune systems than couch potatoes? Dr. James M. Rippe, director of the Exercise Physiology and Nutrition Laboratory of the University of Massachusetts in Worcester, believes the answer is yes. Says Dr. Rippe in *Working Mother* magazine, "The link is there, in some yet-to-be-determined way. For one thing, the body temperature rises slightly during exercise, and the immune system may interpret this as a mild fever and marshal infection-fighting cells."

In fact, a study done at Loma Linda University in California showed that moderate exercise strengthens the immune system by triggering the release of antibodies that attack viruses and bacteria. What's more, endorphins, the mood-elevating brain chemicals released through exercise, may also signal the immune system to work harder.

NASPE's "Shape of the Nation" survey of school physical education programs revealed that children are not getting enough exercise in school, partly due to budget cutbacks that affect school physical education programs. NASPE recommends at least 60 minutes of daily vigorous exercise for children in grades K–12 (as mentioned above, only one state in the United States, Illinois, requires daily physical education classes). NASPE also recommends that schools place more emphasis on lifelong fitness activities, such as running, swimming, and walking, in addition to team sports.

The major responsibility for the fitness of our children rests with parents. They can work to help improve fitness programs in schools and community groups. Parents can be a great inspiration for their kids by being good fitness role models and by making fitness a fun, lifelong family activity.

Here's what parents can do to help their children become more physically fit:

1. Join them in walking or biking more often as a means of transportation; for example, to or from school.

2. Encourage vigorous physical activity over sedentary activities, such as the excessive watching of television or playing of video games.

3. Spend some time each week participating together in fun physical activities, such as running, hiking, cross-country skiing, or playing tennis.

4. If you are an athlete, you can be a role model for your child. If you're not athletic, you can steer your child toward someone who is. Find a program like the ones at NYRR, or a running group or friends who run. Children's fitness classes and programs are also conducted by the YM/YWCAs in every state.

CHILDREN AND RUNNING

It's good to expose your children to running at an early age—but don't force them to run. While most adults run for fitness, kids run because it's fun.

As an exercise enthusiast, you can motivate your child by being a fun running companion. A good way for parents to introduce children to running is to make it a natural part of their play. Youngsters have short attention spans, so break up their runs with walking, skipping, singing, or exploring. Let them run after you while playing baseball, or run up and down hills while playing hide and seek in the park. Very young preschoolers often enjoy brisk walks with a few dashes in between. The key is to integrate running into your child's play.

Older children, like adults, enjoy talking during the run to pass the time. A good conversation on the run is a great way to communicate—and both of you will be surprised how fast the time goes by.

Let your children decide when and how often they want to run. Don't push them. Make the early experience positive, successful, and fun. They may want to run for several days and then move on to other activities, returning on and off to running. The important thing is that they are exercising and having fun.

An important safety note: The American Academy of Pediatrics recommends that children, as well as their parents, be screened by a physician before starting a sports or fitness program.

Preschool Running Tips

For kids age five or under, running is just playtime activity. Parents should encourage fun running and not stress competition at this age. The NYRR Pee Wee running program is designed to develop an awareness and joy of running. Think of it as prefitness for preschoolers. Pee Wees should be encouraged to sprint short distances, not run long distances.

Praise the kids for running, no matter what their pace, or how many times they stop or even fall down. The goal is to begin to establish in their minds that running and exercise are not only good for them, but also fun for the entire family. Sometimes a good storybook helps to reinforce this. Ask for a list of titles on exercise and fitness at a library or bookstore.

Elementary School–Age Tips

Attitudes and habits about fitness and exercise tend to be firmly established in this age group. By adolescence it is already very difficult to change one's style of living, so this is a crucial stage for developing good fitness habits.

Two important factors for fitness development between the ages of six and 12 are having a parent who exercises as a role model and having a good physical education program at school that stresses aerobic fitness, as well as sports. If well administered, youth sports, such as soccer, hockey, basketball, and baseball offer excellent fitness and social benefits.

Fitness running, as opposed to competition, should be emphasized for most kids of this age, and the distance should be limited to one to four miles. There are numerous ways to get your kids involved. Have them accompany you while you run. Go at their pace for whatever distance they can maintain interest. That might be around the block or a loop of a nearby park. You can also encourage your children to participate in activities in which they run a lot without realizing it, such as soccer or tennis.

Biking, skating, dancing, jumping rope, and swimming are other activities you can do together at this age when the children can build a good aerobic base of fitness. Many kids enjoy riding their bikes to accompany parents on a run. This can be a great way to get in your run while chatting with your child.

NYRR encourages children age 12 and under to participate in age-appropriate events. The emphasis is on providing the experience of the joys of running for fitness and fun, as well as participating in a variety of sports and aerobic fitness activities.

NYRR endorses the guidelines established by the American Academy of Pediatrics—preadolescent children should not run long-distance races held primarily for adults. If kids want to try competition, they should run against each other, not adults. Younger children should be encouraged just to take part. This can best be accomplished in low-key fun runs, like those conducted by NYRR.

Children age ten and up can qualify for a Presidential Physical Fitness Award in a total of 58 fitness and sports categories. Among them are "run-

TIPS FROM A RUNNING MOM

Was it because the young lives of my two teenaged daughters were filled with exercise and movement that they became elite athletes? I'd be willing to bet it had a lot to do with it. In order for children to develop good health and fitness habits, whether they become serious competitors or not, it is important that a good example is set at home. Studies show that a parental role model is the number-one influence toward ensuring children's interest and motivation. Here's how you can help:

- Involve your children in your fitness activities. For example, take them on a casual training run, or have them ride a bike to escort you on your run, and if you run races, bring them out to watch you.

- Children are never too young to begin. Toddlers can benefit by being included in the fitness activities of parents and older siblings. Bring them along and encourage even their casual participation. Adapt all activity to include them.

- Don't push. Support your children's exercise or fitness activity, but don't force them. If they are tired or unwilling, scale down the activity.

- Select and promote "active toys" like jump ropes and balls that enable children to develop fitness or coordination skills.

- Set challenging and exciting fitness-oriented goals—like training for a run/walk to school together.

- Use babysitters who, with your support, are likely to promote physical activities—like walking, running, and general physical play.

- Devote time, interest, and enthusiasm to physical education at school. Give it equal priority to "the three R's." You can combine subjects, like finding library books on sports, and doing art projects on the subject.

- Get involved in your children's school to help improve physical education and fitness. If one does not already exist, work toward setting up a school fitness network, or a walk/run program. Volunteer to help lead recreation or free play activities.

- Encourage girls with the same intensity as boys. In fact, you might want to give an extra measure of support to

(continued)

> girls, who are traditionally discouraged or disenfran-
> chised from sports and physical activity.
>
> - Incorporate fun and meaningful movement into all as-
>   pects of life. Examples include creating running, hop-
>   ping, or jumping challenges and "mini relays" while
>   waiting at the school bus stop; and stair climbing in
>   malls or buildings. Use your imagination, or call on chil-
>   dren to do so, to fill dead time with movement.
>
> - Don't lose momentum during inclement weather. Do in-
>   door activities at home, and/or try to get a church or
>   community center to allow you and others the use of its
>   space for recreational purposes during the winter
>   months.
>
> - Make fitness a theme of children's general activities,
>   such as play dates and birthday parties.
>
> *—Gloria Averbuch*

ning," "jogging," and "marathon." Also, you can help your children's schools institute the President's Challenge. For further information on any of these programs, contact the President's Council on Physical Fitness and Sports (see www.fitness.gov/challenge/challenge.html. See also kidsrunning.com).

ONE-MILE RUNNING PROGRAM FOR CHILDREN

The following is a program to build up to running one mile in six weeks, adapted from *Children's Running* by Don Kardong and Jim Ferstle. (For age guidelines, see advice from Grete Waitz at the end of this chapter.)

Week 1: 10- to 15-minute jog/walk on Monday, Wednesday, and Friday

Week 2: 12- to 18-minute jog/walk on Monday, Wednesday, and Friday

Week 3: 15- to 20-minute jog/walk on Monday, Wednesday, and Friday

Week 4: 20-minute jog/walk on Monday, Wednesday, and Friday, and 3 to 4 long (200 to 400 meters) runs at one-mile pace

Week 5: Same as for Week 4

Week 6: 20-minute jog on Monday and 10-minute jog on Tuesday, with 4 to 5 sprints at the end

This is just a sample program. Many others can work just as well. Whatever the plan, though, remember to increase gradually. You might encourage children to keep a training log or diary.

GRETE WAITZ'S TIPS ON RAISING FIT KIDS

- **Have children organize a little road race—from one block to one mile, or ten laps around the block.** The organization of the event, sending out invitations, and arranging refreshments is part of the fun. And everyone, even the youngest, can have a job—as time keepers or race starters, for instance. Then, suggest the children switch roles. "There's always a little task for everyone," says Waitz. "Even the youngest can pour juice." Remember that a big part of having fun is simply having the children spend time together. "Let the kids do the work, not their parents or caregivers. They will learn and enjoy themselves by doing it independently. Offer support but let them do the planning."

- **This is playing, not training.** If races become too competitive, encourage the children to try some noncompetitive games or activities. Slow it down with activities like egg-on-a-spoon.

- **Remember that children know best what they enjoy.** As Waitz says, "What children have fun doing may be very different from what adults consider fun."

- **Be aware that these "games" are also *teaching* children.** Preparing and organizing are tools for understanding and appreciating their activities. When adults go to events, everything is already organized and ready. By doing it from scratch, children learn to understand the total experience.

JOAN SAMUELSON'S TIPS ON HAVING AN ACTIVE FAMILY

- **Cultivate an outdoor life—particularly in the good fall weather.** The Samuelsons have a yard, a basketball net, a backboard to hit a tennis ball, and a driveway that accommodates bike riding. The children also have a tree fort and work in their mom's famous vegetable garden. "They just like to be outdoors," confirms Joan. "This is the way I grew up."

- **Be a role model.**   This is essential, as every expert confirms. "If you lead a fit life," says Joan, "the children will follow." In addition to their running, Joan and Scott Samuelson emphasize activity as a result of what they do *not* do. They do not watch much television, and they have no video games.

- **Don't push.**   "I have a problem with pushing," says Joan, who raises the red flag. "If parents have not met their own athletic goals, they might be inclined to push their children [to vicariously satisfy themselves], rather than for true love of the sport." This may ultimately discourage children from participating altogether.

- **Where you go, they will likely follow.**   "Our philosophy is to do what we love. If the children are interested, great. If not, that's okay. If Abby were to say to me, 'I'd like to ride a bike when you run' (which she did once or twice), that's fine. But the important thing is that we're always doing something physical—stacking wood, raking, mowing."

The most important thing is that the Samuelsons are communicating the right message. When Joan is asked why she doesn't do the obvious—run with her children—she replies with a laugh, "I don't need to 'run' with them. My life is always on the run!"

BILL RODGERS ON FAMILY FITNESS

"I think the most important thing is to support your children's interests. Let them try a variety of sports. I'm not real big on competition for children; let competition evolve on its own. I like to encourage sport for health and fitness. My main interest is that my children will know what it means to be fit and that it should be the rule, not the exception, the way it is now in our society."

COMPETITION

Children run so naturally and gracefully that it seems they were born to do it. There is, however, a big difference between a child's spontaneous running and running for competition. As has been pointed out earlier, NYRR encourages children to participate in age-appropriate events and discourages young children from competing in events designed for adults. In particular, the New York City Marathon first adopted an age minimum of 16, which was eventually raised to 18. This standard had previously been in existence in other countries.

According to author Cliff Temple, "When children undertake training and racing over long distances on the road (e.g., marathon), it can create many problems for the developing body. The growth of the bones around the heels and the knees particularly can be disrupted by excessive training loads, which can lead to problems in later life. The fact that physiologically children can run marathons must not be confused with whether medically they should. It is clear they should not."

Inappropriate training or competition in running (or, for that matter, any sport) is potentially damaging not only physically, but also psychologically. How many child running stars become adult running stars? It is tough to find even one. The theme of this book is the same for children as it is for adults: to make running essentially an enjoyable, lifelong activity.

Grete Waitz, who began running for fun at age 12 and appropriately progressed to serious competition as she got older, provides the following guidelines, based on conferences in which European coaches presented their views on youth running:

1. Specializing in middle distances (800 meters to the mile) should not take place before 13 to 14 years of age; long distances (up to 10K), not before 15 to 16 years of age.

2. Young runners should have well-rounded training before specializing (e.g., at one time, I competed in the high jump, sprints, and even the throwing events).

3. Aerobic, or endurance, training is important for young runners, but it should only be done easily.

4. Young runners should be careful with anaerobic training. Hard anaerobic training should be avoided before puberty, and once begun, increased only in small doses from year to year.

5. Strength and sprint training are good for young runners.

6. Long-term planning is crucial to prevent early peaking and burnout.

PART 10
WOMEN'S RUNNING

37

THE EARLY YEARS

Women's running has evolved from being nonexistent to its current position as a major athletic and social movement. The numbers prove it. Of the nearly 10.5 million Americans who ran regularly in 2002, 44.2 percent of them were female, according to the National Sporting Goods Association (NSGA), and among racers, USATF says the numbers come in at 50 percent female.

The women's running movement continues to gain dramatic momentum. NYRR has seen a rise in female membership every year, and women currently make up 45 percent of all members. NYRR is also still seeing an increase of women running shorter distances, even surpassing the numbers of men at races of four miles to 5K. And from zero women finishers in the first New York City Marathon in 1970, women today make up 32 percent of the field (over 11,000 women ran the New York Marathon in 2003).

NYRR is a worldwide leader in promoting women's distance running. NYRR conducts several nationally and internationally prominent women's road races, including the New York Mini 10K and the Race for the Cure (to promote breast cancer research and education), and other women's races at a variety of distances. The Mini, for a number of years broadcast on network television, is the longest-running all-women's race in the country and the site of several world bests for 10K on the roads.

In addition to the largest women's marathon field in the world, NYRR events have set the stage for dramatic achievements among women runners, including world best times for the 10K, and 10 miles and landmark sub-3:00 and sub-2:30 times in the marathon.

The impact of women's running is felt off the roads as well and is now a part of the consciousness of changing times. Prominent women runners such as Nina Kuscsik, Kathrine Switzer, and Grete Waitz have been instrumental in effecting athletic and social change. After winning the 1979 New York City Marathon, Grete Waitz was the subject of a *New York Times* editorial calling for equality in women's running. The fact that she made the editorial as well as the sports pages illustrated the social significance of her achievements.

> When I started running in the 1960s, I never saw a woman any-
> where. Now, it's understood women can do anything. We are see-
> ing a tremendous increase of women participating in our events
> and joining New York Road Runners. The age bracket in this in-
> crease is 20–30. I think it's because women are getting married
> later, postponing childbirth, and they have careers. They know
> they need to take care of themselves, and they're doing it. Per-
> haps it's also because since Title IX, more women have partici-
> pated in sports in high school and college. Men, on the other
> hand—and this is my personal view—think they're immortal.
> From 20 to 30 they don't do anything, then they get a paunch
> and realize: I better start taking care of myself. So, we get more
> men at the 30- to 40-year-old age group participating.
> —*Allan Steinfeld*

WHERE (AND WHEN) IT ALL BEGAN

By 1971, the second year of the New York City Marathon, women were
making dramatic inroads into the male-dominated world of road running.
That year the first two women to finish the race, Beth Bonner and Nina
Kuscsik, also became the fastest women in the world and the first to break
three hours. (In the 1979 New York City Marathon, Grete Waitz became the
first woman in the world to break 2:30.) In 1971 however, women were not
officially permitted to compete in distance races with men. The irony, and
the disparity, became too great. It motivated Fred Lebow, Kathrine Switzer,
Nina Kuscsik, and others to launch a women-only race. Lebow and company
recruited in schools, bars, and even among Playboy bunnies. The first
Women's Mini Marathon (named for the miniskirt, which was then in
vogue) drew 78 women—a huge turnout for the time. The Playboy bunnies
didn't run the distance, but they generated much-desired publicity. Con-
troversial—and sexist—as this might seem now, Fred Lebow understood
even then the need for media exposure to advance the sport. And if the
bunnies were an insult, real injury was added when, at a press conference
for the event, Kuscsik and Switzer were asked by the press to pose with
their dresses hiked up over their knees. They refused. Today, the New York
Mini 10K, a world-renowned event, draws an international field and has
been broadcast on network television. Bunnies and miniskirts have long
been superseded by gripping athletic competition.

The NYRRC was the first organization to allow women to participate legally in a marathon. But it didn't happen easily, or with even a fraction of the numbers of participants we have today. Once a few women showed the world what they could do, women's running really caught on.

In the early 1970s, Johnson's Wax made a women's shaving cream called Crazylegs®. The company telephoned me, wanting to promote its product with a women's marathon. "But there are only two women who run the marathon!" I explained to them.

"How about a Mini Marathon?" I suggested. The word *mini* was in vogue then. But even with the distance shortened to six miles (it later became 10K, 6.2 miles), it took every bit of creative energy we could muster just to recruit 78 entrants in the first Crazylegs Mini Marathon. Kathrine Switzer and I went to bars— the only places we knew to meet women—and handed out race fliers.

When Bonne Bell got involved in the Mini in 1974, the event grew dramatically. It went from hundreds to thousands. To this day, the question comes up: How can we get thousands of women to run this race when only hundreds come out for a mixed race at the same distance? I think it's because for many women there is a special camaraderie that is part of the Mini. It is their exclusive event. They feel it is their showcase, and rightfully so.

At the time we first held the Women's Mini Marathon, women in sports, including running, were not accepted—that meant socially, as well as politically—by the governing body of the sport. Today women's running is both socially and commercially viable. Major sponsors support the Mini. Partly as a result of women's mass participation in road races like the Mini, the first women's Olympic marathon took place in the 1984 Games.

—Fred Lebow

In 1972, the six women in the New York City Marathon, led by Nina Kuscsik, staged a sit-down strike, protesting a ruling by the Amateur Athletic Union (AAU), the governing body of the sport, that required their race to begin ten minutes before the men's. When the ten minutes elapsed, the women got up and ran with the men. The AAU added ten minutes to their finishing times. Kuscsik launched a lawsuit against the AAU. Simultaneous starts for men and women soon became legal. In addition, the Trails End Marathon in Oregon also filed suit against the AAU for requiring that women, but not men, have a physical exam before running that race.

Back in 1967, Kathrine Switzer symbolically heightened the struggle for women's equality, both as athletes and as human beings. Switzer signed up for the Boston Marathon as K.V. Switzer, got a number, and attempted to run—until she encountered race official Jock Semple, who tried to pull her off the course. Switzer went on to finish that race, win the New York City Marathon, and make a career in women's running and sports.

I began running when I was 13 as part of an effort to make the school field hockey team. The truth is, I wanted to be a cheerleader, but my parents wouldn't stand for it. My father told me, "Life is to participate, not to spectate." He suggested I play field hockey, and military man that he was, he recommended I get in shape by running. I began doing one mile a day, every day.

Immediately, I learned a basic rule of this sport—and of any endeavor—some days are good, some bad. I had to persevere.

Running became my secret weapon. I breezed through team practices with abundant energy. I reasoned that if one mile was good, three miles must be better. Eventually I became disappointed with team sports and decided to quit and focus on being a runner. When a coach at Lynchburg College saw me circling the track, he asked if I would serve as a last-minute substitute for a male runner on the team. I caused pandemonium at the small Virginia school . . . a prelude to the incident with which I will forever be associated.

I had heard of the Boston Marathon; Roberta Gibb had run it. With the help of coach and friend Arnie Briggs, who had run the race 16 times, I prepared myself by training ten miles a day, and even once ran 31 miles in practice to convince a then-skeptical Arnie that "even though I was a woman," I could go the 26.2 miles. To this day, the event is prominent in my mind—the shock and fear when race official Jock Semple attempted to pull me off . . . the course and my boyfriend fending him off. Fortunately, I was able to complete the race.

—*Kathrine Switzer*

Kathrine helped organize the first Mini in 1972 and ran in it and several others, always finishing among the top five or ten. She went on to win the

New York City Marathon in 1974 by the widest margin of any victor (man or woman) in the history of the race—27 minutes, 14 seconds.

"I remember that Kathy ran that race in a tennis skirt, and that she was part of the first television coverage ever broadcast of the New York City Marathon," said Fred Lebow. After winning the New York City Marathon, Kathrine established herself as a spokesperson and TV commentator for running. In 1977, she created and headed the Avon International Running Circuit.

In 1978, the first Avon Marathon, with 124 women, was held in Atlanta. By the end of the circuit in 1985, events had been conducted in 27 countries with over one million women. In one race alone, a 1983 event in São Paulo, Brazil, 11,000 women ran. At that point it was the largest women's race ever held. Today, Avon Running continues in 12 countries and has more than a million participants.

"Particularly in non-Western countries, the Avon races went against local culture, where people (mostly men) thought women competing in a running event was not deemed socially acceptable. But women did participate—and with great joy," says Switzer.

"Avon's involvement in organizing events with so many foreign federations gave us the power to finally negotiate with the International Olympic Committee (IOC) and the International Amateur Athletic Federation to open running events to women competitors," Switzer says. "I think the Olympic women's marathon would eventually have happened, but I believe it was hastened by the Avon women's running circuit."

The Avon Marathon in London in 1980 fulfilled all the Olympic requirements set by the IOC for inclusion of an event in the Olympic Games at the time. Those requirements specified that a sport be practiced in 25 countries and on three continents. In this one race, 27 countries and five continents were represented. This event, which became the prototype for the London Marathon, was ground-breaking in yet another way. It was the first time in history that the streets of London were closed for a sporting event. Switzer recalls the race with satisfaction: "When I watched the women running across Westminster Bridge, and realized the London streets were closed to accommodate them, I knew we were going to see the first women's Olympic marathon in 1984."

Over the years, Kathrine Switzer has also worked closely with NYRR. "After all," she says, "the women's running movement would never have happened without Fred Lebow. The Boston Marathon was certainly a catalyst, but the truth is, the core of the women's running movement was based in New York, with the initiative and support of NYRR."

In 1971, Kathrine Switzer collaborated with Lebow and Nina Kuscsik to make women's running "official." They dispelled the myths that prevented women from taking up the challenge—that running would, as Switzer says, cause overly muscular legs, body hair growth, and even infertility!

Like Switzer, Nina Kuscsik ran against the odds in her pursuit of the sport. "My first marathon was Boston in 1969," she explains. "I entered just like the other 'illegal' women at that time by jumping out of the bushes near the start at the last minute and by hiding among the men runners. I used to fantasize about a legion of women runners in pink T-shirts bearing the slogan 'Long Island Garden Club.' Women could and should be runners and still be able to drink tea at the Garden Club."

In the early 1970s, with the help and encouragement of Vince Chiappetta and Aldo Scandurra, Kuscsik got involved by reading the running rule books and attending AAU meetings. "This was the beginning of the era of NOW (National Organization for Women) and women's consciousness-raising," she explains. "For me, it was the beginning of a 20-year-long fight to rewrite the rules of running."

> I think of the New York Mini 10K more as a celebration than as a race, though I always run hard. It's so inspiring being on the starting line in New York City with such a talented group of women runners. Everyone there is having a wonderful time. When you get that many women on the line, the boys better watch out!
>
> *—Deena Kastor*

In 1972, Kuscsik helped organize the sit-down strike at the New York City Marathon. All the runners, including men, supported the protest, and signed a petition on the starting line arguing for a common start. There were two victories that day: Kuscsik's winning time of 3:08:42 and an announcement from the parks commissioner in New York City saying that races from then on would be started with the command "Ladies and gentlemen, on your marks."

A major turning point for women's running was in 1976, when the men's and women's national championships were combined for the first time.

In the 1980s, runners like Grete Waitz, Joan Samuelson, and Ingrid Kristiansen brought the women's marathon to another level, running times in the mid-2:30s to mid-2:20s. Relates Waitz, "From the time I ran my first marathon (a world record 2:32), in three years the world best improved by seven minutes, when I ran 2:25." In a sport in which improvement of even seconds is remarkable, seven minutes is a revolution. "It was because of the type of training we did," Waitz concludes. "Our times broke barriers for a lot of women. They started to train more, and train harder." Social commentators in Norway have concluded that Waitz's performances, combined with the feminist movement, created change not only in sports, but in all other aspects of life.

In the 1990s, women's world record–setting times remained fairly static, but a handful of women managed to run sub-2:20, and a new influx of talented women from Africa and Asian countries such as China and Japan made the competition more international (e.g., the top three finishers in the 2003 World Championships marathon were an African, followed by two Japanese). By the early 2000s, the big breakthrough came with performances by Great Britain's Paula Radcliffe. Radcliffe's world record marathon runs (the last being 2:15:25 in the London Marathon in 2003) are times that very few believed possible before she ran them.

There are so many levels to the development of women's running. In those early days, women got together maybe to play bridge, but they didn't get together and talk about their feelings or their problems. Now this is commonly done, but it wasn't back then. But running was a special opportunity to do that. Just as it is today, it was a way of getting together. You had miles to go, and you could talk. You made special friendships over the miles.

I remember running a 50-mile race in 1977 and thinking that if I had a different girlfriend to escort me on a bike for those 9.5-mile loops, it would be like having separate telephone conversations with friends. Actually, it was a good thing I didn't try that, as I needed my concentration to run an American record and I didn't want to be accused of being paced!

—Nina Kuscsik

Are women runners more equal with men now? "Yes," says Kuscsik, "but men have had to come a long way, too. In the early days, male runners were simply considered weird. So the sport didn't just open up for women, it also changed for all runners."

But women have come to the sport and train for the sport in different ways than men. For instance, Nina Kuscsik believes the aerobic dance movement of the early 1970s indirectly promoted jogging to improve appearance, thus legitimizing women's running. More directly, the first Women's Mini Marathon and the first women's marathon, the Avon Marathon in Atlanta in 1978, offered women runners from all corners of the earth their own special events. And, of course, money has changed the sport, Kuscsik points out. Women—albeit very few—can actually earn a living by running. And for the casual runner, the exposure of top women runners has placed running among legitimate female pastimes—perhaps like bridge and mah-jongg for generations before.

"There are so many reasons why people run," says Kuscsik. "My advice is to go into it with an open mind. You go to school to get an education, but you can end up getting more of an education from the people you meet than the books you read. The same is true in running. There is untold fulfillment to be gained from the sport, even beyond the exercise angle."

THE FUTURE LOOKS BRIGHT

According to the Women's Sports Foundation, in 1971, one in 27 girls participated in high school sports. Today, that figure is one in 2.5, a more than 800 percent increase. The number of female athletes grew by 40 percent on high school varsity teams in the 1990s, while boys' participation went up only 12.5 percent during the same time. According to the Sporting Goods Manufacturers Association (SGMA), in 2000, 4.3 million females ages six or older jogged or ran.

38

WOMEN'S HEALTH

WOMEN'S HEALTH ISSUES AND CONCERNS

Based on personal and professional experience, Dr. Mona Shangold offers the following information on the variety of health issues and concerns of women runners.

Exercise is even more important for women than for men. This fact runs contrary to the social conditioning women received long ago—the same conditioning many are still receiving today not only in developing countries, but also in the United States. Fortunately, many girls and women have accepted the scientific evidence that exercise is positive. As a result, more women are exercising today than ever before, and the number of exercising women is increasing steadily. The girls who were once labeled, unflatteringly, "tomboy" are now addressed with the complimentary term "athlete."

Although more women are exercising now than ever before, an even greater number should be exercising. Regular exercise decreases susceptibility to osteoporosis and obesity, two conditions that are more common among women than among men. Both aerobic and resistance exercise strengthen bones, and both types also help to prevent fat accumulation. Aerobic activities include running, brisk walking, biking, and swimming. Resistance activities include weight training with free weights or machines. All women should practice both regularly.

Osteoporosis

As humans age, muscles and bones shrink and weaken. This change occurs in both men and women, but the consequences are more serious in women. At any age, the average woman has thinner and weaker bones and smaller and weaker muscles compared with the average man. Losing bone density puts many women into the danger zone in which bones break easily. Although both men and women lose bone with aging, bone loss is greatly accelerated after menopause, when women lose the supply of estrogen that previously protected their bones. Exercise helps to strengthen bones, yet it is not as effective as estrogen. (That is why the bones of athletes shrink and weaken if they stop menstruating at any age, as will be discussed later.)

STEP OFF THE TREADMILL FOR BONE BUILDING

Bone strength, particularly important for women to ward off osteoporosis, is stimulated by impact activities, such as running. For strengthening bones, running outdoors is superior to treadmill running. According to a 2003 study from Hadassah University Hospital in Jerusalem, that's because your feet hit the ground harder outside due to various surfaces and terrains, and this stimulates bone growth.

Weight Gain

Humans get fatter with age, and exercise is the best way to minimize a growing girth. Fat accumulates for several reasons, but mainly because the metabolism slows down. Resting metabolism depends on muscle tissue mass. Aerobic and resistance exercise add and strengthen muscles, speeding up resting metabolism and total metabolism. As a result, more calories are burned, even while sleeping! Because the average woman has less muscle tissue than the average man, and because she usually does less to maintain her muscles, she has a more dramatic decline in her metabolism and adds fat with increasing ease. Most women don't realize that adding muscle will both speed the metabolism and make it easier to do routine chores (e.g., carrying groceries, packages, or luggage).

Women runners are at a definite advantage over their sedentary counterparts. The average sedentary woman in her 30s has 33 percent body fat; in her 60s, 42 percent. By contrast, women runners in their 40s average 22 percent body fat, while those in their 60s average only 26 percent.

Menstrual Irregularity and Amenorrhea (Absence of Menstruation)

Any woman who bleeds more often than every 23 days or less often than every 35 days needs to be evaluated and probably treated for menstrual irregularity. Menstrual irregularity and amenorrhea are higher among women athletes than among the general female population for various reasons, including weight loss, fat loss, alterations in diet, nutritional inadequacy, physical or emotional stress, and changes in hormonal balance. Despite the higher prevalence of menstrual dysfunction in athletes, however, it is dan-

When I entered my first race, the 1977 New York City Marathon, I had a chance to chat with a lot of women runners at the starting area. Many were discussing gynecologic problems that had developed during training. When I revealed that I was a gynecologist, I was overwhelmed with questions about personal problems. I realized that very little was known or discussed about gynecologic problems in runners. Very few doctors had written about these issues prior to that time, and very few women were discussing such problems. The small numbers of women who had been exercising before that time had aroused relatively little interest and promoted few scientific investigations.

I devoted most of my fellowship in reproductive endocrinology to studying the effects of exercise on reproductive function. Some of my studies included questionnaires I distributed to women entering the 1979 New York City Marathon and measurements of hormone concentrations in women runners. (Although I had run the New York City Marathon in 1977 and 1978, the work connected with my study prevented me from entering in 1979.) We were the first to report that luteal phase deficiency, a condition associated with infertility, is more common among runners than among the general population.

Doing more research and speaking to more women stimulated further interest and other questions to answer. Thus, I embarked upon a career in a new field that has grown appreciably since then—sports gynecology. Several hundred doctors now belong to the Sports Gynecology Society of the American College of Obstetricians and Gynecologists, all of whom provide gynecologic care to women who exercise and encourage sedentary women to exercise.

—Mona Shangold, M.D.

gerous to assume that exercise is the culprit. Athletes develop the same conditions that cause menstrual dysfunction in nonathletes, and some of these are serious. Although most athletes with irregular periods or amenorrhea do not have serious medical conditions, a thorough evaluation, including blood tests, is needed to determine whether the cause is serious.

After completion of this evaluation, *all* who have the problem more than a few months (four to six months) should be treated with hormones to replace what their bodies are not making. Of course, they should continue to exercise.

Although many athletes seem to have an aversion to taking hormones, women who are deficient in estrogen have been found to lose bone mass at an increased rate and may lose a significant amount of bone when they have this condition. For this reason, treatment is recommended before six months have passed. Any athlete who has this condition for three years or longer will have lost more than she can regain.

Delay of Menarche

Athletes tend to experience menarche (the first menstrual period) at a later age than sedentary girls. Delayed menarche isn't harmful unless it occurs after age 18. Any girl who hasn't begun to menstruate by the age of 16 should be evaluated and possibly treated. Treatment should definitely be started by the age of 18 if menstruation hasn't started by that time. Although exercise and delayed menarche are related, it isn't clear which is the cause and which is the effect. It is likely that heavy exercise delays menarche and that delayed menarche improves athletic success.

Pregnancy

Much has been made over the years of a woman's ability to continue running—even training—during pregnancy. It began nearly two decades ago with the highly visible case of Ingrid Kristiansen, who, not realizing she was pregnant, continued to train and race for the first five months of her first pregnancy. She even ran a marathon. Kristiansen later claimed she never would have done so if she had known she was pregnant.

Once upon a time, pregnant women were advised to avoid exercise. It is now known that this recommendation was based on fear and lack of data. It has been shown that it is safe to continue exercising throughout pregnancy as long as the pregnancy is normal and uncomplicated.

In 2000, the American College of Obstetricians and Gynecologists (ACOG) issued this statement: ". . . (P)articipation in regular weight-bearing exercise has been shown to improve maternal fitness, restrict weight gain without compromising fetal growth, and hasten postpartum recovery. In addition, the psychological benefits of exercise are undeniable, and should be nurtured by all who care for pregnant women."

The most recent ACOG guidelines, published in January 2002, are slightly less enthusiastic but still endorse exercise: "Recreational and competitive athletes with uncomplicated pregnancies can stay active during pregnancy while modifying their usual exercise routines as medically indicated." As always, consultation with a medical professional is recommended.

Kristiansen made a quick return to top form shortly after giving birth. From world record holders, such as Kristiansen, to average runners, scores of women have successfully run and exercised during pregnancy.

These women illustrate the results of one study that suggests that physically fit women may actually be able to carry out the added work load of pregnancy, labor, and delivery with greater ease to both themselves and their fetuses than sedentary women.

Below are important considerations for pregnant exercisers.

1. **Blood distribution.** Although as yet unproven, blood is less likely to be diverted away from the fetus when exercise is kept at low intensity. Thus, women planning to exercise during pregnancy should attain a high level of fitness prior to becoming pregnant, and should remain fit throughout the pregnancy because exertion is relatively easier for a fit woman. Intense training should not begin for the first time during pregnancy. Since high-intensity exercise is more likely to divert blood flow from the pregnant uterus, it is safest to avoid intense exertion (like speedwork). A proper cool-down after exercise is also important, and safer than stopping abruptly. This will help to maintain adequate blood flow to the baby during this risky time.

2. **Temperature.** In the absence of definitive data, it is wisest for pregnant women to avoid excessive heat accumulation during exercise. High temperatures have been shown to be harmful to the

My philosophy is based on two basic truths about exercise and pregnancy. The first is that we are all an experiment of one. It hasn't been long that pregnancy has been considered a healthy condition and not an illness during which one should remain inactive. And it hasn't been long that a generation of athletic women has been testing this new lifestyle during pregnancy. The second truth is that you should listen to your body with new and more rigorous intensity. Fatigue and pain mean different things now. They may come from hormonal changes, or muscles and tendons that you never knew existed before. And you're a different person in other obvious physical ways—with a belly growing in front of you. Remember that for nine months, your body is not your own. You have given it to someone else.

You have spent a good many years teaching yourself the discipline of pushing through pain and discomfort to achieve your athletic goals. Now you have to reverse that thinking. Being disciplined during pregnancy isn't pushing through pain and fatigue, but forcing yourself to stop, do less, and rest.

Some people feel good running up to the day of delivery, and others, like me, reach a point where it doesn't feel right. That doesn't mean to stop exercising. For instance, I combined swimming, race walking, stationary cycling, and light weightlifting, alternatives I had prepared for well in advance.

Gestation takes nine months, but childrearing is lifelong. One of the unexpected pleasures of my children's development has been their identification with sports and fitness. From a very early age, they understood that when Mom and Dad were out, they were "running." When they saw pictures of runners, they would say, "Mommy" or "Daddy." And when they began to play and run, as all children do, and I played and ran along with them, I realized the legacy I wanted to give to them. It wasn't necessarily to become runners (in fact, they chose soccer), but to embody an appreciation of being physically active, and all of the benefits and joy that come with it. And it is this message I hope is conveyed: that in striving to be fit and strong on the outside, we also strive to be fit and strong on the inside—of heart, soul, and mind.

—Gloria Averbuch

fetus, principally in animals, but probably in humans, too. Keeping a close watch on body temperature is particularly important for fetal development during the first trimester. Heat accumulation can be avoided by such measures as exercising at cooler times of day, exercising for shorter durations in each session, wearing lighter clothing, and maintaining adequate hydration. A pregnant woman should exercise at a comfortable intensity, based on perceived exertion and disregarding heart rate. Check rectal temperature immediately at the end of exercise. It should be 101°F, or less. The maximum safe temperature limit has not yet been determined.

3. **Nutrition.** Pregnant women who continue to exercise must provide enough calories and nutrients for themselves, their exercise, and their pregnancy. Pregnant women require more protein, more calories, and more of many vitamins and minerals than nonpregnant women; however, only thiamine, niacin, riboflavin, and pantothenic acid are needed in higher quantities because of exercise. A balanced diet supplying sufficient calories will provide enough of these vitamins and minerals. All pregnant women need more calcium, more iron, and higher amounts of many vitamins than they do when not pregnant. Most of them will benefit from prenatal vitamin supplements, as well as additional calcium and iron supplements to meet these needs. It is also important for pregnant exercisers to drink extra fluid to replace losses and to prevent excess heat accumulation.

Although most obstetricians usually advise pregnant women to gain 30 to 35 pounds, they do not know whether this recommendation is appropriate for exercisers. Until more precise recommendations are established, this amount seems reasonable. No one knows if pregnant exercisers should gain more, less, or the same amount as sedentary pregnant women. The amount a woman should gain probably depends on many factors, including the change in her exercise habits, and when, during pregnancy, this change takes place. Women who stop exercising during pregnancy will gain more weight and have heavier babies than they would have if they had continued exercising throughout pregnancy.

Hunger is not always a good guide because pregnancy may cause reduced appetite. Pregnant exercisers should eat more than they ate prepregnancy. Consultation with a nutritionist and an obstetrician is a good idea.

It is reasonable for pregnant women to continue exercising in their customary aerobic sports at the same *perceived* level of exertion practiced prior to pregnancy. This will require a slower pace and perhaps a shorter session, since the pregnant woman is doing more work merely by being pregnant. If she exercises at her normal pace with the added weight of pregnancy, she will be doing even more work.

According to *Running & FitNews,* one study showed that calcium absorption from kale is higher than that from milk. Other calcium-rich vegetables include broccoli, collard greens, mustard greens, and turnip greens. Other nondairy sources of calcium are tofu, canned salmon and sardines with the bones. Although dietary calcium is preferable to supplements, Tums® is also a source, as is calcium-enriched orange juice.

If you're taking your calcium and iron supplements at the same time (or within about one hour of each other), you could be reducing the absorption of the iron. Take calcium before bedtime, or take half the dose between breakfast and lunch and the rest before you go to bed.

Iron is best absorbed when taken on an empty stomach along with vitamin C, for example from orange juice. Many people, however, experience stomach pain when they take iron supplements on an empty stomach. They are often advised to take iron with their meals.

If you're a woman who can't stand the cold, you may not be getting enough iron. A woman's ability to regulate her body temperature may depend on the amount of iron in her diet. This is the conclusion of a Department of Agriculture study quoted in *Environmental Nutrition.* The effect of iron depletion on temperature regulation occurs before iron deficiency and anemia are diagnosed. Six women were tested in a temperature-regulated chamber, a cool 64°F, before and after iron supplementation. It was found that before supplementation, the women's internal temperature and external skin temperature were much lower than when tested after supplementation.

It appears safe to initiate an aerobic exercise program during pregnancy. Walking is an excellent choice for most women who were not regular exercisers before pregnancy. After giving birth, a woman can probably resume exercising as soon as it can be done without pain. After a vaginal delivery, this may be as soon as one to three days for light exercise and five to seven days for heavy exercise. After a cesarean delivery, this may be as soon as seven to ten days for light exercise and 21 days for heavy exercise.

Weight training may safely be practiced by all pregnant women with normal, uncomplicated pregnancies, even if they have not previously done it; however, no scientific studies have proved that it is safe or beneficial during pregnancy. The gains in muscle and bone strength from weight training

Carol Howe had an early taste of running fame. By her junior year in high school, the native Canadian was a silver medalist in the 3000 meters at the Pan American Junior Games. But retirement followed at age 20.

Fast forward to age 37, and Howe, now married and with a family and residing in Summit, New Jersey, is on top of the running world again. She was the 2000 NYRR Runner of the Year and in only her second marathon, the 2003 Grandma's Marathon in Minnesota, she ran a personal best time of 2:34:29. She hopes to lower that time even further, and thus gain a spot on the 2004 Canadian Olympic team.

Howe is the mother of two daughters. Seven-year-old Marika was born during her mother's break from running (although she did bike and swim during that pregnancy), but two-year-old Elsalene has already put in a lot of mileage with her mom. That's because Howe ran every day of her second pregnancy. As she puts it, "I exercised because I knew I'd probably return to competition, and I wanted to stay fit enough to expedite getting back into shape."

Howe ran right up until the morning she gave birth, cutting back gradually in distance and pace, until at the end, she averaged only 11 minutes a mile, very pedestrian for a 6–7-minute-per-mile distance runner. "I was very in tune with my body," she stresses. "I wore a heart rate monitor every day, and never went over my limit. I knew my exercise wasn't for quality, and I'd rather be safe than sorry."

If you want to stay active during pregnancy, Howe offers the following tips based on her experience:

- Consult with your doctor. Howe's doctor advised her regarding her heart rate level during training. And make sure you find the right doctor for you. While one was very supportive of her exercise routine, another simply told her: no running.
- Watch your diet. Make sure you eat and drink enough. Howe prides herself on having eaten well while pregnant: "Excellent, plentiful, well-balanced meals—like a marathoner's diet," she says.
- Warm up and cool down carefully. "You shouldn't just stop cold after running. I didn't just hop off the treadmill. I went from running to walking to get my heart rate down before I stopped moving," says Howe.
- Watch your step. Howe restricted her running to a treadmill as her pregnancy progressed, because her equilib-

(continued)

rium and balance had changed, and she didn't want to risk a fall running in the streets, especially challenging since she lives in a hilly area.

- Get back slowly. "I probably tried to come back a little too quickly," says Howe, who, feeling good, started running ten days after giving birth and ended up with hamstring problems. She suggests you consult a chiropractor or other medical professional postpartum to check your alignment and readiness to run, which in retrospect she says she should have done.

may offer many benefits. In addition to bone strength, stronger muscles will suffer less from the strain of the added weight of pregnancy and the altered center of gravity, theoretically decreasing the risk of low back pain and other types of muscular aches and pains. There is no evidence that weight training, when practiced with proper form, is dangerous for pregnant women. In fact, some women runners have chosen to concentrate on weight training while pregnant, preferring to maintain muscle tone, which cannot be achieved as

I ran throughout most of my pregnancy. During the second trimester (the fourth, fifth, and sixth months), running caused uterine contractions that began earlier in each run as the pregnancy advanced. By the end of the sixth month, I stopped running altogether, partly because dressing for winter running took longer than the duration of each running session that was interrupted by contractions, and mainly because I didn't know whether the contractions were significant or dangerous. (I wanted a healthy child and wasn't willing to do anything that might jeopardize my chance of having one.) In retrospect, the contractions probably were not of significance, but I had no way to know that at the time. My son was born by cesarean delivery, primarily because of his large size (nine pounds at birth). Fortunately, he was and has continued to be very healthy. I resumed lifting weights eight days after his birth and resumed running ten days after his birth.

—*Mona Shangold, M.D.*

> You gain all kinds of strengths with motherhood. I lost mental strength when motherhood was new to me. Now that strength is back. I'm always on a fine line, trying to balance my career with my responsibilities as a mother. But I know what I want in the end. Jimmy Connors once said he wishes his children could have seen him in his prime. I hope my children remember me being in my prime as a mother, not as a runner.
>
> —*Joan Samuelson*

well with the light amount of running done during pregnancy. Some also find it more comfortable during pregnancy than running. Another benefit is variety. Pregnancy may be a good time for a woman runner to experiment with cross training, and weight training falls into that category.

Breast Protection

Smaller-breasted women may prefer to run without a bra, while other women may prefer to exercise with a bra that provides good support. The breast is subject to considerable motion during vigorous exercise, and although uncomfortable, this movement is not harmful to women with large breasts.

Tips for Running and Breastfeeding

- Be sure to get medical approval from your physician before you begin to run after your baby's birth.
- Wear a supportive bra that fits well.
- Breastfeed your baby before you run.
- Watch your weight loss. If you are losing more than one pound a week, add nutritious snacks in between meals.
- Eat healthy, well-balanced meals and drink according to thirst.

Dysmenorrhea

Menstrual cramps can be a bother to an athlete, interfering significantly with performance; however, these days, and in most cases, disabling pain is totally preventable. Several medications are available, by prescription and over the counter, but aspirin and ibuprofen should never be taken together. Ibuprofen is more effective for this pain than aspirin. For severe pain, a woman should try ibuprofen first. If this does not alleviate the pain, she may want to see her gynecologist for a prescription, such as Anaprox®. Medication is usually required for only one or two days (at the onset of menstruation). Some women experience less dysmenorrhea during exercise, and some report less since they have been training regularly. Explanations for this remain mostly speculative.

Premenstrual Syndrome (PMS)

In one study, increased exercise was shown to decrease PMS, with greatest improvement noted in breast soreness and fluid retention. Athletes who are significantly inconvenienced may benefit from consulting a gynecologist for evaluation and treatment. Several drugs have been shown to be effective for this condition, but all of them have side effects.

Menopause

Many runners believe that running will protect them from the undesirable effects of aging and menopause. Although regular exercise can retard several aspects of the aging process, it cannot compensate for the estrogen deficiency that follows menopause.

Menopause—a woman's final menstrual period—occurs when the ovaries run out of functioning eggs. For approximately five years before her last period and about five years afterward, she passes through the *climacteric,* a time when her hormone levels are different from the levels before and after. During this transition time, many women have bothersome hot flashes. Estrogen is the most effective way to treat hot flushes. Exercise has no effect on these symptoms.

After menopause, a woman's estrogen levels are lower than they were during her reproductive years. This reduced estrogen level accelerates bone loss, the most serious problem that follows menopause. Although running has a beneficial effect on bone density, it is not beneficial enough to compensate for an estrogen deficiency—in both young amenorrheic athletes and in older menopausal women. Many studies have shown that athletes with low estrogen levels lose bone density at any age, and the bone loss is proportional to the duration of estrogen deficiency. Women nearing

When it comes to women and exercise, sports medicine specialists generally focus their concern on amenorrhea. Needless to say, there's another group of female athletes who also deserve special attention—the athletes who do menstruate regularly. Approximately 30 percent of these women suffer from PMS (premenstrual syndrome) and experience some of the 19 identified PMS symptoms.

Fatigue, hunger, and intense cravings for chocolates and carbohydrates in any form are very common PMS symptoms. Many women can tell the time of the month by their low energy levels and wild eating habits. Premenstrually, they may boost themselves up by devouring bagfuls of candy and dozens of cookies, in addition to bran muffins, bread, and bagels. A woman's dietary intake can certainly vary throughout the month!

In *Physiology and Behavior,* Stephanie Dalvit-McPhillips verified this pattern, reporting that a complex interplay of hormonal changes seems to influence food choices. Premenstrually, high levels of estrogen may be linked with carbohydrate cravings that result in greater carbohydrate consumption. Her subjects ate about 500 more calories per day during the ten premenstrual days, as compared to the ten days postmenstrual—with most of the calories derived from carbohydrate foods.

Women may crave carbohydrates not only because of hormonal fluctuations, but also because they are physiologically hungrier. Hunger tends to create sweet cravings. Premenstrually, a woman's metabolic rate may increase by 200 to 500 calories—the equivalent of an additional meal! Most women athletes, however—being very weight-conscious—try to cut back on calories, since they are feeling fat from premenstrual bloat and water weight gain. The result is double deprivation (higher caloric needs plus restricted caloric intake), and the craving for sweets becomes overwhelming.

To control the premenstrual cravings, a woman can experiment with adding more carbohydrate calories at breakfast and lunch. For example, by eating an additional bran muffin at breakfast, she'll curb the nagging hunger that she'd otherwise resolve with candy that afternoon. She'll abate the PMS sugar splurges as well as other symptoms, such as irritability, headache, fatigue, depression, and mood swings. She'll have more energy for exercise and better enjoy her training buddies, rather than being cranky with them.

—*Nancy Clark, M.S., R.D.*

menopause should discuss having their bone density measured with their physician. Those with low bone density should discuss this with a doctor and should consider treatment. Commonly prescribed are Actonel®, Fosamex®, Evista®, or Forteo®.

Low levels of estrogen also cause many menopausal women to experience vaginal dryness. Some may have no symptoms, but others are greatly bothered by vaginal irritation, burning during urination, and/or pain during intercourse. Estrogen therapy is the most effective treatment for this problem. Again, exercise has no proven effect.

In a study published in the September 10, 2003, issue of the *Journal of the American Medical Association,* women who engaged in regular strenuous physical activity at age 35 had a 14 percent decreased risk of breast cancer. *JAMA* reported similar findings for strenuous physical activity at ages 18 and 50. Women who engaged in the equivalent of 1.25 to 2.5 hours per week of brisk walking had an 18 percent decrease, as compared with inactive women. There was a slightly greater reduction in risk for women who walked briskly for ten hours a week or more. These data suggest that increased physical activity is associated with reduced risk for breast cancer in postmenopausal women, that longer duration provides most benefit, and that such activity need not be strenuous.

Two other menopausal problems may receive benefit from both exercise and estrogen: cardiovascular disease and depression. After menopause, women have a higher risk of heart disease (compared to their risk before menopause), partly due to estrogen deficiency and partly due to the aging process and the cumulative effects of an adverse lifestyle. Because most runners probably have a reduced risk of heart disease compared with sedentary women of the same age, they may be less in need of estrogen for this particular indication. As of 2003, recent studies have disproved the beneficial effects of estrogen therapy on heart disease risk. Studies reporting a higher risk of breast cancer among women treated with hormone replacement therapy (HRT) have raised serious concerns about the safety of HRT for many women.

Similarly, both estrogen and exercise may cause mood elevation in some women. In fact, some depressed runners may be treating themselves unknowingly. While some are no longer depressed because they run regularly, some who are depressed despite regular running may get additional benefit from estrogen. Anyone with suspected heart disease or suspected depression should consult a physician before considering exercise or estrogen as therapy.

Most women experiencing depression will benefit from specific antidepressant therapy and should discuss this with a physician. Questions about treatment for menopausal problems should also be discussed with a physician, and decisions about optimal therapy should be individualized after considering risks and benefits.

Nutrition

Although women athletes have nutritional needs similar to those of male athletes of the same size, they are more likely than men to require calcium and iron supplementation.

The average woman's diet is deficient in calcium. Women require at least 1,000 mg. of calcium daily; women deficient in estrogen (as reflected by amenorrhea or menopause) require at least 1,500 mg. of calcium daily. Inadequate dietary calcium hastens bone loss, which may progress to osteoporosis. Most women need supplementation to obtain the proper amount of calcium.

The average woman's diet is also deficient in iron. Since women lose iron in the process of menstruation and often ingest inadequate amounts in their diet, many women are iron-deficient. Iron deficiency can impair athletic performance, even in the absence of anemia. The blood test that detects anemia does not measure iron stores. The iron stores in one's liver, spleen, and bone marrow can be deficient (the adequacy of iron stores is assessed by measuring blood ferritin), even though a woman has a normal amount of iron in her red blood cells (detected by measuring hemoglobin or hematocrit). Because of the prevalence of iron deficiency among women, it is reasonable for women to take iron supplements.

The only nutrients athletes require in greater quantities than sedentary women are thiamine, niacin, riboflavin, and pantothenic acid. These requirements can usually be met from a balanced diet supplying enough calories.

PART 11
WALKING

39

WALKING FOR HEALTH, FITNESS, AND COMPETITION

Americans everywhere are beginning to realize that as Hippocrates, the father of medicine, once said, "Walking is man's best medicine." So says walking coach Howard "Jake" Jacobson, who for years conducted sold-out walking classes for New York Road Runners. Jacobson goes on to say that Hippocrates prescribed walking in ancient times, in an era when people went just about everywhere on foot. Today, some 70 million people have chosen the oldest and simplest form of exercise—walking—as their fitness activity.

Jacobson, coach to Olympians, is himself a world class age-group competitor in racewalking, which he began doing in 1957 during a successful running career. He introduced "healthwalking" to the nation in 1982. He has contributed the following advice on how to benefit from this common activity. Lon Wilson, Jacobson's protege, has taken over NYRR's healthwalking program since Jacobson's move to Florida. Wilson reviewed this chapter.

WHY WALK?

Why walk? Our bodies were primarily designed for walking, not for sitting or lying down or even running, contends Coach Jake. Because the walking stride involves more muscles, walking can improve muscle tone throughout the body—including the abdominals, thighs, buttocks, calves, arms, chest, and back—even more than running. It's also an excellent cardiovascular activity, and is virtually injury-free.

Walking is a convenient and versatile fitness activity. Walkers have become very inventive; they practice their activity anytime and anywhere. A good example is the popularity of mall walking. Many malls—perfect indoor facilities for walking—are opened for walkers during hours the stores are closed. Lately, other types of buildings have began to accommodate walkers.

WARMING UP BEFORE HEALTHWALKING

It's not just runners who need to warm up carefully before striding out. Just as you'd warm up a car engine on a cold day before driving, your body needs to be properly "warmed" if it's going to function at its best when you walk. This is especially true if you're out of shape. Because connective tissues become less elastic with inactivity, your chances of injury are greater. That's why it's important to stretch your muscle-tendon unit to increase your flexibility and reduce the risks of getting hurt before you begin each healthwalking workout. You can stop to stretch after a warmup walk of three to five minutes, or you can stretch after your entire workout. If you don't stretch mid-walk, you still need to start the walk at a comfortable clip before stepping up the pace.

HOW TO TURN A WALK INTO A HEALTHWALK

"I love to see people get out for a walk," says Coach Jake. "But they can enhance that casual walk and get a better workout using more muscles by learning to healthwalk," he adds. Among the many people he coaches, Jacobson also works with senior citizens through an organized program with a geriatrics center. He tells them, "If you feel good walking, just pick up the pace once in awhile. It will do you more good." Good walking is about positive attitude, he says. "The seniors walk like they mean it. It's beautiful to see."

Coach Jake coined the word *healthwalking,* a copy of the technique of racewalking. To get the full benefits of walking, it helps to put some form and effort into it. In other words, there's a method to turning a walk into a healthwalk. Have you ever noticed people trying to walk into the wind? They lean forward from the ankles, pressing their bodies and legs forward to keep moving. Their arms and legs pump in concert, with quick steps. The best way to accomplish fast walking in an efficient manner is to do what comes naturally—stand tall and stride forward. Reach out for the ground with your heel; plant your heel with a straight leg on an imaginary tightrope and walk with a purposeful stride, with your toes pointed straight forward.

The key to healthwalking is also in the arm carriage. Instead of your arms swinging at your sides as you walk (which actually slows your legs down), bend your arms to a right angle. If you would like to walk even faster, pump them forward and slightly across towards mid-chest. You'll be surprised at how fast you can walk! The opposite arm and leg work together. You are walking with your legs and sprinting with your arms. Feel the rhythm. Short strides and short arm swings work better than long ones, which causes a braking action to the stride.

Walk tall, with a good rhythm, by taking quick steps. The number of strides you take is more important to a good healthwalking pace than the length of each stride. You propel yourself forward by pushing off the toes of your back foot. Remember, brisk walking is an aerobic exercise. You'll get a better workout by breathing deeply and rhythmically during your workouts. Coordinate your breathing with your steps as follows:

Right leg–Left leg		Right leg–Left leg
I-N-H-A-L-E	and	E-X-H-A-L-E

BEGINNING HEALTHWALKERS' PROGRAM

If you're ready to start walking for the "health of it," you may want to begin with Coach Jake's workout below.

Week	Total Time in Minutes*
1. Walk on alternate days briskly	15 mins. to 25 mins.
2. Walk on alternate days briskly	20 mins. to 30 mins.
3. Walk daily, briskly	20 mins. to 30 mins.
4. Walk daily, briskly	25 mins. to 35 mins.
5. Walk daily, briskly	30 mins. to 40 mins.
6. Walk daily, briskly	2 miles or more for 40 mins.
7. Walk daily, briskly	2 1/2 miles or more for 45 mins.
8. Walk daily, briskly	3 miles or more for 52 mins.

* Total time = walk plus cool-down.
Warm up by walking at an easier pace for three to five minutes. Cool down similarly, finishing with five to ten minutes of stretching exercises, such as those prescribed in Chapter 7, Post-workout Stretching Program.

The weeks and months ahead are maintenance. You may gradually work your way up to healthwalking at a faster pace and for longer distances. Just remember, it is better to walk farther than it is to walk faster. It better trains the heart and burns fat.

RACEWALKING

Racewalking, an international and Olympic sport, is the activity from which coach Jacobson adapted his widely accepted practice of healthwalking. Says Coach Jake of his sport, "Racewalking a very viable sport. It is a grueling, physically challenging activity. The athletes at the top level are every bit as

WALK RIGHT

Lon Wilson, the current director of NYRR Healthwalking program, is also a former American masters record holder for the 50K walk, and has racewalked over 100 marathons. He shares the following advice.

Many people assume that the walking they do for transportation is equally good for fitness. This is not the case. There are many benefits of healthwalking over pedestrian walking. The mechanical inefficiency of pedestrian walking creates more wear and tear on the body. The stride of pedestrian walking prevents the muscles from ever reaching a relaxed state, and the long stride of pedestrian walking causes you to sit back on the hips, like you're walking uphill. Also, planting your leg as far in front of you as you can prevents a quicker pace. That's because it causes a braking action. In terms of exercise and fitness, pedestrian walking beats being sedentary, but it won't provide the maximum benefits.

Wilson also provides a tip for both walkers and runners: Concentrate on driving your elbows, as opposed to driving your arms. That focus will keep your arms from tightening, allowing them to remain relaxed and pumping efficiently.

fit as runners. Lab tests of their physiology measures—strength, endurance, maximum oxygen uptake, etc.—are all similar to the results of top marathoners." World class women racewalkers go under 45 minutes for 10K; the men cover the distance sub-42—just under seven minutes per mile. The sport of racewalking is governed by strict rules. These rules have been established by the national and international governing bodies of the sport and are designed to prevent running (called lifting) and bent-knee walking (creeping).

The main difference between healthwalking and racewalking, as Coach Jake sees it, is that "healthwalking is racewalking without the race." In other words, there's no competition involved. He adds, "A good racewalker is a study in power and forward fluidity. We don't sashay or swing the hips; everything is designed to charge forward down the road."

Racewalking for Runners

"I tell people I don't think racewalking is a haven for broken-down runners," says Coach Jake with a laugh. Racewalking, an activity which is virtually injury-free, is often taken up by runners who suffer impact problems or injury. That being said, Jacobson points out the many other ways racewalking can be of benefit to runners:

- Racewalking can help runners remain injury-free by building strength not only in the specialty muscles used in running, but in antagonistic (opposing) and other muscles as well. Running is a pushing activity, working primarily the backs of the legs. Racewalking is a pulling and pushing activity, which strengthens both the fronts and backs of the legs and gives the hamstrings (back thigh muscles) a stretch with each forward extension of the stride.

- Racewalking can also develop greater flexibility in the hips because of the full range of motion employed with each stride. Uninformed people incorrectly think racewalkers swivel their hips. That is incorrect. A good racewalker eliminates lateral sway by reaching forward with the hips as the leg extends, gaining valuable inches with each stride. A good runner, says Coach Jake, should run with the hips as well.

- Racewalking helps build endurance in the chest, shoulders, back, and especially the arms, which swing vigorously with each stride. It will also help a runner develop a better posture by strengthening the abdominal muscles. "Run tall, walk tall" is Coach Jake's motto.

After a runner learns to racewalk, he or she can use it as a tool to improve running form. Says Coach Jake, "When runners have come to me for style advice, I have them racewalk to improve their form. Learning the proper foot-plant that is emphasized in racewalking can be especially important for those with knee injuries from running." The best way to start out is to racewalk one or two miles every other day as a warmup to your regular training. Keep to your regular running mileage; just consider the racewalking as something extra. Once you feel comfortable and fluid with your walking style, you can increase the mileage and intensity of your workouts.

Coach Jake claims that all the runners he has given running/racewalking cross training programs to have dramatically improved their running times. "I've even been known to 'sneak up' on runners and slowly convince them to try competing in the racewalk division. It's good cross training, and they have fun."

Racewalk Technique

To racewalk, follow the form described earlier for healthwalking; however, as you pick up the pace, extend each leg so that it is completely straight as your heel reaches the ground. Plant each foot so that you come down on the outside corner of your heel. Once the heel has touched the ground, your quadriceps (front thigh muscles) will help pull your body over your leg as you transfer forward to the ball of your foot, then use the toes of your back foot to push off. The contracted quadriceps help keep the knee locked, and pull your body over your leg. Remember to walk heel-to-toe. Along with quick steps, concentrate on making short piston-like strokes with your arms, almost like short uppercut punches slightly across your chest. This pumping action will help you to increase your speed and to maintain good balance and forward thrust.

WALKING AS A WORKOUT— DOES IT MEASURE UP?

Many charts describing the caloric burn of various activities have listed walking, but never racewalking. A 1979 study at Columbia University in New York City, in which Jacobson was a participant, indicated that racewalking (and we can assume healthwalking, at varying degrees) not only burns many more calories than walking at similar speeds but at certain speeds, even more than running. This appears to be due to the more dynamic usage of the arms in racewalking than in running, and to the taking of more steps, producing more muscular contractions per minute.

At a certain speed, there is a crossover in which racewalking becomes more difficult than running at the same pace. That difficulty translates to more steps, greater use of muscles, and thus higher calorie burning. Here are some examples.

At five miles per hour (12-minute-per-mile pace) running burns 480 calories per hour. At the same pace and same distance, racewalking burns 530 calories.

At six miles per hour (10-minute-per-mile pace) running burns 660 calories per hour. At the same pace and same distance, racewalking burns 734 calories.

At seven miles per hour (8:30-minute-per-mile pace) running burns 690 calories. At the same pace and same distance, racewalking burns 960.

Walking may pose less of an injury risk than running, but surely running provides a better workout. Or does it? The Institute for Aerobics Research once performed a six-month study of more than 100 young women to find out. What they discovered was that 12-minute-mile aerobic walkers, speeding along with an arm-swinging, hip-swaying gait, improved fitness as much as joggers. By covering three miles a day, five days a week, they boosted their fitness levels by 16 percent—almost twice as much as brisk walkers and four times more than strollers.

RUN, WALK, RUN

Should you take walking breaks during training and racing?

Many beginning runners walk before they run. Brisk walking is an excellent cardiovascular and strength-building activity on its own merits, and can also help ease the transition from inactivity to running. NYRR's beginner running classes start with 20 minutes of brisk walking and progress to periods of easy running interspersed with walking breaks. Over the course of the ten-week session, most participants build up to running for 20 minutes without a break—and they do it without injury or overexertion, both of which can end a commitment to running before it's even firmly in place.

But once a running lifestyle is established, what then? Should runners continue to incorporate walking into their training and racing? What advantages can walking offer, and what are the best strategies for making it part of a running program?

Walking Breaks in Training

When running, each footstep strikes the ground surface with three to five times the runner's body weight. Over time, runners with biomechanical problems, such as over-pronation, may develop injuries as a result of this repeated pounding. Walking, which keeps one foot on the ground at all times, considerably reduces the impact forces. In addition, by giving a respite to running muscles, walking breaks can help keep muscles fresh and injury resistant. Thus, it is possible to safely complete longer workouts with walking breaks than without them. Longer workouts have many benefits for runners, including more calories burned and greater gains in muscle strength.

Walking breaks can be particularly useful in long workouts, such as marathon training runs, because they conserve the body's stores of carbohydrate, its primary fuel for exercise. The harder you exercise, the greater percentage of carbohydrate your body uses. Carbohydrate stores are limited, while stores of fat, the main exercise fuel burned during low-level activity, are not. Walking breaks allow you to burn fat and conserve carbohydrate. This carbohydrate-sparing can be crucial in long, hard efforts, where it's possible to deplete your fuel stores completely.

Walking breaks have psychological benefits as well. One, they provide a restorative time-out—a chance to assess progress, monitor the body's feedback, and then continue. They are also motivating: Walking briskly isn't the same as stopping in the middle of your workout, or failing to complete it. You're eager to pick up the pace again after a brief interlude.

The length and frequency of walking breaks depend on your fitness level and overall training. You might try walking for one minute for every five to 15 minutes of running. The important thing is to plan your breaks and take them as scheduled, rather than running until you are forced to walk.

Walking Breaks During Races

Walking breaks can serve the same purposes in races that they do in training. They are particularly useful in longer races where carbohydrate depletion—hitting the wall—can be a major issue. With intelligently planned and carefully executed walking breaks during your race, you're likely to pass hundreds of struggling runners in the late stages of a half marathon or marathon.

As you do in training, plan your race-day walking breaks. Many runners choose to walk for a minute or so every mile, or at every aid station—which also simplifies the task of drinking a paper cup full of water or sports drink! As a courtesy to your competitors, move toward the side of the course while walking, and avoid sudden changes in pace.

Walk On!

You may reach (or already be at) a point where you no longer need or desire walking breaks. That's fine, but you should never hesitate to use them out of concern that "real" runners don't walk. Walking breaks are simply a way of maximizing your physical potential and increasing your odds of success—and isn't that what running is all about?

(Adapted from "Run, Walk, Run," by Gordon Bakoulis, *New York Runner,* Fall 2003.)

PART 12
THE RUNNING LIFESTYLE

40

RUNNING AND TRAVEL

One of the most appealing aspects of running is how portable it is. Where you go, it goes. With a bit of planning and experience, not only is running a convenient travel companion, but it can also be a wonderful adventure.

NYRR is truly an international organization in this regard, and travel is one of its major areas of expertise. Over the years, NYRR has coordinated travel and accommodations for the thousands of international runners in its events. NYRR covers every detail, including the recruitment of 350 volunteer translators for the international runners in the New York City Marathon.

In addition, NYRR is an active AIMS (Association of International Marathons) member, and has programs for fitness vacations. Many NYRR staff have attended and/or participated in races all over the world as part of their work.

Many runners are travelers, for either business or pleasure. Having traveled extensively around the world on running business, often as the guest of marathon race directors, Fred Lebow was an expert in this area. His advice is below, followed by tips from other traveling runners.

ON THE ROAD WITH FRED LEBOW (1992)

"During my tenure at the NYRRC, I have been fortunate to travel all over the world. At last count, I have run races and roads in over 50 countries, putting in the miles on every continent. Some of the techniques I have developed over the years for travel and running may seem a bit unorthodox, but they work for me. At the very least, you can adopt (and adapt) some of these methods to suit your needs.

Speaking of suits, I used to travel with one. I arrived at the 1977 Boston Marathon with my two suitcases, one of which contained a suit, tie, and dress shoes. Eventually, after significantly more travel experience, I worked my way down to one soft bag, which must have a shoulder strap. Instead of a suit, if necessary I take just a jacket and tie. And I never check a bag. Everything is in a carry-on. The point is, I have found it easiest and wisest just to pack enough to get by, and to take it with me on the plane."

I never make a big deal out of what I wear while I'm away (nor, frankly, do I make a big deal about my clothes at home, either!). But that required breaking a habit I had going all the way back to my youth. When I was young, my family used to go to great lengths to have us bathed and always dressed in clean, fancy clothes. Even when we were hiding from the Nazis during the war, we dressed up nicely. Crazy.

I always pack my all-weather running gear. Even though I prefer singlets in hot weather, I also pack long-sleeved shirts and long pants, depending on where I'm going. I have been to places such as Istanbul, Morocco, and most Arab countries where it isn't appropriate to dress without having my arms and legs covered (not to mention that one can't get into various sightseeing spots without being dressed this way).

Having proper clothing is probably even more important for women. There are many countries where it is not advisable for women to run in shorts. Unless you are familiar with the site, it is probably wise for every runner to take long, lightweight running pants. And in all cases, it is also advisable to check with one of the locals about the proper customs before going out to run or tour. In my experience, this doesn't apply to just the Third World. It includes places in some European countries as well.

When I travel, I never worry about jet lag. I have found that the best way to approach any trip is to go out for a light run after arriving. (I take a shower beforehand if I'm feeling especially groggy.) I learned this from many of the elite runners who come to our races in New York and do the same. In addition, according to an article in *New York Running News,* experts on jet lag recommend that travelers begin following the schedule of the new place—meals, sleep habits, etc.—as soon as possible. It's especially helpful to engage in an outdoor activity like running, so the body is exposed to sunlight, which seems to send a time signal. This is particularly true if you arrive somewhere in the early morning, having flown from a place where it's late in the day.

Even though I always run upon arriving, I take my running very easy because of the stress of travel. Going for a run may sound rough when all you feel like doing is lying down. My feeling is, experiment; try to run anyway. You can always stop and walk, or take a rest. When I've been tired mid-run, I go with the feeling. I stop and take a break. I've even taken a short rest in the middle of a marathon. Beware, however, of doing it in a strange place. Taking my shoes off for a relaxing catnap in Chicago, I awoke to find they had been stolen. I had to make my way back to the hotel in my socks.

Before you take off for a run in a strange place, get a general understanding of where you are and how and where it is most appropriate to run. You can do this by asking a cab driver, someone at your hotel, a native, or a friend who has visited the place. I remember arriving in Teheran, and I was so anxious to run, I went out immediately. And just as immediately, Iranian soldiers stopped me. I never saw another person running in Iran.

Once you get acclimated to your surroundings, running can be wonderful. It's new, it's fresh, and it's adventurous. But beware of getting carried away in a new location, which is very common. On a beautiful day in Barcelona, I found myself about 13 miles out, having left my map in a pocket back in my hotel room. My mind went blank; I couldn't even remember the name of my hotel. I went to a police station for help. After a dozen calls, they finally located my hotel and drove me back. Imagine seeing a guy walking out of a police car wrapped in a blanket! To assure everyone I wasn't a criminal, I did what I always do—I gave out race T-shirts. I always carry a stock of those as souvenirs.

In the past few years, the world has really changed. When I used to be at a hotel on business and ask about places to run, or if there was a fitness center, they would look at me like I was speaking a different language. Now, every hotel has a fitness center; some are minimal, but often they're very large. When you ask the concierge where to run, he or she will give you a running map.

I was also struck by a commercial for a cruise line. It shows a beautiful scene of a boat on the water, and then a close up of two people running around the deck. Running is not as "kooky" as it was, but rather, it's very mainstream. It's expected. You can see it especially in hotels; at 6 A.M., the business people go for a run, and then they go about their business. Wherever I go around the country, and around the world, the streets are full of walkers and runners.

—Allan Steinfeld

Most travel veterans advise running early in the morning; however, I think this depends on where you are. Surely it is easiest and in busy cities makes sense in order to avoid crowds and traffic. But I have had great runs in spots like along Lake Michigan in Chicago where, at sunset, the light casting its reflection on the water is a beautiful sight.

Where are the best locations to run a race? There are so many places that are good for different reasons. Many feel the place, rather than the race, is most important. I have run a half marathon in Cairo in terrible conditions for a good time, but the course—run down roads and past buildings that haven't changed in 2,000 years—was amazing. Early mornings in China were fascinating, passing other runners and those practicing t'ai chi. I've always wanted to experience running the marathon in California through the redwoods.

But for me, it's not just the city, it's the people that make the race. I ran the first Oslo Marathon about ten years ago, and the crowds were incredible. I ran the very difficult (and lonely—there were no spectators) Aruba Marathon, which had the potential for being a disaster, until I met some friends (animal and human). There were no spectators, only goats. I actually have a special feeling for goats, as we used to have them at home when I was growing up. But they don't make for a great cheering section. Fortunately, I was spotted by coach and running administrator Tracy Sundlun, who paced me and gave me encouragement over the entire final ten miles. Aruba was a very memorable race, and place.

Running can make for some great sightseeing. One of the nicest features of travel running is going through famous parks in places like Vienna and London. And running can also be a great challenge, or a way to experience history. I once ran in the Colorado Rockies, where it started out hot and we ended up in high altitude with snow. In Greece, I ran the original marathon route, and in Rome I began a run from the Vatican.

Unlike the "old days," now there's a lot of good help and advice on travel running. Some major hotels, particularly in big cities, have running maps. In the United States, you can check on locations, running groups, or races by contacting local running clubs, the YMCA or YWCA, or the Road Runners Club of America. There is even a road running club in Paris.

Lebow's Rules of Travel

1. Get away with as little clothing as possible. A nice running suit doubles for me as leisure wear. You might want to bring two of them.

2. You don't have to dress up while traveling. Why get all done up just to get all sweated up? I've been to Paris, Rome, London, New York—and I've realized you can dress down and still be acceptable in all those places. What's most important is to be comfortable, and you can do that with a moderate amount of style, too.

3. Ask a hotel concierge (or other local) where to run. Take with you a map and the telephone number and address of where you are staying. You can use the business cards most hotels keep in their rooms or at the front desk. During your run, look for landmarks to navigate by along the way. And be precise. After getting lost, one friend of mine told a Casablanca resident, "I remember my hotel; it was a white building." The gentlemen replied, "Do you realize what 'Casablanca' means? Every building here is white."

4. Try laundering your running clothes the easy way—while you're in them. I learned this trick through rather unpleasant circumstances—after I stepped in animal "waste" in Marakesh, Morocco. I couldn't bear to touch my shoes, so I took a shower in them. Now I take a shower with all my running clothes on, at least in summer gear. I know of a number of other runners who do this, even at home.

If a certain nonperishable food is part of your pre-race preparation (bananas or bagels), bring it with you to be sure you'll have it. Sometimes, this isn't just to have some extras. You may not like the local fare, or in some cases, even have access to it. One NYRR staffer toed the starting line of an eastern European marathon hungry after spending days on scant rations of tea and rice. Rather than standing in long lines during limited hours for questionable results, he ate what his host had on hand.

FOR RUNNERS WHO FLY

Runners who fly should be aware of new information on blood clots, or deep vein thrombosis (DVT). In fact, all flyers are warned, as publicity and itineraries e-mailed to passengers from some airlines list Web sites to read up on the subject. DVT.net, an Internet resource on the topic, states that although the condition is rare, experts advise all air travelers to flex their legs at half hour intervals during flights. During air travel blood flow slows down, especially in the lower legs, and the possibility of coagulation rises steadily. Clots form in five to ten percent of passengers, usually in the calf (deep vein thrombosis), where they can cause swelling and pain, which often becomes chronic. In some cases, a clot moves to a lung, causing pulmonary embolism (PE), producing pain, fainting, and death.

According to an article in the June 2002 issue of *Running Times* magazine, data show that being athletic accounts for ten times more victims than any of the usual risk factors for blood clots, such as a previous blood clot (but some sources list other risk factors, such as older age and obesity).

The theory is that athletes with lower resting pulse rates have greater risk of stasis: stagnant blood subject to clotting. Another theory is that athletes are more likely to fly with bruises or sore muscles, which can trigger clotting. Some even recommend that runners wear compression stockings and flex their legs every fifteen minutes during flights. Speak with you doctor, and/or check on the Web for further information.

Airlines provide information for passengers on their own Web sites, such as www.continental.com/travel/specialneeds/health.asp. See also www.dvt.net/ and www.airhealth.org.

TIPS FROM A RUNNING TRAVEL AGENT

Travel agent Thom Gilligan tempts New York City Marathoners at the expo with running tour packages. Gilligan urges runners to consider using a travel agent, who represents all airlines, hotels, car rentals, and other companies that offer services to travelers. "If you know one who is a runner, all the better." Another option to use when planning a running vacation is the Internet. Here are some of his inside tips on travel.

Special Travel Gear

- **Woolite.** A small pack, or travel-size bottle, of Woolite is a good idea. It works in cold water and can be used not only on wool but also on cotton and synthetics.

- **Water purifiers.** The tap water in many countries is unsuitable. It is either not palatable or contains bacteria that can cause all types of illness. You can purchase a water purifier that filters out any impurities for about $30 in most camping equipment stores. They are lightweight and can just about slide into a running shoe.

Airline Flights

- **Upgrades.** There's nothing like the luxury of first-class or business class. Even if you do only a small amount of air travel, it pays to join every possible frequent flyer program. That's because when seats are full in regular coach, you may get "upgraded" to first or business class. Priority is given to those passengers who have a frequent flyer number in their reservation record. In addition, frequent flyers also receive periodic mailings of special discount certificates, two-for-one fares, etc.

- **Carry-on luggage.** Pack your running gear in your carry-on bag. This not only keeps you on the road if your luggage is lost, but in some countries running gear is quite valuable and is often stolen from checked luggage. Running shoes, shorts, Gore-Tex® suits, and other gear are "hot commodities." Always watch your bags.

  You are allowed only one carry-on bag plus a laptop computer, pocketbook, camera, or some other valuable, non-checkable item. Never pack in your carry-on any item that might be potentially used as a weapon such as scissors, Swiss army knives, nail files, etc.

- **Checked baggage.** You are allowed only two pieces of checked baggage. You will be charged about $80 or more per extra piece. The maximum weight of any piece is 55 lbs. Never lock your bags. X-ray screeners may need to open your bag if they see an item that they want to examine more closely. If they cannot open your bag, they have the right to refuse loading it.

Hotel Rooms

- **Nonsmoking rooms.** Many hotels now offer nonsmoking rooms, which should be requested when making a reservation.
- **Secret deals.** Most city hotels offer special weekend rates that are available only if you are smart enough to request them.
- **Running maps.** Special running maps are now produced by some hotels, such as the Park Lane in London and the Park Plaza in Boston. Many Hyatt hotels also provide them.
- **Plastic bags.** Plastic laundry bags, most often located in hotel room closets, are a convenient place to stuff wet running gear when you pack your bags. Just make sure to empty them as soon as possible after arriving at your destination.

On my bulletin board is a postcard I sent to myself from a faraway country. "See the world—it matters," the card says. And one of the greatest ways to see the world is by running, a sport you can practice anywhere. Whether just to maintain fitness, as a unique mode of transportation or sightseeing, or to take part in a race, running in new territory makes you realize just how universal the sport is, and how unique it can be as a travel companion.

I have been fortunate to visit nearly 30 countries, and to run in many of them. Here are some tips based on what I learned while running around the world.

1. Be flexible. The stress of travel and sightseeing will likely necessitate a reduction in training. It's important to accommodate this added stress, both to prevent illness and injury and to enjoy your trip. During travel it's especially important to practice a runner's cardinal rule: Listen to your body.

2. Find a travel agent sympathetic to your needs as a runner. If it's someone who specializes in running, ask about races, clubs, or running areas. In addition, for general running or race information in different countries, you can contact that country's Sports Federation (the equivalent of USATF in the United States); or for American cities, look on the Internet for local races and running clubs.

3. You might want to try to run before you fly, even if it means getting up with the sun. That way you won't have to attempt to overcome fatigue and the challenge of a new spot immediately after arriving because you feel compelled to get in a run.

4. During airplane flights, walk around, stretch out, eat lightly, and drink plenty of water.

5. Bring versatile running gear that's easily washable and quick-drying. Carry shoes and clothing in plastic bags so you have a place to repack the gear when it's wet. Take the insoles out of running shoes to speed drying time. If you pack wet gear after a run, remember to remove it first thing on arrival.

6. If you fear the absence of your runner's diet, bring some of your staples along as insurance. Cereal and powdered milk are lightweight and portable, as are whole-grain crackers or pretzels. When eating out, don't be shy about asking for your food prepared "light." Just be polite.

7. Speaking of bringing things along, running paraphernalia makes great gifts. I learned from Fred Lebow—who took running presents everywhere—

that running T-shirts, patches, and pins are unique and greatly appreciated "thank you" items for people who show kindness or do you favors. In a crunch—so to speak—American candy and gum are good gifts in many countries.

8. You'll probably be better off running in the morning. Business or sightseeing often present unexpected scheduling and fatigue, and mornings are the best time to avoid pedestrians and traffic in major cities. Early morning runs are also a great way to really see a city.

9. Allow for jet lag, especially for races or hard training. The general rule is that it takes about a day of adaptation for each hour of change in time zone.

10. Allow time for your total workout, including proper warmup and cool-down. Many people compromise important warmup and cool-down routines when time is short or when it's inconvenient to do them. To make it more convenient, adapt exercise routines to hotel rooms. For example, instead of the fence or tree you normally use to stretch, try bedposts or staircases. The same adaptation holds true if you can't run. Warm up and run or walk flights of the hotel stairs instead.

11. Be especially alert to cars and traffic lights. As an American running in England, for example—where traffic travels in the opposite direction than in the United States—my first, and last, lapse in concentration nearly proved fatal!

12. Carry identification, including the name and telephone number of where you are staying. If you're setting out to run alone, tell someone where you're going and when you plan to return. Take money and a local cell phone, and if you're running more than 30 minutes—especially if it's hot—don't stray from accessible water, or a place to buy a drink if necessary.

13. If you're on business, try breaking up meetings with a run. In fact, this can be smart business sense, as runners are generally respected for their discipline. In addition, a run with business associates often creates a refreshing new rapport.

14. Learn important words and a few pleasant greetings in the native language.

—Gloria Averbuch

GUIDELINES FOR INTERNATIONAL MARATHONERS

Tips from a group of well-traveled marathoners in the "72nd Street Marathoning and Pasta Club."

1. Decide what you want to get out of your international marathon experience, then choose the city accordingly. "The fastest" course may not be in "the most entertaining" city.

2. Don't expect all international marathons to be conducted with the slick efficiency of New York or London. Be prepared for the odd snafu, and roll with the punches.

3. Don't underestimate the effects of jet lag. Leave early enough to give yourself sufficient recovery time. On arrival you may feel fit enough to trot around the museum, but running a marathon is something else.

4. Check out the likely weather and temperature ranges for the race and take several combinations of clothing.

5. Pack a personal care kit that includes the basics you need, e.g., petroleum jelly, aspirin, granola bars, moleskin. Some of these may be tough to find abroad.

6. Check out the international visa requirements long before departure. Some countries won't let you in with just a passport, and you can't make it to the starting line unless you can first get on the plane.

7. If you need an inoculation before you go as part of an overseas health requirement, get it done well in advance to avoid any stiffness or allergic reaction too close to marathon day.

8. If you want to run an international marathon with other runners from the United States, check out whether a group trip is being organized. This may save you some money, too.

9. If you want to run abroad but don't feel up to a marathon, check out the half marathons and 10Ks. Many marathon events incorporate these and other shorter races.

10. Take some time to check out the course beforehand. If it isn't well marked, learning the way ahead of time may help you feel more secure. You'll also learn about the terrain in the process, such as where the uphills are, to plan your pacing.

11. Eat prudently the night before the race and stick to familiar foods. By all means experiment with the local fare, but wait until after the marathon.

12. Be prepared for water stops that don't exist, or have run out of water. If in doubt carry your own bottle.

13. Watch out for ankle-twisting surfaces. Cobblestone streets or uneven paving is not unusual.

14. Talk to local runners along the route. Few situations offer such a great opportunity to enjoy a friendly and informative exchange. It's amazing how much you can learn about your "host" country—even with minimal language skills—from a local marathoner.

15. Watch out for cavalier drivers and cyclists. Sideswiping marathoners is still an accepted sport in some countries.

16. For encouragement from the crowd, wear a T-shirt with your name and country written on it. Both translate into most languages, and the crowd will root for you.

17. Standards of fair play can vary, so don't get thrown if you see a local runner get a bit of help from a friend on a bicycle. Consider it all part of the local experience.

18. Unless you're in it for a winning place, make time to take in your surroundings as you run. Marathon courses often go through neighborhoods and locations off the tourist track. This will give you a real feel for the country.

19. Carry the name and address of your hotel or where you are staying with you. If you get stuck far from the finish line, you may be better understood showing someone the address than trying to pronounce it.

20. Take enough money for a cab or bus or train fare back home.

21. Be courteous to local marathoners. Be careful, especially in a crowded start, not to shove or push.

22. Wash your souvenir international marathon T-shirt with care. It may well run and fade faster than you did!

23. Make up your mind to have fun. The actual race is only one part of the entire international marathon experience. If you're interested in only the race itself, it's cheaper and more convenient to stay home.

24. Start training for the next one as soon as you get home.

RUNNING U.S.A.

Peter Roth has been involved with NYRR and the running movement for many years. Part of his contribution has been to travel around the country to locate the best running sites. You can also visit the Road Runners Clubs of America and Running in the U.S.A. Web sites for information on clubs and races across America: www.rrca.org, www.runningintheusa.com.

Following are some race and contact information for major cities.

Atlanta

Atlanta Track Club, (404) 231-9064, www.atlantatrackclub.org

Phidippides Running Store, Ansley Mall, (404) 875-4268, Sandy Springs Landing, (404) 255-6149, www.phidippides.com

The famous Peachtree Road Race course is close to most Atlanta hotels and the downtown area. Many local and visiting runners ply back and forth along Peachtree Street, testing the course as well as getting to and from Piedmont Park, just two miles from downtown. For a more direct route to the park, head out Piedmont Avenue. The Grady High School track is adjacent to the park and is used for speed workouts on Tuesday nights. To be closer to the park, stay at hotels in the midtown Colony Square area.

Atlantans desiring more serious workouts head for the Kennesaw Mountain trails about 20 miles northwest of town. Also, Stone Mountain, 15 miles east, is a favorite for its five- and eight-mile loops.

Boston

USATF New England, (617) 566-7600, www.usatfne.org

Boston Marathon (BAA), (617) 236-1652, www.bostonmarathon.org

Bill Rodgers Running Center (running store), (617) 723-5612, www.billrodgers.com

With the tradition of the Boston Marathon and the large universities throughout the city, Boston has many excellent courses to satisfy its active running population. Close to the downtown hotels and offices is the Charles River. Its riverbank pathway gives you many distance options, depending on which of the 11 bridges you want to use. The longest loop can take you 16.78 miles; if you want a shorter 3.79-mile loop, use the Charles

River Dam to the east and the Harvard Bridge to the west. For a shorter run of 2.82 miles, use the Longfellow Bridge to the east instead of the dam.

To the west of Boston, in the Brookline/Newton area, you can run around the popular Cleveland Circle Reservoir next to the marathon route. The reservoir is close to two miles around but has very little shade. Many runners hop over the fence to run closer to the water. You can extend the run onto Commonwealth Avenue and challenge the famous Heartbreak Hill. This is a series of four medium-size hills covering about three miles on the marathon route.

In Cambridge, many runners congregate at the Fresh Pond Reservoir's parking lot before heading out for the 2 1/4-mile paved loop around the water. Every Saturday morning at 10:30 A.M. you can find a small race of 2 1/2 or 5 miles here. You don't need to register in advance. If you are looking for group workouts, try calling the BAA office.

Chicago

LaSalle Bank Chicago Marathon, (312) 904-9800, www.chicagomarathon. com

The answer to finding great runs in Chicago is simply to head east to the lakefront. Its beauty and accessibility make this the foremost place to enjoy your workouts in Chicago. Surprisingly, the water in Lake Michigan is pure enough to attract throngs to its downtown beaches. Many local running clubs schedule their workouts here, and you are bound to find runners congregating in Lincoln Park to the north of downtown along the shoreline. The best spot is a few blocks north of Fullerton Avenue, where you will also find a bulletin board with notices of local races.

Lincoln Park is about a five-mile strip, yet you don't need to be confined to its boundaries. If you head south, the Gold Coast covers 1 1/2 miles to Navy Pier, and you can go another 7 1/2 miles to Jackson Park, where there's a 2.2-mile loop adjacent to the University of Chicago and its excellent track. There are a few other small parks around the city.

About 1/2 mile east of the O'Hare Airport hotels is the heavily wooded Des Plaines Forest Preserve. Here you will find a 5 1/2-mile-long dirt trail along the east bank of the Des Plaines River. Most of the trail will be south of where you will probably enter the preserve.

Cleveland

Rite Aid Cleveland Marathon, (800) 467-3826,
www.clevelandmarathon.com

This lakeside city offers some convenient downtown running, although weekend activity is in outlying parks. The lakefront, known as the Marginal Area, has miles of flat, unremarkable, shadeless terrain. You will have some good views of the Cleveland skyline. An old warehouse and steel mill area, known as the Flats, lies next to the Cuyahoga River and provides another downtown running opportunity. There are several little bridges to run over, and the streets are winding and confusing, but you can always work your way back along the river to where you began.

At a minimum of eight miles from downtown, the Emerald Necklace is an unbroken chain of parks that is also known as the Metroparks System. It runs in an arch from east to west around Cleveland for a distance of about 100 miles. Different clubs use different parts of it, the largest of which is the Cleveland West Road Runners, which uses the Rocky River, Lakewood area. They have a group run every Saturday morning at 7:30 A.M.

Dallas

White Rock Marathon, (214) 372-2068, www.whiterock-marathon.com

Lukes (running store), Oak Lawn, (214) 528-1290

Running in this city is focused on two locations: Bachman Lake, six miles from downtown, next to Love Field Airport; and White Rock Lake, a bit farther away, northeast of town. On weekends, a large group meets at White Rock Lake at 7 A.M. and starts running 11 minutes later. They call themselves the 7-11s. The grand meeting place here is Big Thicket Cabin on East Lawther Drive along the northeast side of the lake. One loop around the lake is nine miles. Other runners meet here informally throughout the mornings. Bachman Lake has a smaller but popular 3.1-mile loop.

Running downtown is complicated, with no easy route to follow. The hotels near and along the Stemmons Freeway offer some opportunities to follow service roads or run on the Trinity Riverbed Levee. It is recommended that you do not run in this area alone.

The Cross Country Club of Dallas puts on races the first Saturday of every month. Lukes on Oak Lawn is a well-known resource for local information.

Denver

Rocky Mountain Road Runners Hotline, (303) 871-8366, www.rmrr.org

Runners Roost (stores), (303) 759-8455, www.runnersroost.com

Gart Bros. Sports Castle, (303) 861-1122

This is an easy city to run in, with beautiful vistas of the Rocky Mountains and long, even, flat, unimpeded routes. Weather is seldom a problem, but the high altitude can slow you down, especially if you have just arrived. There are a number of popular areas in town. The lunch crowd can be found at Cheesman Park, where a wood chip trail offers views of the capital dome. One loop is a little less than a mile. Washington Park, a couple of miles to the southeast of downtown, gets the early, late, and weekend crowds. Here, a shaded, mostly flat road loops around for 2.2 miles.

Cherry Creek Trail is a beautiful course that runs along Speer Boulevard and out to Cherry Creek Reservoir after about nine miles. This is a paved trail with no intersections to interrupt your run. The reservoir attracts many runners as well. The Platt River Greenway connects to the trail and can add many more miles to your run.

For mountain runners, there are three great courses close to downtown. The most challenging is Lookout Mountain, which goes five miles uphill. The most interesting is Genesee Park, which contains an animal preserve, including buffalo. The closest is Red Rocks Park, only about seven to eight miles west.

Detroit

Detroit Free Press/Flagstar Bank Marathon, (313) 222-6676, www. detroitfreepressmarathon.com

Motor City Striders, (313) 544-9099, www.motorcitystriders.com

This is a friendly running town that takes advantage of a large forested island in the Detroit River. Belle Isle is a 2 1/2-mile run from downtown, and once you are over the bridge, you can use a perimeter road of 5 1/2 miles or use trails through the woods. You will see a lot of natural wildlife here. A large group of downtown runners sets out every Tuesday at 5:30 P.M. The meeting place changes every week, so you need to call ahead.

The beautiful Elmwood Cemetery lies just off Jefferson Avenue before you get to the Belle Isle Bridge. It was designed by Robert Olmstead, who also designed New York's Central Park. Here you can run a 1 1/2-mile loop and wander over dirt paths on the only hills (man-made) in the city.

Local runners feel this is a safe city to run in, and a lot of old crime-ridden neighborhoods have recently become gentrified. Only 20 minutes to the west are wonderful rural areas for your long weekend runs.

Houston

HP Houston Marathon, (713) 957-3453, www.hphoustonmarathon.com

Memorial Park Tennis Center, (713) 861-3765

Houston is one of those few cities that has a favorite running spot where everyone likes to meet. Memorial Park is said to attract as many as 10,000 runners on weekend days. Many begin their workouts at the Tennis Center, doing their warmups and socializing in the parking lot before heading out on the crushed granite three-mile trail. A big campaign succeeded in funding night lighting for 24-hour use of the trail. The Tennis Center also has information on local clubs, races, etc. The closest hotel is the Houstonian, and there are other hotels in the nearby Galleria area in uptown Houston.

From downtown, you can run west through the greenbelt along the Buffalo Bayou River. After 2 1/2 miles you'll reach a residential area, and after another 2 1/2 miles west you'll be at Memorial Park. A loop from downtown to the bridge at Sheperd Drive and back on the other side of the river will give you a five-mile workout.

Kansas City

Kansas City Track Club Hotline, (816) 333-RACE, www.kctrack.org

Mid-America Running Association, (816) 746-1414, www.mararunning. org

This busy running town has three parks that attract local runners. Liberty Memorial Park, the most convenient, lies adjacent to Crown Center. This is a small park, but you can do about 1 1/2 miles without repeating yourself. Mill Creek Park, also small, is located in the Country Club Plaza Area. Here you will find an undulating 0.8-mile loop.

The most popular, Loose Park, is located about 3 1/2 miles south of downtown. Runners usually park and meet at the tennis courts on the west side. Although the park has only a one-mile paved loop, extra miles are covered in the neighboring residential communities.

The Kansas City Track Club has, perhaps, the oldest consecutive weekly group run in the country. Its Wednesday Night Run (WNR) includes from 25 to 60 members each week. During standard time they meet at 6 P.M., and during daylight savings time they meet at 6:30 P.M. Call ahead to find the meeting place, which changes. A potluck dinner follows the run.

Los Angeles

Los Angeles Marathon, (310) 444-5544, www.lamarathon.com

This spread-out city has no central running courses, and the favorites are hard to reach except by car. Run early and you will avoid the poor air quality Los Angeles is known for. About 5 1/2 miles north of downtown, Griffith Park has a vast 53 miles of trails that zigzag in seeming disarray. The 15 miles of paved roads are easier to follow, and you'll find many runners working their way along them. If you run up to the observatory, you'll appreciate the spectacular views below. Only three miles from downtown is Elysian Park, but the roads there are hard to follow. It's best to go there with someone who knows the way.

A favorite local route is San Vicente Boulevard for a pleasant run to the ocean in Santa Monica. To avoid more traffic, you can also run a parallel course three blocks south on Margarita Avenue past many palatial homes. Once at the ocean, you can head south along the beach and, if you have the time and endurance, you need not turn around for about 30 miles. Los Angeles Airport lies along this waterfront course. To find the most runners at any one time in any one place here, head out to Balboa Park in Encino, where you will have a choice of flat routes from three kilometers to seven miles.

Miami

Miami Runners, (305) 227-1500, www.miamirunnersclub.com

This warm, mostly flat city has an active running community, and the Miami Runners Club puts on frequent races. There are two very popular routes that local runners use, and they are worth the short trip to get to them. To run from downtown, there is easy access via Biscayne Boulevard to the Venetian Causeway, which will give you a pleasant 2 1/2-mile run over to Miami Beach.

Southwest of the city at Tropical Park you can find a five-kilometer and a five-mile out-and-back course that is in constant use. This is the busiest spot, except on Saturday mornings, when hundreds of runners gather at 6:30 A.M. at Parrot Jungle for a long workout. They take Old Cutler Road and the Rickenbacker Causeway to get to Crandon Park in Key Biscayne. One way is a mostly shaded, well-marked 13.1 miles. Of course, you can turn back at any point. There is plenty of water supplied by volunteers along the route.

Minneapolis

Minnesota Distance Running Association—Raceline, (952) 925-4749, www.runmdra.org

Twin Cities Marathon, (763) 287-3888, www.twincitiesmarathon.org

The Minnesota Distance Running Association is a venerable and active running club that can get you plugged in to whatever local events are going on. This is a busy running community, although with 22 lakes in the city, everyone is spread out enjoying the beautiful neighborhoods near their homes. Winter running is a challenge here, but the elements have nurtured many local world-class runners. The joy of toughing it can be seen in the popularity of the springtime Mudball Run, held when the terrain is particularly sloppy.

Most hotels are situated in downtown, and the best routes are out at the three lakes southwest of town. Loring Park is on the way to the lakes, with a loop that is close to one mile around. The first lake you'll reach is Lake of the Isles—2.8 miles around on a flat, paved path. Next, heading south, is Lake Calhoun's 3.2-mile circumference, and last is Lake Harriet's three-mile loop.

Native runners also use the River Road loops along both sides of the Mississippi. This course starts 3 1/2 miles from downtown, and distances vary according to which bridges you use.

New York

New York Road Runners, (212) 860-4455, www.nyrrc.org

New York has some of the best and most convenient running sites in the country. Central Park is the gem of the city, and from the dark hours of early morning until the late hours of night it is flooded with runners over the myriad routes that its 840 acres provide.

Of course, in New York, as well as most other cities, you must run with caution, especially during off-hours. The favorite meeting places in the park are the Engineers' Gate at 90th Street and Fifth Avenue, near the reservoir (a block from NYRR headquarters at 9 East 89th Street), and at 67th Street on the West Drive, next to Tavern on the Green, where the marathon finishes. At the Engineers' Gate there is a gatehouse that is staffed part-time by an attendant. In addition, brochures on NYRR events and programs are on display and available at all times. Numerous hotels are within a short jog of the park, which features a six-mile loop, although shorter routes taking the 72nd Street or 102nd Street transverses are available. In the center of the park is a 1 1/2-mile loop on a flat dirt path around the reservoir. On Saturday mornings, a group run with stretching instruction is conducted for the public at 10 A.M. at the Engineers' Gate.

NYRR holds races just about every weekend year-round. It also sponsors a safety program in Central Park that provides a patrol throughout the day and evening. You can usually find running partners by stopping at the club building and there are group runs conducted twice a day at 6:30 A.M. and 6:30 P.M. It's a great place to pick up race fliers and other running information. NYRR also has a store that sells gear (not shoes).

There are other great places to run in New York. Riverside Park begins at 72nd Street along the Hudson River and extends up to the George Washington Bridge, about 5 1/2 miles to the north. Most runners stay within the promenade areas between 72nd and 120th Streets where an up-and-back route is about 4.8 miles. In Brooklyn, Prospect Park is a popular running site that offers a pleasant, rolling 3 1/2-mile loop on the Park Drive.

Philadelphia

Philadelphia Distance Run, (215) 564-6499,
   www.philadelphiadistancerun.org
Rittenhouse Sports, (215) 569-9957

This city has one of the biggest urban parks in the country, Fairmount Park. Only a short distance from Center City, you can find some natural trails here that seem to have distant rural settings. The main route, though, is along the Schuylkill River, just north of the Philadelphia Art Museum. Here, runners meet at Plaisted Hall, the southernmost building along Boat House Row. They run up to Falls Bridge and come back on the other side of the river and around the Art Museum. This is a safe, flat, 8.4-mile loop.

A couple of miles north of Falls Bridge, you can reach a gravel bridle path, Forbidden Drive, which runs close to Wissahickon Creek. It's called "Forbidden" because no vehicles are allowed. This will take you through scenic wooded and flat terrain until you come to the end at the northwest border of the city, 5 ¹/₂ miles away.

About 15 miles north of Center City lies Pennypack Park, which is well utilized by the Northeast Road Runners. A paved path runs east to west for about 11 miles over gentle terrain until the west end becomes very hilly. If you can get to Valley Forge National Park, 25 miles from town, you'll enjoy some beautiful, hilly runs through its 2,255-acre terrain. Local runners meet at the Covered Bridge on Route 252.

Phoenix and Scottsdale

Runner's Den, (602) 277-4333

Arizona Road Racers, (602) 775-7897, www.arizonaroadracers.com

Running is hot in this city—literally and figuratively—due to the desert environment and the easy access to unimpeded routes. There is no central location at which to meet other runners, but there are frequent events put on by the Arizona Road Racers. Most mileage is tread along the Arizona Canal's 23.67-mile length. Recently the pathway has been reconstructed to pass under intersecting roads and allow you a nonstop workout. Downtown running is limited to fairly busy streets and small Encanto Park.

A new running path has been built along a dry creek bed called Indian Bend Wash. Its 15-mile length starts in North Phoenix and runs right through the heart of Scottsdale, ending at Arizona State University in Tempe. The pathway goes under most cross streets.

Phoenix contains the world's largest park within a city. At the South Mountain Preserve, seven miles south of downtown, you can enjoy many trails within its 15,357 acres. If you head seven miles north of downtown, you can reach the North Mountain Preserve for interesting runs that include Squaw Peak Park. Both preserves have well-marked trails, and maps are available at the gates.

Pittsburgh

Pittsburgh Citiparks, (412) 255-2539, www.city.pittsburgh.pa.us

At the confluence of three large rivers—the Allegheny, Monongahela, and Ohio—sits the Golden Triangle, with its downtown office complexes.

Numerous bridges cross the rivers and runners enjoy looping over them in many configurations. Point Park at the Triangle, Roberto Clemente Park, and Three Rivers Stadium can be included in these loops.

The most popular venue in town is Schenley Park. Close to downtown and adjacent to Carnegie-Mellon University, its 456 acres offer a ten-kilometer cinder and dirt trail and a perimeter sidewalk. East of Schenley Park, you will find the 499-acre Frick Park, with many nature trails that wind through ravines, along creeks, and over hills. North Park is also a popular hangout, where a mostly flat five-mile bike trail circumvents a lake. This park is 14 miles out of town on Route 19.

There is a lot of street running in Pittsburgh. The downtown is quite flat, but once you are in the suburbs there are hills galore. These are long hills, and when you get on top of them, you can stay there for a flat run. Of course, intersecting streets can be a distraction.

St. Louis

Spirit of St. Louis Marathon, (314) 727-0800, www.stlouismarathon.com

St. Louis Track Club, (314) 781-3726, www.stlouistrackclub.com

Although two major rivers flow together just north of town, there are no decent courses that put you close to either the Missouri or the Mississippi. There is a small park at the Gateway Arch where you can get a few miles in if you are limited to that part of town. Local hotels have maps that will facilitate your needs.

Six miles from the arch, at the western edge of downtown, is a large, wonderful 1,400-acre park that was the site of the 1904 World's Fair. Forest Park is the major focus of running here, and its well-marked paths give you a perimeter run of 6.2 miles, with a .9-mile add-on through a wooded area. There are some interior paths available as well. There are many local tourist attractions at the park for you to enjoy. Runners meet at the Lindell Pavilion Fieldhouse along the northern edge of the park.

Shaw Park, a few miles farther west, offers a two-mile loop. There are many corporations nearby, and at the lunch hour it's a busy runners' thoroughfare.

San Francisco

San Francisco Chronicle Marathon (415) 284-9653, www.
    chroniclemarathon.com

Golden Gate National Recreation Area, (415) 561-4700, www.nps.gov/ goga/

Few cities have the dramatic climate and terrain that you can find here. The ocean, bay, bridges, and hills offer exciting vistas and venues for a variety of opportunities. Local runners gravitate to the Marina Green and the adjacent Golden Gate Promenade, which take you along the bay and up to Fort Point, under the Golden Gate Bridge. You can also run up to the bridge and then across it to Marin County. A run from Marina Green to Marin County and back is a little more than 7 miles. Not far from the Green, on Chestnut Street, is the Fleet Feet Store, which is a good place to stop for local running information.

Most local clubs use the magnificent Golden Gate Park for their regular group workouts. You will find it about 3 1/2 miles southwest of downtown. There are many different meeting places and complex routes, although an easy course would be to follow the North and South Drives, which form a loop. The park is about three miles long. Kezar Stadium, just outside the park, has been rebuilt with a new 400-meter track, which is open to the public.

Seattle

Super Jock 'n Jill, (206) 522-7711, www.superjocknjill.com

Harris*direct* Seattle Marathon, (206) 729-3660/1, www. seattlemarathon.org

This city lies on a strip of land between Puget Sound and Lake Washington. Many of the long routes can be found along the eastern edge of the city on the shores of the lake. Next to the sound, on the western edge, there is a downtown 2 1/4-mile waterfront run between the Aquarium and Pier 89. Across Elliot Bay you can run on the Alki Beach roads and enjoy their great views of the city skyline.

As great as these runs are, nothing beats the attraction of Green Lake, located a few miles north of downtown. Its 2.78-mile loop gets very crowded each morning, and often by 5:30 A.M. the parking lot is full. Many runners head south to the adjacent Lower Woodland Trails for extra mileage, zigzagging over its hilly, grassy fields.

An old railroad right-of-way has been recycled into a long, flat, traffic-free path known as the Burke-Gilman Trail. It begins along Lake Union, heads east through the University of Washington campus, and then winds toward the northeast, eventually hugging the lakeshore at the northern tip, a 16.6-mile journey. From here, a 12-mile extension on the Sammish River Trail will take you to Marymoor Park in Redmond.

Washington, D.C.

Montgomery County Road Runners, (301) 353-0200, www.mcrrc.org

Marine Corps Marathon, (800) RUN-USMC, www.marinemarathon.com

Running in this city offers many important landmarks to enjoy as well as beautiful and convenient parks. The Mall, between the Lincoln Memorial along the Potomac River at the west end and the Capitol to the east, usually has a busy crowd of lunch runners seeing and being seen on this flat, open, grassy terrain. There are few intersecting streets along the two-mile stretch. If you head west past the Lincoln Memorial and then south, you can run about a mile along the river in West Potomac Park, then make a four-mile loop around the adjacent East Potomac Park. Running around the east side of the Tidal Basin can deliver you back onto the Mall near the Washington Memorial.

If you head north along the river, you will pass the Kennedy Center and wind up in Rock Creek Park. The park is a thickly wooded area along both sides of Rock Creek, which flows into the Potomac. A bike path will keep you close to the park roads as you wind your way about nine miles northward to the Maryland boundary. The park extends another ten miles into Maryland.

WORKADAY RUNNING

Running becomes a lifestyle, an integral part of the day, when it's no longer a chore. Eventually, it becomes like brushing your teeth; you no longer think about it, you just do it. And you *need* to do it, like you need to brush your teeth.

> Think of taking a shower. That's just the point. It's so natural, you don't even think about it. Do you think about what arm you wash first? Do you know if you washed your neck?
>
> The sound of the running water puts you in a secluded environment. It's meditative. Your thoughts come in and go out. That shower may be the only private time you have all day. Are you truly dirty if you don't take a shower every day? No, but you feel that way. It's the same with running. Just like a shower, running is part of my daily life.
>
> —*Nina Kuscsik*

TIME MANAGEMENT

There is hardly a runner—no matter how dedicated—who doesn't wonder on certain days, "Just how am I going to fit it in?" Many of those who run took up the sport because it is the easiest and most convenient and effective exercise; however, with busy lives and responsibilities, even the easiest activity can become difficult.

Here are some helpful time management techniques from busy NYRR members.

Running, working, and living in New York City is definitely a balancing act. Although I ran at a highly competitive level, I always worked as well, usually full time. I would choose time periods when running was my top priority, usually leading up to a major competition such as the Olympic trials. I was fortunate to be able to support myself through freelance writing and editing, which allowed me to keep my schedule flexible and turn down assignments when necessary.

Now I work full time at New York Road Runners, am the parent of two young children, ages 4 and 6, and run mainly for recreation and fitness. It's still a struggle to fit in all in, and to be honest, I don't know how I managed to train and compete so intensely for so many years without losing my sanity! I definitely didn't sleep as much as I should have to support such a physically intense lifestyle. Though I am blessed with a good constitution and was seldom ill, I often felt run down, as if I were fighting something off. I'm sure I could have performed at a higher level if I'd devoted myself full time to running, but that would not have suited my personality and overall life goals.

These days my running consists mainly of my 1.5-mile commute to and from work. It's a lovely jaunt through Central Park, and I take it at a leisurely pace because I have no reason to push myself. I'm fortunate to have a supportive employer; it's not at all unusual here at NYRR to arrive at or leave from the office in running gear, and there's a shower on the premises. On the weekends I try to run for about an hour each day, usually on woodland trails so there is less pounding on my aging body. These runs restore me, body and soul, and I hope to continue them for years to come.

Running is a wonderful way to enhance my life. To people who say they don't have time to run, I say, make the time. Just try it (you can walk before you run) for two weeks, and see if it doesn't make you so much more efficient and productive that you don't know how you functioned without it. Enlist the support of people around you—your spouse, children, neighbors, friends. Even 20 minutes, three or four times a week, can change your life.

—Gordon Bakoulis

WELCOME TO THE REAL (RUNNING) WORLD

Running is one of the most time-effective ways to exercise, a fact that appeals to our ever–time-constrained culture. Yet for young working professionals, the sudden change from post-college life often puts running on the back burner, or off the stove completely. Back in school, it seemed like there was always that extra time between classes to get outside for a run, but once out in the professional world, those elusive hours are quickly filled with deadlines, meetings, and all the responsibilities that come with a full-time job. It need not be this way.

As a recreational runner in college, I enjoyed jogging around the rural Vermont roads where I went to school. Following graduation, I went to work full-time in journalism, and I feared my running interests would have to be put on hold. By being creative with my time, however, I have run five marathons in the past three years, finishing most recently with a 2:56:53 at the 2003 Boston Marathon.

I have found that the busier my schedule gets, the more I enjoy the release that running affords. Living in New York City can have its stressful moments, and the solace provided by a run in Central Park allows me to refocus my perspective and benefits all other aspects of my life. Running in a big city is a great way to meet people, and training for a marathon gives focus and structure to my time outside of work.

Below is a list of tips designed to help young professionals incorporate a running routine into their busy schedules. Indeed, you don't have to give up running with a stressful nine-to-five. With a little planning, our great sport can have a positive role as you set out to build your career—and your miles.

- Run in the morning. By getting out the door before work, the boss's deadlines won't derail your running plans.

- Bring running to your job by creating partners and groups among co-workers, and by entering events together like the JPMorgan Chase Corporate Challenge (see page 498, Corporate Running).

- Join a running club. Running clubs are a perfect way to meet groups of runners, training partners, and friends, and the motivation provided by group runs will get you out the door on those days when your motivation wanes.

- Pick a race—and train for it! It doesn't have to be a marathon. By picking any race distance, you'll boost your motivation to get out there and stick to a consistent running schedule.

- Make a day of it. Gather a group of friends at the same race, or even after training, and follow it with a relaxing brunch. There is nothing more rewarding than a delectable and leisurely meal with friends after a race.—Gabriel Sherman

EVERYONE IS BUSY

These days, everyone is busy. As runners, we're adults playing a children's game; it isn't supposed to be a priority. So when people inevitably ask me why I run, I answer quite simply: it's either running or Prozac (and I'm only half-joking). Fitting my running into my schedule is not a matter of choice, I explain, but rather, of personal survival.

I began what was then called "jogging" in 1969. When all-comers road races gained in popularity, I graduated to running, and have been at it ever since. Over the years, of all the reasons I run—physical health, competition, working at NYRR—it eventually came down to something pretty basic. I run to maintain sanity, and out of gratitude.

After a certain number of years, running becomes like brushing one's teeth—how do you NOT find the time? That being said, I do have my work, a home to keep up, a husband (understanding, as he is also a serious runner), and two studious, athletic teenaged daughters in whose lives I am deeply involved. Just shuttling the girls to daily soccer practice and watching their games eats up a large portion of the day.

Yet, I'm a daily runner (or occasionally cross train as an alternative), and I lift weights twice a week. Here is how, and why, I get it done:

Efficiency—Whether it means getting up very early (I'm a morning person, and so is my exercise), or doing errands on the run (to save a drive, I might run a video to be returned or with money to purchase a couple of bagels, running with one in each hand), or logging miles while other parents wait out the long pre-soccer-game warmup. While I enjoy a gym, and have had a membership, I use the neighborhood roads (or grass or softer surfaces), and the communal medicine balls and free weights that are scattered around the house. The weights I can't lift in our low-ceilinged basement, I lug upstairs. Then there's lugging the equipment back down. I consider this tiring task, which leaves me breathless, (not to mention the agility and balance it takes not to whack a lamp or window with a weight bar), part of my workout.

Letting Go—While running in the morning remains inflexible (to train for a marathon, I've started out as early as 4:30 A.M., compensating for lack of sleep with catnaps, even behind closed doors or under my desk when I worked in an office), if I can't get it in, I have learned to let it go. I've also gotten more flexible. Frozen eyelashes and rain-soaked gear are testimony to the fact that I used to run in any weather, but now, if it's really bad, I'll jump rope indoors, or use a ski machine. I used to be a purist: Nothing replaced running. But I can be satisfied just getting in general fitness. If I'm away, and running is compromised, I use the hotel, do repeats of hotel staircases, or take the long way carrying heavy bags. These days, it all counts.

Science—I try to practice what I preach. Working with NYRR, and writing this book, has been a tremendous education. Like the many other aging athletes interviewed here, if I feel the need to prepare for a race, I now emphasize quality running over quantity. I watch my running surfaces; I employ variety in my training. There are things we know from science, like the need to preserve muscle mass, which declines with age, so I lift weights.

Priorities—To put the time into running, something's got to give. There are fewer friendships and free time. I make only sporadic use of an actual recipe, or a hair salon. My idea of a nice outfit is clean sports gear. I'm sure I'd look better (my teenaged daughters remind me of this quite often) with more care taken to my appearance. But you can't be everything.

Smelling the Roses—I think of what Nina Kuscsik, a contributor to this book, once said: "Our bodies are meant to be used." Particularly as I get older, I pay my respects when I run. It's how I express my gratitude for my life, and my good health. My two daughters, Yael and Shira, ages 17 and 14, are elite soccer players, and two of the fittest people I know. The day I wrote this, I did a fitness run with Yael, part of her training program as a member of the USA Under-19 National Soccer Team pool. When we started out, I struggled. Glancing over at her, the thought went through my mind: I should have had children when I was younger. Then, as we warmed up, I managed to hold the pace. "Wow, you ARE fit," she said to me. And every minute I have ever stolen out of every day to take a run became golden.

—Gloria Averbuch

Put It on the List

"I'm a list maker," proclaims George Hirsch, who for years has adhered faithfully to his routine of making nightly lists, then crossing out tasks as he completes them. "I get great pleasure from seeing things crossed off the list," he says. But while most runners who are so religiously governed by a list would surely need to include their daily workouts, Hirsch never does. He knows he will put in the miles. "Running is automatic. It's closer to something like washing my face when I get up," he concludes.

In the business world, George Hirsch is known for starting up successful magazines. He founded *New York, New Times,* and *The Runner*—which merged with *Runner's World* in 1987. Hirsch became the publisher of *Runner's World* at that time. Recently, he was named worldwide publisher emeritus of *Runner's World* and *Men's Health* magazine. (Hirsch was the first publishing director of *Men's Health.*)

Hirsch is a busy executive, and as a runner, he's no slouch either. Although he puts in a relatively modest 40 miles a week for someone competitive, he managed to win a NYRR Runner of the Year award in the 50-plus age category—which means that in his age group, he won the majority of New York races in which he competed. A few month's before his 60th birthday, he ran a sub-three-hour marathon. Hirsch is still training in Central Park and running marathons.

Hirsch, who gets in his training any time of day during which meetings are not scheduled, admits that for doing his sport, being publisher of a major running magazine "makes my life easier." Wherever business travel takes him, from the magazine's headquarters in Pennsylvania to consulting with advertisers around the country, he can be assured of finding running time. In fact, he even conducts specific business agendas while racking up the miles with some of his co-workers.

Even though running is an integral part of George Hirsch's life, he is often compelled to sacrifice training time. In 1986, when he ran for the United States Congress from his east side New York district, he had a hard time fitting in any running at all. One of the problems was being a novice at campaigning. "I've been a magazine publisher for 35 years. I know what I'm doing. But as a political candidate, I was learning every step of the way." During the 24-hour-a-day schedule of political campaigning, Hirsch would forego a run in favor of catnaps, which he took whenever and wherever he could. He claims he perfected the art of a 15-minute snooze during mid-Manhattan cab rides.

Hirsch says he learned most acutely that life often presents us with more tasks than we can possibly accomplish when he was a business student at Harvard, where he was inundated with work. "You understood you were not going to get every assignment read. I soon realized that was the philosophy: to give us more work than we could possibly do, to be faced with some tough choices, just like the real world."

Even doing the familiar job in which he is comfortable, and within the supportive atmosphere of a running magazine, Hirsch is often forced to sacrifice his run. As he travels a great deal—traversing busy streets—he uses this analogy: "There are traffic jams in life, both literally and figuratively." Although Hirsch is a serious runner, he keeps the time and energy he devotes to the activity in perspective. "I don't make my living as a runner. I'm not training for the Olympics, so running is not my highest priority—although staying fit is."

Hirsch has recently come up with a solution to those times when he can't get out to run, which is made tougher at many hours because he must cross busy Manhattan streets for several miles until he reaches Central Park. The purchase of a low-impact treadmill has allowed him the opportunity to train comfortably in the evening and save his legs from some pounding at the same time.

But perhaps George Hirsch's real gift—which is often rare among serious runners, not to mention high-powered business people—is his ability to relax. "I'm pretty good at it," he says. "After days I've been busy, I will not set my alarm on weekends in order to get up and run. I'll sit in bed with the newspaper, coffee, and a bagel. I take it easy on myself."

Yet, when it's time to buckle down, he puts in the training time. When he takes on the marathon challenge, for example, he plans six weeks worth of long runs, with at least three 18 to 20 milers. But the real secret of his success is knowing exactly how and when to be serious. Although Hirsch says he would never drop out of a marathon once he's started, if he doesn't find time to do the training, he'll change his plans and not toe the starting line. "Life is forgiving," says the man who has mastered perhaps the ultimate balancing act.

TREADMILL TIPS

Whether to beat bad weather, or just enjoy the comforts of a health club, many runners turn to using a treadmill. The popularity of treadmills skyrocketed in the 1990s, and their use remains steady. Here are some treadmill tips to consider.

If you've never used a treadmill, give yourself time to adjust. Experiment by changing the pace or elevation.

Keep in mind that since a treadmill has motors in it, it is doing some of the work for you. You don't have to push off as hard on a treadmill as you do on a road surface or track. However, there's a way to compensate for this. By elevating your treadmill to about a two percent grade, you can more accurately simulate real outdoor running.

Although treadmills are a good way to make running easier and more relaxed (you can watch television or listen to music while using them), they can also be used quite effectively for interval or uphill running, which you can do by setting the computer controls to your desired pace or elevation.

However, due to factors such as dust, humidity, and the friction associated with each strike of a runner's foot, frequent adjustments may be necessary in order to maintain a treadmill's accuracy. If you suspect your treadmill is off in its calculations, you'll have to do your workout on perceived exertion.

Buying a Treadmill

If you are thinking of buying a treadmill, there are several factors to consider. Among them are impact cushioning, stability, smoothness of speed and incline adjustments, control layout, noise, and warranty. If you have pets or small children, also be sure your treadmill has an easily accessible emergency shut-off switch. Some treadmills even require the user to insert a safety key before turning them on. Remember, the most important rule is to experiment before you buy. Although the price range varies widely, don't necessarily assume you need the highest-priced model. Many runners find that a treadmill in the medium price range sufficiently meets their needs.

(Adapted from "Running in Place," *New York Runner*, Jan./Feb. 1998.)

CORPORATE RUNNING

Work and running, real life and play—never the twain shall meet? Not so, if the largest running series in the world is held up as the example. The JPMorgan Chase Corporate Challenge is a series of 3.5-mile road races open to employees of corporations, businesses, and financial institutions. The series, which includes over 250,000 runners from 6,000 corporations, is international in scope, with events overseas as well as in the United States. The largest single event is in Frankfurt, with 5,000 runners. The largest version is conducted by NYRR in Central Park, which was also the site of the first Corporate Challenge back in 1977.

Barbara Paddock, vice president of corporate sponsorship for JPMorgan Chase and also a runner, oversees the series. She emphasizes how the event has integrated running into the workplace on every level. The Corporate Challenge isn't just a road race; it's an institution. Through participation, publicity, or by word of mouth, says Paddock, "If you're part of the corporate world, you've heard of the JPMorgan Chase Corporate Challenge."

Paddock explains the nature of the event: "The race is more about company camaraderie than athletic achievement. It is an opportunity for employees to have fun in a noncompetitive, nonworking atmosphere." A look at an overflowing Central Park on race day is testimony to her claim. Banners, banquet-style picnics, company uniforms and photos, cheerleading sections of fellow employees—all testify to the fact that running and work need not be isolated pursuits.

To see if there is a JPMorgan Chase Corporate Challenge event held in your area, check out jpmorganchasecc.com.

Business and Running

Can successful running be translated to business—and vice versa? One person seems to have made it very clear it can. Alberto Salazar, the former multi-event American and world record holder, was still in serious training when he delved into the restaurant business—immersing himself much in the way he had done in his running. In June 1987, he co-purchased a Eugene, Oregon, restaurant. During his tenure, the Oregon Electric Station became one of the most successful restaurants in the entire Pacific Northwest. In November 1991, Salazar brought his athletic and executive abilities together when he became a major player in the world of international road racing and track and field as an executive with Nike. In 2003, NYRR established the Alberto Salazar award, to be given annually to the top American male and female finishers in the New York City Marathon. Salazar was the last American to win New York, which he did three consecutive times, 1980–1982, with a world record in 1981.

"I think there is a correlation between running and business success. In fact, sometimes I make too direct of a correlation. I tend to be a bit simplistic: Just work hard and it will result in success. In running, however, the rewards are much more directly related to the work you put in. You've got to train smart, but there is a much greater correlation between the amount of effort and the amount of success.

"In business, there are a lot of other variables. It's not quite so simplistic. At first I tended to think that running and business were both regulated by the same effort. But I realized that in business you've probably got to be even smarter, because you're dealing in various ways with a lot of other people. That's resulted in the hardest adjustment for me in the business world. I tend to be a little too confident, or to move a little too quickly.

"Nevertheless, I think there is some similarity between the two in terms of overall philosophy. You have a job to be done and you do whatever it takes to accomplish it. You have to fight the inclination to be negative. That's one of the things I've noticed in the business world. You bring up an idea or a solution to a problem, and the first thing people think of is why it can't be done. I think the proper way is first to see why something will work, and then deal with the hurdles as you go along. Being optimistic can get you past a problem.

This aspect of running and business is similar. Good runners should be the same way. They should be optimistic, envision themselves winning or running a goal time. Then they go about doing the work to accomplish that goal. If you don't look to the ultimate goal—be it financial or otherwise—if you look merely at all the problems along the way, you'll never get it done. Sometimes you can be naive or simplistic and overlook what may become major problems later on, but overall, you're still better off having the same attitude in business as you have for successful running."

24 TIPS FOR ENVIRONMENTALLY-CONSCIOUS RUNNING

Running writer Welles Lobb points out that runners spend a large chunk of their lives outdoors breathing fresh air and bounding over land. Through their close contact with the natural world, many develop an appreciation of nature and sympathy for its well-being. So, as we stride through this age of vital environmental concern, here's Lobb's list of 24 new and recycled conservation tips, which appeared in *New York Running News,* for individual runners and clubs to consider. Although not every tip is practical for everyone, if we all do our share, we can make our world a better place for running.

Reduce Unnecessary Driving

1. Run from either your home or place of work instead of driving to a workout spot. If safety or training reasons require you to drive, try to combine this trip with others (for example, grocery shopping or banking) to consolidate use of your car. You can also run or walk to a nearby workout site for your warmup, if that's possible.

2. Measure your running routes by bicycle odometer, rather than by car.

3. Consider commuting to and from work by foot. With coworkers who are also runners, take an active role in installing a locker-and-shower facility at your workplace.

4. Clubs should encourage members to carpool or use public transportation when traveling to races. Assign a member the job of organizing carpools for club members traveling to out-of-town races. Also, consider renting a van or bus for group trips to races.

Keep Training and Racing Sites Clean

5. Try to pick up at least one piece of litter at workout or race sites. Carry personal garbage home in your car and dispose of it properly.

6. Clubs should organize a club "Cleanup Day" at a local park or popular running route. Combine it with a fun run and social event.

Use, Don't Abuse, the Land

7. Run on established trails. Trailblazing and taking shortcuts can cause damaging erosion.

8. In an emergency, if no public toilet is nearby and you must relieve yourself, don't do so near an open water source or on fragile vegetation. Also, bury solid waste.

Support the Cause

9. Support races that contribute to environmental causes like park-land acquisition, clean water, or clean air.

10. Write to your elected officials to express your views on the importance of clean air and public land acquisitions, especially the establishment of trails for nonmotorized traffic.

11. Clubs should get political! Endorse pro-environment candidates for public office in your club newsletter. Also, include a conservation tip of the month in your newsletter.

12. Clubs should organize a club environmental committee to brainstorm about running/conservation projects. Also, invite a public official, conservation officer, or environmental activist who is a runner to speak to your club about running and the environment.

Save Natural Resources, Reduce Waste

13. Bring your own supply of safety pins to races. This relieves the race director of potential shortages and expenses, and may ultimately reduce the demand for manufactured metal. Also, donate your accumulated collection of race safety pins to your club for future use.

14. Consider a "no shirt" option when filling out your race application. Chances are you already have a stockpile of race T-shirts at home.

15. Donate your old shirts, sweats, and shoes to charities. Clubs should organize an old clothing and running shoe collection drive for charity.

16. Clubs should print their newsletter on recycled paper.

17. Wear your running clothes two or three times before machine-washing them. Remove perspiration odors with a quick rinse after daily use. Air-dry clothes instead of using the dryer.

18. Carry your own water supply to races. This stretches the race director's supply and reduces the number of thrown-away cups.

Recycle

19. Share running magazines or newspapers with friends, then recycle them.
20. Buy sports drinks or bottled water in containers that your state accepts as recyclables.
21. Clubs should raise funds by collecting and selling members' aluminum and glass recyclables to local buyers.

Eliminate Plastics

22. Request environmentally-benign products at races, for example, paper drinking cups, nonplastic awards, and paper bags for packets.
23. Clubs should use ceramic, metal, or paper dishes, cups, utensils, etc., at socials.

Last But Not Least

24. Save water. Keep showers brief and use a water-saver head.

FRED LEBOW ON THE RUN-TO-WORK MOVEMENT (1992)

Since starting work at the NYRRC, I generally run everywhere—to work, to meetings, to receptions. In fact, by 1974, I began to realize I could get everywhere so much faster by running than by subway, bus, or taxi.

That's when we started the Run-to-Work movement at the club. But it really escalated for a time a couple of years later during a New York City transit strike. First of all, we set up a water station on the Brooklyn Bridge with a "RUN-TO-WORK" sign for people walking or running to work. To spread the message, we sent out press releases on how to run to work. People seemed to get the idea; they were running to work by the hundreds. We began to have conversations with various companies about accommodating runners, by installing shower facilities and changing rooms, for example.

Unfortunately, when the strike was over, the Run-to-Work movement lost momentum. But the health and fitness movement lived on and did help affect the management at many companies, which now have extensive gyms and workout and health programs.

The New York City transit strike and Run-to-Work helped popularize wearing running shoes to walk to work, or any other place. And some people still run to work. In addition, in places like New York, it's very easy to run to work because the paths and distances are convenient.

PART 13
RUNNING EQUIPMENT

42

RUNNING SHOES

Running is easy, the common refrain goes. Just lace up your shoes and head out the door. Just lace up your *running* shoes, that is. They're the only protection you've got from the impact of hard surfaces on long stretches of road.

HOW TO CHOOSE RUNNING SHOES

Once an elite runner and now an accomplished masters runner, Gary Muhrcke began selling running shoes in 1976 from the back of a van. Now he owns six Super Runners Shop stores in the New York metropolitan area, which, he emphasizes, specialize in the technical aspects of running shoes. In other words, says Muhrcke, "I stress shoes used by athletes, not just those that look good." The most important thing, echoes Muhrcke, is to stay with a shoe you've used successfully in the past. If the worry is that your favorite model has changed, or will do so in the near future, relax. Muhrcke says most of the good companies create shoes that evolve, and that it is this evolution that has produced the most successful shoes on the market. Therefore, if you need motion control, for example, you'll be able to fulfill that need with increasing effectiveness in future generations of shoes.

If the name or the look of a shoe changes, knowledgeable salespeople can determine which shoe is most like the one you currently wear. It's a matter of knowing the characteristics and the fit. "If you're wearing a shoe that rates an A-minus grade," claims Muhrcke, with evolving shoe technology, "a smart salesperson can offer you one that gets an A-plus."

If you are trying on a shoe at the Super Runners Shop, you are allowed to test that shoe by running outside the store on the sidewalk. Muhrcke claims that nothing will better reveal if the shoe is right than a true test run. What if your store doesn't allow it? "Tell them to change their policy," says Muhrcke. To help you find that perfect pair, look for durable, comfortable running shoes that will be strongest and give support where you are weakest or tend to have problems or injuries.

Before going to the store to buy shoes, determine what you need. Do you want a sturdier, more supportive, heavier training shoe, or a racing shoe (also known as a flat) that is lighter, and has more flexibility? You may be tempted by a combination shoe, called a racer-trainer, but it is usually not as good as either one separately. Have a price range in mind and shop in a store that specializes in running shoes. Employees there should be able to recommend a few different shoes in your price range. In addition, they can assess which shoe might suit your build, your running style, and your running goals. They can also show you how to prolong the life of a shoe with proper care (e.g., using shoe glue products).

If the Shoe Fits

Don't overlook socks. If you don't wear them when running, fine. But if you do, bring them with you to try on with shoes. Another plus to a running shoe specialty store is that you can become acquainted with the various lines of sports socks and their properties (some of which are mentioned in this chapter).

A training shoe should be long enough to fit a thumb-width at the toe end of the shoe. A racing shoe can be snug; the toe can almost touch the end of the shoe. The width should be comfortable when standing. Keep in mind that feet tend to be larger later in the day.

Should Women Buy Men's Shoes?

Once upon a time, claims Muhrcke, there was, in fact, more variety and quality to men's running shoes than women's. "Years ago women thought their shoes weren't as good. Now I think women's shoes are superior for them and make more sense than buying men's shoes." Top companies make both men's and women's versions of shoes. Women's shoes are made lighter than men's, and thus serve women better. But if a woman has a wider or larger foot, says Muhrcke, she shouldn't hesitate to try men's shoes.

Although separate shoe models are made for men and women, a man with a narrow foot can try a woman's shoe and a woman with a wide foot can try men's shoes. Women should check the heel width though, as it may be too wide in a men's shoe. The shoe lacing can also help with width sizing.

Do You Need More Than One Pair of Running Shoes?

"I don't know about you, but I can't put my foot into a wet pair of shoes," says Gary Muhrcke. So, if sweat or rain plague you as a regular runner, you need more than one pair of running shoes. You probably should not buy two pairs of a new model at once. Try the shoes for at least a few weeks to make sure they work for you.

Do You Need Separate Racing Shoes?

The technology of training shoes has evolved to the extent that lightweight models may well serve for most runners' purposes, including races. "The biggest factor is weight," says Muhrcke. "You may save only two ounces in a racing shoe, but for the serious runner, two ounces over 10,000 meters is a lot." Most would benefit from racing shoes, he concludes, if not for the physical aspects then for the psychological ones. It's the ritual. "Putting on racing shoes is the thing you do on race day that psychologically prepares the body to race."

Construction Details

Before buying your running shoes, consider the construction of the shoe as well as the fit.

- **Lasting.** The last is what a shoe is shaped around. The type of last greatly affects the flexibility and stability of the shoe. Slip lasting allows for increased flexibility and characterizes lighter shoes. Board lasting increases stability and the integrity (resistance to deformity) of the shoe. Combination lasting includes the advantages of both methods. There are two shapes used in lasting, curved and straight. Most people find a slightly curved last to be most comfortable.
- **Flexibility.** Flexibility refers to the bend of the shoe in the area surrounding the ball of the foot. Racing shoes should be very flexible and training shoes should be slightly stiffer. Most shoes can be made more flexible by bending the shoe across the ball horizontally.
- **Shock absorption (cushioning).** The two parts to shock absorption are front (or forefoot) and heel (or rear foot). Generally, softer shoes (air shoes) exacerbate problems for runners with structural

imbalances. People who have impact-related problems (e.g., heel bruises) benefit from soft shoes. If you have a specific problem, select a shoe that provides appropriate cushioning.

- **Insoles (sock liners).** Insoles add to shock absorption. These are removable and replaceable and either come with the shoe or are purchased separately. Foam rubber or canvas insoles are unacceptable. Some, like antishearing insoles, can be purchased separately. These reduce friction to prevent blisters. If necessary, to prevent slipping, insoles can be glued into the shoe.

- **Heel counters.** The heel is cradled in a cup that is called a counter. It should be stiff, especially in a training shoe. The counter resists excessive heel motion. If you have any imbalances causing a problem, look for a strong heel counter made of plastic.

- **Toe box.** If your toes are thick or slide forward, look for a high toe-box shoe. If you still have toe problems after purchasing the shoes, the toe box can be cut to allow room. The cuts should be vertical, not horizontal.

- **Quality control.** The shoes must be balanced. They should not rock or tilt to the sides when placed on a flat surface.

- **Caveat emptor.** Gary Muhrcke advises that you can get the most from your purchase, and best protect yourself by being on the lookout for shoe wear. Muhrcke's Law states, "Repair shoe heels as soon as necessary." The basic sign of the need for repair is if the outsole has worn down to the midsole. You should be able to bring your shoes into a running shoe store for repair.

In the past, NYRR has made collections of used running shoes to donate to homeless shelters or to those who have been a part of its various other programs. Why not find a good use for your shoes in your own community? Make a collection and bring them to a local homeless shelter or other charitable organization. T-shirts are also often coveted, particularly by children.

Farther afield, you can donate your running shoes to worthy causes through long-running programs, such as Shoes for Africa (www.shoesforafrica.com) or Nike's Reuse-a-Shoe program (www.nikebiz.com, under "responsibility," click on "environment").

After one year, even if your shoes do not appear worn-out, they probably are. "The elements alone—heat, salt that melts snow, pavement—wear out shoes," claims Muhrcke. Even a shoe that still looks good can lose shock absorption. With one repair of the outsoles, a shoe that is used constantly should last 800 to 1,000 miles.

There are two common mistakes that Gary Muhrcke has seen over the years that receive little attention. The first is that people don't understand pronation, the act of the foot rolling inward on footstrike. Customers tell Muhrcke that they need antipronating shoes when many times they have normal footstrike. "To a degree, to pronate is to run normally," explains Muhrcke. "Pronation is part of foot function; the 'hit and roll' of the foot disperses energy, as it should." Runners continually point to wear on the outer shoe heel as a sign that they need special shoes. "The eventual wear of shoes on the outer heel is also normal," says Muhrcke. Obviously there are categories of runners who may need a more specialized shoe; for example, those who are large or heavy, or who increase their mileage and subsequently suffer injury. But generally this is not the case.

The other mistake is made by women who want to buy top-of-the-line shoes. They correlate price with quality, but pricier running shoes are those with more features, which add weight. But, as Muhrcke points out, women are lighter than men and don't need the heavier shoes. "They're doing themselves a disservice," he says and suggests that these women stay with a sparer, simpler model. "The bottom line," says Muhrcke, "is that running is a very simple sport. After all, even two-year-olds run. A lot of people try to complicate it." With today's technology and expert help, it should be easy to buy the appropriate running shoe.

Shoes and Injury Prevention

Running shoe manufacturers now produce shoes not only designed to reduce the risk of injury, but also to help eliminate the cause of (often chronic) injuries that may already exist. True, much of injury-free running depends on biomechanics, but the correct choice of a running shoe is very important, especially for those prone to certain types of injuries.

Most running shoe designs emphasize either shock absorption (which provides mainly cushioning) or motion control (which provides mainly stability). Generally, the more a shoe is designed for motion control, the more rigid it is and the less it absorbs shock. Conversely, the better the shock absorption, the less motion control. The challenge for today's shoe manufacturers is to provide shock absorption and motion control in one shoe.

Manufacturers today realize the importance of shock absorption, even for people who need shoes with good motion control, for example, people who have stability problems or flat feet.

You should choose a shoe that will best accommodate your feet—and your potential foot problems. If you have supination (feet roll to the outside) and, therefore, tend to have bowlegs or suffer from iliotibial band syndrome, stress fractures, shin splints and plantar fasciitis, choose a shoe that offers plenty of shock absorption. Look for a slip-lasted shoe with a soft midsole. If you have excessive pronation (rotation or torque to the inside), choose a shoe with good foot control. Choose a straight-lasted shoe with a firm midsole, particularly on the inner (medial) side of the shoe, which also may have a firm board last.

MONITOR YOUR SHOES

From the beginning of shoe use, the wear of the outsole should be noted, and later midsole compression should also be monitored. Although most people incur injuries because of improper training, if an athlete becomes injured or sore in the first two to four weeks after changing shoe type, the shoe must be considered the likely cause. In this case, it is best to resume using the old shoe model.

The wear on the shoe pattern on the bottom of the sole (ridges, waffles, etc.) tells you about your footstrike and thrust (how your foot pushes off the ground). This is what a shoe dealer assesses when looking at your old shoes. Shoe wear can be valuable to discover what a normal pattern of shoe wear is for you, and to determine which brands and models wear better or longer.

Wear on the sole of the shoe is not always the first indication of shoe deterioration. Some runners compress the midsole before they wear out the outsoles. Learn to assess compression. While outsole wear is more obvious, many runners don't check for compression (called "bottoming-out" by dealers). Thus, many customers wonder why, although the shoes don't appear to them to be worn-out, they don't feel the same cushioning. Gauging the effectiveness of cushioning will help you from running in shoes past their prime.

Pronators wear out the midsole fast; also, the medial sides of the shoes compress quicker. Forefoot strikers (those who land first on the ball/toe of the foot) can also compress or compact the midsole material more quickly.

ADDITIONAL SHOE TIPS

1. Shoes generally lose their shock-absorbing qualities anywhere from 500 to 700 miles, or about six months of running five to ten hours a week.

2. Take your old pair of running shoes to the store with you to show the dealer.

3. When buying running shoes, ask to try on several different types for comparison. After buying a pair of shoes, wear them for casual walking for at least a few days before running. According to guidelines from the International Marathon Medical Directors Association, training with a new pair of shoes should be done slowly and gradually, and competing should be done only when you are absolutely sure that the shoes are trouble-free.

4. Choose shoes that are roomy enough. For one thing, your feet expand during running. You should purchase shoes that have about a thumb-width between the longest toe and the front of the shoe, and make sure the toe box allows enough room to wiggle your toes. Try to buy the shoes in the afternoon, when your feet are bigger.

5. You might consider treating your shoes with a protective coating, like Scotchgard®, or some other product made specifically for this purpose.

6. Cliff Temple suggests that you look carefully at the inside of the shoes for rough seams or other possible causes of blisters.

7. Temple also advises beginners not to buy cheap shoes, such as sneakers not specifically designed for running. But don't buy the priciest model to begin with either.

8. Look down at your feet. How are they shaped—long and narrow ("needle feet") or square and short ("thimble feet")? Now go for a shoe in that shape. People tend to buy shoes in the shape of their feet, even if they don't realize it.

43

RUNNING APPAREL

Just like the running movement, running clothes and accessories have evolved. And they continue to be improved upon with remarkable technological developments. In what has developed into a growing and competitive industry, the race to create the ultimate in both functional and stylish running gear sprints on.

The latest running attire catchwords are simply, "Don't sweat it!" And they are meant to be taken quite literally. The days of running in old-fashioned sweatshirts and sweatpants are long gone, and for good reason. Although they were once regarded as staple running equipment, sweats, in essence, accomplish everything you don't want as a runner. They cling to moisture, keeping you uncomfortably wet while you run, and actually become heavier as a result. Additionally, they offer no protection from wind, rain, or snow. In fact, running in sweats these days is the equivalent of using a rotary-dial telephone. Sure, it'll work, but why on earth would you want to use it?

This section focuses on the latest technological advances in running attire, as well as some of the more popular accessories available to consumers. Much of this information is provided by Beth Creighton, NYRR's merchandise director since 2000. Creighton's views are formed by her task of stocking NYRR's Running Gallery, a year-round store dedicated to New York City Marathon and NYRR apparel. In addition, she heads the enormous store set up at the Marathon Expo, which generates 30 percent of NYRR's yearly sales during a one-week period. NYRR sells worldwide to over 100 countries. The appeal of NYRR merchandise is its functionality, design, and logos, particularly the cachet of the New York City Marathon.

"Running wear is both functional and fashionable," says Creighton. "High tech gear has been developed for any type of running in any kind of climate. It has also expanded to accommodate trail and off-road running." Creighton says women's gear is an increasingly larger part of NYRR sales. That's likely because of the significant increase in the number of women runners. Other developments include the fact that running gear is now made for multisports participation, like mountain biking or hiking.

"Runners are also savvy consumers" she says. "They look for clothing made with technologically-advanced fabrics." Quality is the number one consideration. The clothing should be able to hold up under demanding circumstances, such as a 15-mile run in snow or rain. Go for the brand names, experts advise.

Fall and winter present runners with the challenge of staying warm, dry, and protected from the wind without wearing so many clothes that they can't move or risk getting overheated. Diane Magnani, former running store owner and a 2:49 marathoner, frequently answers runners' what-to-wear questions. "A good rule of thumb is that you should dress to run as if it were about 20 degrees warmer and you were going out for some activity not designed to raise your heart rate," she says. That way, you may feel chilly at first, but you'll warm up considerably after the first five to ten minutes.

You'll save yourself a lot of sweating if you remember to dress in layers, especially when the weather is unpredictable. For example, you might start an early-morning run wearing a polypropylene top under a long-sleeved shirt under a lightweight shell, with polypropylene tights or thicker pants on the bottom. As you warm up and the sun gets high in the sky, you can remove the shell, pants, and cotton shirt and tie them around your waist or carry them in a small pack.

"You'll also be able to get away with fewer and less bulky clothes," says Magnani, "if you wear a hat and mittens or gloves. At least 50 percent of the heat your body loses is lost through your head. If you get warm, just pull the items off and tuck them in a pocket."

If you're trying to run a fast time in a race, you may want to opt for a bit of shivering on the starting line in order not to be burdened with extra items in the later miles. If you can, have a friend with you to whom you can hand your extra gear just before the race starts.

It's a misconception, Magnani notes, that it's healthy to sweat excessively when you work out. People used to believe that one of those suits that makes you sweat was a way to lose weight. All it does is make you dehydrated. Of course, you will perspire some, no matter how cold it is. The best way to deal with that is to make sure the layer next to your skin is made with a material that "wicks" moisture away from the skin, such as polypropylene. To keep moisture away from the outside, wear a fabric that also "breathes."

TOP OF THE LINE RUNNING GEAR

Running apparel is available for all weather conditions. Warm-weather cloth-ing is meant to keep you cool and dry, cold-weather clothing to keep you warm and dry. Winter wear is particularly essential to the majority of run-ners. For years, a persistent dilemma for the inclement-weather runner—and for companies producing active wear—has been to come up with running gear that not only prevents moisture and wind from getting in, but also allows moisture (i.e., sweat) to get out.

There are a number of well known and popular moisture-management fabrics currently on the market that do just that. "Moisture management," also called "wicking," is the ability of the material to pull sweat from the body so it dissipates and dries quickly. The fabrics that achieve this effect are made of synthetics, like polyester and nylon (as opposed to cotton, which holds moisture) and come in a variety of brand names. They are lightweight, breathable, insulating fabrics that are effective in wicking mois-ture away from the body. These fabrics also transport perspiration vapors outward while preventing precipitation from penetrating inward.

DRESS FOR SUCCESS

Cool-Weather Wear

It's a good idea for runners to go for a good jacket and various pairs of run-ning tights with different thicknesses.

Because high-tech fabrics are in everything from shirts to jackets, the key to successful dressing is to layer. You might wear a lighter-weight "inner shell" and a heavier material with the same properties as an "outer shell" (such as in a turtleneck shirt covered by a jacket). Look for this clothing made with performance fabrics like Supplex® and Lycra®, perhaps with a lit-tle cotton mix.

Jackets are definitely high-tech, and can be divided into various levels of protection—with the maximum being a heavy-duty material that is made for weather extremes and activities less heat-generating than running, such as hiking. For maximum warmth, Thermolite® is best, and Creighton says it's a huge seller.

Tights come in a variety of thicknesses and styles. They are usually made of Lycra/nylon blend, which is a stretchy, supportive material. For those who prefer less formfitting legwear, looser pants are available. They still come in polyester/cotton blend, but they also feature more technical fabrics, like polyester and/or nylon.

Some clothing remains classic. Hooded sweatshirts are still available at The Running Gallery (as are crew necks and quarter zip pullovers). They are often polyester/cotton blends. Although not made of performance materials, they are, nonetheless, staples as memorabilia and for casual wear. For example, the hooded sweatshirt at The Running Gallery is 90 percent cotton (the more cotton, the heavier the item) and 10 percent polyester. It will last you for years.

> You can eliminate some excess perspiration altogether by shedding extra layers as you warm up during winter runs. But where are you going to put the scarf, mittens, and hat that all seemed essential when you first set out? Try creating a modern-day chatelaine. Tie a soft piece of sash cord around your waist (a leather belt will chafe). Add a few large safety pins to the sash. When you want to take off the scarf, just wrap it around the cord. Your gloves and hat can be pinned to the sash while you continue running at a cooler, less encumbered pace.
>
> —*Kay Denmark*

Lighter-Weight Running Wear

NYRR sells a CoolMax® Alta which features UV protection and low-pilling durability. It is so successful that The Running Gallery added long-sleeved CoolMax® shirts. You'll pay a bit extra for this material, but not much. In terms of performance it's definitely worth the investment. Although the cotton T-shirt is a standard, it is good in only the most ideal weather conditions. That's because it holds moisture. As soon as you begin to perspire, the slightest breeze will give you a chill.

Shorts are also huge sellers in The Running Gallery. Typical running shorts offer the greatest freedom of movement. They are short and have ample splits on the sides to allow for a full stride. Compression shorts are quite popular, and looser soccer/basketball shorts are made for running as well. Many of the looser shorts have a cross-over appeal—that is, they are used for other sports. All of these styles come in high-tech fibers, such as—CoolMax® liners, with Supplex on the outside. Bicycle shorts are Lycra/Supplex blend, look like a short version of running tights and are also used for running. Also popular are compression shorts, which you can wear under running shorts. "They prevent chafing, and hold you in," says Creighton.

Singlets are also a running essential. They are made almost exclusively of CoolMax®. The material is so effective that you can run a race and a short time later, the singlets and shorts are bone dry.

HEAD TO TOE

Hats and Gloves

Headwear is extremely important for runners, since in cold conditions the majority of the body's heat loss is through the head. In hot weather, shielding the face with a visor (as opposed to a hat, which retains heat) is a good idea.

Mild conditions call for bandannas or baseball caps. The New York City Marathon bicycle cap, a trademark worn by Fred Lebow, who pioneered the design, is a top seller at NYRR. The Running Gallery sells a popular headband made of polar fleece. It keeps the ears warm without overheating by covering the entire head. In very cold weather, ski hats (an old standby) are useful.

A Buff® is a single piece of fabric, made from polyester (for its wicking properties) with no seams. This tube-shaped garment can be used as a hat, headband or neck warmer. It's mostly seen in cycling, but it's crossing over to runners. Its new popularity resulted in it being made available at the 2003 New York City Marathon, featuring Marathon colors and a picture of a Marathon bridge.

Hands are another important extremity to keep warm. Thermax® gloves are popular sellers at NYRR. Their thin fibers are hollow in order to trap heat. In extreme cold, you can wear heavier gloves, or layer gloves by adding a pair of mittens.

Socks

The Running Gallery sells socks made from CoolMax® for summer, and a heavier sock, made with Thermax for winter. You should have socks made from performance materials because the fabric keeps moisture off your feet. Saturated cotton socks will likely give you blisters. Sales at NYRR have reflected the popularity of lower cut socks over higher cut ones. The choice of sock styles depends on personal preference and how they fit with an individual's running shoes.

Most running socks have blister protection. But what to choose: double or single-layered socks? Beth Creighton says it's personal preference. "On NYRR staff, it's about 50/50."

FOR WOMEN ONLY

"You can't run without a sports bra," claims Beth Creighton. "Having one is a given. And as they have increased in popularity, companies are paying more attention to the level of comfort and support."

It used to be that only one manufacturer sold sports/running bras. Now they are made by sportswear companies, as well as traditional bra manufacturers. These bras are a must, not just for running, but for any athletic activity. The latest revolution is in sports bras made especially for larger-breasted women (some sports bras even feature underwires).

Since this item is so important for a woman, it is essential to shop smart when choosing a bra. Try it on—run in place, move, stretch. Make sure the bra is snug, but not so tight it interferes with your breathing. Rub your fingers along the seams to determine that they won't chafe. Replace bras when the elastic has broken down. Some experts suggest line drying (as opposed to using the dryer) helps keep the materials from prematurely breaking down.

REFLECTIVE WEAR

When running in dark, or even near-dark, it is essential to "see and be seen." Especially in or near traffic, you should make an effort to help people see you. Almost all technical merchandise has reflective properties—either as part of the fabric, as piping, or as printing. Reflective vests are popular. Many running shoes and clothes feature reflective strips. You can also buy this material to adhere to your clothing. The latest trend in reflective wear is built-in all-over reflectivity—materials that are built right into clothing and offer maximum visibility.

SUNGLASSES

Running during the day has its share of hazards, too, namely, exposure to the sun's ultraviolet (UV) rays. Extended UV exposure can cause retinal and corneal problems, impair night vision, and lead to eyestrain due to constant squinting. Also, the skin around the eyes can be vulnerable to skin cancer.

If you wear vision-correcting lenses of any kind (eyeglasses or contact lenses), it's important that you maintain your ability to see clearly when running, says Dr. Michael Fedak, a Manhattan ophthalmologist and accomplished ultrarunner. This can be done easily, he says. Most people have little or no trouble wearing their corrective eyewear on the run, and doing so has a number of advantages.

The first is safety. "Especially running in the city, you need to be able to see traffic, obstacles, and other people," says Fedak. Some people get used to running without glasses because they find them inconvenient or uncomfortable, then are amazed at the difference in their perception when they wear them. Another advantage is that glasses protect the eyes from airborne particles—"another hazard of urban running"—as well as wind, insects, branches, and other potentially damaging or annoying objects.

Runners have two main complaints about wearing glasses: they can fog up, and the bouncing or slipping around can be distracting. The former problem gets serious only when running at an all-out pace, claims Fedak, who wears glasses for protection while running even though he doesn't need them to correct his vision. "If you can, just take them off and wipe the lenses."

As for slipping and bouncing, there are several solutions. One is to simply wear glasses that fit snugly. You can either get your pair tightened or consider buying a pair of lightweight "sport" glasses, many of which can be fitted with prescription lenses. "That's what I wear, and I never even notice them," says Fedak. Or if you can, try a strap that wraps around the back of your head.

Contact lenses are favored by many runners for their convenience, and, according to Fedak, all but the old "hard" types will stay securely in your eyes under most conditions. "It's very rare to have them fall out," he says.

Sunglasses are popular among runners because of concerns about the damaging effects of the sun. The problem can even occur on overcast days, when Fedak suggests wearing orange- or yellow-tinted lenses for improved clarity, as well as UV protection.

Look for "100% UV protection" on the label. In general, the darker the lens, the more the protection. Other features include lens coatings to minimize scratching and prevent fogging. Try glasses on for fit and comfort; they should be snug but not so tight as to pinch or fog up.

"You've got nothing to lose with sunglasses, as long as you use a pair with maximum UV protection. Shop around—they don't have to be that expensive, even the ones that are specially designed for sports. I once bought a pair of bright yellow ones for $9.95 that are protective and virtually indestructible."

To protect runners' eyes, manufacturers have created sunglasses that are not only effective in blocking UV rays, but are also "sportsworthy"; they won't fall off your face. Most sports sunglasses come in a wraparound style to ensure maximum UV blockage. Adjustable ear stems, interchangeable lenses, and adjustable frame angles are other options you may want to look into. As for the color of your lenses, gray is recommended for bright sunlight, brown or bronze for a hazy sun, and amber or yellow for cloud cover or fog. Some sports sunglasses also come with a removable foam strip on the top of the frame that absorbs perspiration and prevents the glasses from slipping or bouncing.

RUNNING STROLLERS

Baby-sitting has never been so much fun! These days you can see runners and walkers everywhere using these strollers—three-wheeled carts that are lightweight, but sturdy. Strollers come with a variety of features, and because they can be expensive, it is good to get the feel of one before buying. You can check them out online, in ads in various running magazines, or head to a specialty running store. Baby stores carry them as well. The important features to look for are a hand brake, canopies for sun protection, and quick release wheels for folding or storing the stroller.

WHERE TO FIND IT ALL

No matter what type of running accessory you're interested in, excellent shopper's guides and reference sources are the many mail-order companies advertised in the back of major running magazines or by going online. On-line mail order is NYRR's primary source of business. By using mail order, you can outfit yourself for the entire season without even leaving your home.

You can order NYRR merchandise by phone (1-800-405-2288) or online at nyrrc.org/merchandise. You can also visit The Running Gallery during NYRR hours.

The days when a solitary road runner was viewed as "a nut running through the street in his underwear" are now a distant memory. Once considered a poor man's sport (after all, the only special equipment you really needed was a pair of sneakers), running has transformed itself into a sometimes costly venture. A quick glance at the advertising pages of running magazines provides a small sampling of the products currently available to the consumer—everything from baby joggers to computer software to log your miles.

In this land of opportunity—and entrepreneurial frenzy—two words remain as clear and all-important as ever: caveat emptor! With the proliferation of products available to the consumer, it is sometimes exceedingly difficult to distinguish between gimmickry and usefulness. The only advice that seems clearly prudent is to do your research before spending your money. Read magazine articles about specific products, talk to your running friends about accessories they use, and, most important, ask questions of the salespeople you deal with. Generally, runners do like to help other runners.

FRED LEBOW ON THE POWER OF A T-SHIRT (1992)

It seems T-shirts are a runner's most cherished possession. They certainly are a race director's! We started giving out T-shirts to several hundred entrants in the 1973 New York City Marathon. Now, for races alone, we make about 160,000 T-shirts a year, and we sell an additional 75,000 a year.

People ask me all the time how we get over 7,000 volunteers for the Marathon (not to mention the 6,000 others along the course, and volunteers for our 100 other events). I answer "Never underestimate the power of a T-shirt." Even heads of corporations who earn six-figure salaries call me to ask for a T-shirt.

> Perspiration stains make even the most beloved T-shirts look especially grimy. But that old faithful cleaning cure-all, borax, can often do the trick. Before laundering, soak the shirt for an hour in hot water with approximately a half cup of borax.
> —*Kay Denmark*

For some reason, the rich and not-too-rich alike treat a T-shirt like gold. Once, the filmmaker Spike Lee was directing a movie near the NYRRC. We met, and I gave him a shirt. He checked carefully to make sure he had the right size. He was really happy with it.

Sometimes people say they are tired of getting T-shirts in races, so at one point we tried something else. We tried giving out watches, shorts, hats, headbands, shoelaces—nothing worked like T-shirts. People complained, "Where are the T-shirts?" Even though many of the racers have dozens of T-shirts in their drawers, they always want more.

A T-shirt can be sort of a bribe, but it's a legal bribe. In 1976, the first year the Marathon went through the city streets, a group of hoods from one of the neighborhoods paid me a call. It turned out part of the route was on their turf. I was nervous, to say the least. I handed each of them T-shirts and made them the guardians of that part of the course. It worked. On the day of the race, there they stood, "on guard" in an organized line along the roadway, wearing their T-shirts.

We give T-shirts as goodwill gifts in other countries. I give them out at meetings with city agencies. I gave a shirt to the pope, to presidents. A T-shirt not only opens doors, it widens them.

(Beth Creighton adds, "Everyone still talks about this. Even all these years later, I hear these T-shirt stories.")

RESOURCES

1. New York Road Runners resources
2. Bibliography
3. Running and fitness publishers
4. Magazines
5. Organizations
6. Internet Running-Related Resources

1. NEW YORK ROAD RUNNERS RESOURCES

New York Road Runners is located in New York City at 9 East 89th Street (between Madison and Fifth Avenues), less than a block from Central Park. NYRR is open weekdays from 10:00 A.M. to 8:00 P.M., Saturdays from 10:00 A.M. to 5:00 P.M., and Sundays from 10:00 A.M. to 3:00 P.M. For members, there are changing facilities, lockers, toilets, and water fountains. The Running Gallery store (weekdays from noon to 7:00 P.M., weekends from 10:00 A.M. to 3:00 P.M.) stocks the latest in running gear and accessories.

President and CEO: Allan Steinfeld

Headquarters: New York Road Runners
9 East 89th Street
New York, N.Y. 10128

Telephone: 212-860-4455
NYC Marathon Hotline: 212-423-2249
E-mail: webmaster@nyrrc.org,
marathonmailer@nyrrc.org.

Web sites: www.nyrrc.org
www.nycmarathon.org
www.fast-women.com
www.mensracing.com (race results)

Membership:

New York Road Runners serves 250,000 runners and walkers annually, including 40,000 members from every U.S. state and dozens of countries around the world. With comprehensive fitness programs including races, classes, clinics, and community services for people of all ages, abilities, and fitness levels, New York Road Runners is also the organizer of the renowned New York City Marathon.

NYRR membership dues start at $35 per year ($20 for juniors and seniors). NYRR offers a variety of membership options and packages that fit every budget and lifestyle.

Membership Benefits:

- Eligibility for guaranteed entry into the New York City Marathon*
- Reduced fees for NYRR races (up to 35 percent discount), fitness classes, special events, and parties
- Discounts on NYRR merchandise
- Regular mailings, including *New York Runner,* plus newsletters, race applications, e-mail bulletins, and special announcements
- Free informational clinics and lectures on fitness-related topics
- Annual discount Benefits Directory, listing New York City stores, gyms, and health care providers offering NYRR member discounts
- Use of free lockers and water fountains convenient to Central Park

NYRR membership also helps to support numerous community programs and safety initiatives, and offers many ways to get involved.

NYRR Programs:

- The New York Road Runners Foundation
- Group Runs
- Central Park Safety Program
- Senior Fitness Program

*Individuals who are NYRR members by January 31 of a given year, run nine qualifying NYRR races within that same calendar year, and maintain their membership the following year will be eligible for guaranteed entry into that second year's New York City Marathon.

Printed Materials:

- *New York Runner*, the official quarterly magazine of NYRR
- New York City Marathon Participants' Handbook
- Bimonthly races mailing, includes race applications and information
- Member newsletter

Classes:

New York Road Runners has a variety of offerings throughout the year. Ranging from four to ten weeks, the classes have been designed by leaders in their fields to help participants meet their fitness goals. All classes are taught in group settings by experts at Manhattan venues.

All classes are open to NYRR members and nonmembers. Members are entitled to reduced fees (approximately 10 percent off). Advance registration is required unless otherwise specified.

- Running Classes
- Power Yoga
- IM=X Pilates
- Active-Isolated Stretching
- Deep Water Running
- Healthwalking
- City Sports for Kids

Library

The Albert H. Gordon Library is available to NYRR members at NYRR Headquarters in New York City. Named for its generous benefactor, Mr. Albert H. Gordon, the library has numerous volumes of books, videos, and magazines covering running history, road racing, cross-country, and track and field, as well as health, nutrition, and fitness. Featured authors include Grete Waitz, Bill Rodgers, Joan Benoit Samuelson, Frank Shorter, Roger Bannister, George Sheehan, Hal Higdon, Kathrine Switzer, and Joe Henderson.

2. SELECTED BIBLIOGRAPHY

Allen, Mark, and Bob Babbitt. *Mark Allen Total Triathlete*. Chicago: Contemporary Books, 1988.

Applegate, Liz. *Power Foods,* Emmaus, PA: Rodale Press, 1991.

Athletic Achievements (editorial staff). *The Almanac of Sports Contracts.* Little Canada, MN: Athletic Achievements, 1997.

Averbuch, Gloria. *The Woman Runner,* New York: Simon and Schuster, 1984.

Bakoulis, Gordon. *Getting Real about Running.* New York: Ballantine, 2002.

———. *How to Train For and Run Your Best Marathon.* New York: Simon and Schuster/Fireside Books, 1993.

Bannister, Roger. *The Four-Minute Mile.* New York: Lyons & Burford, 1955.

Battista, Garth A. *The Runner's Literary Companion.* New York: Penguin Books, 1996.

Benjamin, Ben E. *Listen to Your Pain.* New York: Viking Press, 1984.

Benyo, Richard. *Making the Marathon Your Event.* New York: Random House, 1992.

———. and Joe Henderson. *Running Encyclopedia.* Champaign, IL: Human Kinetics, 2001.

Bingham, John. *No Need for Speed.* Emmaus, PA: Rodale Press, 2002.

Birch, Beryl Bender. *Beyond Power Yoga.* New York: Fireside Books, 2000.

———. *Power Yoga.* New York: Fireside Books, 1995.

———. *Beginner's and Intermediate Practice.* (audiotapes).

———. *The Primary Series of Astanga Yoga.* (audiotapes).

———. *Everyday Mindfulness: Meditation.* (audiotapes)

Bowerman, William J., and William H. Freeman. *High Performance Training for Track and Field.* Champaign, IL: Human Kinetics, 1991.

Brody, Jane. *Jane Brody's Good Food Book.* New York: Bantam Books, 1992.

Brown, Richard L., and Joe Henderson. *Fitness Running.* Champaign, IL: Human Kinetics, 1994.

Carr, Gerry A. *Fundamentals of Track and Field.* Champaign, IL: Human Kinetics, 1991.

Chodes, John. *Corbitt: The Story of Ted Corbitt.* Los Altos, CA: Tafnews Press, 1974.

Christman, Paul. *The Purple Runner.* Tallahassee: Cedarwinds, 1983.

Clark, Nancy. *The New York City Marathon Cookbook.* Nashville: Rutledge Hill Press, 1994.

———. *Nancy Clark's Sports Nutrition Guidebook*. Champaign, IL: Human Kinetics, 1994.

Cohen, Neil. *Jackie Joyner-Kersee*. Boston: Little Brown, 1992.

Coleman, Ellen. *Eating, for Endurance*. Palo Alto: Bull, 1992.

Colfer, George R., and John M. Chevrette. *Running for Fun and Fitness*. Dubuque, IA: Kendall/Hunt, 1992.

Daniels, Jack. *Daniels' Running Formula*. Emmaus, PA: Rodale Press, 1998.

Derderian, Tom. *Boston Marathon: The First Century of the World's Premier Running Event (Centennial Race Edition)*. Champaign, IL: Human Kinetics, 1996.

Drinkwater, Barbara L. *Female Endurance Athletes*. Champaign, IL: Human Kinetics, 1986.

Durbin, Bruce, Sr. *Portrait of an Athlete*. Champaign, IL: Human Kinetics, 1992.

Elliot, Richard. *The Competitive Edge*. Los Altos, CA: Tafnews Press, 1991.

Ellis, Joe, with Joe Henderson. *Running Injury-Free*. Emmaus, PA: Rodale Press, 1994.

Fahey, Thomas D., and Gayle Hutchinson. *Weight Training for Women*. Mountain View, CA: Mayfield, 1992.

Fixx, James. *Jim Fixx's Second Book of Running*. New York: Random House, 1980.

———. *The Complete Book of Running*. New York: Random House, 1977.

Floyd, Patricia A., and Janet E. Parke. *Walk, Jog, Run for Wellness Everyone*. Third edition. Winston-Salem: Hunter Textbooks, 1998.

Freeman, William F. *Peak When It Counts*. Los Altos, CA: Tafnews Press, 1991.

Friel, Joe. *The Triathlete's Training Bible*. Boulder, CO: Velo Press, 1998.

Galloway, Jeff. *Galloway's Book on Running*. Bolinas, CA: Shelter Publications, 1984.

Gallup, Davia Anne. *Running with Man's Best Friend*. Loveland, CO: Alpine, 1986.

Gambaccini, Peter. *The New York City Marathon: Twenty-Five Years*. New York: Rizzoli International Publications, Inc., 1994.

Glover, Bob, and Shelly-Lynn Florence Glover. *The Competitive Runner's Handbook*. Revised edition. New York: Penguin Books, 1999.

———. *The Runner's Training Diary*. New York: Penguin, 1997.

———. *The Runner's Handbook*. New York: Penguin Books, 1996.

Green, Sammy. *Recipes for Runners*. Garden City Park: Avery, 1991.

Greene, Laurence S., and Russell R. Pate. *Training for Young Distance Runners*. Champaign, IL: Human Kinetics, 1997.

Grisogono, Vivian. *The Knee: Problems and Prevention*. London: John Murray, 1998.

Harris, Raymond, and Lawrence J. Frank. *Guide to Fitness after 50*. New York: Plenum Press, 1977.

Heinonen, Janet. *Sports Illustrated Running for Women*. New York: Penguin, 1989.

Hendershott, Jon. *Track's Greatest Women*. Los Altos, CA: Tafnews Press, 1987.

Henderson, Joe. *Marathon Training*. Second edition. Champaign, IL: Human Kinetics, 2004.

——. *Running 101*. Champaign, IL: Human Kinetics, 2000.

——. *Best Runs*. Champaign, IL: Human Kinetics, 1998.

——. *The Running Revolution*. Tallahassee, FL: Cedarwinds, 1998.

——. *Better Runs*. Champaign, IL: Human Kinetics, 1995.

——. *Fitness Running*. Champaign, IL: Human Kinetics, 1994.

——, with Bill Rodgers and Priscilla Welch. *Masters Running and Racing*. Emmaus, PA: Rodale Press, 1991.

Higdon, Hal. *Run Fast: How to Beat Your Best Time Every Time*. Emmaus, PA: Rodale Press, 2000.

——. *Boston: A Century of Running*. Emmaus, PA: Rodale Press, 1995.

——. *Marathon: The Ultimate Training Guide*. Emmaus, PA: Rodale Press, 1999.

Jacobson, Howard. *Racewalk to Fitness*. New York: Simon and Schuster, 1980.

——. *Healthwalk to Fitness*. Levitttown, NY: Walkers Club of America Press, 1997.

Jacoby, Ed, and Bob Fraley. *Complete Book of Jumps*. Champaign, IL: Human Kinetics, 1995.

Jamison, Neal. *Running through the Wall: Personal Encounters with the Ultramarathon*. New York: Breakaway Books, 2003.

Jarver, Jess. *Sprints and Relays*. Los Altos, CA: Tafnews Press, 1995.

—— (ed). *Middle Distances*. Los Altos, CA: Tafnews Press, 1991.

Jerome, John. *The Complete Runners Day-by-Day Log and Calendar, 2004*. New York: Random House, 2003.

Johnson, Alice. *Half a Mind: Hashing.* Camden, ME: Yankee Books, 1989.

Johnson, Joan. *The Healing Art of Sports Massage.* Emmaus, PA: Rodale Press, 1995.

Jordan, Tom. *PRE!.* Los Altos, CA: Tafnews Press, 1977.

Kardong, Don. *30 Phone Booths to Boston.* New York: Penguin Books, 1985.

Kislevitz, Gail Waesche, editor. *First Marathons.* New York: Breakaway Books, 1999.

———. *The Spirit of the Marathon.* New York: Breakaway Books, 2003.

Kowalchik, Claire. *The Complete Book of Running for Women.* New York: Pocket Books, 1999.

Lawrence, Allan, and Mark Scheid. *Running and Racing after 35.* Boston: Little, Brown, 1990.

———. *The Self-Coached Runner.* Boston: Little, Brown, 1987.

Lebow, Fred, with Richard Woodley. *Inside the World of Big-Time Marathoning.* New York: Rawson Associates, Ltd, 1984.

Lewis, Carl, with Jeffrey Marx. *Inside Track.* New York: Simon and Schuster, 1990.

Lewis, Frederick, and Dick Johnson. *Young at Heart: The Story of Johnny Kelley—Boston's Marathon Man.* Waco, TX: WRS Press, 1992.

Marra, Reggie. *Quality of Effort.* New Rochelle, NY: From the Heart Press, 1991.

Martin, David, and Peter N. Coe. *Better Training for Distance Runners, Second Edition.* Champaign, IL: Human Kinetics, 1997.

Martin, David E., and R. W. Gynn. *The Marathon Footrace.* Springfield, IL: Charles C. Thomas Publishers, 1979.

Meagher, Jack, and Pat Broughton. *Sports Massage.* New York: Doubleday, 1989.

Melograno, Vincent J., and James E. Klinzing. *An Orientation to Total Fitness.* Dubuque, IA: Kendall/Hunt, 1992.

Micheli, Lyle J., with Mark Jenkins. *The Sports Medicine Bible.* New York: HarperResource, 1995.

———. *Healthy Runner's Handbook.* Champaign, IL: Human Kinetics, 1996.

Murphy, Frank. *A Cold Clear Day: The Athletic Biography of Buddy Edelen.* Kansas City: Wind Sprint Press, 1992.

Murray, Frank. *Happy Feet.* New Canaan, CT: Keats, 1990.

Nelson, Mariah Burton. *Are We Winning Yet?* New York: Random House, 1991.

Nideffer, Robert M. *Athlete's Guide to Mental Training.* Champaign, IL: Human Kinetics, 1985.

Noakes, Tim. *Lore of Running.* Forth Edition. Champaign, IL: Human Kinetics, 2003.

Paish, Wilf. *Nutrition for Sports.* North Pomfret, VT: Trafalgar Square, 1991.

Parker, John L., Jr. *And Then the Vulture Eats You.* Tallahassee: Cedarwinds, 1990.

Pritt, Donald S., and Morton Walker. *The Complete Foot Book.* Garden City Park, NY: Avery, 1992.

Reber, Deborah. *Run for Your Life: A Book for Beginning Women Runners.* New York: Perigee, 2002.

Rodgers, Bill. *The Complete Idiot's Guide to Jogging and Running.* Indianapolis: Alpha Books, 1998.

——. *Bill Rodgers' Lifetime Running Plan.* New York: HarperCollins, 1996.

——. and Priscilla Welch. *Bill Rodgers and Priscilla Welch on Masters Running and Racing.* New York: St. Martin's Press, 1991.

Roth, Peter. *Running U.S.A: A Guide to Running in 125 American Cities.* New York: Simon and Schuster, 1979.

Runyan, Marla, and Sally Jenkins. *No Finish Line: My Life As I See It.* New York: Putnam, 2001.

Samuelson, Joan Benoit, and Gloria Averbuch. *Joan Samuelson's Running for Women.* Emmaus, PA: Rodale Press, 1995.

Sandrock, Michael. *Running with the Legends.* Champaign, IL: Human Kinetics, 1996.

Santos, Jim. *Sports Illustrated Track and Field Guide.* New York: Penguin, 1991.

Shangold, Mona M., and Gabe Mirkin. *The Complete Medicine Book for Women.* New York: Simon and Schuster, 1992.

——. and Gabe Mirkin. *Women and Exercise: Physiology and Sports Medicine,* second edition. New York: Oxford University Press, 1994.

Sheehan, George. *Running and Being.* Twentieth Anniversary edition. Second Wind, 1998.

——. *Going the Distance.* New York: Villard, 1996.

——. *Personal Best.* Emmaus, PA: Rodale Press, 1992.

——. *Running to Win.* Emmaus, PA: Rodale Press, 1992.

——. *This Running Life.* New York: Simon and Schuster, 1980.

Shorter, Frank, with Marc Bloom. *Olympic Gold—A Runner's Life and Times.* Boston: Houghton Mifflin, 1984.

Sillitoe, Alan. *The Loneliness of the Long-Distance Runner.* New York: Penguin, 1959.

Sparks, Ken. *The Runner's Book of Training Secrets.* Champaign, IL: Human Kinetics, 1997.

Stones, D., G. Joy, J. Wszola, and D. Martin. *The High Jump Book* (2nd edition). Los Altos, CA: Tafnews Press, 1987.

Tanser, Toby. *The Essential Guide to Running the New York City Marathon.* New York: Perigee, 2003.

Temple, Cliff. *Running from A to Z.* Los Altos, CA: Tafnews Press, 1987.

——. *Marathon, Cross Country, and Road Racing.* North Pomfret, VT: Trafalgar Square, 1990.

Traum, Richard, with Michael Celizic. *A Victory for Humanity.* Waco, TX: WRS Group, Inc., 1993.

Tricard, Louise Mead. *American Women's Track & Field, A History.* Jefferson, NC: McFarland & Co., 1996.

Ullyot, Joan L. *Running Free.* New York: G. P. Putnam's Sons, 1980.

Waitz, Grete, and Gloria Averbuch. *On the Run, Exercise and Fitness for Busy People.* Emmaus, PA: Rodale Press, 1997.

——. *World Class.* New York: Warner Books, 1986.

Watts, Denis, and Harry Wilson. *Middle and Long Distance/Marathon and Steeplechase.* Los Altos, CA: Tafnews Press, 1985.

Wells, Christine L. *Women, Sport and Performance.* Champaign, IL: Human Kinetics, 1991.

Wharton, Jim, and Phil Wharton. *The Whartons' Back Book.* Emmaus, PA: Rodale Press, 2003.

——. *The Whartons' Cardio-Fitness Book.* New York: Three Rivers Press, 2001.

——. *The Whartons' Strength Book.* New York: Times Books, 1999.

——. *The Whartons' Stretch Book.* New York: Times Books, 1996.

Whitsett, David A, Forrest A. Dolgener, and Tanjala Mabon Kole. *The Non-Runner's Marathon Trainer.* Chicago: Masters Press, 1998.

Williston, Floyd. *Johnny Miles.* Tallahassee: Cedarwinds, 1990.

Yudkin, John. *The Encyclopedia of Nutrition.* New York: Penguin, 1985.

3. RUNNING AND FITNESS PUBLISHERS

Cedarwinds Publishing
Runners' Books and Smartware
Books, videos, accessories
P.O. Box 352 Medway, OH 45341
800-548-2388
513-849-1624 (fax)
balbert@aol.com

Human Kinetics
Books, videos
P.O. Box 5076
Champaign, IL 61825
900-747-4457
www.humankinetics.com
humank@hkusa.com

**McGraw-Hill Health Care
Publications**
1221 Avenue of the Americas
New York, NY 10020
212-512-2000
212-512-4100 (bookstore)
www.bookstore.mcgraw-hill.com

**New England Sports
Publications**
Books, magazine, newsletters
P.O. Box 252
Boston, MA 02113
617-891-1844
www.runningnet.com/nerunner

Road Race Management
RRM, Inc.
newsletters, reports, race procedures
4904 Glen Cove Parkway

Bethesda, MD 20816
301-320-6865
301-320-9164 (fax)
www.rrm.com

Salmini Films
Running films, videos, and NYC
Marathon highlights
440 Commercial Avenue
Palisades Park, NJ 07620
201-767-0268
201-944-0365 (fax)

Sportswords Ltd.
Books, magazines, collections
1475 Third Avenue
New York, NY 10028
800-778-7937
212-772-8729

**Tafnews Press/Track and
Field News**
Books, newsletters, and magazines
2570 El Camino Real, Suite 606
Mountain View, CA 94040
415-948-8188
415-948-8417 (editorial)
www.trackandfieldnews.com

Trafalgar Square Publishing
Books
P.O. Box 257
North Pomfret, VT 05053
802-457-1911
tsquare@sover.net

4. MAGAZINES

American Track & Field
83 D'Onofrio Drive, Suite 203
Madison, WI 53719
608-827-0806
608-827-0810 (editorial)

**The Harrier and The Harrier's
High School Cross Country
Report**
P.O. Box 41
Marlboro, NJ 07746

Inside Texas Running
P.O. Box 19909
Houston, TX 77224
281-759-0555
www.insidetexasrunning.com

MetroSports Magazine
259 W. 30th Street, 3rd Floor
New York, NY 10001
212-563-7329
www.metrosportsny.com

National Geographic Adventure
104 W. 40th Street
New York, NY 10036
212-790-9020

New England Runner
P.O. Box 252
Boston, MA 02113
617-891-1844
www.runningnetwork.com/
nerunner

New York Runner
9 East 89th Street
New York, NY 10128

212-860-4455
www.nyrrc.org

Northwest Runner
4831 NE 44th Street
Seattle, WA 98105
206-527-5301
www.nwrunner.com

Outside Magazine
400 Market Street
Santa Fe, NM 87501
505-989-7100
www.outsidemag.com

Runner's Gazette
67 West Jupiter Lane
Lewisburg, PA 17837
570-524-9713
570-524-9748
www.RunnersGazette.com

Runner's World
33 East Minor Street
Emmaus, PA 18098
610-967-5171
www.runnersworld.com

Running Research News
RRN P.O. Box 27041
Lansing, MI 48909
517-371-4897
www.rrnews.com

Running Stats
704 Mohawk, Suite 19
Boulder, CO 80302
303-494-1362 (fax)
www.runningstats.com

Running Times
213 Danbury Road
Wilton, CT 06897
203-761-1113
www.runningtimes.com

Track and Field News
2570 El Camino Real, Suite 606
Mountain View, CA 94040
650-948-8188
www.trackandfieldnews.com

Trail Runner Magazine
1101 Village Rd. UL-4D
Carbondale, CO 81623

970-704-1442
www.trailrunnermag.com

Triathlete Magazine
328 Encinitas Boulevard, Suite 100
Encinitas, CA 92024
760-634-4100
www.triathletemag.com

**University of California at
Berkeley Wellness Letter**
P.O. Box 420148
Palm Coast, FL 32142
904-445-6414
www.berkeleywellness.com

5. ORGANIZATIONS

Achilles Track Club, Inc. (ATC)
42 West 38th Street, Suite 400
New York, NY 10018
212-354-0300
www.achillestrackclub.org

Amateur Athletic Union (AAU)
PO Box 22409
Lake Buena Vista, FL 32830
407-934-7200
www.aausports.org

**American Anorexia/Bulimia
Association**
165 W. 46th Street, Suite 1108
New York, NY 10036
212-575-6200
www.4woman.gov/nwhic/
references/mdreferrals/aaba.htm

**American Chiropractic
Association**
1701 Clarendon Boulevard
Arlington, VA 22209
800-986-4636
www.amerchiro.org/contact.shtml

**American College of Sports
Medicine**
P.O. Box 1440
Indianapolis, IN 46206-1440
317-637-9200
www.acsm.org

**American Dietetic Association
(ADA)**
120 South Riverside Plaza, Suite
2000
Chicago, IL 60606-6995
800-877-1600
www.eatright.org

American Fitness Professionals and Associates (ARPA)
P.O. Box 214
Ship Bottom, NJ 08008
609-978-7583
www.afpafitness.com

American Massage Therapy Association (AMTA)
820 Davis Street, Suite 100
Evanston, IL 60201-4444
847-864-0123
www.amtamassage.org

American Orthopedic Foot and Ankle Society
2517 Eastlake Avenue E
Seattle, WA 98102
206-223-1120
www.aofas.org

American Osteopathic Academy of Sports Medicine (AOASM)
7600 Terrace Avenue, Suite 203
Middleton, WI 53562
608-831-4400
www.aoasm.org

American Physical Therapy Association (APTA)
1111 North Fairfax Street
Alexandria, VA 22314-1488
703-684-APTA (2782)
800-999-APTA
www.apta.org

American Running Association
4405 East West Highway, Suite 405
Bethesda, MD 20814

301-913-9517
800-776-2732
www.americanrunning.org

The Armory Track and Field Center
216 Fort Washington Avenue
New York, New York 10032
212-923-1803
www.armorytrack.com

The Arthritis Foundation
P.O. Box 7669
Atlanta, GA 30357-0669
800-283-7800
www.arthritis.org

Association of International Marathons and Road Races (AIMS)
Hugh Jones, AIMS Secretary
10 Theed Street, Suite 3
London SE1 8ST
England
+44 207 928 6200
www.aims-association.org

Association of Track and Field Statisticians (ATFS)
President Paul Jenes
23-25 Grandview Road
Victoria 3113
Australia
+61 39 844 1644
jenesp@ausport.gov.au
http://easyweb.easynet.co.uk/
~rsparks/atfs.htm

The Asthma and Allergy Foundation of America (AAFA)
233 20th Street, NW, Suite 402

Washington, DC 20036
202-466-7643
www.aafa.org

Boston Athletic Association (BAA)
40 Trinity Place, 4th Floor
Boston, MA 02116
617-236-1652
www.baa.org

Center for Women's Health and Sports Gynecology
c/o Director Mona Shangold
1601 Walnut Street, Suite 1200
Philadelphia, PA 19102
215-988-4754

Deep Water Running and Swim Clinic
700 Columbus Avenue, #9J
New York, NY 10025
212-222-0720
http://transitiontimes.com/
dougstern.htm

Eating Disorder Resource Center
24 East 12th Street, Suite 505
New York, NY 10003
212-989-3989
http://users.rcn.com/dps.
interport/edrc/main.html

Enviro Sports
P.O. Box 1040
Stinson Beach, CA 94970
415-868-1829
www.envirosports.com

Hash House Harriers New York City
212-427-4692
www.hashhouseharriers.com

Institute for International Sport
The Feinstein Building
University of Rhode Island
3045 Kingstown Road
P.O. Box 1710
Kingston, RI
02881-0104
800-447-9889
www.internationalsport.com

International Amateur Athletic Federation (IAAF)
17 Rue Princesse Florestine
B.P. 359
MC 98007 Monaco Cedex
+377 93-10-88-88
www.iaaff.org

Johns Hopkins Medical Center
550 North Broadway, Suite 1100
Baltimore, MD 21205-2011
410-955-1050
800-829-0422
www.hopkinsmedicine.org

Marathon Tours and Travel
261 Main Street
Boston, MA 02129
800-444-4097
www.marathontour.com

Melpomene Institute
1010 University Avenue
St. Paul, MN 55104
651-642-1951
www.melpomene.org

Metropolitan Athletics Congress (MAC)
395 Pearl Street
Brooklyn, NY 11201
718-488-5711
www.mactrack.org

National Alliance for Youth Sports
2050 Vista Parkway
West Palm Beach, FL 33411
561-684-1141
800-729-2057
www.nays.org

National Association of Anorexia Nervosa and Associated Disorders (ANAD)
P.O. Box 7
Highland Park, IL 60035
847-831-3438
www.altrue.net/site/anadweb/

National Collegiate Athletic Association (NCAA)
700 W. Washington Street
P.O. Box 6222
Indianapolis, IN 46206-6222
317-917-6222
www.ncaa.org

New York Road Runners (NYRR)
9 East 89th Street
New York, NY 10128
212-860-4455
www.nyrrc.org

National Youth Sports Safety Foundation
One Beacon Street, Suite 3333

Boston, MA 02108
Phone: 617-277-1171
Fax: 617-722-9999
NYSSF@aol.com
www.nyssf.org/

President's Council on Physical Fitness and Sports
Department W
200 Independence Avenue, SW
Room 738-H
Washington, D.C. 20201-0004
202-690-9000
www.fitness.gov

Road Race Management, Inc. (RRM)
4904 Glen Cove Parkway
Bethesda, MD 20816
301-320-6865
www.rrm.com

Road Runners Club of America (RRCA)
510 North Washington Street
Alexandria, VA 22314
703-836-0558
www.rrca.org

USA Track and Field (USATF)
One RCA Dome, Suite 140
Indianapolis, IN 46225
317-261-0500
www.usatf.org

USATF Road Running Information Center
5522 Camino Cerralvo
Santa Barbara, CA 93111
805-696-6232
www.usaldr.org

United States Department of Agriculture Food and Nutrition Information Center (USDA)
Agricultural Research Service, USDA
National Agricultural Library, Room 105
10301 Baltimore Avenue
Beltsville, MD 20705-2351
301-504-5719
www.nal.usda.gov/fnic

United States Olympic Committee (USOC)
One Olympic Plaza
Colorado Springs, CO 80909
719-866-4500
www.usoc.org

USA Triathlon
616 W. Monument Street
Colorado Springs, CO   80905
719-597-9090
www.usatriathlon.org

Women in Sports and Events (WISE)
244 Fifth Avenue, Suite 2087
New York, NY 10001
212-726-8282
www.womeninsportsandevents.com

Women's Sports Foundation
Eisenhower Park
East Meadow, NY 11554
800-227-3988
www.womenssportsfoundation.org

6. INTERNET RUNNING RELATED RESOURCES

www.active.com
www.coolrunning.com
www.everydayrunner.com
www.letsrun.com
www.marathonandbeyond.com
www.marathon-world.com
www.run-down.com
www.runnergirl.com
www.runningnetwork.com
www.runnersweb.com
www.runnerscorner.com
www.runtheplanet.com
www.trackwire.com
www.ultrarunning.com
www.ultramarathonworld.com